MONEY RAISING MASTERCLASS

How I raised $40 million in 2.5 years
from investors; took my company public
and created a $300 million company.

NORMAN MEIER

authorHOUSE®

AuthorHouse™
1663 Liberty Drive
Bloomington, IN 47403
www.authorhouse.com
Phone: 1 (800) 839-8640

Published by AuthorHouse 05/08/2020

ISBN: 978-1-7283-6085-0 (sc)
ISBN: 978-1-7283-6084-3 (e)

Print information available on the last page.

This book is printed on acid-free paper.

CONTENTS

PART 3
THE $100 MILLION BLUEPRINT

Money isn't everything but it ranks right up there with oxygen.
(Rita Davenport, motivational speaker)

INTRODUCTION

Million Dollar Knowledge

> I have done some terrible things for money...
> like getting up early to go to a job.

What I am about to teach you can normally not be found in a book. You can't find it in a course, seminar or any other way.

What I am about to teach you is a very specific knowledge that is literally worth millions of dollars.

If you truly understand how this process works and keep learning and improving, then there is nothing that can stop you.

Read everything very carefully and write your ideas and notes into a personal journal.

If you are serious about creating a $100 million company, then this book is a good starting point.

We don't find books by accident. It is actually the opposite. Books find us. You probably heard of the quote: When the student is ready, the teacher will appear. The same is true for books. When you are ready for your next level in life, the right books will appear.

This is one of those moments.

Money Raising

> I raised $40 million in 2 1/2 years from investors; created a $300 million company and became a self-made millionaire in the process.

How do you find investors? That's the million-dollar question! If you have millions of dollars from investors available, you can make any dream or project work. Finding the money is the hardest part.

I have raised millions of dollars from investors, took companies public and dealt with many great sales people who also raised a lot of money from investors. I have invested millions in resource projects all around the world and hired geologists who worked on these projects.

The lessons in this Money Raising Masterclass are real and authentic. They come from actual personal experience and from many sales people and stock brokers that I have had the privilege to work with.

The knowledge in this book is very special and it took years of trial and error until I figured out how best to go about it.

Raising money is not easy. It is hard work and it is a numbers game. But once you know what to do, there is no job like it. The ability to make lots of money and turn your business ideas into reality is a great accomplishment and satisfaction.

Listed and established companies can raise money from investment funds, private equity companies or other financial companies. But if you are just starting out with an idea, you have no other choice but to get the money from private investors.

Raising money is a combination of the knowledge of how to do it, technical knowledge and sales skills. I have seen average non-financially educated people raise millions of dollars because they mastered the art of money raising so well by developing great sales and communication skills.

In the end money raising is like selling any other product. It is all sales. But the benefits are much bigger.

In this book I am going to cover the process as well as the sales side of the business.

In the end you can really only raise money by talking to people and trying to convince them of your investment ideas. The better you learn to communicate, the more people you can convince to invest.

Some people are better suited to talk to investors and others are better when it comes to managing projects. You have to find out what you do best and find good partners that can do the things were you have weaknesses.

In the end you have to build a company and you can't do it alone. You will need a team. In the beginning raising money is the most important function because without money to fund your projects and ideas, there is no company. Even if you have not a "sales person" you will have to learn how to raise money from investors if you want your company to get financed.

The $100 Million Dollar Secret

> Trust that there is a future waiting for you that is beyond what you might be able to grasp at this present moment.

There are a total of 46.8 million **millionaires** worldwide at the beginning of the year 2020, and they collectively own approximately $158.3 trillion.

In the 33rd annual Forbes list of the world's billionaires, the list included **2,153 billionaires** with a total net wealth of $8.7 trillion.

There are millions of millionaires in the world and the number is increasing with each year. The only question that you should ask yourself, is why you are not one of them yet?

How did those people become millionaires or even billionaires? Did they have a great 9 to 5 job that paid them really well? Most definitely not!

They are all business owners and **own shares of their own public company.** No one becomes a billionaire by simply earning a salary from a job each year. People become wealthy by owning a significant share position in a company that is listed in the stock market.

But how did they start out? How do you become a multi millionaire?

They all started with a business idea. Then they incorporated a corporation, issued shares for themselves and raised money from investors. Eventually, they took the company public in the stock market and it was valued a several hundred millions of dollar.

I have raised $40 million in 2.5 years from 500 investors and his company was valued at over $300 million in the stock market. Actually, I raised over $400 million from private investors and $600 million from institutional investors in my career since 1995.

But the goal of this book is to teach you the things that you need to know to raise the first one or two million dollars by yourself so that you can take your company public in the stock market and attract millions more afterwards.

This book will teach you everything about this process and how I have done it.

SPECIAL THANKS
to Mariano Duyos

Mariano is my designer. He has designed all of my programs, created lots of beautiful brochures and corporate materials and he is one of the main reasons why I have been successful. I would have been lost without him at times.

Mariano is not just a business partner but also a personal friend. Thank you so much for everything that you have ever done for me. You are truly the greatest designer and person! I hope we will continue to work with each other for many years.

You helped me to put my ideas and visions into beautiful materials. Your work is so important and helpful. Part of the secret of my success, is having you as my designer. Ideally, I want to keep this secret to myself but I wouldn't do you justice if I didn't promote how excellent you are.

You are not just a designer who makes things looks pretty but you are also very smart and you understand what I am looking for if I come to you with an idea.

I am glad to have found you and thank you from the bottom of my heart.

Also thanks to…

… the people who are no longer in my life but who have taught me many valuable lessons about business and life.

… the haters and people who wanted to see me fail. I gained more resolve and strength from your negative comments.

…my father Prof. Dr. Edwin Meier who has always been a free spirit and who was not afraid to live his life his way. He was always self-employed and chasing his vision. I am glad you didn't follow a corporate or government career. Your example taught me to be freethinking and independent.

…my business partners and friends who have worked with me over the last few years. I could not have been successful without your support.

… Christian, Julian, Oskar, Jules, Philipp, Yves, Igor, Bojan, Adrian, Mischa, Hammer, Alex, Bernhard, David, Marco, Duty, Oemercan and many more. You know who you are… sorry if I didn't forgot someone…

…my wife Ursula who supported me all these years and took care of our children when I was traveling.

…Kayleen Grey for always believing in me when things got difficult – especially when it felt like I had the whole world against me.

… to the people in this industry who have no integrity. Thank you for teaching me how NOT to do business.

LEGAL DISCLAIMER

Statement

The information in this book is based on my personal experience, my knowledge and influenced by many books that I have read. Everything that I have written is done with the best intentions. The strategies and tips have helped many people to improve their lives. I hope you understand that NMI, Inc. or I cannot be made liable for any statements made. If you would like to copy some of the content, please ask at www.normanmeier.com first for written permission. If you like what you read, please refer us to other people.

Every bit of advice about making money, Private Equity, public companies, etc. is based on my personal experience and is not typical. You should consult a lawyer before you start any kind of money raising activity. I do not take any kind of responsibility for statements made. Any kind of statement may have errors, may not legally be viable, laws may have changed and the accuracy of my information might be false. The information cannot be used as proof in legal matters as some of the information might have been changed or altered to protect certain people involved. This information comes with the best intentions to educate and help other people.

Do not duplicate or distribute without permission

The products and contents offered by Norman Meier contain proprietary content and must not be duplicated or distributed without written permission. No portion of this material may be shared or reproduced in any manner under any circumstance whatsoever without advanced written permission from Norman Meier and NMI, Inc. No portion of this brochure or any Norman Meier or NM International, Inc. product or material is intended to offer legal, medical, personal or financial advice. NMI, Inc. has been taken every effort to ensure we accurately represent these strategies and their potential to help you grow your business. However, we do not purport this as a "get rich scheme" and there is no guarantee that you will earn any money using the content, strategies or techniques displayed in the NMl, Inc. products. Nothing in these products is a promise or guarantee of earnings. Your level of success in attaining similar results is dependent upon a number of factors including your skill, knowledge, ability, connections, dedication, business savvy, business focus, business goals and financial situation. Because these factors differ according to individuals, we cannot guarantee your success, income level, or ability to earn revenue. You alone are responsible for your actions and results in life and business, and by your use of all the Norman Meier and NMI, Inc. materials and/or products, you agree not to attempt to hold us liable for any of your decisions, actions or results, at any time, under any circumstance. The information contained herein cannot replace or substitute for the services of trained professionals in any field, including but not limited to financial or legal matters. Under no circumstances, including but not limited to negligence, will Norman Meier, NMl, Inc. or any of its representatives, employees or contractors be liable for any special or consequential damages that result from the use of, or the inability to use, the materials, information or success strategies communicated through these materials, or any services following these materials, even if advised of the possibilities of such damages.

Results disclaimer

The results of using these products will vary depending on your circumstances, time commitments, and overall application of these programs. Based on these factors it is possible that the use of this product will generate little or no results for you. The use of these products does not guarantee financial improvement, business improvement, or personal improvement. Anything that you apply from the materials you learn, is done at your own risk

MY STORY

How I became a self-made millionaire in 2 ½ years

Hi, my name is Norman Meier.

When I was in my twenties, I was hungry for money and success like most young men. I had a dream and that dream was to become a self-made millionaire by the time I was 30. But by the time I was 30 I was still broke.

Even though I was making good money at the time, I was still far from being a millionaire. I earned over $120,000 per year but I had no money saved.

And then I started to ask the question why is it that some people are more successful than others. And especially what is it about some people that enable them to become millionaires?

> There are over 24 million of millionaires in the US alone and the number worldwide is growing rapidly (even in difficult economic times).

24 million millionaires! And the number is growing! If that many people have achieved financial success, you can do it, too, I thought.

I started to read and study everything about self-made millionaires. I listened to motivational audio programs, read books and wrote ideas in my daily journal. I tried to find the answers so that one day I could hopefully be one of them as well.

My last job interview

One day I applied for a job with UBS, the biggest bank in Switzerland. They offered me a job for $150,000, which would have been a step up financially and the job description seemed also interesting. Any normal person would have accepted that offer and been happy about it.

But then I did the math. I needed $100,000 per year to live comfortably and I could put away about $50,000 per year. So after 10 years I would have $500,000 in savings.

My initial thought was that half a million is ok but it is still not an entire million. I considered it for a few minutes and then I told the guy at UBS that I wasn't interested in the job.

I knew I had to do something different if I wanted to become a millionaire. I needed to play in a different league and think outside of the box. I wanted to achieve something great and I didn't feel that taking on a better job would help me to accomplish my dream.

So my options were:

1. Work harder and better at earning commissions with my sales job
2. Save money for the next 30 to 40 years
3. Take on another job that pays better

The problem was still that I didn't have the answer that I wanted. I wanted to become a millionaire in a short period of time and in order to do that I needed to have a different strategy.

The meaning of life

Then there was also something else that happened that same week that changed my life forever. In one week there were 3 deaths: A person from payroll died, a friend's brother that I just met died and one night I got home and there was a dead cat on the street.

I was confronted with death and the meaning of life. Logically, I wondered about the meaning of my own life. I thought if I worked in a regular job working for someone else I would "waste" my talents and my life and it became even more clear to me that I had to go into business for myself even though I wasn't sure what I should be doing exactly.

Change your mental mindset

Then I asked myself what I should do differently? If I continued to do things that way I did them, nothing would change. I realized that I needed to change something. I read a lot of books, went to seminars and listened to audio programs. Eventually, it hit me. I realized what I needed to change.

Once I made that decision, I became a self-made millionaire only 2 ½ years later. It was quite astonishing. It was unbelievable. When I look back in time, I realize now how quickly everything happened. This was more than 15 years ago.

What let me to go there? What does it take to become a millionaire in such a short time? The answer is that is a **MENTAL MINDSET**. It is the way you think that determines how much money you make. Let me explain further...

When I went to a seminar from a German motivational speaker by the name of Bodo Schaefer, there was one statement that changed my life forever. Bodo Schaefer developed the program "How to make your first million in seven years". He told us that at one point in his life, he was completely broke and depressed and didn't know how to pay his bills anymore.

In a personal conversation his coach told him to plan to become a person who can make $100,000 per month.

At first, this seemed very unrealistic and he came up with all kinds of excuses why this was impossible. But his coach also told him that you don't actually NEED $100,000 per month to enjoy a great lifestyle. No one really needs that. But it is the PERSON that you need to BECOME that is capable of making that kind of money each month.

I liked that and it became my primary motivation. I also wanted to become this person. I asked myself, too, what I needed to do or to change in order to make $100,000 per month.

Clearly, I needed to **think outside of the box** because the conventional ways of thinking don't work if you want to attract that kind of money into your life. You can't expect to work in a regular job and become a millionaire.

What do you need to **change in your mental attitude to become this person**? Which habits do you need to develop and get rid of? What is it that you need to **CHANGE**? This is the key factor here.

I was really motivated by that because I really wanted to make a $100,000 per month. This became my primary motivation and driving force. I wanted to become the person who was mentally strong and capable to achieve this goal and of course I wanted the money. But the money was secondary.

Brian Tracy

The next important mental shift came from Brian Tracy. Brian Tracy is one of the top motivational speakers and business trainers in the world. I actually once got the chance to meet him once in Switzerland even though he lives about 15 minutes away from me here in California.

He told us to write down our current income. My current income at the time was $140,000. Then he asked the question if we believed that it was possible to increase our current income by 20% in the next 12 months.

20% more equals $160,000 per year. Then he asked the question if we believed if this was possible and realistic. What do we need to do or change to increase our income by 20% in 12 months? A little bit more effort, a few more sales and I could achieve it. Yes, of course it is possible, I thought.

Then his next question was: What if you took your current income of $140,000 and you DOUBLED it within a year to $280,000. What would you have to do differently in order to achieve that number? Is it possible?

Yes, it was possible but I was hesitant. It was a big number. This is exactly the point where most people start to block. They come up with excuses and reasons why it is not possible or realistic to make this kind of money. It might have taken you a long time to get to a certain income level and doubling it within 12 months seems to be a big step.

And of course if you believe that you can't do it, then you are right. You won't be able to do it.

Think about it. What do you have to change in order to double your income in 12 months? You will have to start to think in **NEW WAYS and NEW POSSIBILITIES**.

And that is the **BIG SECRET**. You have to **OPEN UP YOUR MIND**. You can't have a regular 9 to 5 job and hope to become a millionaire. It is simply not possible. It doesn't work. It is the WRONG SYSTEM to have a regular job.

But then Brian went on and said the following thing: What if you were to increase your current income of $140,000 by 10 times so that it would be $1.4 million?

Most people at that point will say: Ok, that is all nice but let's stop dreaming here. This is totally unrealistic. It took me years to get to $140,000. Getting to $1.4 million was completely out of the question.

This calculation or example was actually the second thing that got me motivated. I asked myself how could I make $1.4 million per year, which is a little bit more than $100,000 per month? And how would I be able to pull this off?

"The quality of your questions will determine
the quality of your answers."
(Anthony Robbins)

One thing I realized is that there are people out there who make $1.4 million per year or more **right now**. What is it that they know or do differently? What is their secret? How can I learn the same things so I can become one of those people?

The first thing that I have done is to write myself a personal check for $1.4 million. I signed it, I looked at it and I dreamed about it every day. I still have that check today. I put it into my journal and where I started to write down all my ideas, insights and strategies that could lead me to my goal. I took the number of $1.4 million and made it my goal and after 2 1/2 years I made it happen.

HOW did I do it? That is the million-dollar question, right?

How I built several businesses and financed them with millions of dollars

All successful people are big dreamers.

I knew I needed to start my own business in order to be financially successful. But at first I really didn't know what to do exactly. It was just a dream.

At the time I was still living in Switzerland. Almost by chance I heard of a company that would do incorporations. So I decided to call the number and I incorporated a company in Nevada.

Because I didn't know exactly what the purpose of the company was going to be I decided to give it my cat's nickname "Hemis". My cat's name was Hemingway but I called him "Hemis" sometimes. I thought I would change the name later when I knew what it was going to be. So there I was, owning a company with the name Hemis Corporation but no business model or product.

At that time I was helping a friend of my father's to get a gold company back listed onto the stock market. The company got delisted and because he couldn't speak English and didn't know how to get it done, he had asked me to help him. As a former stockbroker I had a general idea but no specific knowledge about taking a company public. So I flew to North America and talked to a securities lawyer, an accountant and an auditor and finally I was able to get it back listed again. The company had a gold project in Africa and they were raising money from private investors to get the project financed. They raised over $12 million from private investors in about 3 months.

So then I thought: If I did all this work for them and I now figured out how to get a company listed then why not do it myself instead of working for someone else?

I was able to get a gold project in Mexico from a friend who was in the gold business in Vancouver, Canada. I put the project into Hemis and then I started to sell shares of the company or basically to raise money.

At first I only raised a few hundred thousand dollars but eventually, I won several more people for "my cause" and the team grew. I was able to develop the project and we got great results from the initial tests and drilling results.

In the end we ended up with several companies, 25 exploration projects, about 60 people, 3 sales organizations, 10 geologists, 500 investors and about $40 million in raised capital.

I got paid a salary from five companies and with some bonuses, etc. my income grew to over $100,000 per month, while I was raising about $1 to $2 million each month.

I took the company public and it got listed with a market capitalization of over $300 million. I was the main shareholder with more than $123 million in stock value. The stock price of my company went from $0.27 to $3.50 and all of my investors made money.

I also built a second company that was listed at $150 million and the share price went from $0.50 to $2.00 in a matter of weeks.

I built 5 companies that paid me a salary of $10,000 each per month and I earned about the same amount in commissions from my sales organizations. I had saved $1.3 million in cash and I bought a house for $1.5 million. I leased two Porsches: one for me, and one for my wife. I was renting a luxury apartment overlooking the city for $10,000 per month. Life was great.

I felt on top of the world. In a very short period of time I had achieved success that was out of the ordinary. I was really proud of myself. I thought that I had it made in life. I thought that I never had to worry about money ever again.

Everything can change in an instant

> The keys to success are a single piece of information, a single idea at the right time, in the right situation that can change your life.

The main reason why I write these books and programs is to encourage others. I know that most people read books of successful authors and many things that I write about are not new pieces of information.

But what I am hoping is that you will get one insight, one single piece of information that will change your business life for the better. One idea or strategy can change everything.

Sometimes we are doing everything right but the results are not satisfactory. By changing one thing or getting one piece of advice, things will improve.

Therefore, I urge you to read and study all my materials. I hope it will help you to improve your life. You can find my programs at www.normanmeier.com

Setting yourself apart from the crowd

> 5% of people are financially independent and 95% are not.
> How can you belong to the 5%?

Have you read all the books about success, attended all the seminars or listened to all the success gurus? And despite all this info are you still not any further in life?

Interestingly, you are not alone in this situation. Thousands of people like you are searching for success and spend thousands of dollars on material but do not earn one more cent.

Many people are living in a dream world and have unrealistic hopes and illusions. Even though they are willing to learn and to think positively, they are not getting ahead financially. What is it that most of the success gurus are not telling you? Are you still dreaming of millions but are you worried how to pay your bills next month?

I don't think that the main problem is a lack of motivation. I believe that the main problem is that most people don't know HOW to go about it.

The world is full of opportunities and times have changed. But we have too many choices and this leads to confusion. And because of too many choices, people do what they have always done – they look for a better job.

But if you keep doing what you have done in the past, you will get the same results.

The rat race

> You were born to do more than just go to work, pay bills and die.

Get out of the rat race. I want to show you now how you can get out of the rat race or "break out of the hamster wheel" like I prefer to call it. If you keep spinning your wheels and go from paycheck to paycheck, then I want to give you the solution to fix your problems.

> The definition of the rat race: A competitive struggle as an employee to be able to buy a fancy house and an expensive car to impress your "friends" and neighbors while struggling financially every single month.

Most people have a life similar to this: They go to school, get a degree, get married, buy a house, have kids and get a job. After a life to financial struggle, they retire with almost nothing.

Most people are spinning their wheels like a hamster in a wheel but they are not getting ahead financially because they have to pay bills, mortgage payments, credit cards, etc. and because of that they are always in the same position.

Combined with a poor spending habits and the belief in false advertising of buying things on credit, they dig themselves deeper into a financial hole of debt.

Most people have been working hard in a job or career and are not getting ahead in life.

They are stuck in what I call **"the hamster wheel trap**".

A lot of people live paycheck to paycheck. They cannot stop working because in that case their income will also stop and their whole life is going down the drain. They have created your own financial prison and they cannot get out.

Just like a hamster that is in his hamster wheel you are moving really fast but you are still in the same place. You can even try to run faster but you will still not move forward.

Most people have been working hard in a job but they are not getting ahead in life.

They might even have a high income but very little or no money is left at the end of the month.

Basically, they have created your a **golden cage** and put on the **golden handcuffs**.

They cannot stop working because in that case their income will also stop and their whole life is going down the drain.

They have created your own **financial prison** and they cannot get out.

Unfortunately, we live in a world where money matters and most people probably won't leave the civilized world to build a house in the woods and eat worms to survive. Whether we like it or not, we will have to deal with money.

It also doesn't occur to most people that there are other options because this is what everybody seems to do. And there is also the feeling of inferiority and self-doubt because they don't think they know enough.

Breaking out of the hamster wheel or the rat race

> When I was young I thought that money was the most important thing in life; now that I am old I know that it is. (Oscar Wilde)

We all want a better life. We all have goals and dreams. How can we achieve most goals and dreams? The answer in most cases is: with money!

So the main question is then: How can you make more money?

You have two options:

1. Work
2. Investing

Let's look at what happens when people turn 65 years old:

80% of people are dependent on the state to take care of them
15% have a little bit of money saved
5% are financially independent from the state

Most people are in the hamster wheel of life. They go to work, pay bills and when they turn 65 they are broke.

The problem is that if you do what everybody else is doing, you will end up where everybody else is: nowhere. Therefore, you need to do something differently!

> We all create our own reality and the key is to change your reality and start to think differently than you have done so far.

Unfortunately, saving a little bit of money every month is not the solution, either. You need to have great financial success to get ahead and to be free.

Why is money so important?

> You will not help poor people by becoming one of them yourself.

A doctor once said that the biggest problem with sick people is wallet cancer. If you have to worry about money all the time it has a bad influence on your health. Most marital problems have to do with lack of money.

The Wall Street Journal once published the following statistics:

70% of people are living from paycheck to paycheck
62% of people say that the lack of money is their biggest problem
95% of couples fight over money issues on a regular basis

If you have to work hard anyway, you should
do something that makes you rich.
(T. Harv Eker)

No matter how much you don't like it, money is a necessary evil because in our society you cannot function freely if you don't have money.

Why is it so important then? It doesn't mean that you should buy a sport's car and throw money out of the window. It gives you the freedom to spend time with your kids, to do good things, to support your charity of choice, to create jobs for others, to have the time to spend with your family, to be able to travel the world and to do the kind of work that you really enjoy.

No money = uncertainty, stress and problems

There are very few things in modern life that are doable and possible without money. If you have money in our society and time, you will have a much better life. You can "fight it" or be "against it" but it won't help. Unless you move to the woods and eat worms and berries all day, you will never be truly happy.

I want to encourage you to be all you can be and to have money as a supporting role in your life.

Positioning

You need to get into the right position in order to become rich. What do I mean by that? Most people have a job and go to work from nine to five. The only way to make more money is to do overtime, get a second job or to get a better job.

People still think that if you go to school, get good grades and get a good job that everything will work out in life. But this kind of thinking is not going to get you ahead. To have a job is nothing bad but if you would like to be financially free you need a different strategy. A job will help you in the beginning of your career but it is not a strategy for the entire 40 years of your working life.

> If you dream of having a million dollars as an employee then it is the same of standing in the middle of the Sahara and trying to see the ocean. You are simply not in the right position to see it.

Let's compare the next three statistics with each other:

<u>At retirement</u>

80% of people are dependent on the state at the age of 65
15% of people do have a little bit of money but they are not financially independent
5% of people are financially independent

<u>Job or no job?</u>

85% of people have a job
10% of people are self-employed
5% of people are entrepreneurs

> Your boss cannot make you rich!

<u>Millionaires in America</u>

10% of millionaires are in the top management of large companies
5% of millionaires are self-employed specialists like doctors, lawyers or other professionals
5% of millionaires are top sales people
74% of millionaires are entrepreneurs

And only 1% of millionaires are in the show business, musicians, people who made money in the stock market, inventors and lottery winners

Control your own destiny or someone else
will control it. (Jack Welch)

I was using the **wrong vehicle** to make money. I tried to become rich by working in a job. I realized that I would only really excel if I started my own business.

Being successful in business and in life requires certain skills and the right mental attitude. Once you have learned what it takes to get on top, you can repeat it over and over again.

The main skills are:

- Sales skills
- Marketing skills
- Business skills
- Leadership skills
- Financing knowledge

A successful businessman once said the following thing: "You can take away all my money and all my things. One year later I will have everything back again. And the reason is because I know exactly what it takes mentally."

I can teach you this kind of mental attitude.

The following book represents the most important lessons from my point of view based on the last **25 years of my business and personal experience**.

I have started many businesses and took several companies public in the stock market. I financed them with millions of dollars and I became a millionaire in very short period of time once I decided to go out on my own.

You don't have waste 10 years of your life to figure
out what works and what doesn't work.

You can learn how to be successful from people who have done it before you.

I became a millionaire in very short period of time, lost everything and then built myself back again. I can show you how I did it so that you can do it as well – only better and without losing it.

But in order for you to do this you will need to **change your mental attitude and learn some new skills.**

The American Dream – The money lies in the streets

What is the American Dream? It is a life that describes how you can make a lot of money from nothing and enjoy a great lifestyle.

And the best way to become a millionaire is **to start your own business**. Let me teach you what I know and help you to build your dream business.

There has never been a better time in all of human history to start your own business to become financially independent.

Most people never get started and that's why they don't have success.

I don't have all the answers – I only have my answers. But my strategy created a multi-million company. I hope you can achieve similar financial success or more with my knowledge.

Sales skills are the foundation of every great success story

> Everybody wants to be successful and make a lot of money. But it is not intelligence or technical knowledge that make you rich. It is the ability to sell yourself, your ideas and products.

Most people hate selling (and salespeople) but they never realize that they are always selling - whether or not they realize it. Asking for that promotion, convincing your kids to listen to you, getting that date; if you want to be successful in life, you need to master sales and communication.

Knowing how to sell it's useful for EVERYTHING in your life, not just business.

Whatever business idea you might have, in the end it all comes down to selling a product or service to a customer. The more sales you make the higher your profits will be. The foundation of every business transaction has to do with selling.

If you want to know the secret of making money you should study everything there is to know about **sales, communication, psychology and marketing**. It will give you the tools and the understanding in dealing effectively with other people.

> If others have done it before, you can do it, too. Find out what they have done and then copy their actions.

I have found that almost anybody can become a sales person. Sales skills are learnable and I have seen average people turn into great sales people.

In the end you need to do the things that other successful people have done and then copy their strategies and actions.

> 74% of all self-made millionaires are directly involved in sales.

The science of influencing others

> Influencing others isn't luck or magic – it's science.

Being able to influence other people is power. You will have the power to get what you want by influencing other people. And it doesn't matter if it is your clients, family or co-workers.

Interestingly, most people function based on the same principles. We all have the same motivations, behavioral patterns, emotions or thoughts.

Once you have understood all these psychological factors you can use them to influence others. Once you have understood the basic principles and secrets, the world will never be the same.

Being able to communicate effectively can make you a lot of money. Top sales people use a lot of these techniques to earn six or seven income figures. Marketing professionals know and understand what messages will trigger buying signals and therefore they can use that approach in their businesses.

In order to influence someone you need to touch him or her on an emotional level.

In my program and book "Sales Psychology" you will learn the basic techniques to motivate and influence other people. The goal is to apply them with integrity so that you can achieve your personal and financial goals as an entrepreneur, businessman or sales person. This book focuses solely on the process of dealing with investors and money raising. But in order to become an even better sales person, you should absolutely learn everything there is to learn about sales. This is one of the secrets. You need to become a specialist in sales (which is a learnable skill) to raise millions of dollars. You need to be able to convince investors as well as your sales people.

Influencing others isn't luck or magic – it's science. There are proven ways to influence other people. And it doesn't matter whether you are a marketing expert, sales person or a politician.

In order to influence and persuade someone there are a number of principles and techniques that need to be applied. Those principles can be learned.

Communication is the key to personal and career success

Everything that we want to achieve in life whether it is personal or professional has to do with some sort of communication. That is why it is important to learn to communicate exceptionally well so that you can achieve all your goals. The most famous people are successful because they have learned to present themselves in the best possible way and because they can communicate better than others. The better you can communicate the better will be the quality of your life. Communication is everything.

In school, kids learn algebra and calculus but they ought to learn communication skills. Knowing how to communicate can make all the difference between a good life and a bad life. In extreme cases it can decide if someone lives or dies.

If you are serious about becoming a millionaire, then improving your sales skills will put you on the path to becoming a successful businessperson. I will teach you the most powerful strategies ever discovered in sales effectiveness.

The sales training program in this book on money raising is not based on theory. It is practical knowledge that has been used in over 3000 face-to-face meetings and thousands of phone calls.

I also call it the "Million Dollar Sales Secrets" because it teaches you the skills you need **to make a million dollars as a sales person or business owner**. How do I know? I was one of them!

The source of your success

We live in the age of computers. Each year new and faster computers enter the market place. Imagine you had absolutely the best computer in the world. This computer is better and faster than any other computer that you have ever seen. This computer is years ahead in its development and capabilities.

Now imagine that you were using software on this computer that is from the 80s. The performance power of the computer would be useless because the old software would slow down the computer.

Now the same thing is true when it comes to your brain. You have the absolutely best computer in your head but if you use the wrong software, it won't be very effective. This software is the reason why you are held back from the life that you could have. So delete your old software and be ready to upload new software.

> I am offering you new information (software) for your brain. I want to help you to start your own business, make it a financial success and live your dream!

Your brain is a super computer

> The human brain has an estimated storage capacity of 256 billion GB, which is the equivalent of 1.2 billion average PC hard drives.

The amount of connections that your brain can make is 1 with eight pages full of zeros. This number is greater than the combined number of molecules in the known Universe. What you can think and do is literally beyond belief. You are so smart and you have so much potential that it is really unbelievable.

The biggest enemy that you have is **fear and self-doubt**. Basically, you are your own worst enemy.

In order to become successful you need to feed your brain the right kind of information. You can compare it to a piece of land that has an old house on it. First, you need to clear the land of all the old stuff so that you can build a new house.

The knowledge that I teach will provide you with new and better information that will help you to become successful in business and in life. You need to reprogram your mind with better information.

What can you expect from the book?

It has been my mission in life to help other people just like you to achieve their personal goals. Over the last 20 years I have written 12 books and developed over 50 audio and 80 video programs.

I have produced many programs in the areas of money and finance, sales psychology, online marketing, leadership, personal and business success.

And in my programs I explain in detail HOW exactly I was able to GO FROM ZERO to becoming a self-made millionaire in only 2 ½ years.

There is no quick and simple answer. Becoming a millionaire this quickly is NOT EASY but it is POSSIBLE. It is very possible if you read this book carefully and apply its lessons.

I would also love to meet you personally at one of my seminars or workshops and share with you my lessons and insights so that I can help you to become successful as well.

This is what you can expect to find there:

- No BS, no hidden agenda, no cheap sales tricks
- This is my REAL LIFE story and the lessons that I have learned are real, authentic and honest
- It is also the story of how I became rich quickly, lost everything and rebuilt my life
- I will teach you how I became a mentally stronger person and what you can do to achieve similar results
- My success was NOT BECAUSE OF THE INTERNET
- It is not a rich quick scheme system but a fundamental shift in the way you think and the skills that you have to develop
- I have many great ideas for you to make money and I explain in detail how those ideas work

Start your own business and live your dream

Why haven't you achieved all your goals including financial independence yet?

Did you already try several other moneymaking programs before and you are still not closer to your dreams?

Have you asked yourself the question: When is it finally YOUR turn?

If so, don't worry. I have been there, too.

What seems impossible today will one day become the new normal.

Since I started my career in 1995 in the financial services industry, I have taken several companies public in the stock market, I have raised over $400 million from private investors and $600 million from institutional investors.

I have created countless companies and marketing materials, I have trained hundreds of sales people personally and I have dealt with thousands of investors.

I know what sells and how investors think. I understand what motivates them and which ones are good ones to target.

I also understand how sales people think and how to attract them for my cause.

I currently work with sales people and sales organizations in five different countries. I have companies and bank accounts all over the world.

I have raised money for all kinds of projects and companies. Some industries include gold, uranium, oil and gas, biotechnology, alternative energy, etc.

The technology today allows me to live anywhere in the world and work from home if I want to. I have four children and one of the benefits of job is that I can spend lots of time with them. Once I in a while I travel and visit my sales teams in a different country.

I have built an international Private Equity firm with offices and sales teams all over the world who are raising money for my projects.

My income is higher than a normal person can grasp and I own shares in all the deals that I finance.

I remember when I started with just one idea and zero investors. If you are at the same place then my example should encourage you to believe in yourself and to keep moving forward.

> Self-doubt and fear are the only things that are holding you back from a life of greatness.

I only have one question for you: What are you waiting for?

PART 1

MONEY RAISING MASTERCLASS

CHAPTER 1

RAISING MONEY FOR YOUR COMPANY AND THE $100 MILLION BLUEPRINT

How I raised $40 million in 2 1/2 years from investors; created a $300 million company and became a self-made millionaire in the process.

How to create a company, get it financed and listed in the stock market for $100 million

What I am about to share with you can literally change your life. The title of this program is quite intriguing. The term "$100 million" sounds almost to good to be true and I am sure that you have an even mix of emotions of some reservations and doubts as well as some level of curiosity.

But what I am about to share with you is not for everyone. Not everyone is able to do what I am going to explain and not everyone wants to achieve it, either.

But for those who want to change their life, this is for you.

Why do you think successful people can start and build one successful company after another?

1. They have the knowledge
2. They have the money

What if I told you that the money is not the problem?

What if you had between one and ten million dollars available in 12 months? Would you be able to turn an idea into a successful business? Would your chances be higher than if you had no money to start out with?

Are you willing and committed to learn and play in the big league with the big boys?

This is not normal

> Daughter: "Mom, what is normal?"
> Mother: "It is just a setting on the dryer, honey."

Why am I qualified to talk about this subject and why should you even listen to me?

Unlike other people who offer programs about success, I have actually done it. I have built several public companies that were worth more than $100 million in the stock market. I know exactly what I am talking about and I can show you how it is done. My goal is to teach you how to create a multi-million dollar company.

Let me give you some proof and actual numbers. But before I do that I want to let you know that I have put together a program to explains step by step how to build and structure a new company, find the right projects, get it financed with money from private investors, take it public in the stock market so that it can become at least a $100 million company.

Why is this knowledge important and how can it help you?

There are lots of business owners who struggle financially because their business is lacking money. They are unable to expand their businesses and execute on their business plans. Knowing how to attract the right investors is key and this knowledge make all the difference between a striving business and a failing business.

There are people out there who have great ideas or inventions but they have absolutely no idea how they can ever get the money to develop these ideas and to turn them into a reality.

Others come across a situation and they say something like "*Hey, someone should come up with a product that can do this or that…*" But because they have no access to money, they dismiss that thought immediately.

And finally there are people out there who dream of making millions but they have absolutely no idea where to start. It remains a complete mystery and a pipedream.

I have three questions for you:

- Do you have a great business idea that could change the world but you don't have the money to make it happen?
- Do you have access to projects that could become multi million dollar deals but because you don't have enough money, you don't even start to entertain the thought to acquire them for yourself?
- Do you look at successful entrepreneurs and wonder how they were so "lucky" to create such great companies?

> If you want something you have never had, then you have to do something that you have never done before.

Let me tell you my own story.

Back in 2005 I decided to start a new company called Hemis Corporation. Hemis was a gold exploration company with projects in Mexico and USA. I raised over $40 million from private investors in about 2 ½ years. I raised this capital from about 500 individual investors. But I didn't raise all that money by myself. I had built a sales team who sold the stocks of my company over the phone.

I had acquired several gold exploration projects and I had a team of 10 geologists who worked on these projects.

I also worked with a securities lawyer, accountant, auditor and market maker to get the company listed by doing all the necessary filings with the SEC (securities and exchange commission) and FINRA (financial regulatory authority).

I first offered the shares of Hemis for $0.27 to private investors. The company's first public price on February 9th 2007 was at $0.80 and the price of the stock went as high as $3.50 per share.

In the first year over 50 million shares were traded and the highest market capitalization (value in the market) was over **$300 million.**

The company was doing well in 2007 and 2008 and was actively trading more than 50 million shares. All of the initial private investors made money if they sold their stocks in the first two years. In fact, most people sold their positions between $1.00 and $1.50. They bought the shares at $0.27 and therefore they made 4 times or 6 times what they had invested.

Another deal that I took public was Tecton Corporation. It was a company that was valued at over **$150 million**. There were over 75 million shares outstanding at a price of $2.00 per share. Most people bought the shares at $0.50 and therefore made about 4 times what they had invested.

Over the years I have been involved in many other companies and deals. Some did well, others didn't.

Ideally, you want to build a company that lasts and that will maintain on its own but there is never a guarantee. If you business model works you can build a company long-term and enjoy the benefits of getting capital from outside sources.

Ideally, you want to own a majority share position in your company and create real value so that your personal share position will one day be worth millions.

In my case, I owned over 35 million shares of Hemis at $3.50, which was equivalent of $123 million. And I owned 20 million shares of Tecton at $2.00, which was about $40 million.

> They say money doesn't bring you happiness –
> but neither does being broke!

Starting small

Even though I raised millions of dollars, the start was very humble and small. It all started when I was working for Claudio who needed help with a company that got delisted from the stock market. He had a gold deal in Africa and raised about $12 million in 3 months from private investors. He had bought a publicly listed shell (=company without any projects) and needed help to get it back listed onto the stock market.

Even though I was a stockbroker in the past, I had no idea how to take a company public. It requires a whole different kind of knowledge. But by talking to accountants and securities lawyers and by simply "learning by doing it" I figured it out.

And then I thought to myself: If I am doing this for someone else, I might as well do this for myself.

I asked my friend Bruno who used to work for a big bank but was now washed up and broke if he wanted to join me in starting a new gold company. To my surprise he said "yes" and so we began.

We didn't even have a gold project at first and honestly had no clue about gold. But over time and again with "learning by doing" we learned a lot.

We started to sell stocks of our company and got the first two investors in the first month for a total of $16,500. The second month we didn't raise a cent and I almost quit.

But after that we got lucky and raised about $160,000 in the third month. This gave us the necessary capital to secure a gold project in Mexico.

After that things started to take off and more and more people joined our organization. Eventually, our team was over 60 people strong and we raised about one to two million dollars per month.

The Wolf of Wall Street

> The BS stories that we keep telling ourselves are the reason why we don't achieve our goals.

Maybe you have seen the movie the Wolf of Wall Street with Leonardo Di Caprio and asked yourself how you could make money just like him.

The real Wolf of Wall Street, Jordan Belfort, has raised over $200 million from investors but unfortunately he has done it in a fraudulent way – even though 95% of the things he did were actually legal.

Basically, the process is selling stocks from a company to investors, earning a commission and getting the company funded. What I can teach you is the same principle to make money but to do it in a 100% legal manner and with integrity.

I have "only" raised $40 million from private investors for private companies but I am sure that I can teach you many valuable things when it comes to this topic! In total I raised over $400 million from private investors for all kinds of financial products and $600 million from institutional investors like banks, investment houses and others.

Since you are dealing with **new start-up companies there is always risk involved** for the investors. That is simply the nature of this business. But at the same time it is one of the most lucrative investments if the deal goes right. With some deals investors can even make 10 times of what they have initially invested. In the end it is up to the company and the management to make that happen.

The main principle is always the same: how well you can sell your idea (= your company = shares of your company). The better you can position it, the more you will sell. The more you sell, the more money you will make.

> If you want to achieve the same result as other successful people, simply copy what they have done and you will get the same results. (Tony Robbins)

Lack of money is the most common problem with new business ideas

Let's say you have a new business idea. In order for you to turn this business idea into reality you will need money.

Now the first step that most people do is to go to the local bank and ask for a loan. The problem is that most banks will not lend anyone any money if there is no security or collateral.

This usually ends most business dreams because without any money you can't turn your idea into a reality.

But even if you have some money saved and use your own money to start your own business, most people will eventually run out of money because they underestimated how much longer it takes to make a profit and how much more it will cost to run a business.

> Most business undertakings **cost twice the amount** than originally anticipated and **take twice as long.** (Brian Tracy)

Then the next problem is that even if you have some money to get started, most people have no idea how to get more money into the company through financings or investors.

And if they approach investors, they usually have **no clear plan or strategy** on how the investor will get a good performance, **if** he will get his investment back and more importantly **when** he will get his investment back. Simply saying, *"Hey, this is a great business idea"* is unfortunately not enough for someone to invest into a company. You will need a clear strategy for an investor so that he is motivated to invest.

And finally, if you go to a professional Venture Capital Firm because you have a great idea, the firm will very often take over control of your company and end up owning more than 80% of your business.

But this is not what most new entrepreneurs want. They have an idea that they believe will make them rich and they want to stay in control of their own company. They don't want to keep their freedom and do things on their own terms.

Unfortunately, with all these problems and obstacles most people resign and go back to the "security" of a regular job and their business dreams end up staying dreams forever.

There are many problems and challenges when someone is starting a new business. Most people feel overwhelmed and give up because of these initial problems.

Here are the ten most common problems:

<u>Summary of problems</u>

Problem 1: Banks won't lend you any money without collateral
Problem 2: You will eventually run out of your personal savings (=personal financial ruin)
Problem 3: No knowledge about corporate finance, share structures and securities laws
Problem 4: Venture Capital Firms will take over company and entrepreneur loses control
Problem 5: Venture Capital Firms will dictate direction of company = having a job
Problem 6: Venture Capital Firms will get rich – not entrepreneur
Problem 7: Entrepreneurs has no clear strategy how to attract private investors

Problem 8: Entrepreneurs have no clear strategy for selling part of the company
Problem 9: Entrepreneurs usually give away too much of the company in the beginning
Problem 10: Entrepreneur has to go back to regular job = end of dream

> Don't downgrade your dream just to fit your reality.
> Upgrade your conviction and chose a new plan.

The power of Private Equity – Keeping the business dream alive

Luckily, there is an alternative. It is called "Private Equity".

Instead of going to a bank and getting a loan or getting money from a "Venture Capital Shark", you can raise money from private investors to finance your business idea.

Imagine if you had for example $2 million in the first 12 months to run your business...

How much different could your potential success be instead of starting with very little or no money?

Do you think that if you knew that there is money in the bank and you could pay yourself a monthly salary from your own company that you would be less stressed and could fully focus on working on the business?

> Do you think it would dramatically increase your chances of success if you had for example $2 million for your business ideas?

I can personally tell you from experience that it will change EVERYTHING! I raised over $40 million in 2 ½ years and a lot of positive things happened.

Not every business idea requires necessarily that much money. Sometimes you can create a great business with only one or two million dollars that will change your life for good. The main goal is to use the initial money to make your basic concept work and then you can get more money from an investment house later.

This program is about teaching you how to make all this happen.

> Mitt Romney the Republican presidential candidate has an estimated net worth over $240 million. How did he get it? He made his career in Private Equity!

He was working for the Private Equity company Bain Capital and that is how he made his millions. Do you want to know how you could do the same?

I often get the following question: "*Hey, if it is so lucrative, why are you selling these programs to us? Why don't you just make millions for yourself?*"

Answer: I have earned millions and I enjoy this topic so much and get so excited about it that I want to share my excitement with the world. And I still continue to make money this way. But I remember how I was lost and confused and really wanted to become successful in my life. I had no idea how to make it happen back then. But today I feel that money alone is not fulfilling. I want to help people. I want to teach people who have that inner burning desire but need to knowledge and tools that they are lacking. By making others successful I get a sense of accomplishment and feel that I can give back to the world.

What is the Private Equity Business System and how does it work exactly?

Private Equity is money that comes from investors of companies that are not yet listed on a public stock market. Or in simple words: Investors buy shares of a private company.

The basic concept of the Private Equity Business System will teach you the following things:

1. How to find investors, raise money and create a multi-million dollar company.
2. How to structure your company so that you can attract private investors
3. How and where to find private investors
4. How to take your company public in the stock market and give your investors an exit strategy for their investment
5. How to create a publicly listed company and turn your personal share position into millions
6. How to create a successful business with the power of Private Equity
7. How to make money for yourself using the system of Private Equity

> The main goal of this program is to have it explained in a simple, clear and easy to understand format so that regular "non-finance people" will get it.

Don't be intimidated if you have no finance background. You can compare it to driving a car. You need to learn how everything works so that you can drive the car and move forward but you don't need to know how the engine works. In that case you will hire a mechanic.

When it comes to Private Equity you will need the help of professionals as well. You will need a securities lawyer, an accountant and other professionals. But you don't have to know everything yourself. But more details later.

The foundation of our economy

Take a good look at the world around you. Everything that you own, see or eat comes from a company. The food you eat, the clothes you wear, the car you drive and basically everything around you was produced and sold to you by big corporations.

Some big brand names like Coca Cola, Microsoft, McDonald's are worth billions of dollars and can't almost be found all over the world and in every country.

But how did it all start?

Let's take Coca Cola as an example. One day in 1886, a pharmacist from Atlanta had an idea and came up with a drink. A drink? That doesn't sound like a million dollar idea at first but we all know how popular it became.

Walt Disney imagined his amusement park and put it on a piece of paper. But by getting money into the company to finance the idea, it became the biggest entertainment company in the world.

Or what about Microsoft? Bill Gates created software that is on 80% of all the computers in the world today.

But there are also thousands of unknown companies that are successful and that have created great products. Many of them are totally unknown by the general public but worth millions or billions of dollars.

A corporation is a tool to create something big. And by choosing the right model and financing structure you can accelerate the progress. If you know how to properly organize it so that you can attract investors who will give you their money and trust, they will take on the risk for you.

> A corporation is the greatest invention of our time. Someone has an idea and it will take on a life of its own.

Creating something substantial out of thin air

Think about the basic foundation of our economy. If you have an idea for a business, it is first merely a thought. You will take that thought (or idea) and manifest it into the real world. You will form a corporation, put in a business model, create the right share structure, finance the company, take it public in the stock market, get additional financing from institutional investors and finally create a multi-million dollar business.

> Thoughts are energy. They are real and they have power.
> Every business was originally just a thought or a dream.

Think about it. All the big companies in today's world were first just a thought or a dream and then turned into big corporations that sell products or services and employ thousands of employees. The more time goes by the bigger and more valuable the company gets. And if you were the founder of this business with the majority of the shares in the company, not only will the company be worth millions but your personal net worth as well.

I will teach you several exciting business models that will be ideal for private equity and public companies. Resources deals like oil and gas, gold, silver are a great choice, for example, but also biotechnology and other new technologies. I will show you a typical company and how you can put together a similar deal without any previous knowledge about the industry. You don't have to be a specialist yourself in that field. You can hire specialists or scientists. All you have to do is to organize it and lead it.

I will show you how to find investors and build sales organizations that exclusively sell the shares of your company to raise capital for your projects. I owned several sales organizations during my career. One of them continually raised about one to two million dollars each month for several years. How cool is that? Knowing that there is a constant flow of money available for your business!

Excited enough? Ok, let's get started with the basics.

> Good things will happen not because of "luck"
> but because you work hard to get them.

What is a stock?

A stock or a stock certificate represents ownership in a corporation. Your stock will only have value if the company has value. Otherwise it is simply a piece of paper.

But here is where you come in. Your job is to **put a project or product into the company** that increases the value of the company and will eventually make a profit.

Basically, **your business idea or business model** is what drives the company. The corporation is like the car. You will learn how to create and build the car so that will have more and more horsepower over time.

> The cool thing about founding a company is that you give life to something that was simply a piece of paper and you put the value into it.

Multi-millionaires and billionaires

If you take a look at the richest people in the world, you will find out that they have one thing in common. Not one of them had a job. They owned companies that went public in the stock market, expanded and got valued at millions or billions of dollars. And that is the answer. You will only become very rich if you decide to have a business that becomes big.

How does someone become a multi-millionaire or even a billionaire? Well, it wasn't by working in a 9 to 5 job with a boss and a salary. And it wasn't by working two jobs or working overtime. Only 1% of people became rich because they can sing, act or won the lottery. Only 10% were doctors, lawyers or other professionals.

The answer is pretty simple. Over 74% were entrepreneurs. Nobody has done it by having a regular job or an income. The only way that people become billionaires is by **owning a big share position** in a company.

If you really look at people like Bill Gates or other billionaires, you will find that there is really only one way to become a billionaire. A person had an idea and built a business. The company eventually went public in the stock market and the company grew over time. The founders had a majority share position in the company and because of it they became billionaires. That is the only way it is possible unless they inherited it from a person who has done it just like that.

Ideas are the beginning points of all fortunes. (Napoleon Hill)

Let's make an example:

You start a company and you own 10 million shares (= 10%) of a company that has issued a total of 100 million shares. At first, the price per share is $0.10 when you start out. Once the company is public is it $1.00 per share. Over time you develop the company and after 20 years the stock price has gone to $100 per share – that's a billion. Of course, this is very simplified but I guess you understand the main idea.

How many companies do you know that have a share price of more than $100 per share? Typically, those companies also have much more than 100 million shares issued. So basically, there is a billionaire or at least a multi millionaire "hidden" in there somewhere.

If you are the founder of a new company, you will automatically be the main shareholder. If you structure it the right way, you can raise money by selling some of the shares of the company but still maintain the majority of the company. If your company is successful, your shares will gain in value and this could potentially mean that you will own several million dollars because of your share position.

Why not put yourself into a position that could allow that to happen?

Well not everybody is going to become a billionaire. And not everybody is going to be a millionaire – even though there are over 24.2 million millionaires in the United States alone today.

You can still have a public company and make money with it. You can use all this knowledge and make a nice income from operating the company. You decide how much your income will be by the size and efforts of your capital raising abilities and on how well you develop your company.

There are thousands of people who have done it before you and now enjoy the life they always wanted. You just need to know how it is done and then do the same things so that you will get the same results. If you follow through, your life will never be the same.

Job vs. being an entrepreneur

Joke:

The owner of the company where I work pulled up in his brand new BMW this morning.

ME: "*Wow, that's a really nice car boss!*"
BOSS: "*Let me tell you something: If you set goals, work hard, and act determined, I can get an even better one next year!*"

No matter how hard you work as an employee, you will never have the financial opportunities that owning your own company will give you.

Let's talk about "job security". Most people are scared of leaving their job. But as the owner and president of a company you can pay yourself a salary, a bonus, dividends, get more shares, loan money against your shares and so on. There are many options to make money. I have covered and explained all the options how you can make money later on in this program. There are two ways how you can earn money using Private Equity: 1. **Before** the company is public and 2. **after** the company is listed.

But you can also start small while you make your business happen. You raise $1 million in the first year, pay yourself a salary of $100,000 per year and use the $900,000 for the business.

Raising $1 million per year is pretty easy. It is about $85,000 per month. If you get about 4 investors per month (or one investor per week) who invests $20,000 on average, then you will reach that goal. When I raised money for Hemis the average investment per investor was $55,000. Some people invest $5000 others $100,000.

But the main goal is to build a company will eventually have real value so that your shares will become valuable. You can also choose not to pay you a salary at all but because you believe so much in your own project you hope that your shares will eventually be worth millions.

Example: You own 5 million shares personally and you hope that they will be valued at least at $1.00 per share when the company goes public (= $5 million) and several dollars in the years to come.

> The trick is to realize that the only long-term success that you should focus on is to build your own company that will turn into a multi million-dollar business.

Take a look at the people around you

In my opinion, the greatest invention of all time was to be able to form a company. But it is not just for you to make money. It can change the world and do great things for other people as well.

Think about it. Someone has an idea, incorporates a company, hires people, sells products and makes a profit. It provides hundreds of people with an income for themselves and their families. People can send their kids to school, buy houses and save for their retirement and it was all because you provided them with a job or an opportunity. It starts to take on a life of its own. If you do it well enough, and often enough, it will expand and grow.

Microsoft Corporation

Microsoft was not just a leader in computer innovation and software but it also changed the lives of its employees for the better. Many of the employees received stock options and shares of the company as a bonus. Some regular secretaries even became millionaires because of it.

Microsoft went public on March 13, 1986. If you were able to participate in the initial public offering and buy 1000 shares at $21 for $21,000, your shares would be worth over $7 million today. The stock has split nine times since the beginning.

Amount of shares at IPO	1000
Price per share	$21
Amount of shares today	288,000
Share price of Microsoft today	$46
Value of shares today	$13.24 million

What if you had shares of Microsoft **BEFORE** it was offered to the public?

You might have $26 million instead of $13 million. Or who knows, maybe even more! That is the attractiveness for investors to buy private shares of companies before they are listed. If you have a good story, you will get the money from investors to finance your business and therefore your dream.

What exactly does Private Equity mean?

Private Equity is a type of investment. The word "Private" refers to a company that is **not listed in a stock market.** If a company is public it is listed, if it is not listed, it is considered a private company.

The term "Equity" refers to **capital** or investments.

Therefore Private Equity means that it is an investment into a company that it not yet listed on a stock exchange.

How does Private Equity work?

A new start-up company is looking for initial capital to grow its business. In order to raise money for the company, the management of the company sells shares of the company to private investors (= to raise money).

Example:

ABC Corporation is in the oil business. In order to buy a piece of land, drill the holes and put an oil field into production, the company needs $2 million.

Since the company is very new and has no track record, no bank in the world will lend the company $2 million. There is no collateral or security for the bank in case the project doesn't go as planned.

But the management of ABC Corporation believes in its project and raises the money from private investors by selling a part of the company (= shares of the company) to private investors.

This way, the company can organize $2 million to make the project work. The investors invest into ABC Corporation, receive shares of the company and if the company is successful, the shares will go up in value.

Private Placements – Several financing rounds for investors

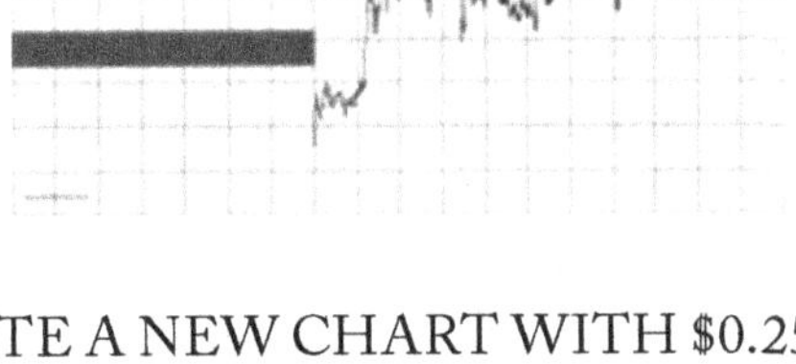

(PLEASE CREATE A NEW CHART WITH $0.25, $0.50, $0.75 and $1.00 IPO – MAKE IT SIMPLE AND CLEAR TO UNDERSTAND)

Before the company goes public it will do several "private placements" (= financing rounds) for private investors.

Example:

Financing round 1: \$0.25 per share – 1 million shares - \$250,000
Financing round 2: \$0.50 per share – 1 million shares - \$500,000
Financing round 3: \$0.75 per share – 1 million shares - \$750,000

Total money raised before IPO: \$1.5 million

IPO / first price: 1.00 per share

Explanation:

Let's say that a new company wants to raise \$1.5 million in the first year. The management decides to do three financing rounds to raise capital for the company.

The price per share in the first round is \$0.25. If someone invests \$10,000, he will get 40,000 shares of the company.

The first price is always the lowest price because the company is still very new and doesn't have a lot of assets. This means that an investment at this point in time is very risky because the company could fail. But if the company can raise the capital, execute its plans and go public at \$1.00 per share, the investor has quadrupled his investment. At the IPO his 40,000 shares will be worth \$40,000.

It is very attractive for an investor to get such a great performance but it is also good for the company because it will get capital into the company.

Once the company is public and trading in the stock market the price of the stock could potentially go from \$1.00 to several dollars in price. In this case the investors will really have made a lot of money.

After the IPO, the price will be driven by supply and demand. In any case, the price will be higher than at the beginning. Investing into a pre-IPO stock is an exciting adventure, especially if you have a stock that will go through the roof.

Even though big companies have a lot more money than new start-up companies, smaller companies have much more growth potential than larger companies. That is why it is so attractive to invest into them. Being able to be invested at the beginning before the company has become big can make a huge difference. Imagine if you had held stocks of companies like McDonald's, Cisco, Apple or Google 10 or 20 years ago, how much big would your personal net worth be today?

If only I had bought...

What are the top performing stocks of the past quarter century? They include some very familiar names like Dell, Microsoft and Home Depot, but also some surprises including the No.1 stock, Franklin Resources, which is up 64,224 percent since 1982.

A $100 investment in each of top 25 stocks in their infancy would have turned your $2,500 investment into a whopping $650,000.

Conclusion: The biggest grow potential of a company is in the beginning. This is the opportunity that you will give your investors.

Gold project example to get started

Let's assume that you have access to a gold project that could potentially have 1 million ounces of gold in the ground. One million ounces of gold at a gold price of $1200 per ounce is equal to $1.2 billion. The gold doesn't have to be produced – it is available and given to you by Mother Nature. All you have to do is to find it, dig it out of the ground and sell it. And in order to do that you must acquire a land position that potentially has gold in it.

<u>Example: how to acquire a land position to search for gold</u>

A farmer, who is the landowner, holds the legal rights to this property. You approach the farmer and ask him to acquire the mineral rights to his land position. A lawyer draws up a contract, which gives you the right to acquire the property's mineral rights. (= Option to buy the minerals rights, the farmer still owns the land)

In the beginning, the first contract with the landowner is simply an option. You pay the landowner $10,000 for an exclusive option to acquire his property in 3 months by paying $50,000. The landowner receives $10,000 now and in return you get an option. Your job is now to organize the remaining $50,000 within 3 months so that your option will be turned into a contract.

The contract will give you the rights to the property to do exploration and to do the necessary geological work to identify the gold resource. The farmer will still participate financially over the next few years.

Now in order to successfully acquire this project, you will have to do a first round of financing to get at least the $50,000 into the company. You can do a financing round at $0.10 per share and raise the capital from your family and friends.

There is actually a financing round called "family and friends". It is at the very beginning when you have zero capital and no project that the people that love you most and believe in you will give you their money.

But once you have acquired the first project, you have added value into the company and now the company is worth more.

Based on that initial success and value, you can now do a first public financing round at $0.25 per share and raise $250,000 for example. The $250,000 will be used to do work on the first project so that the company can have even more value and first positive successes.

After the first round you can do a second and third round and with each financing round you will increase the amount of money in the company and the value of it. You build up a company by creating assets.

Basically, this is the groundwork or also called "proof of concept" and "proof of management". You proof that you were able to do what you set out to achieve, acquire your first projects, develop your first prototype and proof that your idea or system is working and making a profit. But at the same time you have proven yourself as a good manager and shown that you can make it happen.

Now, after the initial phase is done, you will have a lot more options to acquire more capital from professional investment firms and banks.

Summary of advantages of Private Equity

Advantages of Private Equity for a company

- Getting the capital it needs to execute its plans (e.g. $2 million)
- Not having to give up control over the company (you make all the decisions)
- Cheap capital (no interest payments or loans, etc.)
- No interference from investment firm
- No risk to the company if project fails (investors carry the risk)

Advantages of Private Equity for an investor

- Low entry point for investor (e.g. $0.50 entry and exit at $1.00)
- High return potential (investors can potentially double or triple their money)
- Being part of a new and exciting company
- Short investment horizon (1 to 2 years)
- No price fluctuations (not trading in the market, not exposed to market crashes)
- Exit strategy is given with IPO (they can sell their shares in the stock market)

Advantages of Private Equity for an entrepreneur

- Capital for company and project is available to execute the plans
- Entrepreneur doesn't have to give personal guarantee (= no risk to him)
- Entrepreneur can pay himself a monthly salary and quit his full-time job
- Entrepreneur can live his dream and build something out of nothing

- Entrepreneur is major shareholder of the company and if the project succeeds then he could become a millionaire

The $100 million blueprint explained

> When you try to achieve something big, it is hard to fail completely. (Tim Ferriss)

The following text is an explanation and description on how to create company with a market capitalization of $100 million or more in the stock market.

$100 million is actually a very small number for the stock market. Here is how the professionals look at it:

Micro cap company	below $100 million
Small cap company	$100 million to $500 million
Medium cap company	$500 million to $1 billion
Large cap company	more than $1 billion

The word “cap” stands for “capitalization” or market capitalization. This means basically valuation or how much the company is worth in the market.

Choosing the right project / product

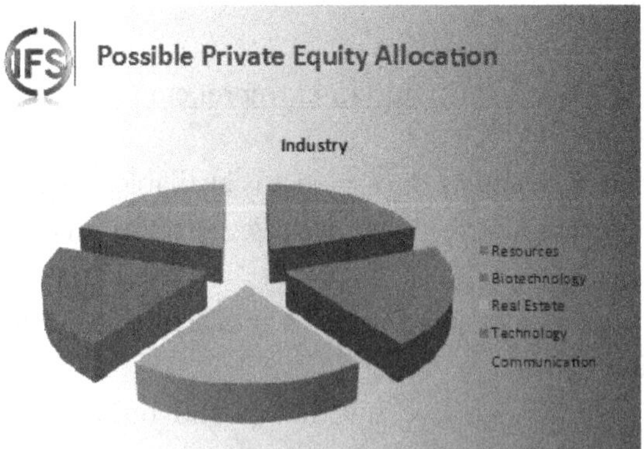

The next step is to find a project. This can basically be any project from any industry but there are some things that you need to consider if you want to have a $100 million company in the future. There is no right or wrong project but not every business model is ideal for the stock market or a good choice to attract investors.

Therefore you should focus on industries or products that investors like and that have a potential to grow into a multi million dollar business. Good choices are: Natural resources (gold, silver, oil, etc.), biotechnology, real estate and modern technology. If you have a concept for a company that cannot eventually be turned into a $100 million deal, then you should not choose it.

Once you have your project, you need to know how to raise capital and attract investors.

In general, you need to raise the first couple of million of dollars yourself to get started. Once you have raised the initial capital to prove that your business model or prototype works, it is much easier to get $10 million or $20 million in financing from a financial institution.

Thoughts about risk

Famous quotes about risk

- *Risk comes from not knowing what you're doing.* (Warren Buffett)
- *Nothing happens without risk, but without risk nothing happens either.* (Walter Scheel, former German chancellor)
- *People, who avoid risk, risk the most.* (George Frost Kennan, Diplomat)

There is basically no investment without risk. The higher the possible return, the higher the risk.

Risk is always relative. There is the famous triangle of risk, return and time. You can never have all three things in an ideal relationship. Typically, the shorter the investment horizon, the less return and the more risk. The longer the time, the less risk and the more return can be expected.

The cool thing about Private Equity is that you have a very short time frame (1 to 2 years) and a high return potential (several hundred percent). Now when it comes to the risk that is can be very high or if you work with a group who has done deals successfully before and they know what they are doing, then the risk can be much lower. So basically, if the deal works out, the company goes public, the risk can be relatively low.

In general, it is advised not to invest more than 5 to 10% of your total portfolio into Private Equity investments. Here is why:

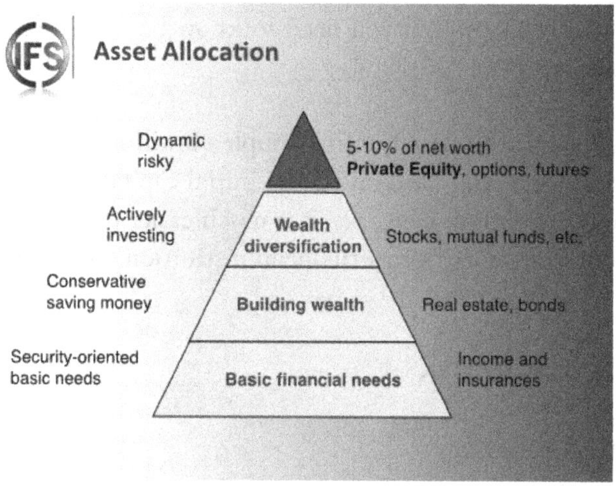

A "textbook portfolio" should look like this:

<u>Example: $100,000 total money available to invest</u>

40% = conservative investments (cash, bonds, insurances, real estate)
30% = balanced (mix of bonds and stocks, mutual funds)
20% = growth-oriented (individual stocks)
10% = dynamic / risky (Private Equity, options, futures)

Since not every Private Equity deal is a success, an investor should not put more than 5-10% into this type of investment.

Why most new companies fail

1. Lack of capital
2. Poor management choices or inexperienced management team
3. No real merit for products in the market place (= wrong product)

How to eliminate or reduce risk factors

Unfortunately, there is always some degree of risk when it comes to investments. Nothing is 100% secure. But when it comes to Private Equity there are certain things that you can do as an entrepreneur to increase the chances of success and therefore reduce the potential risk factors.

Risk 1: Lack of capital
Solution: Make capital raising your number one priority next to developing your business. My having your own sales team to raise capital, you will always have enough money in the company.

Risk 2: Management mistakes
Solution: Everybody makes mistakes as a manager. That is normal. But by utilizing the experience of professionals like a securities lawyer or me as your independent consultant for example, will dramatically increase your chances of success.

Risk 3: Poor product choice
Solution: Not every product is an ideal candidate for Private Equity. You should only pick a product that has a multi-million potential. Certain industries are better than others in the beginning. Also, if you have to first create the market need by spending millions in marketing for five years first to make your product known, then you might want to rethink your choices.

Risk 4: Keeping control of the company
Solution: If I gave a scientist $5 million who invented and developed a great new product or cure for cancer, he might have created a great product but he is really not a specialist when it comes to financing, stocks, taking a company public and marketing. Therefore it is smarter to have someone in charge that has done the process before and has different skills and

knowledge. When it came to my deals, we always made sure that we would keep the control of the company in the first couple of years so that we could ensure the successful development of the stock and the corporation.

Top IPOs and examples of successful stocks

> Money may not buy you happiness but I would rather cry in a Mercedes than on a bus.

The biggest IPOs in the last few years were Alibaba Group, Agricultural Bank of China, Industrial & Commercial Bank of China, VISA, General Motors and Facebook.

Google, zynga, LinkedIn or Groupon also did very well. But there are also other successful companies that are less known like for example Fabrinet (FN), MakeMyTrio (MMYT), Molycorp (MCP) and others who tripled their stock price after the IPO – just to mention a few.

Some of those companies have been around for many years. But there are hundreds of companies that "no one knows about" that did extremely well. Typically, there are in a nice market or an industry that is not consumer based.

Examples:

- Greystar Resources went from $0.70 to $13.00 (1500%)
- Energy Metals went from $0.25 to $6.25 (25x times up!)
- Alumina Copper offered as a Private Placement and sold for $425 million
- Universal Uranium went up 400% (discovery of Uranium deposit)
- Hemis first financing round was $0.27 and the stock went up to $3.50 (1200%)
- Tecton was sold at $0.50 first and went up $2.00 (400%)
- Linear Gold went from $1.80 to $9.00 in 12 months. (500%)
- ILG was first offered at $0.50, then $2.50, then $10.50 and the company was finally valued at $14.50 per share.

- Halo Resources was first offered at $0.10; got listed at $0.50 went to $1.50.
- Arc Energy went from $6 to $20 within 6 years.
- Cumberland went from $0.50 to $9.50 in 7.5 years. (1900%)
- El Dorado was first offered at $1.00; went to $10.50 in 4.5 years. (1000%)

> There are thousands of successful entrepreneurs living among you with companies that did really well in the stock market. Just because you have never heard of them, doesn't make them less successful.

Choosing the right project and industry

Not every industry is a good choice for a Private Equity product. I personally like natural resources. The reason for this is that you don't have to first produce them. All you have to do is to acquire a piece of land and the land already contains the natural resource. Your job is to get it out of the ground. But the earth provides the product for you. In case of gold or oil, you just have to find it and bring it to the surface. Then you call sell it for a profit. And usually finding a gold reserve is a multi million dollar discovery. The same is true for finding oil.

Example: Oil and gas

Oil and gas prices have increased greatly over the last 30 years. Many of the richest people in the world made their fortunes from oil.

Oil is a natural resource that has been developed by nature over millions of years. It is something that doesn't have to be produced first. It is available by Mother Nature for free and all you have to do is finding it.

Once you put up a rig, an oil well can produce anywhere from 10 to 20 years. Natural gas is usually a bi-product that comes with an oil deposit. The great thing about this industry is also that there is already an established market and many pipelines available and selling the product is easy – unlike with a new technology where a market first needs to be established and takes years to create.

Over the last 30 years the oil price has multiplied and the same will happen for the next 30 years to come. Experts believe that half of the world's oil supply has been found and that the second half will soon be used up. The world cannot survive without oil at this point in time and alternative energy sources will take at least one or more generations to replace oil and the main energy source.

Now is the perfect time to invest into oil. If you are part of it for the next 5 to 10 years, you will benefit from a huge up-trend. After that it might be too late.

As an entrepreneur you might decide to acquire a piece of property, hire a geologist and start your first project.

Let's assume that you invest $1 million into a well and that this well produces 100 barrels per day. If the oil price is $50 per barrel, you will earn $5000 per day or $150,000 per month. About half of this will go to production cost and taxes and therefore you will end up with about $75,000 per month. This is a net profit of $900,000 per year.

It takes about 3 months to put the project into production and after 13 months of production you will have recouped your initial investment of $1 million.

If the well will produce for the next 20 years, you won't have to invest another dollar into it and you will make $900,000 per year or $18 million after 20 years.

If you are able to create not just one but also seven of those wells, you will have approximately $7 million per year as profits. Based on the valuation formula (annual earnings x P/E ratio of 15) you will have a market capitalization of $100 million.

Once you can proof that your oil well is producing in one place, it is usually possible to find more drill targets nearby.

This is just one example of how you could create $100 million company by acquiring oil projects. Finding oil projects is not as difficult as you might think. You can find projects online or by talking to geologists. Getting a project is easy. The "hard part" for most people is getting the money to finance those projects. But if you apply the knowledge of Private Equity that you have learned here, you will be able to organize the first million with no problems.

Conclusion:

You can build a $100 million company if you and a few sales people (3 to 4 guys) raise $2 million in 12 months to fund the initial project.

- Do you think that is realistic?
- Do you think it is possible that a group of 4 people could organize $500,000 each in a matter of a year?
- Do you think that finding 2 or 3 investors per month per person is doable?

Of course it is possible!

Minimum example

Let's say that you offer your shares for $0.50 and raise $1 million in 12 months. The $1 million will enable you to generate an oil well that produces 100 barrels per day or about $1 million per year in earnings.

Your company is now worth about $15 million (with P/E ratio of 15). If you only issue a very small number of shares, let's say 15 million shares in total, then your share price is $1.00 per share. If your investors invested their money at $0.50 per share and now have $1.00 per share, then they have doubled their investment. Cool, isn't it?

Looking at this example and utilizing the vehicle of oil, it seems very easily doable.

Inventions, gadgets or technological concepts

There are many people out there who create and develop new inventions. Typically, those people are technology nerds who love to come up with a new concept or prototype to make the world a better place. Some people invent new solar panels; others develop other technological things that they believe in.

The main problem of those inventors is lack of money (like always!). But if you can make a deal with them and get the rights to their invention, you can start a new company, let them be in charge of the product development and you will raise the money to make it happen.

The inventor will be able to fund his research and develop the product and live his dream. You profit from the existing product and make money by being a major shareholder. This is a win-win situation for everyone.

Biotech deal example

Another way to find a good project is to go a University and check out the research department. A professor or a person studying for his PhD is working on a cure for cancer. It is a new idea / approach and he is writing a paper on his research.

A professor usually has no clue about organizing millions to turn his research into a reality. But luckily you do!

You can find amazing projects that can change the world and be a part of it. You help to finance a cure or a new medication and help with the development of the company by raising capital.

Choosing the right management team

> Just because you can cook doesn't mean
> that you should run a restaurant.

What I am teaching you is not to cook food but how to run the restaurant. Building a company happens on several levels. Developing a great product and selling it to customers is just one part. The other part is to build the financial structure, raising money and taking the company public.

A scientist or specialist should not automatically be the CEO. Sometimes it is better than someone else is running the company and the scientist is responsible for the production or operations.

One of the most important lessons that I have learned is that there can only be one boss. If two people decide to start a company together then they must first decide who the boss is and who is responsible for other things.

You can learn how to run a gold company without having a degree in geology. You can hire specialists (e.g. geologists, biotech guy, IT developer, etc.) for the technical part and operations.

Business plan and development

In order to create successful deal, you need to have a business plan. A typical plan for a Private Equity company would look something like this:

Month	Going public plan	Operations
1.	First round of financing	Start
2.	Create financial statements	Acquire 1st project
3.	Financial audit	Add important management member
4.	Second round of financing	Option for 2nd project
5.	SEC Filing: S-1 Registration Statement	Acquire 2nd project
6.	Answer questions from SEC	Develop 1st and 2nd project
7.	FINRA – Form 15c2-11 (market maker)	Work program I
8.	Answer questions from FINRA	Geological report NI 43-101
9.	Third round of financing	Option for 3rd project
10.	Assignment of trading symbol	Acquire 3rd project

11. Preparation of news releases	Work program II
12. First price / start trading	Work program III

<u>13-24 months</u>

- Positive share price development from \$1.00 to \$2.00
- Develop projects further
- PIPE financing (Private Placement into Public Entity)

<u>After 24 months</u>

- Exit for initial investors
- Option for mega project
- Capital acquisition from institutional investor for \$20 million

As you can see, the first year is the most important year. While you are preparing for the IPO you also have to develop the company at the same time. Sometimes it is smarter to wait 6 to 12 months and to give the company a little bit more time before it goes public so that it can develop the projects further.

The share structure = \$100 million blueprint

The skeleton of your company = the share structure

Just like there are bones inside your body to hold everything in place, a company needs a good skeleton or share structure to be in good shape.

If you fail to do this, you will lose control over the company or create a share price valuation disaster and your company will fail due to poor planning and initial set-up.

All your efforts, reputation and money will be gone if you screw this part up. But luckily you are not alone: I am here to help you.

Components of a company

In order to create successful business there are a number of components that need to be present and they all must fit together.

- Shell (corporation)
- Management team (You and your key members)
- Financing (money from Private Placements)
- Specialist team (e.g. geological team)
- Projects / products (land, contract, option, prototype, etc.)
- Legal counsel and knowledge (securities lawyer)
- Administrational support / team (your assistant)
- Accounting (accountant and auditor)
- Financial knowledge about Private Equity and IPO plan (this text)
- Promotion (marketing of shares when company is publicly traded to create volume)
- Contact of networks (market makers, project access, financing partners, etc.)
- Strategic action plan and exit (business plan)

<u>Example of a share structure:</u>

Price	Who	shares	money raised
$0.001	par value (management)	10 million	$10,000
$0.10	family and friends	500,000	$50,000
$0.25	1st round of financing / private placement	1 million	$250,000
$0.50	2nd round of financing / private placement	1 million	$500,000
$0.75	3rd round of financing / private placement	1 million	$750,000
$1.00	First price at IPO		
$2 - $3.00	12 to 24 months after IPO		

Total money raised before IPO: $1.56 million

Amount of shares	Owners
10 million	Management key members
500,000	family and friends
3 million	Investors (3 rounds @ 1 million shares each)
13.5 million shares	**Total issued**

Little trick / hint: The 10 million shares of the management team are preferred shares (= special shares with 10x the voting rights of common shares so that the management won't lose control over the company). The shares of the investors are common shares with one vote per share. You can also give those shares special dividend rights.

Typical set-up:

100 million shares	Authorized (maximum that can be issued)
20 million shares	Preferred shares (for management with 10x voting rights)
80 million shares	Common shares (for investors)

Valuations, market capitalization and set-up

Every great company that is publicly listed had humble beginnings. It first needs to get incorporated and shares needed to be issued. That is the starting point.

But you can't just do it like everybody else. You need to know from the beginning where you want to end up. Therefore you need to know how to structure it the right way so that your share structure will help you to raise capital without losing control.

Of course, there are many different ways on how to choose the perfect share structure but to keep things simple, we will assume that a public company will get incorporated with 100 million shares authorized but only 50 million shares will be issued.

Incorporation

100 million shares authorized (maximum amount that can be issued)
Par value - $0.00001 per share (minimum amount per share at the beginning)

When you incorporate a new company you have to decide what the maximum number of shares will be and what the lowest possible price is.

When public

Goal = $100 million value / market capitalization
50 million shares issued and outstanding
Share price = $2.00 per share

If your goal is to create a $100 million company you plan on issuing 50 million shares in total, then you must make sure that your share price will be $2.00. You can create a $2.00 share price by making sure you have generated enough earnings or assets in the company.

Basic calculation

50 million shares x $2.00 per share = $100 million total value / market capitalization
(Amount of shares) x (share price) = market capitalization

There are two basic valuation formulas that you should understand:

Formula 1: Amount of shares outstanding x share price = market capitalization
Formula 2: Annual earnings x P/E ratio (price per earnings) = fair valuation

In general, when it comes to building a public company you must start with the end goal in mind. Then, you have to go backwards and define the individual steps. This also have a big effect on your share structure and at what prices you will raise capital.

Example: $10 million annual earnings x 10 (P/E ratio) = $100 million valuation

So in this case you need to build a business that will generate $10 million in annual earnings.

Explanation

Assuming a company has issued 50 million shares and a current share price of $2.00 per share, and then the market capitalization is $100 million. (See formula 1)

This calculation is not based on the success of the company or any other factor but is solely based on math. The share price might be too high or too low based on the operations of the company but if the market is willing to pay $2.00 for a stock, then that is what the price is and therefore the market capitalization or value of the company is.

In order to get an idea whether the valuation is fair, we need to apply the second formula. Let's assume that the company is having earnings of $10 million per year and if you multiply this number with the P/E ratio of 10, you will get a fair valuation of what the company should be worth. (See formula 2)

The P/E ratio is a number that varies from industry to industry. It is simply a factor of many years of earnings a person would be willing to pay to buy the whole company.

Let's look at an example: Assuming you were interested in buying a business that generates $1 million per year in earnings. How much would you be willing to pay for it? If you were willing to pay $5 million for it, you would have amortized your investment in 5 years. The P/E ratio is the factor 5 (or 5 years).

When it comes to private companies being bought, the P/E is anywhere from 3 to 5 but when it comes to listed companies, the average P/E ratio is 15. With more conservative businesses or old economy industries it is around 10 and with more dynamic industries it is around 25.

If we now consider that $10 million (annual earnings) is multiplied by 10, then a fair valuation would be $100 million. In order to get the share price you need to divide the $100 million with the amount of shares outstanding (the shares that the company has issued) which is 50 million in our example and therefore the share price is $2.00.

Based on these simple calculations you will get a guideline of whether a company is over or undervalued in relation to its annual earnings.

Of course other factors can also be important for the valuation. Some things are intangible and cannot be taken into consideration with a formula. These might be factors like ability to increase earnings, stability of the company, market position, etc.

This also means that a company can be valued higher because of its positive outlook even if the current numbers are not reflecting it. If someone is convinced of the long-term potential of the company, investors or the market is willing to pay a higher price today.

Generating annual earnings out of the money raised

The goal is to create earnings of $5-10 million per year with the money that you will raise. So the question is this: Do you think you can create a business that will eventually generate $5 million in earnings per year with about $5 million that you have raised?

> Entrepreneurship is living a few years of your life like most people won't so that you can spend the rest of your life like most people can't.

Based on our numbers and the goal of wanting to have a company with a market capitalization of $100 million, we must create annual earnings of $5-10 million per year to achieve our goal.

Proof of concept example with a small business

> Don't give up too easily now – you are probably closer to success than you think.

But you can also **"start small and finish big"**.

My sister-in-law had a business idea. She first thought that it would be a great idea to develop a small business that she could operate on the side while working as a nurse.

Her idea is to create picnics for other people. She is a great cook and knows how to put together a nice looking picnic. She is convinced that other people would want to surprise their loved ones with a surprise picnic for special occasions.

She believes that she can charge anywhere from $150 to $300 per picnic depending on the package. She wants to call it "Perfect Picnics".

Let's say that she makes an average of $100 in profit for herself per picnic.

Let's assume that she could market it in such a way that she could book five picnics per day. This would give her $500 in profit per day.

Because the idea is so popular she eventually needs to get help. She decides to hire two employees and pays them an hourly rate to do the work. Let's say that 50% of her earnings go toward the employees' wages. In that case she would make another $500 per day for the two employees.

So in total she has the potential to earn $1000 per day.

Now because the system is working so well, she decides to duplicate the concept and expands the business to ten different cities where she has three employees each.

In that case she would make $10,000 per day. If she is fully booked on 25 days per month, then she makes $250,000 per month in pure profits.

This equals $3 million per year.

She has come a long way from a small business idea that she could operate on the side, wouldn't you agree?

Now, let's take it even further!

If she decided to sell the business, she could probably ask for $10 million. After three years the buyer would start making a profit. If the buyer believes in the business concept and thinks that it could be expanded to 100 locations, then this would be a small price to pay.

There is, however, an even better way for her to sell her company. She could take her company public in the stock market. In the stock market the valuation goes up. This is called the P/E ratio. The P/E ratio on average in the stock market is 15. This means that the market is willing to pay 15 times the annual earnings of that business. So if you multiply $3 million with 15 you end up with a market valuation of $45 million.

A bigger company decides to buy her out and offers $30 million.

This example is no utopia or fantasy. A woman who started an indoor play facility for kids eventually ended up with over 200 locations and sold her business for over $80 million.

Sometimes a small business idea that doesn't appear to have a lot of potential for growth can become something really big. It is the little, every day ideas that people are willing to pay for that make a business successful. Think about Starbucks: all they do is sell coffee! Subway sells only sandwiches. What could you sell?

Start with something small that you have a passion for and develop it into something that works. It needs to be something that people are willing to pay money for, makes a profit, can be duplicated, multiplied and be operated by others. All you need to do is to create a basic business concept that works and generates a profit.

Conclusion:

> If you can create a business that generates annual earnings of $10 million you can create a company with a valuation of $100 million.

The process step by step

Setting goals for the company and for yourself

You have to start with the end goal before you begin. Basically, you will have three options at the end:

1. You can stay on as president and CEO and run the company for several years
2. You can step down and simply be a main shareholder but someone else is running the daily operations
3. You can sell the majority of your share position and make a lot of money

In regards to the company you can…

1. Make millions by owning shares of the company
2. Have a monthly income as a director or consultant for many years to come
3. Create many happy investors that you can re-use for your next deal
4. The business is functioning and making a profit. This creates stability financially and you will have created a success story.

Incorporation, set-up and structure

When you incorporate a new company you want to start with the end goal in mind. You should set it up with all the pre-IPO financing rounds in mind and assign yourself enough shares and voting rights so that you won't lose control to bigger investors.

You know already how much money you want to raise and at what price.

Business Development

The main goal in regards to your actual underlying business is to do one of the following things:

1. Proof of business model or business concept
2. Create a prototype or develop the product (robot, software, etc.)
3. Acquire and develop something (e.g. land position, company, software, etc.)

The goal is to develop the company to a certain level so that a bigger investment house can see that you have done the groundwork and that your concept works so that they have less risk to invest $10 to $20 million into your company.

Going public process and SEC filings

The going public process will take about 6 to 12 months. You will need the help of a securities lawyer. You don't have to hurry, though. Make sure that you give yourself enough time to develop the company and raise enough money before you go public. Sometimes it is better to wait to have a greater impact when you are trading.

Professional Team

You will need a number of professionals to help you with the entire process:

Transfer Agent: Independent company that issues shares and keeps track
Registered Agent: Required in each state when you incorporate a company
Market Maker: Member of FINRA who will sponsor you to get a trading symbol
Stockbroker: To help you to sell shares and help when publicly trading
Accountant: To make your financial statements every 3 months
Auditor: Required to check your financial statements every 3 months
Legal Team: To help you with the entire process
Consultant: To help with business development

Creating marketing material and legal contracts

You will need the following legal material / contracts:

- SSA (Share subscription agreement) = contract to buy shares
- PPM (Private Placement Memorandum) = legal document that describes all details and risks about the company
- Minimum of 35 shareholders buying at least 100 shares each (proof of SSA, purchase and identity)

You can create the following marketing material to help sell your stocks:

- 2 pager summary
- Marketing brochure
- Power Point Presentation
- Website

Exit after IPO

The main goal for you is to create successful exit for your initial investors. When people first buy your stocks, the stocks will be restricted from selling because there is no market to sell them. Once the company is public and trading, the investors can sell their shares into the open market. Basically, going public is your exit strategy.

One of the biggest challenges is to create enough volume so that people can actually sell their shares. There are a number of promotional activities that you can do to create more volume in the market.

Dealing with investors

Some people are easy, some as difficult to handle. You will always get one or two assholes out of a hundred investors. That just comes with the territory. My advice: Be legally airtight secured with the right contracts and don't take every investor! If you feel someone is going to be a pain in the butt, refuse to take his or her investment. Typically, it is not the person who invests $100,000 who makes problems. It is always the ones that invested $5000.

Potential pitfalls or why things go wrong…

- CEO is a technical specialist or scientist but not a businessman
- No exit strategy or plan for investors to sell their shares
- Company will not be able to raise enough capital to execute the business plan
- No experience of management in capital markets and how to finance and structure the company and share structure
- Sales projections are too optimistic
- Valuations are too optimistic
- Company will run out of money if costs are too high
- Company is dependent on outside capital / equity
- Dilution of share structure (too many shares have been issued)
- Projects or products have no merit in the market place
- Marketability and attractiveness for public shareholders (sexy enough story)
- Bad promoters (sharks) associated with the company
- Integrity of management team and track record of past
- Ability of management to present well and to convince institutional investors later

Consulting and help

The whole topic is quite complex and if you have never been involved in a deal like this you will definitely need help. That is why I am offering my consulting services.

Ways to make money with Private Equity

Making money before the company is public - Earning examples of Private Equity

As an entrepreneur you can build a new company, get it financed and take it public in the stock market.

> You can make money with your deal BEFORE the company is public and AFTER the company is public.

Private Equity is a way to sell shares of your company and in return people will put money into the corporate account. If you do your job well, you will be able to raise several hundred thousand or a few million dollars. This money is intended for the operations of the company, of course. However, there is no company if there are no people who operate it. So if you are the president of this company, you can pay yourself a salary. You can decide yourself what this salary should be. As a director of a company you can also pay yourself a bonus or issue additional shares as compensation.

As long as you do things that are reasonable and don't hurt the company, you should get paid for the work that you put in. Everybody understands and agrees with this.

There are a few ways to earn money:

- **Salary:** You can pay yourself a monthly salary. Example: $5,000 to $10,000 a month. For a CEO of a company that is very reasonable and on the low end.
- **Bonus:** You can have a plan and if the business reaches a certain milestone or goal, you will get a bonus: Example: $20,000
- **Consulting services**: Instead of being part of the company as management, you could work as an external consultant.
- **Expenses:** If you need to travel a lot, you can charge your expenses to the company. These could be things like air travel, your car, your phone, hotels, etc. If you are actively traveling and doing things this could easily be a few thousand dollars a month.
- **Selling shares:** You sell a portion of your own share position to new investors. You could for example sell 200,000 shares for $0.50 that you originally paid $0.0001 for. This would give you an additional $100,000.
- **Acquisition:** Depending on your business, you could acquire a piece of land privately or through one of your companies and then sell it for a higher price to the company. The difference would be your profit.

- **Promotion:** You can plan on selling a nice portion of your share position once your company goes public. You could for example sell 500,000 shares for $1 per share in the first month of going public.

(Before doing any of the above things please discuss it with your lawyer.)

As the owner you can pay yourself a salary, a bonus, dividends, get more shares, loan money against your shares and so on. The possibilities to make money are endless.

These are some great opportunities to make money before the company is public as long as you keep the best interests of the company and your investors at heart. Keep also in mind that if you can make your investors happy with the first deal, almost all of them will invest what they did before and more into your second deal.

How to create personal wealth with a listed company

If you personally own 10 million shares of your company and your company goes public at $1.00 per share, then your personal wealth is $10 million. If you can sell your share position in the market and turn it into cash, then you have it made.

> So the plan is to build a company, sell shares to investors and raise money for the company, go public and then sell some of your shares in the stock market to turn your share position into cash.

The real secret of our economy: public companies

> Have you ever wondered how people make millions in the stock market?
> Have you ever heard of someone who sold their business for millions of dollars?

You can sell your own stocks in the market and turn them into millions. This happens after your company is public. Here are some examples of how people make money with companies:

<u>Owning shares in public company</u>
How do you get to own shares in a public company? You have to be one of the founders at the beginning. Example: If you form a new corporation and issue **5 million shares for you personally** and the company gets financed and goes public **at $1.00 per share**, then your personal net worth will be **$5 million.**

<u>Raising money for your company BEFORE and AFTER it is public</u>
If you have a good business model and the right legal vehicle to raise capital for your business, you can earn a commission for every dollar that you raise for the company.

Let's say that you are able to raise $10 million from 100 private investors in the course of 12 months. If you pay yourself a 10% commission on monies raised, you will have earned **$1 million!** This is called doing a private placement into a private company.

But you can also do it AFTER the company is public. You can have your company listed first with almost no investors in the beginning. You start with the public shell and then you do what is called a PIPE financing: Private Investment into a Public Entity. It is exactly the same process of raising money and selling shares to investors but with the only difference that your company is already public.

<u>Brokering a deal between a company and a financial group</u>
Depending on the connections that you have you could earn **$1 million** simply by putting two parties together. Assuming that you have an agreement with a company who will pay you a 3% finder's fee for finding the right financial institution who will fund their company, you can make lots of money, too. All you have to do is to find the right two parties, make an agreement and bring them together.

<u>Selling your own share position</u>
Assuming you own 10 million shares in a company that you are about to finance through investors. You decide to keep 8 million shares and sell 2 million shares privately for a discount of 50%. If your company's stock is priced at $1.00 per share and you sell 2 million shares at $0.50 you will have made **$1 million** in cash. (Depending on your jurisdiction there are legal ramifications about the process but it can be done.)

<u>Having a long-term stock position in a deal</u>
You could start a company and issue 100 million shares to investors. You personally keep 10 million shares in the company that you decide not to sell right away. Assuming that your business will grow over time and become more valuable (with or without your involvement), it could eventually turn into a company that is worth $500 million in the stock market. By maintaining your 10 million shares you could end up with a net worth of **$50 million.**

<u>Doing a promotional stock campaign</u>
This can be the fast track to becoming rich. Once a company is listed on an exchange you can initiate a promotional program to make your stock more known. The goal is to create a lot of attention and volume in the stock so that a lot of new investors will buy the stock in the market. If you are the only person selling initially and you are offloading your entire share position, you could make millions in a very short period of time. I have seen many promoters that were able to sell 10 million shares over the course of 3 months into the market at an average price of $3 to $4 per share. By selling the entire 10 million shares into the market, they made over $30 to $40 million in as little as 3 months.

Once a company is listed on an exchange you can initiate a promotion program to make your stock more known. The goal is to create a lot of attention so that new investors will buy your stock via their broker. This will create a lot of volume in your title.

Without any new buyers your stock will not be actively traded and nothing happens. There is no point in having a public company if no one knows that it exists. There are over 13,000 listed companies in the US and you need to do something that brokers and investors will be attracted to your title.

There are a number of marketing strategies that you can use to create market awareness. Things like newsletters to potential investors, research reports or online presence in stock portals are just a few to mention.

The main goal of a promotional program is to sell your or the company's shares. Typically, a company hires a promoter that is the only person with free trading shares. The promoter has for example 10 million shares available and initiates a marketing program. Usually, he has a lot of contacts of potential buyers or lists of people that are interested in buying new issues. He puts the company in the best light possible and sends out marketing material to those potential buyers. The buyers get interested and put in orders through their brokers to buy your shares. Since you or the promoters are the only people who are sellers you sell your positions to new investors.

I have seen many promoters that were able to sell ten or even twenty million shares between $2 and $4 per share and make millions like that in a few months only.

The company releases news releases every week and by showing that the price of the stock keeps going up and up it is able to attract more and more investors.

Here are some examples of companies that had a high volume over a certain period of time with a reasonable price:

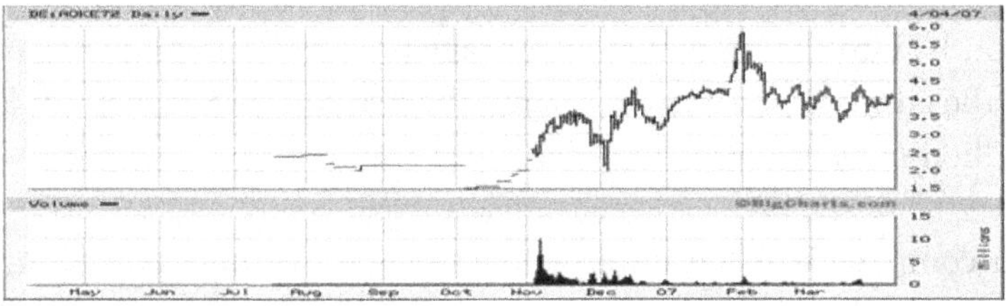

In the month of November there were over 20 million shares traded with an average price of $3 per share. That is $60 million!

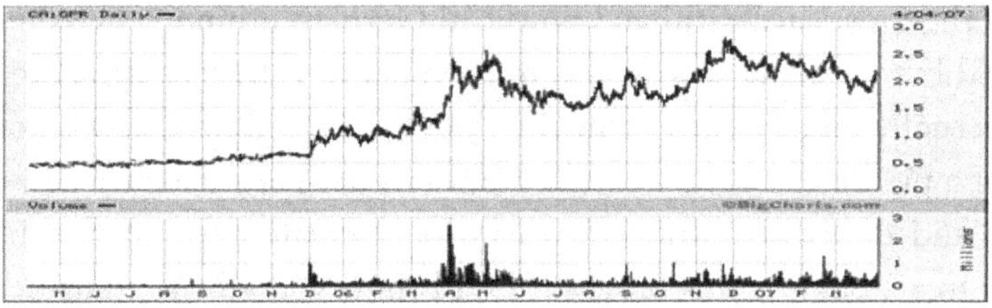

In April the average price was about $2 per share. I would say that at least 12 million shares were traded that month. A total of $24 million!

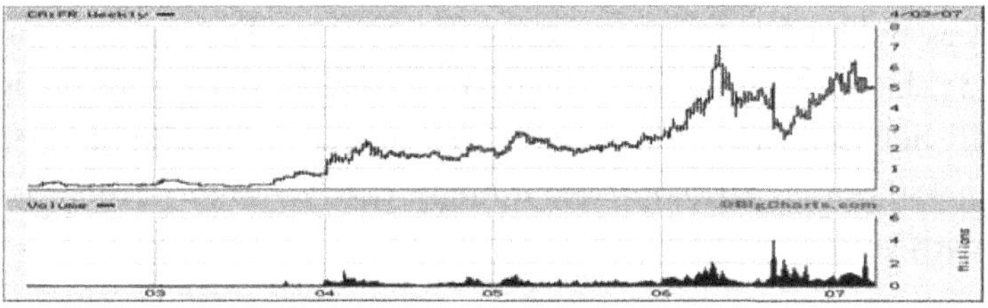

In the last year of this chart with an average price of $4 per share I would guess that at least 50 million shares were traded. That is over $200 million!

So if you are able to build a company, take it public and then be the only party that can sell, you can become very rich in a matter of days. If you are able to sell 10, 20 or 30 million shares in a few months between one and two dollars, then you are set for life!

Even if you are able to sell a few hundred thousand shares or a million in three months, this can make you a lot of money.

Depending on your stock marketing budget, the quality of your company and therefore the daily average trading volume, you should be able to sell at least anywhere from 2000 to 5000 shares per day without hurting the stock price.

Assuming that your average price per share is $1.00 that would result in $2000 to $5000 daily income. If you trade stocks on 20 days in a month, it could be up to $100,000 in one month.

One of the most successful and powerful German promoters was only 26 years old but he made at least $10 million per deal that he promoted. He never actually founded any companies but he learned how to promote the stock of a public company to attract new buyers. He signed up newsletter writers and developed strategies that would create a lot of new buying volume in a stock. In this program I will show you all the strategies that people like him are using.

Building public companies and selling the shells

In order to go public you can make the necessary filings with the SEC (Securities and Exchange Commission). You will need a company, a project, at least 35 shareholders, audited financial statements and a securities lawyer who will help you with the process. You might be looking at spending between $50,000 to $100,000 and it might take you 6 to 12 months to go public with your company.

But there is also a faster way to go public. It's called reverse merger. You can buy an existing publicly listed shell and merge your company into this shell. This way you are public right away and you don't have to wait 6 to 12 months. But to buy a shell like this you will need about $500,000.

The way you can get this money is through investors by selling them shares of your own company. I will show you how this is done exactly.

There are people out there who specialize in building public shells and sell them to people who are looking to go public. You could learn how to do it and create 4 new shells per year and sell them for $500,000 each. **You would make $2 million per year by simply doing this.**

The process of raising capital

You could structure your company in such a way that you issue 10 million shares for yourself and sell another 10 million shares at different levels to investors. If you go public you will have issued a total of 20 million shares and if your share price is at $1.00 per share your company will be worth $20 million in the market. If you were able to raise capital at an average price of $0.50 per share you will have raised $5 million for your company.

With this money your goal is then to expand your company and do your best to increase the value of your share price.

Once your company is public you are able to get money from institutional investors and investment houses. This will open up a whole new world of financing options.

A securities lawyer will prepare an offering memorandum (legal prospectus or also called PPM) and a share subscription agreement (a contract to buy shares from the company) to that you have the necessary tools to sell shares.

All you need next is a corporate account for people to invest their money into.

Ways to sell your shares

There are several ways to sell investments to clients:

1. Telephone sales – get a good list with the right names / potential
2. Personal sales – face-to-face (referrals from existing contacts)
3. Presentations – organize a presentation once a month with 20 to 30 people
4. Online – free PDF report – follow up by phone
5. Existing clients

<u>Typical sales process (telephone sales)</u>

A marketing person makes the first call to a list of potential clients. This is a general cold call. The main goal is to send some general information to a potential client (= the initial marketing info package). A typical call goes something like this:

"Hello, I am calling from ABC. I would like to send you some general marketing information about our company. It is a great investment opportunity. The company will go public in 6 months and we are very excited about the development. Where can I send you the info? Blah, blah, ..."

I don't want to offend anyone but women have actually a higher success rate when it comes to cold calling. A study has shown that the highest rates were women around 45 years of age with a British accent. This is why we have mostly women in the marketing team.

A few days after the potential client has received the marketing info, a sales person (= typically a man) who is more experienced will follow up and start to build a relationship. He will explain more about the investment and it typically takes 2 or 3 conversations until a client is ready to invest.

> You can sell vacuum cleaners, subscriptions or other things – but you will make most money by selling shares of private companies to investors.

In the end it is all sales but the commissions and the ability to earn money is much higher with financial products. Normally, a sales person can earn about 10% in commissions. I have met many Private Equity sales people who were earning more than $500,000 per year.

Isn't 10% too much?

The price of the stock is relative when the company is private. It is much more important for a company to have enough capital in the beginning and therefore the management is willing to pay a higher commission to its sales people. If the price of the private placement is $0.50 instead of $0.40 per share, it is already a difference of 20% in price. Therefore, the price and the commission is not always a clear science or calculation.

It is much better for a company to have 90% of $2 million for example, than to have 95% of $500,000. If the sales people are more motivated and willing to sell shares, it will benefit both parties.

There is not really any rule or law that defines the exact amount that can be paid in commissions. Some companies pay even more commission than 10%. Just make sure that you keep the best interests of the company and the investors at heart and that you act with integrity when it comes to this topic.

(If you have seen the movie "Wolf of Wall Street", I am sure that you would agree that 50% is obviously too much in commissions.)

Selling shares to investors

You can decide to raise capital all by yourself or to get the help of a few more people. The task becomes much easier if the people around you are helping and are confronted with the same challenges.

I have created a training program to educate and train "Private Equity Brokers". This training includes basic knowledge about stocks, Private Equity and sales skills.

A Private Equity broker is technically not a stockbroker. He will only advise people when it comes to investments related to Private Equity. Now, in order to do this, he has to either be licensed or a director of the company of the company that he sells.

The main objective of the job is to get investors to buy shares of private companies – basically to raise money. The job is sales and relationship focused because the broker is dealing with clients. The broker will sell shares to clients and advise them on how to invest into Private Equity stocks.

There is lots of telephone activity involved because clients live all over the country. A broker will establish a lot of client contacts and will have lots of face-to-face meetings with investors. He will make investment recommendations and grow a client base over time.

The goal is to build up a number of clients that will invest into several deals. A client will invest into one deal at first, grow his investment and then invest into more deals in the future. By having successful deals, the broker will not only grow his client base but also the money under management.

A broker will earn a commission on capital raised and by selling shares. If the broker raises for example $100,000 per month from private investors, he can earn anywhere from 5% to 10% in commission.

Since it is not an easy challenge in the beginning, a new broker should be aware that he might face a number of difficult situations. He has to deal with a lot of rejection and needs to be determined to succeed. Especially in the beginning of his career until someone has built up a substantial client base, there is a lot of prospecting involved.

> Most people are holding themselves back because of fear of rejection, fear of failure and laziness.

You need to understand that this is one of the most difficult jobs that are out there. Selling investments over the phone to people that don't know you can be quite the challenge. Unfortunately, not everybody is cut out for it. 80% of the people who start in this industry fail in the first three months because they are not closing any deals. If you are willing to learn and grow and never give up, you can potentially turn into a great sales person.

> People in this industry who have decided to become the best can easily make more than one million dollars per year.

This industry is really tricky. Once you get hooked, you will never get out of the industry. You might change companies but it is very hard to change the profession once you were successful once. People who made the experience of earning $20,000 or $50,000 in a month will never go back to a regular job that pays $5,000 or even $10,000 a month. Once you have figured out how it works you will never have to worry about money again. If you know how to sell Private Equity and you have a good product to sell, you can always make a lot of money in a short period of time and turn your life around. It is almost like a secret knowledge that you must obtain and you must have experienced a phase where you made a lot of money. Once this is the case you can always go back to selling private stocks – no matter where you are in life.

<u>A typical earning example of a team of 25 sales people</u>

5 people	raised $0 in a month	10% = $0
5 people	raised $200,000 to $500,000	10% = $20,000 to $50,000
15 people	raised $50,000	10% = $5,000

The interesting thing is that it is never the same people that don't raise anything. In sales you have a great month and then a bad month.

Being part of a sales team can be entertaining. Here are some *extreme* examples:

- There was a story of a guy who raised $5 million and earned $500,000 with one deal. He was partying with girls for 3 days straight. When he got back his sales manager fired him. He had to earn back his job again. Even though he was the best sales person, his "bad behavior" was not tolerated.
- One of my sales managers was a crazy but a brilliant sales person. He came to me when he was $50,000 in debt. I gave him a chance and gave him a job. In his first year he earned over $500,000 but after this year he still had the $50,000 loan because he spent all his money on girls and partying.
- There is another guy that I know personally that takes half of a pill of ecstasy and watches movies all day. Then all of a sudden, when he has a "normal" moment for about 20 minutes, he picks up the phone, calls up an investor and raises $500,000.
- There was a guy who raised $1 million in one month and invited the whole team for dinner in a fancy restaurant. One of the sales guys couldn't take it because he didn't want to be the second best. Then he went back to his office and called this famous surgeon and basically "forced him" to immediately make a transfer of $3 million online. He returned to the dinner and told in front of everyone that now he was the best of this month. (Talking about stupid pride and people with too much ego…!)

The story of the Wolf of Wall Street is not a myth. It really happens and I have seen it firsthand. A lot of those sales people are extreme and crazy. But of course you don't have to be part of such a crazy group or organization. You need to be 100% focused on the business and have a clear head. In fact some of the best people in this business are highly self-disciplined. I guess you have to be self-disciplined in any job if you want to get to the top.

If you build a sales team you might end up with *"a stable full of wild stallions"* competing against each other. But the good side of this is that you will have millions of dollars for your companies.

There are people out there with no real education and the only skill that they have is selling. If they made $5000 in a previous job working on a construction site and then all of a sudden they make $20,000 per month, then it is hard for them to ever go back to the old job.

Once you have "licked blood" you will never get out of this industry because no other job pays that much with so little effort.

I know people who are in this industry for more than ten years and they "hate dealing with customers" but because they make so much money, they can't stop.

My friend and I once made a funny observation. All of the sales people that we knew simply rotated from one sales organization to the other but no one ever left the industry.

How can you legally raise capital in the US?

In order to sell stocks to private investors you must be a licensed broker with a Series 7 if you live in the US. Otherwise you will be breaking the law.

However, there is a loophole.

> As a director of the company you are legally permitted to sell shares of your own company to private investors.

Tip: Make all your key sales people a **VP of business development and director** of the company. This way they are legally able to sell shares.

It is actually better not to be a broker if you sell shares to clients because you are representing your company you can almost say anything about how great you think the company is. As a stockbroker you are very limited to what you are allowed to say.

As a director of the company you can either sell shares on your own or get the help of a broker dealer who can help you with selling the shares to investors. If you can convince a stockbroker who is licensed with a Series 7 and is working for a broker dealer, he or she can help you to finance your company much faster because he usually already has established client relationships.

Another way to do this legally is to hire only marketing people who "prepare" the clients as much as possible without actually doing the contract and you as the director of the company will close the deal.

In order to raise capital, you need to write a prospectus about your company. This prospectus is called a PPM (Private Placement Memorandum). A PPM is a document that describes every single detail about your company and has an offer to raise capital in it. It is also called a legal prospectus. For example, it could say in your offering that you would like to raise $5 million by issuing 10 million shares at $0.50 per share in a specific time frame (mostly 2-3 months).

The investor is involved at the beginning of a new venture with a high return potential. Usually, the investment horizon is relatively short – anywhere from a few months to three years. The main motivation for someone to buy a new start-up company lies in the potential gain.

> A big company like McDonald's is unlikely
> to double in price within one year.
> But a small start-up company can double, triple or go up ten times.

Why people buy Private Equity stocks

> Greed is the number one reason why people buy pre-IPO stocks

People always believe that there is something out there in the financial world that can make them rich overnight. Most people believe that there is a secret investment or strategy that is kept from the average person and if they only found a way to access this kind of investment, then they could become rich, too.

Of course, Private Equity deals can offer such a great investment but most of them are also very risky and often losing money is more likely than hitting it big. Despite all the warnings in the contract, people still choose risk over security.

I actually did a test once. I created two different products. Both were Private Equity based but one product had a capital guarantee of 100% if you kept the investment for 10 years. Guess what? No one wanted the safe product with the capital guarantee! Everyone chose the product that had the most risk but also a higher return potential. That was very interesting for me to observe.

Typical sales process

1. Cold calling – Lead Generation (first call)
2. Follow up call (general information, explanation and creating interest)
3. Sales call and contract
4. Dealing with objections and questions
5. Closing the deal
6. Loading the client (= getting him to increase his existing position)

> Selling stocks is no different than selling any other product – it is all sales!

The people who make most money in this business are the people who are very good at sales. This means that they are very good in dealing with other people, they understand exactly what kind of concerns and objections clients have, they are basically psychologists in disguise who know a lot of techniques to influence other people. If used with integrity then they help other people to make the right decisions and to get them to move from the security based low performance thinking into better choices.

Everything is a numbers game

Selling a product or service has a lot to do with the law of probability. Whatever it is that you sell, it is always a numbers game. That means that you might have to offer your product or service to many prospective clients in order to make a sale.

So the more people you talk to, the more sales you will make. You can literally calculate how much money you want to make. Selling is like math.

Building your own sales organization to raise capital

> Successful people are 100% convinced that they are the masters of their own destiny. If they don't have the right circumstances, they create them!

Depending on your business model you might have built up a sales team that sells your products or services to clients. The sales that are generated help you to advance your business and therefore your company.

Depending on where you are in your development, you might not have enough money to move forward faster and expand your company.

> Besides getting money from financial companies, I would strongly suggest you build a **second** sales team who solely focuses on raising capital for your company.

When I first started my company, I actually had built up a separate company with 25 sales people who only contacted investors and raised capital for my deal. This sales organization became the driving force to finance my own deal and all they did all day was talk to potential investors. Because I owned this company, the sole purpose was to raise capital for my deal only and not for anybody else's deal. With this sales organization, I was able to raise $10 million alone in the first year.

Depending on your jurisdiction, your sales people might have to be licensed by the local authorities and pass an exam. It is even possible that your sales organization might have to be licensed as a financial company. But the advantage of having a company that only raises capital for your deals is priceless. It can make all the difference.

There is only so much time in a day and so much effort that you can put into selling the products yourself. That is why you need to get additional help or leverage. Ten people will sell much more than you will be able to sell. If you build a sales team you can focus on improving the company and its products.

The key to building a sales team is to find a good sales manager first. This person must be an experienced sales person who knows everything about selling and can train and motivate other people.

You should focus your efforts on getting as many sales people as possible. Create a sales organization that is motivating and that will not make you go broke. You can have people on straight commission or organize the sales team in such a way that you ensure by the law of averages that a certain amount of sales is inevitable.

You can create two types of sales teams. First, there are the sales people that actually sell the product that your company has to offer. And second, you can create a sales team that only raises money by selling shares of the company to investors.

Building a sales team is easier than you think. There are a lot of people out there that would like to improve their lives and make more money. You can offer them a job with the opportunity to make a lot of commission and at the same time they help you to achieve your business goals.

You need to rent an office with several phone lines and then you will be amazed how much faster and bigger your results will be.

You can pay $10 per hour per person who is doing marketing calls. I would also add a certain percentage 2-5% of the sales commission to motivate them to make more calls. If they get the right clients prepared who will do a big investment, the bigger will their own paycheck be.

Let's do the math:

You could hire 10 marketing sales people and you pay them $10 per hour. If they work 5 hours per day, 5 days a week and 4 weeks a month, your cost per person will be $1000 in base salary.

10 marketing sales people will cost you $10,000 per month. Office rent and expenses might also add another $5000 and therefore your operation will cost you $15,000 per month.

But what will be the benefit? You should create 1000 new leads for new potential clients each month. If you can turn 10% of those leads into 100 good prospects and you only close 20% of those prospects, you will create 20 new clients per month.

Now, based on the quality and ability of your clients to make an investment, you could have a conservative average investment of $10,000 per client, which will lead to an overall investment of $200,000 per month.

The $200,000 will go directly into the bank account of the company. It is there where you can deduct the $15,000 investment as a marketing expense to finance your sales team.

$15,000 plus 10% in commissions for the sales people will end up costing the company $35,000 per month. But the amount of investments that you have received will be well worth it.

If you intend to raise $2 million in the first year to finance your projects and take your company public, you will be able to accomplish this with hiring a sales and marketing team of 10 people.

Math backwards

A broker or sales person should have a clear plan on how much money he wants to raise and how much money he wants to earn.

Example:

A broker wants to make $250,000 per year in personal income. If he earns a 10% commission, he needs to raise $2.5 million from investors for the company. That means that he needs to raise an average amount of about $200,000 per month.

He can do it the following ways:

- 1 client with 1 investment of $200,000
- 2 clients with an investment of $100,000 each
- 10 clients with an investment of $20,000 each
- 20 clients with an investment of $10,000 each
- A mix of different amounts

Based on his strategy he has to target different clients. If he only needs one investment of $200,000 per month, he should only focus on people who are very wealthy.

If he wants to get 10 to 20 clients who will make a smaller investment, his approach will be a bit differently.

> The first couple of millions are always the hardest for new companies to organize. Once you have proven your basic concept, getting 10 to 20 million dollars is much easier.

Learning how to set up a company so that you can attract investors is relatively easy. Getting money into the company is the bigger challenge. That is why you must focus on raising capital and make it a priority. Hire a good manager for the operational side of the business but make sure that there is always enough money coming in the door.

In my career I have raised a lot of money from private investors. If you make raising money a priority there is no limit to what it possible.

Howard Schultz, the founder of Starbucks, has a net worth of $2.9 billion because of his majority share position in the company. But when he started, he got turned down 242 times by banks. In the end, 11 people wrote him a check to get started.

Howard Schultz (book title: *Pour your heart into it*). This is one of the best business biographies I have ever read. It is truly inspiring.

Fred Deluca, the founder of Subway, wrote another very inspiring book. It is called: "*Start Small Finish Big: Fifteen Key Lessons to Start - and Run - Your Own Successful Business*".

I highly recommend both of these books to get inspired.

The company has to be public for institutional investors to invest

Private investors will give you money if they believe in your story. They won't be able to sell their shares until the company publicly listed and trading. Institutional investors, like mutual funds, pension funds, banks, investment banks, etc. will not buy shares of a private company. The reasons are because they need to be able to sell their position into a liquid market if the stock loses value and that they need a valuation on their books for accounting reasons. A private company does not yet have a proper valuation and therefore would be listed as zero value in their books.

Therefore you will need a public vehicle to get institutional financing.

The process of getting money from an institutional investor is always the same. They will do a due diligence process. Basically, they want to know everything and see everything. You will have to provide financial statements, SEC filings; business plans, marketing material, etc.

An institutional investor wants to buy a deal that is undervalued and has growth potential. Therefore, they want to see if the company has the ability to increase sales and market share. The money that they will provide should solely be utilized to expand the business and therefore the valuation of the company and its share price.

An institutional investor is all about the numbers and not much about emotions. A $25 million financing is considered a small investment for an institutional investor and therefore if you ask for financing make sure to ask for a larger sum of money and try to make a business plan that will show how this money can be used to fulfill this plan.

Conclusion: Playing in the big league

Why should you even have a $100 million company? Besides that this is considered still a small company, there are many positive benefits that will come along with it.

> If you have to work hard in any business anyway, then you should choose a model that will eventually make you rich.

Benefits for you:

- **Job security:** because you are your own boss and pay yourself a paycheck from the company
- **Financial freedom:** never worry about money again
- **Success story:** You create something that you can be proud of
- **Making a difference in the world or people's lives:** Improve the world with your products and give jobs to many people

Why should you settle for a life of mediocrity? You can play in the big league, too. All you need to do is to learn how to play the game. And the game is called public companies!

Everything you need – will come to you at the perfect time. Now is that time!

> Everyone you will ever meet knows something you don't. (Bill Nye)

We don't meet people by accident. They are meant to cross our path for a reason. There is a reason why you are reading this right now. You were meant to learn about Private Equity!

They say, "The teacher will appear when the student is ready". So here we are!

If you really understood the power of his knowledge then I am happy to teach you more about it. I believe that this knowledge can literally change lives, create many jobs and be a blessing for the world if done right.

> 97% of the people who quit too soon are
> employed by the 3% who never gave up.

So how much is all this knowledge worth?

Once you really understand that process you will realize how the world was built and how fortunes were made. You can use that specific knowledge to build a fortune yourself.

Everything that is a big today was once only a thought or an idea. Somebody believed in that idea and found others who were willing to support that idea as well with money.

Every big corporation today started with someone who believed in an idea and finally got the money to make it happen.

> The only person you are destined to become
> is the person you decide to be.
> (Ralph Waldo Emerson)

The minute you choose to do what you really want to do, you start living a different kind of life.

The specific knowledge that I will teach you in this program cannot be bought anywhere else or learned in books. It is so unique that the only way that you can get it is through an actual learning experience. It has cost me years of my life, lots of energy, sweat and blood to get to that point. I spent over $1.4 million alone for my lawyer in three years to acquire the specific knowledge on how to properly finance a company or a deal and then to take it public.

The value in this program is literally worth millions of dollars.

Basically, I am giving away all my secrets for free. Everything that I have learned to become a millionaire and exactly how I did it is now available to you for an unbelievable low price.

I have decided to give my knowledge to the world and make it affordable for everyone. I believe that it is now time for others to be encouraged and to live the lives of their dreams.

<u>I will teach you the following things:</u>

1. How you can **raise money** to grow your company and **go public**
2. How to **sell your stocks** in the market and **turn it into cash**
3. How to **find investors** that will buy stock in your company and give them a good return on their investment
4. How to build, structure and organize a new public company so that it can become **a $100 million company**
5. How to **market and promote the stock** of your public company so that many new investors will buy your stock
6. How to avoid common mistakes and pitfalls and stay 100% legal
7. How to turn **a business idea into a real company** that is publicly listed and **gets millions in institutional financing**
8. How to put together the right marketing material so that investors will buy your company's stock

9. How to **create a real exit strategy for your investors** so they make money and keep coming back to you for **new deals**
10. How to **choose a business model and industry** that will sustain good and bad times

Success is really easy when you think about it

> The fears we don't face become our limits. Life begins where fear ends. (OSHO)

Think about all the possibilities and options there are. If you don't believe that then you will be struggling your whole life. In the first world countries the money basically lies in the streets. You just have to do something and pick it up.

There are all kinds of options for you to make money in this world. We live in the richest and best time ever. Never before has it been easier to create wealth. Technology has made it possible for everyone with little or no money to create a business that can grow internationally. The Internet has opened up options that have never been there before.

> To build a public company and to raise money for it is possible for anyone. All you need to have is an idea, a business plan, the right set-up and then the skills to sell shares and raise capital.

For every difficulty that supposedly stops a person from succeeding there are thousands who have had it a lot worse and have succeeded anyway. So can you!

> It is better to try something and maybe get disappointed than to never have the courage and always wonder.

Personal experience and help

I have been applying this system for the last 10 years and have successfully been involved in many deals. I have made lots of money, created a lot of happy investors and gained tons of experience in this field.

I love the business of Private Equity and I can't imagine not being involved in it. If you are interested in starting your own business and need help in the process, I am happy to be at your service.

The next step...what else can I help you with?

Maybe now that you have finished this text you will say something like this:

"Hey, all this sounds great and I am excited to get started. But I will really need your help and more details to make it happen."

Well in that case I can offer you the following things:

- **Sales skills:** I can teach you and your team how to sell stocks to investors.
- **Building a sales team:** I can help you to build a sales team and help with training
- **Marketing material:** I can help to create perfect marketing material for your investors (writing and design)
- **Companies:** Incorporation and set up of your company
- **Consulting:** Ongoing business consulting and strategy

Let me be clear about one thing: It is very possible to learn everything about Private Equity and how to raise capital. But it is not easy and it is not a short-term thing. If you really want to learn this, you must be willing to invest time, energy and money.

You should give yourself at least 12 months to learn the basics. If all of this it too much for you, then please don't even get started and pursue a different career. I will only work with people who are seriously interested in learning all this. But if you decide to move forward, I will help you in any way that I can.

> Setting a goal to create a new company is the first step to turning the invisible into the visible.

Here is how I can help you to achieve your goals and dreams of owning a multi million-dollar business:

1. **Workshop / seminar:** The $100 million blueprint (Initial training and knowledge)
2. **Personal coaching** (personal assistance as external consultant)
3. **Corporate business services** (Tools, contracts, legal, etc. to make it happen)

If any of the things that I just explained has caught your attention and curiosity I suggest it is time to take it to the next level.

Don't worry if you didn't understand every last term or detail. The main thing is that you are motivated to learn how to build a multi million-dollar company.

I can only show you the door – but you have to open it and take the next step.

I would love you see you at one of my seminars or to meet you in person!

> The ones who are crazy enough to think that they can change the world are the ones that do. (Steve Jobs)

CHAPTER 2

HOW TO BECOME A MILLIONAIRE WITH YOUR COMPANY AND PRIVATE EQUITY

> Human beings have the remarkable ability to turn nothing into something. They can turn weeds into gardens and pennies into fortunes.

In this brochure I would like to explain how you could raise money for your business, take it public and become a self-made millionaire in the process.

Step 1: Incorporate a new company

The first step is to incorporate a new company. Ideally, since you want to go public in the US, you should choose to incorporate in the following states due to tax reasons and flexibility:

1. Nevada
2. Wyoming

You can use an online provider to help you with the process and for a few hundred dollars you can get set up.

Step 2: Create the right share structure and issue shares for yourself

You can choose any share structure but ideally, you want to have the following structure:

Number of authorized shares: 100 million
Number of preferred shares: 20 million
Number of common shares: 80 million
Par value: $0.0001 or $0.00001 (possible in Nevada)

The preferred shares are for the founders and the key management members. Make sure you include in the bylaws that those shares have the 10x voting rights compared to common shareholders. You can also add special dividend rights.

The par value is the initial value of the shares. If you acquire 10 million shares at $0.0001, then you have to put $1000 into the corporate account and buy the shares just like any other shareholder with a SSA (share subscription agreement).

You want to start with the end goal in mind when you start. How much money do you intend to raise before you go public?

Example

Founders:	$0.0001
Family and friends:	$0.10
First round of financing / private placement:	$0.25
Second round of financing / private placement:	$0.50
Third round of financing / private placement:	$0.75
First price when listed:	$1.00

If your goal is to go public at $1.00 and you own 10 million shares, then you will have $10 million.

Step 3: Acquire a project

The main thing is to build your company. For this purpose you will need a project, a prototype or a product.

Let's say you use the funds from the first round of financing to acquire the first project or option to buy the project. This step will now increase the value of the company and you can justify doing the next round of financing at a higher level.

You don't always need a completely finished project. Sometimes all you need is a contract, LOI or an option to acquire a project.

Not every product or project is a good fit for the public markets. You should choose a project that has a multi-million dollar potential. Your company should eventually be worth several hundred millions of dollars. You can achieve this well with natural resources for example.

Step 4: Do a private placement

Let's say this is your plan:

First round of financing / private placement:	\$0.25 – \$250,000 – 1 million shares
Second round of financing / private placement:	\$0.50 – \$500,000 – 1 million shares
Third round of financing / private placement:	\$0.75 – \$750,000 – 1 million shares

Total: \$1.5 million raised and 3 million common shares issued

Depending on your project, you will need to spend money for salaries, commissions, legal fees for the going public process and general office expenses.

The majority of the funds should go to the project so that it can be developed and become an asset.

You should make a financial plan and know from the start how much money you will need to spend and how much money you will need to raise before you go public. In our example $1.5 million is not very much money and it can be spent quickly. Most projects need more money.

Remember the following rule: "Things often **cost twice as much** and **take twice as long** as originally anticipated."

The goal has to be to use the money wisely so that it will either generate more money for the company in the future or turn your project into a valuable asset.

Step 5: Start raising money

Before you start raising money from private investors, you should set a goal.

<u>Example</u>

- 1-year goal: $1 million from private investors
- Goal per month: $100,000 from private investors 2 months off per year (summer and winter)

How can you achieve this goal? There are several ways:

<u>$100,000 per month</u>

- 1 investor who invests $100,000
- 2 investors who invest x $50,000
- 4 investors who invest $25,000
- 10 investors who invest $10,000

<u>$1 million per year</u>

- 1 investor = $500,000
- 3 investors = 2 x $100,000
- 4 investors = 4 x $50,000
- 10 investors who invest $100,000 each

Loading the same clients

- You can usually load every client at least a second time (load = invest again)
- Start with $25,000 and load again with $25,000 per investor = $50,000

Weekly goal

- 1 investor per week who invests $25,000
- 4 weeks x 10 months = 40 investors x $25,000 = $1 million

Depending on your average amount that a client invests, you will have a different marketing strategy to generate those kinds of contacts. A smaller investor who invests $10,000 is typically an average person / worker who you get through lots of cold calls.

An investor who invests $100,000 has a more specific profile than an investor who invests $10,000. You have to find and target these high net worth individuals in order to get them.

Always ask the following question: Who is my ideal client? What kind of profession, income level, sex, age or interests does he or she have?

In general this is an ideal investor:

- Male
- Age between 40 and 70 years old
- Manager, self-employed, businessman, professional
- Income over $100,000 per year
- Home owner

But don't just limit yourself to this profile. One of my business partners did really well with farmers. Find out what works for you.

Step 6: Pay yourself a salary of $100,000

Money raised:	$1,000,000
Salary paid:	$100,000
Money for the company:	$900,000

The most important person in the company is you. Without you there is no company. That's why you must be well taken care of so that you can focus on bringing in money.

> You have to focus all your time and energy on sales and raising money for the first year.

I used to pay myself a monthly salary of $10,000 per company. This way I could focus all my attention to developing the company without any worries. At one point I had five different companies that paid me $10,000 per month plus a percentage of my sales organizations, which ended up being $100,000 per month in income.

This way I didn't worry about getting a commission from the monies that I raised. My head was free and I could focus on building the company, bringing investors and building my sales organizations.

Step 7: Make your project work

Use the money wisely to generate more money or sales. It takes money to make money. This is true when it comes to creating assets for the company.

If you have a gold exploration project, then you must spend the money on drilling, geologists, etc. so that you can prove a resource. You could spend $1 million on your drilling programs and then find a 500,000 ounce gold deposit.

A 500,000 ounce gold deposit x $1200 per ounce equals $700 million in assets in the ground. Once you are able to prove this resource, you can easily get $50 million from a bank to go into production and get the gold out of the ground.

As a valuation in the public markets, they say that for each proven ounce of gold, you can take $100 as a valuation. In this case you can declare about $50 million as assets. In this case you have used $1 million to generate an asset of $50 million.

That's why it is so important that you choose an industry that has a multi-million dollar potential. Not every business is suitable for the public markets unless you have lots of sales.

Step 8: Take your company public

There are two ways to take your company public in the stock market: Either you go through the process with the SEC or you buy an existing listed company (shell).

The normal process to take your company public is anywhere between 6 and 12 months.

1. Buy a listed Pink Sheets shell for $100,000 (non-reporting company)
2. Buy a listed OTCQB shell for $400,000 (SEC reporting)
3. Do a regular filing S-1 Registration Statement filing with the SEC and then get a market maker who is a member of FINRA to sponsor your company.

Ideally, you want to have a SEC reporting company that files its financial statements every three months. This way you can attract more money from the public markets and grow as a company.

If you choose a Pink Sheets company who is non-reporting then you can also trade your stocks and make money but it probably won't be a long-term success.

Step 9: Go public at $1.00 and create market valuation of $100 million

In order to create a $100 million market valuation you must focus on four things:

1. Amount of shares issued and outstanding
2. Annual earnings
3. P/E ratio
4. Share price

<u>Share structure</u>

10 million shares issued and outstanding
1 million shares x $1.00 = $1 million (your net worth)
9 million shares x $1.00 (from investors)

$1 million in earnings x p/E ratio of 10 = $10 million
$5 million in earnings x p/E ratio of 20 = $100 million

Step 10: Do a PIPE financing and acquire more money

A PIPE financing is a private placement after the company is public. PIPE means "Placement into public entity". Let's say your stock is trading at $2.00 per share, then you can do a PIPE financing at $1.50.

Once your company is public you can easily attract institutional investors. But before you are eligible to get the big bucks (e.g. $10 million or more) you must make sure that you have two things taken care of first:

1. Proof of concept
2. Proof of management

Proof of concept means that your business model works and can be expanded or duplicated.

Proof of management means that you were able to raise initial funds, take the company public and make the project work. This means that you can be trusted to do the same process again but on a bigger scale.

In order to get a $10 million financing you will need to do these things first:

1. You need to be public (listed) in order to get more financing (from institutional investors and mutual funds)
2. You need to raise the first $1 to $2 million first trough private investors pre-IPO before you can expect institutional investors to invest
3. Don't use a Private Equity or venture capital firm because they take 80% of your company and then you basically created your own job and work for them
4. Focus on quality in your products / projects
5. Develop a vision to create $100 million company in the short-term but a $1 billion company in the long run.

Other ways to become a millionaire with your own company:

1. **Dividends:** You pay yourself (preferred shareholders only) a dividend from the earnings
2. **Bonus:** You can take out money and pay yourself a bonus
3. **Stock options:** You can issue yourself stock options
4. **Forward split 2:1** – now you own 2 million shares at $0.50 and now to goal is to increase the share price to $1.00 again (vacuum effect)
5. **Sell a new project to company for $1 million:** You can issue yourself 1 million shares for the acquisition or $1 million cash
6. **You sell shares into the public market:** Sell 500,000 shares with your stockbroker for $2.00 on average and make $1 million – Keep the other shares for long-term gain
7. **Loan against your shares:** If you own 10 million shares at $1.00 for $10 million, a bank or lender might 10% loan against your position and give you $1 million in cash.
8. **You use your shares as a collateral to buy real estate:** Instead of putting any money down, you put 0% down and use your shares

as collateral. Then you sell your piece of real estate for a higher price later on.

9. **Stock marketing and promotion:** You sell 10 million shares into the market over 3 months into high volume at an average price of $1.00 and make $10 million
10. **You raise $3 million pre-IPO** and take out $1 million as a commission or salary for yourself – the rest stays in the company ($2 million)

Great marketing materials – the foundation for your success

One of the most important people in your team is the **designer**. You need impressive marketing materials that look professional if you want to succeed in this business.

Next to impeccable looking marketing materials you will need **great content**. The key is to have financial terms in your material as well as easy to understand texts that explain what your company does so that **regular people will be motivated to invest** into your deal.

You can have a weak or empty company with little assets but if your marketing materials look great, then you have a chance to raise money from investors.

On the other hand if you have poor looking marketing materials but a great company, it makes it harder to convince people to invest.

What goes out to clients, matters. Everything must be perfect. Every detail counts.

Call center marketing team to generate leads

It is much easier to make phone calls to people who have already received your company information and show a general interest.

I would suggest that you hire 5 marketing people can create a small call center. Those people make 100 cold calls per day and generate 5 good leads per day. This is 25 leads per day or 125 per week or 500 per month.

Your job is to follow up and try to close a deal. This works really well and is the main strategy to raise money from private investors.

Build a sales organization

I used to have several sales organizations consisting of sales people as well as marketing people. A sales person tries to close a deal and a marketing person generates a lead.

I used to have 25 sales people in one organization in Zurich, Switzerland. We typically raised between $1 million and $2 million per month.

You will need a general manager and a sales manager (drill sergeant like person).

Start out small with 3 to 5 people. Continually grow the team until you reach 25 people.

Intermediaries

Be selfish so you can be generous.

You don't have to raise all the money by yourself. A great way to get investors is to use the help of financial advisors who already have clients (= intermediary).

I have worked with many different financial advisors who have several hundred clients and manage over $100 million of client money.

You have to make a commission agreement with them and pay them 10% for all the monies raised.

One advisor, Michael, brought me $500,000 in the first week. Another one, Richie, brought me a couple of millions and my friend and broker David brought me $1.2 million for two different deals.

> Things can move really fast with the right contacts and with a good project.

Getting back into sales after many years

> Just do it. Just call 100 people today and see what happens. Don't overthink it. Just act.

One of my strongest skills is sales. In fact I was so good at it that I became the number one sales person and team leader in an organization of 5000 people when I was in my twenties.

But for a while when it came to making client phone calls myself, I tended to avoid them. I felt like I was better than others and I didn't have to go down to a level where I felt humiliated on a daily basis. Basically, I let my EGO get in the way of success.

But I soon realized that this was a mistake. Here I was, successful businessman and entrepreneur, taking companies public, leading 60 employees and now I have to make 100 calls per day myself to potential clients that I hate doing so that I move forward again? The answer is: YES!

> Don't let your EGO get in the way of success.

You can fight it as long as you want but in the end you are in sales. You have to make sure that money comes into the company and since you know most about your project, you are the best and most knowledgeable sales person.

If you have a system that generates leads for you, then make 10 sales calls per day. 8 can be bad and 2 will be good (worst case scenario).

If you do these calls 5 days in a row (Monday to Friday) you will have 10 great leads and your level of self-confidence will skyrocket. You will feel like you are in charge and in control of your life and destiny.

You will automatically have a nice surprise when you make lots of sales calls.

After a long break I decided to make sales calls again. My first deal was $50,000. It was so easy. I couldn't believe it.

Don't overthink it. Just act. 100 calls will give you100 opportunities. Someone is always going to invest.

> A day of worry is more exhausting than a day of work.

The rule of 100/5

> Dreams don't work unless you do. (John C. Maxwell)

<u>Here is how the rule works:</u>

- Make 100 calls per day
- Generate 5 leads per day (95 say no)
- Do this 5 days per week (Monday to Friday)
- In one month (or 4 weeks) you will have 100 new leads
- Out of 100 leads you will generate 5 new clients per month

Once you have generated leads, the "Pareto Principle" usually applies (also know as the 80/20 rule). 80% of the people will not be interested and 20% will become clients.

> A person of average intelligence with clear goals will surpass a genius who is not sure what he really wants.

Daily numbers and tasks

You need a DIG = Daily Income Goal

What is your daily income goal? $5000 or $10,000?

$2,400,000 divided by 240 working days equals $10,000 per day. If you raise $10,000 from one investor per day, you will have your project financed, are able to take your company public and make all your dreams come true.

Be realistic about your plan:

- 1 month = 20 working days (MO to FR) x 4 weeks
- Rest = buffer, other things planned, free time, unexpected things, etc.

Make sure you plan your week well. Reserve slots in your calendar for sales calls. Do it every single day and watch your life change.

The best way to gain self-confidence is to do what you are afraid to do.

Clarity leads to success

You don't always need a plan. Sometimes all you need is balls.

My friend and business partner Philipp came back to work after a longer break. His initial intention was to generate 7 new leads each day so that he would have 35 new leads per week or 140 per month. According to his math, he would surely close 3 or 4 deals per month.

But then he had an epiphany. He changed his thinking. He asked himself how he could immediately close a deal and generate money without having to generate 140 leads first. He decided to call up two leads that told him a few months ago that they needed to think about it or wait for whatever reason. He called them up and within 1 hour, he closed two clients for $50,000 and $20,000. His focused changed from "I need to generate leads" to "I need to close a deal". This kind of clarity helped him to move ahead so much faster.

Another employee of mine wasn't doing so well financially. He was struggling and was about to get kicked out of his apartment for not paying his rent.

Because he was under so much pressure, he needed to close a deal by the end of the day or else he would lose his apartment. His only focus was to get one client who can invest $10,000 by the end of the day. He went straight for the "kill" and because of his focus he closed one deal that ended up saving him.

Sometimes we lose time and energy because we have no clarity or focus. We just go about our day and waste time with unnecessary things. If you are clear about your main daily income or sales goal for the day, you will achieve far more than if you just "work" without a clear target.

If you don't design your own life plan, chances are you will fall into someone else's plan. And guess what they have planned for you? Not much!

Being a good boy doesn't equal money

> The Universe does not favor good behavior and condemns bad behavior. There is no moral compass when it comes to the law of attraction.

If you are a good boy, then you will be rewarded. If you behave badly, then you will be punished. Unfortunately, this is not reality.

You can behave immorally or badly and still become rich.

It is important to recognize that the two things don't go hand in hand. In order to become rich, you need to do the things or actions that are necessary to attract money.

If you are good person and act with integrity, then that is your choice. Of course, I feel that acting with integrity is the right thing to do. And I am convinced that it is the only way for long-term success.

Unfortunately, I once met a guy called Ahmad. He was very rich but he was a real criminal. He would deliberately cheat people out of money. He was the perfect example for me that you can be rich and not be a good, moral person at the same time.

I also met a lot of rich people who had a lot of integrity. My former mentor David, for example, was also very rich but had a lot of integrity.

You see, the two don't necessarily have anything to do with each other. But the one thing that you should ask yourself is who you want to become as a person. How does it feel to always have to look over your shoulder? True success is only possible if you can feel good about how you made your money.

Invest into your employees / sales people

> Train your people well enough so they can leave. Treat them well enough so they don't want to. (Richard Branson)

Pay them well enough so they don't want to leave. If you pay them more than your competition, then they won't leave you. If they chose to be in this industry, then they are money-hungry sharks anyway.

Having a good team is the most important key to your success. You can't do it alone. You can't build a $100 million company and raise millions of dollars all by yourself. It is not possible. You will need employees and business partners.

> CFO asks CEO: "What happens if we invest in developing our people and then they leave us?"
> CEO: "What happens if we don't, and they stay?"

When things don't work out

Often, the main reason for failure is **plain laziness**. You start to blame people and circumstances. It is not the market, it is not the competition, it is not the product – it is you! Decide never to be lazy. This motto alone will improve your life a lot.

> Laziness will kill your chance at success. (Dennis James)

As Tony Robbins says your worst day can become your best day. Boris Becker, the tennis legend, said that losing is just as important as winning.

In 99% of the cases the problem is lack of sales in any business. No business has ever gone under with high sales.

Your job is to make sure that you have lots of sales (= lots of investors who invest money by buying the stock of your company).

> One of the best places to start to turn your life around is by doing whatever appears on your mental "I should list".

"I should call more clients…" NO! I **must** call more clients!

Before you give up – try! Really try it! Make a pact with yourself and decide to call 100 new clients in one week. Do this for one month and watch how everything will improve.

If you are not afraid of failure and rejection there is nothing that you cannot achieve. You can't lose if you don't quit.

Ever feel like giving up? If so, you are not alone! I am here to tell you that…

> **Giving up is not an option!** That decision alone, not to give up no matter what, is the most empowering choice that you can make.

When money is tight

> You don't have a spending problem – you have an income problem.

Don't save $5 for a Starbucks coffee. You can't get rich with pennies. You don't have a problem with your lifestyle or your spending habits.

The main problem is your income. You need to focus on making more money. You need to focus on sales. You need to talk to new clients every single day and raise money.

> A penny saved is still only a penny.

Don't say: I can't afford that.
Ask yourself: **How** can I afford that?

This business has the ability to make you rich. You can earn $100,000 per month if you work hard. You can afford anything you like. The main problem is only your fear. You are afraid of rejection, failure and putting in the hours.

Set some exciting goals and pick up the phone!

> I work harder than an ugly stripper.

Working 10 hours a day calling potential investors is greatly underestimated. Hard work is necessary to reach your goals.

Break the barriers

> Someone just called me "normal"...I have never been so insulted in my entire life.

Many want to point out "reality" to you. They say "face the facts" and only look at "what is". If you are able to see only "what is", the by the Law of Attraction, you will only create more "what is". You must put your thoughts beyond "what is" in order to attract something that is different.

How was I able to raise $40 million in 2.5 years from 500 private investors? How was I able to take my company public and create a $300 million company?

It was certainly not by being "realistic" in the general sense. I had **absolute clarity**. But I also had a **courageous vision** and I was **not afraid of big numbers**.

Don't listen to other people. Especially, if they have never achieved financial success on a high level.

> When a flower doesn't bloom you fix the environment in which it grows, not the flower.

Surround yourself with positive people. Create a work environment where you can succeed and be motivated. Do what is necessary. Change your location, change your office, remove people, add people, etc.

In order to succeed you need a positive encouraging environment where you can follow your dreams and succeed without any negative influences.

Believe in yourself. Believe in your vision. I believe in you!

CHAPTER 3

HOW TO TURN AN IDEA INTO A LISTED COMPANY

Turning an idea into reality with Private Equity

> Private Equity has the power to fund any business dream that you might have.

If you understand how to raise money for your ideas, then anything is possible in this life for you. The trick is to understand that **each business is a corporation with shares**. In order to finance your ideas, you need capital. And you can get the capital by selling shares to investors who believe in your idea. Once you understand how this process works, you can organize the money and try out any business idea that you might have.

The cool thing is that you don't even have to invest your own money (if you have any). Most people don't have any money but just a dream. I believe that all business dreams are doable. You just need to convince enough people to give you money and motivate them with returns. That's why learning about Private Equity and public companies is so important.

Once you learn about the principles of Private Equity and how you can create the right share structure so that investors are motivated to invest, there is nothing that you cannot do.

The business of Private Equity gives me the freedom to work when I want and from where I want. I can work from anywhere in the world. As I am writing these pages, I am in Northern Ireland where my wife was born. It always was her dream to live here for a while and because of my independence and flexibility, we have been here for the last 2 years. Of course, we are planning to go back to America but there is no pressure or stress to do it because of what of Internet and technology these days. I can reach investors, sales people or financial advisors by phone or Skype and it really doesn't matter anymore where I am located in the world.

Of course, it is always easier to convince someone to invest when you meet them in person but most investors are convinced to invest through a conversation on the telephone. In America, where distances are much bigger than in Europe, it is literally impossible to meet all of your investors in person. That's why the telephone is so important. Once you have mastered the art of selling over the phone, there is nothing that you cannot achieve.

Your idea

> Do you suffer from **paralysis analysis**? Do you have brilliant ideas but unable to get started?

Are you confused like so many people? Do you have certain hobbies, passions or interests but don't know how to make money with it?

The key to getting started is **clarity**. You need to take a pad of paper and a pen and write your thoughts down.

If you have several ideas or passions but you are unsure which one to choose, then you must pick only one at first. You must focus on one business idea first.

> Most of the time we feel tired not because we have done too much but because we have done too little of what makes us come alive. (Jim Kirk)

Clarity – let the Universe help you

Lack of time is never the problem. The real problem is lack of direction.

Decide exactly what you want to achieve. The most important factor for my personal success was without a doubt: clarity.

> Especially now, in the age of the Internet, it is ten times more difficult not to get distracted and develop clarity.

Make it your number one goal to develop your goals in as much detail as possible. This step alone will help you more than you can imagine.

If you want to use the law of attraction and you are absolutely clear in regards to what you really want to be, do or have and you can say it out loud, it will be easier for the Universe to give you exactly what you wish for. If your wish is fuzzy, then you won't achieve anything because you send out mixed messages.

Step 1: Creating a product / finding a project

> Don't wait for opportunities. Create them.

When you are young and you are looking at the world of business, you see a lot of big, established companies that are worth billions of dollars in the stock market and it appears quite daunting to compete against that.

But how did all those big companies start? How did they get so big? The answer is over time and with lots of money.

Every business that is big today was small at some point in time.

You should go 40 or 50 years in the future and imagine yourself and being the chairman of the board or a Fortune 500 company.

Your goal should be to choose a business or industry that will eventually be huge and where your company can become a leader. You should think big and create a multi-billion dollar company.

But how do you go about doing this? In this program I will explain how you can create and structure a public company that can raise millions of dollars from investors and from the market and be valued and hundreds of millions of dollars in the stock market.

How do I know all this? Because I have done it before! I will teach you the process and hopefully it will inspire you to do the same but hopefully even better.

Step 2: Incorporate a new company

A year from now you may wish you had started today.

Incorporating a new company is easy these days. I typically incorporate a company online with a service provider. I either choose the state of **Nevada or Wyoming** because of their tax laws and their flexibility. Nevada recently added a $500 per year business license, which makes it more expensive. Wyoming is much cheaper and you don't have to file the directors in the first 12 months. This means that your directors are private and not public knowledge. I often use www.shieldcorp.net because it is very cheap and I know what I am doing. Others use www.incfile.com or www.incparadise.net. I would strongly recommend NOT using www.incorp.com. I have had many bad experiences with them.

In any case, I often use a nominee director, which costs me about $300 to $500 per year. This helps to keep the company anonymous and if your name is somewhat "infamous" and you have people who don't like you, then they won't be able to write anything badly about your newly formed company on the Internet.

Another easy and extremely cheap way to incorporate a new company is in the United Kingdom (www.companieshouse.gov.uk). I use a service provider called www.companiesmadesimple.com

If you incorporate a new company in another country, it is often easier to use a service provider and these days there are many to choose from.

Incorporating a Swiss company costs CHF 100,000 (approximately $100,000). The laws there are also not as flexible as the laws in the US or other countries. But having a company in Switzerland can of course have its benefits (e.g. having a Swiss bank account).

Incorporation companies USA

Silver Shield Services, Inc.
www.shieldcorp.net

EastBiz.com, Inc.
www.incparadise.com

Step 3: Create the right share structure – acquire your own shares

You need to start with the ideal end goal in mind.

When you incorporate a new company, you should always start with the end result in mind. If your plan is to take the company public one day and you don't want to lose the control over the majority, then you must plan accordingly.

One way to ensure that is to issue preferred shares and give them 10x the voting rights over common shares.

A typical structure looks like this:

100 million shares authorized

80 million common shares
20 million preferred shares

The 20 million shares are for you and for the management team. The 80 million shares are for the investors.

In order for you to acquire your own shares, you also have to pay for them just like a regular investor would do. But the big difference is that you can acquire them at par value or $0.0001 per share. If you bought 10 million shares for yourself at par value for $0.0001 then you only have to transfer $1000 into the corporate bank account. You also have to fill out a SSA (Share subscription agreement).

Since it is the very beginning of new company, there is zero value in the company and that's why you can acquire them so cheaply.

Once you go public and your share price is at $1.00 for example, you will have $10 million personally. You probably can't sell them all at first but your net worth is technically speaking $10 million. Maybe you are able to sell 1 million shares in the market eventually (cash out) and keep 9 million shares in the deal.

You can also give yourself 5 million options to acquire preferred shares at par value or a bit more (for example $0.001) with a time frame of 3 years to issue shares later on.

> In any case, issuing shares for yourself in the beginning is what is going to make you a multi-millionaire if your company does well in the future and gets listed.

But you absolutely need to start with the end goal in mind first. You need to plan every step of the way in advance and see how it affects your financing and share structure.

Step 4: Open up a corporate bank account

> Position yourself strategically with several companies, different banks, several accounts and in different countries.

It is very important, which bank you work with. Some banks get really difficult when you accept money from investors and make lots of international wire transfers.

If you get a big bank that does a lot of international business transactions and is not constantly on your case about potential fraudulent activities but you pay more fees, etc. then choose that one.

Most banks are iffy when it comes to transactions that could jeopardize their reputation.

Don't mention anything about investors when you first open up the account. Once it is open and you have a relationship with your bank established, you can be more open.

I have had banks close my accounts for no particular reason just because they suspected that a transaction was suspicious. The main goal is to have options available when one bank is giving you a hard time. Don't ever just rely on one banking relationship.

To open up a corporate bank account in the US you will need:

1. Articles of incorporation
2. EIN (Employer Identification Number) – also known as TAX ID
3. Business address and phone number

You can obtain an EIN online here:

https://www.irs.gov/businesses/small-businesses-self-employed/apply-for-an-employer-identification-number-ein-online

Step 5: Create the basic marketing materials

> The difference between winning and losing lies in the details.

Having good-looking marketing materials is key. If it can impress investors, then it makes your job to convince them a lot easier.

Often, good marketing materials can make up for a company that is still young and that has flaws.

Years ago I was lucky to find Mariano Duyos, a designer from Argentina. He has helped me to create numerous brochures and marketing materials that made my success even possible. Without him, I would have been lost. Having a great designer makes all the difference in the world.

<u>You should create the following marketing material for your potential investors:</u>

1. 2-Pager (Summary about the company, details about the private placement)
2. Corporate Summary or brochure (Colorful marketing brochure about the company)
3. Business Plan (numbers, details, strategy, EBITDA projection)
4. PPT (Power Point Presentation)
5. 10 reasons to invest into *ABC* – 10 reasons to invest into *this industry* (e.g. oil)

<u>Designer</u>
Mariano Duyos
www.marianoduyos.com

<u>Online services for hire</u>
www.upwork.com

Step 6: Creating all the necessary legal materials

> With INTEGRITY you have nothing to
> fear since you have nothing to hide.

Before I even got into the Private Equity business I did wanted to do some consulting work for a guy named Claudio. Claudio was crook who deliberately cheated people out of their money. I didn't know that when I first met him.

I was supposed to meet him for a second meeting in his office and instead of him greeting me at the door, the place was full of police officers. A legal prosecutor greeted me at the door and he asked me if I would give him a statement, which I did.

Luckily, I did not get involved with Claudio. But when I found out how fraudulently he was conducting his business by raising capital from investors, I was shocked.

So early on I was confronted with the law and the legal side of this business. I decided right then and there that I would protect my company to the best possible degree. I made sure I had a proper contract written up by a securities lawyer. I created a "consulting protocol document" that made it clear for a second time that the person who invests money was at risk of losing it. I even translated it into German for my German speaking investors.

I went into this business right from the start with the attitude that assuming that I prosecutor would try to attack me, I would be adequately covered. My contract was airtight and the way I went about my business was 110% legal.

Most people screw up because they get greedy and think they can transfer the money to an offshore account or similar.

You have to assume that your deal doesn't go as planned and then you could potentially land in jail. So how are you going to protect yourself in case things go south?

Luckily, I was so well protected that I never got into any legal trouble.

You can still make a lot of money but make sure you do it the right way and that you do it 100% legal.

You need to do the following things:

1. SSA – Share subscription agreement
2. PPM – Private Placement Memorandum
3. Form D – SEC Filing and registration / Announcement to raise capital
4. Accounting – Financial Statements / do not mix personal and business
5. Proper contracts for projects
6. Management agreements (for you and your officers)
7. Consulting agreements

Step 7: The management team

It is important that you understand the difference between officers and directors of a company. There are only three official titles when it comes to a company:

1. President
2. Treasurer
3. Secretary

Those positions are directors and they have the real power in a corporation. You can always add an additional director if you like.

An officer is a member of the management. For example a CEO, the Chief Executive Officer, is a management title. He doesn't have the same legal power as the president of a corporation.

Often, you can see that the CEO and president are the same person but technically they don't have to be.

A CFO (Chief Financial Officer) is also just a management title. The real person with power is the Treasurer.

One person alone can be President, Treasurer and Secretary or it can be three different people.

You can use a nominee director to protect your identity. A nominee director is listed as the director when you do your initial filing of the directors and then immediately steps down. This way no one really knows who is in charge of the corporation. This is a great way to protect your name, reputation or assets from people who want to hurt you financially.

An unknown person once targeted me online. He immediately started to write badly about me as soon as a brand new corporation was founded. This made it almost impossible for me to build up a company and make it successful. So instead I decided to use a nominee director and it was impossible to find my name attached to any of my companies.

If you have a company that has a technical background, then you ideally want to have a couple of experts in your management team. If you have a gold exploration company, then one of your directors should be a geologist. If you have a biotech deal, then you should have PhD in biochemistry as one of the directors.

> Ideally, you want to be in charge as the president and CEO and hire experts to use their name and reputation for the company.

When I started my first company Hemis Corporation, I ended up with about 10 geologists in my organization. Most of them had over 20 or 30 years of experience and had a PhD in geology. The reason why I was able to get them to join my team was because I was excited about the company and simply had **the courage to ask them** if they would join. I offered them 20,000 shares and I would pay them $150 per hour or $800 per day if they needed to do any work for the company (like writing a report, etc.). But if I didn't need them, I didn't have to pay them. In return, I was able to put them on the advisory board and use their CV and picture in my marketing materials. This gave the company a lot of credibility and it made it easier to raise money because all these experts were part of my company.

There are many young scientists working in the research departments at Universities with great ideas or projects. They are not getting paid a lot and they have no idea how to attract investors to fund their ideas. It is easy to partner with a scientist who has written a study about a certain topic and then you can use his dissertation including the name of the University as your own.

Step 8: Private Placement financing rounds - Raise money from private investors

It's going to be hard. But hard is not impossible.

In order to raise money from investors, you need to be able to motivate them. An investor wants to double or triple his investment and he wants to know when he can get his money back.

Ideally, you can motivate an investor with an IPO (=initial public offering). Let's say you have a great business idea or concept and the investor is able to buy shares at $0.50 per share, then your projected IPO price could be at $1.00.

The investor will double his investment by buying the shares in a private placement and selling them into the public markets when the company is listed.

But this is not enough. Your story must have enough potential so that the share price has a potential to be $5 or even $10 in the near future.

A typical private placement plan could look like this:

1st round: $0.25
2nd round: $0.50
3rd round: $0.75
IPO / first price when public: $1.00

It depends how much money you want to raise in each round. If you want to raise $500,000 per round, then the amount of shares that you will issue, looks like this:

1st round:	$0.25 - $500,000 – 2 million common shares issued
2nd round:	$0.50 - $500,000 – 1 million common shares issued
3rd round:	$0.75 - $500,000 – 666,666 common shares issued

Total shares issued for investors: 3,666,666 common shares
Total amount of money raised: $1.5 million

Raising money from investors is one of the most difficult things you can do. But once you have mastered the art of raising capital, it is also the most financially rewarding. You can fund your company / business idea and you can't make money for yourself as well. If you own 5 or 10 million shares as the founder and your company goes public at $1.00, then you have got it made!

The main goal has to be to speak to enough people every day and present your story. If you speak to 100 people a day and ask them to send them some information, you might be able to continue talking to 10 afterwards. Out of those 10 interested leads, maybe 1 or 2 will end up becoming an investor. The whole process is hard work but it is very possible if you are not lazy or afraid of rejection.

Ideally, you also want to use leverage by building a sales team or by using existing financial advisors who already have clients. A sales team of 20 people can raise anywhere between $1 and $2 million per month. An individual person might only raise $50,000 to $100,000. If you are working alone in the beginning, then your plan will just take a little bit longer than anticipated. If you don't give up and continue to speak to enough potential investors, you will eventually reach your goal.

Step 9: Generating new leads

There are four ways how you can generate leads for potential investors. In general, the best way to convince is person is face-to-face. The second best is on the phone.

> The reason why entrepreneurs are struggling is
> because they use HOPE as a STRATEGY.

1. Make calls yourself
2. Marketing team
3. Online strategy
4. List broker, existing lists, clients, former investors, referrals, etc.

If you are alone, then you have to be in charge of raising money first. In that case you have to make 100 cold calls. You can use the telephone book, yellow pages or make your own list. Your goal is to generate 5 to 10 leads per day where you are able to send the initial information package to the client and get him interested in the deal.

The second method is to hire 2, 5 or 10 marketing people who generate leads for you to follow up. If you hire 5 people and they make 100 cold calls each and generate 5x 5 leads per day, then you will have 25 leads per day to follow up with. This method is usually much easier and better because you already know that the person showed some initial interest and is open to talk to you.

> Use online marketing to generate leads.
> Use the telephone to follow up.

The third option is to run an ad online. If a person clicks on your ad, he gets redirected to a landing page and in exchange for his telephone number and email, you will give him a report about investing. Your job is then to follow up with a call after that person has read the report and try to sell him the shares.

The fourth option is to buy leads from a list broker. A professional marketing company can sell you a lead for $5 to $100 per lead. These lists can be really good because you have the perfect target group of people who have the right age, income and who are interested in investing. But be careful that you don't buy a list where 5 other companies have called them.

In general, the best list consists of former investors. These are people who already once invested into a private placement and bought shares elsewhere. Most of these people are risk-takers and somewhat naïve or greedy.

Once a gambler – always a gambler!

Step 10: Acquire the first project

Start small – finish big. The first project will give you momentum.

In order to have a compelling story for your investors, you will need to have a project, product or prototype.

Many great ideas require you to have millions of dollars. But it is important to note that you don't necessarily need it in the beginning. Often, a simple option agreement or LOI to acquire it, is all that you need at first.

Example: One of my companies has three oil projects. The total amount to acquire all three projects and put them into production is over $9 million. The $9 million initial investment could potentially put those three projects into production so that they would generate about $40 million per year from the sale of the oil.

The company has zero capital but I was able to strike a deal with the holder of the leases to give me the projects for no down payment. No I can go out to investors and tell them that I have three projects and raise the money. All that I had was a written option agreement that says that we intend to acquire the projects in the near future.

In the past I had to pay about $10,000 to acquire an option for a gold project. The first payment of $10,000 would give me 3 months to raise an additional $50,000 to pay for it fully. As you can see you don't always need a lot of money to acquire a project.

You can use the following things for your first project:

- LOI (Letter of Intent) – $0 upfront
- Option to acquire a project / property – $0 to $10,000
- Prototype – only the cost of the first prototype
- Contract – deal that you make with another party
- Patent – approximately $5000 to register a new patent

Project acquisitions mining exploration projects

www.bcgold.com
David Zamida

Step 11: Issuing shares with a transfer agent or through the company

> A transfer agent is a company assigned by a corporation to maintain a list of investors.

You can either issue shares directly from your company by printing a share certificate or you can get registered with a transfer agent who will do it for you professionally.

If you intend to go public in the future, you will need a transfer agent. A transfer agent will make sure that the correct of shares are issued, will help with lost certificates and will issue a CUSIP number when you go public.

The setup fee for a transfer agent is about $500 and then each certificate costs about $20.

If you are starting out, you won't necessarily need a transfer agent in the beginning. But I would strongly suggest that you do it anyway because it looks professional and later on when you have to do your financial statements and audit, it will be an important factor.

Here is a list of transfer agents that I used to work with:

Island Stock Transfer Agent (Florida) – www.islandstocktransfer.com
Pacific Stock Transfer Agent (Las Vegas) – www.pacificstocktransfer.com
Quicksilver Transfer Agent (Nevada) – www.qstransfer.com

Step 12: Creating financial statements and audit

Don't ever mix personal expenses with business expenses.

One of the most important things to get listed is to have proper financial statements. You must first hire an accountant that has experience with public companies and share issuance. Not all accountants know how to do this properly.

Once you have financial statements according to GAAP (General Accepted Accounting Principles), you must then send them to an auditor. The auditor then will double check the financial statements and sign off on them so that they can be used in an SEC Filing.

Accountant Canada and USA

Gerald Wong
3740 Albert St 701
Burnaby, BC V5C 5Y7
Canada
Tel: +1-(604) 294-2818
Email: geraldwong@telus.net

- Gerald Wong has prepared over audited financial statements for over 200 public companies.

- He is self-employed and works from home.
- He is a great accountant who is extremely diligent and can help even with challenging financial statements.
- He has contacts to auditors for public companies.
- He is reasonably priced but requests a retainer before he starts working.

Step 13: SEC Filings (S-1 Registration Statement)

> Get registered and set up with the SEC. This will give you credibility and trust with your clients.

First, you must get registered with the SEC and their EDGAR system. In order to get registered, you must file the Form ID, which you can download from the SEC website (www.sec.gov).

You can use a filing agent or a securities lawyer to submit this form with the SEC. I always use a company in Canada called Computershare (www.computershare.com). They are considered an "e3 Filing Professional". Even though they are located in Canada, they do US filings, too.

The next step is to file the SEC Form D. The Form D says basically that you intend to raise money from private investors according to SEC Rule 506. You must announce it 15 days in advance before you can accept money from the public by filing the Form D. In this form you will state the total amount of the private placement amount and how much commission you will pay out.

After you have done these two filings, you will file the **S-1 Registration Statement**. This is your filing to go public. The S-1 Registration Statement is basically the same content like your PPM plus your **audited financial statements**. In this filing you will also mention the company's goals, all the potential risks involved, the shareholders, the management team and basically every single important detail about the company.

The key here is transparency and **disclosure**. The most important factor here is disclosure. The goal is to create a document that mentions all facts and potential risks so that an investor can make a proper decision whether he wants to invest or not.

The SEC is not looking for a "good business model". It just wants to make sure that all facts are mentioned and that the investors are properly informed.

Step 14: Market Maker – Form 15c2-11

You can set the first public price together with the market maker.

The term "Market Maker" often gets confused with "Market Promoter". The market maker is a member of FINRA (Financial Regulatory Authority) and they are necessary to get listed. **A market maker will sponsor your company** and help you to obtain a **trading symbol.** They don't promote your stock. They simply set a first price (bid and ask) so that a market is created.

The market maker will file the Form 15c2-11 with FINRA so you can obtain your ticker symbol. The filing with FINRA happens after your S-1 Registration Statement from the SEC was declared "effective".

FINRA will make sure that there is a fair market. This means that the biggest 10 shareholders of free trading shares will not control more than 90% of the free float.

You need a market maker to get listed. For the first 30 days you will only have one market maker and then about 10 more will come automatically.

You can set the first price for the company in accordance with the market maker. The first price has to be close to what your last round of financing was.

Market Maker

Spartan Securities Group, Ltd.
Member FINRA/SIPC
15500 Roosevelt Blvd
Suite 303
Clearwater, FL 33760
Office: (727)502-0508
Fax: (727)502-0858
Main person: Micah Eldred

Step 15: Budget for IPO, project and personal income

Always pay yourself first as an employee of the company.

It is important to understand that going public is expensive. I paid about $250,000 with my first deal and it took my about one year. But of course there are cheaper options once you know what needs to be done. You can go public with $50,000 initial capital if you have very basic financial statements.

Here is an approximate list of costs for the whole process:

Initial set-up:

- Incorporation - $500 to $1000
- Bank account
- Legal set-up to raise money - $5000
- Project acquisition / option / contract - $10,000
- Management - $10,000
- SSA, PPM, Form D (SEC), EDGAR - $5,000

Legal fees:

- Retainer from securities lawyer: $5000

- S-1 Registration Statement: $25,000
- Additional work for comments: $10,000

Accountant:

- Financial statements and book keeping: $5000 (per quarter)

Auditor:

- Audited financial statements: $10,000 (per quarter)

Market Maker:

- No money
- Legal fees for comment for FINRA: $10,000

Transfer Agent:

- Set-up - $500
- Issuance of share certificates - $5000
- CUSIP number - $500

Employees:

- CEO / president: $5000 per month
- CFO / treasurer: $5000 per month
- Administration: $5000 per month

Total estimated expenses for 12 months: **$307,000**

General and administrative expense

A general and administrative expense (**G&A**) refers to expenditures related to the day-to-day operations of a business. In the company's income statement, these expenses generally appear under operating expenses.

Office expenses: $100,000
Marketing: $50,000

Sales commissions: $100,000 (10% on capital raised)
Project investment: $350,000
Cash reserves: $100,000

These are numbers based on about $1 million raised in 12 months. Ideally, you want to invest as much money into the actual project or product of the company but in the first year, you will have a lot of other expenses as well.

Step 16: Taking the company public at $1.00

> Have the courage to think big. You don't need to ask anyone for permission.

Be bold and courageous. Be the first to think big and act accordingly. You will find out that if you have the courage to go big, you will have no competition and people will follow you because they look up to you.

When I took my first company public, I had about 75 million shares issued and outstanding and the opening price was $0.80 per share. This equaled a market capitalization of about $60 million. Within a very short period of time, the stock price went up to about $4.00 USD and the value increased to over $300 million.

Initially, my first investors were able to buy the shares at $0.27. The jump from $0.27 to $0.80 was already 3x of what they had invested but when it went even higher, the ratio was about 12 times of what they had invested. Most investors sold their position between $1.00 and $1.50 though.

The second company I took public had a first round for the private placement of $0.50 and an opening price of $1.25. The stock went up to about $2.00. This company also had about 75 million shares outstanding and a market capitalization of $150 million.

In general, a company with a market capitalization of $100 million is considered a small cap or even micro cap company in the eyes of the stock market. $500 million is a small to mid cap company. $500 to $1 billion is a mid cap company and over $1 billion is a large cap company.

Elizabeth Holmes, the founder of Theranos, came up with an idea to patent a device that could test blood levels and administer medicine. Her idea seemed so revolutionary that she was able to raise $6 million in the first year from investors. Once her idea became more publicly known, the company raised over $600 million and received a market capitalization of over $9 billion.

She was a University dropout and simply had an idea. Even though it turned out that her idea didn't end up working and the company eventually got dissolved, it shows that **if you are courageous, believe in your idea, promote it properly that you can create a multi million dollar company.**

The point that I am trying to make is that you need a great idea that has the potential to be huge, raise the initial capital and then create a company that is public. Once your company is public, you will get access to more funds much more easily.

I once turned down $1.5 million from a fund in London because they wanted my shares as personal collateral. Looking back, I should have taken the deal. They offered me that deal simply because I had a public company and a promising project.

The hardest part is to raise the first $1 or $2 million. Once you have done that, it is much easier to get $10 million afterwards.

Most investment funds are not allowed to invest into a private company because they need an actual value in their books. They need a listed company that shows a tradable and sellable share price. But once you are public, those mutual funds will buy your stock and help you to grow.

Step 17: Buying a listed shell (reverse take-over)

> You can go public immediately by buying a listed company and do a reverse take-over.

There is even a website where you can buy a listed company. It is like a market place for "shells".

You need to distinguish between a **reporting company** and a **non-reporting company.**

A reporting company is a company that does filings with the SEC (EDGAR system) and files its financial statements on a quarterly basis. A reporting company is usually traded on the OTCQB (Over-the-counter quotation board). The trading symbol could be something like this: ABCD.QB

A non-reporting company is a company that does **no filings with the SEC**. A non-reporting company is also trading but is trading on the OTC Pink Sheets. You can buy and sell shares just like on any other exchange but there are no regulations. It is like the "Wild West". The trading symbol could be something like this: ABCD.PK

An OTCQB shell costs about $350,000 and a Pink Sheets shell costs about $100,000.

Here is an example for an ad that I found online:

OTCQB Ready Fully Reporting Pink Trading Public Shell For Sale

- Selling control block (30,000,000 restricted shares)
- Has symbol, trading and quoted on the OTC Pink w/piggyback status OTCQB READY!
- **FULLY REPORTING - FULLY AUDITED BY PCAOB ACCOUNTING FIRM**
- 100,000,000 shares authorized.
- 33,272,311 shares issued and outstanding (includes 30mil shares control block)
- 33,019,811 Restricted Shares
- **252,500 CURRENT FLOAT**
- No regulatory issues
- Have shareholder list and current with transfer agent
- Approximately 124 shareholders of record
- Nevada Corp. incorporated 1989
- Current director will appoint new director(s) and step down
- DTC Eligible!
- **All corp. articles, bylaws, minutes and financials in order, securities attorney maintained**
- **Recent stock quote $0.20 Bid X $0.66 Ask**

Cash & Carry - Ask $349,500.00

Email us for the symbol and details

***** WE ALSO HAVE AVAILABLE CLEAN PINK OTC NON-REPORTING AND/ OR DELINQUENT REPORTING PUBLIC SHELLS PRICES RANGING FROM $90,000 - $115,000 EMAIL US FOR DETAILS**

OTC listing requirements
www.otcmarkets.com
(Official site for OTCQX, OTCQB and OTC Pink Securities)

Buying a listed shell
Deal Stream (formerly MergerNetwork.com)
www.dealstream.com

Buying a broker dealer
Bdmarket.com

Step 18: Making money with your share position

You only have to be right ONE TIME! (Mark Cuban)

You can start 10 different companies and fail 10 times. And it is possible that the 11th time you will break through and be successful.

You never know which deal will take off. Typically, 4 out of 5 deals fail. It is usually with the one deal that you will make your money.

That's why it is important to have a big share position in each company that you start.

If you own 5 million or 10 million shares in a deal because you started it, then you will have a few million dollars once the company is public and trading.

If you own 5 million shares and your company goes public at $1.00, then you have $5 million. You probably won't be able to sell all 5 million shares and cash out. But you might be able to sell 1 million shares over the course of 12 to 24 months and keep 4 million shares.

I used to own 35 million shares of Hemis with a share price $3.50. Theoretically, this was worth $123 million. The problem was that I could not sell all those shares because the volume was not big enough. I could only sell a couple of thousand shares per day not to bring down the share price.

If that is the case, then you need to wait and work on building the company into a solid deal that will sustain the value. You might be able to sell the shares in the future.

Step 19: Making money with raising money (post-IPO)

> Promotion and stock marketing is a separate skill. This knowledge can make you millions of dollars next to what you are already earning.

You can become a millionaire by selling shares into the market. This means that you are "cashing out".

Example: You sell 5000 shares per day times 20 days per month for 3 months.

5000 shares per day
100,000 shares per month
Average price: $2
Total after 3 month: $600,000

If you want to sell shares into the market to cash out, you need to generate volume. This means that you need to hire newsletter writers, do lots of marketing, do 2-3 news releases per week, etc. to attract new investors. If you are the only person (or one of the few) who can sell shares, then most new buyers (that you don't know personally, coming from the market) will buy the shares from you.

Step 20: Making money with raising money

Get up every morning and remind yourself: I CAN DO THIS!

Making 100 cold calls each day is hard work emotionally. If you get rejected 95% of the time, it can be quite frustrating. That's why you must know exactly WHY you are doing what you are doing or you must have a better STRATEGY to approach potential investors.

You can pay yourself a 10% commission or a 50% commission. It all depends on your deal, structure, legality and set up. You can raise money for the company and get rich at the same time. If you raise $200,000 per month and get 10%, then your annual income is $240,000. If you pay yourself 40%, then it is $1 million per year.

And here is where ethics come into play. Are you working in the best interest for the company or for yourself? Is it even legal to take out so much money?

I have seen a lot of great sales people who earned 20% or 30% and became millionaires.

Some organizations divide the money up this way:

20% commission for sales person
10% costs, marketing, office, salaries, etc. (for sales organization)
30% sales and marketing costs in total

70% company / project (actual money that goes into deal)

The SEC will typically allow no more than 10% in commissions. You could pay 10% in commission and 20% in marketing expenses (separate consulting agreement), leaving the company with 70% of the raised capital. In order to make it economical for a sales organization to sell your deal, you have to pay them at least 30%.

Become a great sales person.
Your sales skills will determine how much money you will earn.

Step 21: Building a money raising sales organization

Life is too short to think small.

Another important factor for success is **leverage.** If you have a sales team of 10 people who sell your products to clients, then they will achieve a better result than you just by yourself ever could.

When I built my own sales organizations, we were able to raise $40 million in about 2 years from private investors. In total we had about 500 private investors. My sales organization in Zurich had about 25 sales people and my other two organizations were smaller but they also contributed to the overall result.

Intermediaries are another important group. An intermediary is an independent financial advisor or group. If I pay a commission to financial advisors who already have several hundred clients and manage already millions of dollars, then it is much easier and quicker to raise capital for my companies. Their clients already trust them and I don't have to convince them or gain their trust.

We are currently talking to a group that would guarantee between $1.2 and $1.5 million per month in new investments.

This **one contact alone** could finance my entire deal and I don't ever have to talk to one single investor myself. That's why you should contact as many different people as possible. You never know which contact will be the jackpot.

Having the right people as your business partners is key. If you have average people around you, then your results will be average or low. If you work with great people, then you will do much better and this kind of momentum will motivate you even more.

But even if you don't have any contacts of intermediaries or sales organizations right now, you should also make regular calls to broker dealers, financial advisors and other contacts who could potentially help you to raise the money for your deal.

Step 22: Repeat the process and build more companies until you made it

> The MARKET doesn't care about your feelings. Get up and do it again.

Even if you fail the first time, get up and do it again. When my first deal failed, I fell into a depression and wanted to give up.

It was my securities lawyer who said the following thing to me: *"All the great people in this business screw up big time once. If you learn from your mistakes, recover and do it again, you can come out as one of the great ones. I have seen it happening many times."*

This was very encouraging because I come from a culture in Switzerland where people are very unforgiving when you fail in business once. You are always considered a failure in their eyes. But luckily it is the complete opposite in America. It is almost expected of you to fail many times and overcome adversity in order to become great. Failing is no shame. Not getting up and trying it again is.

I want to encourage you to get started. If you fail, then do it again but better. The most important thing is to believe in yourself and in your vision. If your **desire is strong** enough and your **business model makes sense**, then **you will always find investors** who are excited to support you.

CHAPTER 4

MONEY RAISING MASTERCLASS

22 steps to successfully raising money from private investors

> If you can find ONE investor, you can find a million more.

How do you find investors? That's the million-dollar question! If you have millions of dollars from investors available, you can make any dream or project work. Finding the money is the hardest part.

I have raised millions of dollars from investors, took companies public and dealt with many great sales people who also raised a lot of money from investors. I have invested millions in resource projects all around the world and hired geologists who worked on these projects.

The lessons in this Money Raising Masterclass are real and authentic. They come from actual personal experience and from many sales people and stock brokers that I have had the privilege to work with.

The knowledge in this program is very special and it took years of trial and error until I figured out how best to go about it.

Raising money is not easy. It is hard work and it is a numbers game. But once you know what to do, there is no job like it. The ability to make lots of money and turn your business ideas into reality is a great accomplishment and satisfaction.

Listed and established companies can raise money from investment funds, private equity companies or other financial companies. But if you are just starting out with an idea, you have no other choice but to organize the money from private investors.

Raising money is a combination of the knowledge of how to do it, technical knowledge and sales skills. I have seen average non-financially educated people raise millions of dollars because they mastered the art of money raising so well by developing great sales and communication skills.

In the end money raising is like selling any other product. It is all sales. But the benefits are much bigger.

In this program I am going to cover the process as well as the sales side of the business.

In the end you can really only raise money by talking to people and trying to convince them of your investment ideas. The better you learn to communicate, the more people you can convince to invest.

Some people are better suited to talk to investors and others are better when it comes to managing projects. You have to find out what you do best and find good partners that can do the things were you have weaknesses.

In the end you have to build a company and you can't do it alone. You will need a team. In the beginning raising money is the most important function because without money to fund your projects and ideas, there is no company. Even if you have not a "sales person" you will have to learn how to raise money from investors if you want your company to get financed.

Lesson 1: Setting a goal

Set clear, measurable goals. A goal properly set is halfway reached.

Where do you start? Just like anything in life you should start with a goal. Raising money is hard. Raising money is a numbers game. Learning how to raise money takes time. But it is very possible in any market condition and any economy.

If you have never raised any money before, you should not try to raise a specific number but focus on activities.

Examples activities / goals for beginners:

- Make 100 calls per day
- Generate 5 good quality leads (sending out information and good conversation)
- Telephone time: 5 hours per day

Being on the telephone and trying to sell can be mentally exhausting. Most people can't make phone calls for 8 or even 10 hours a day. It is not efficient. That's why I recommend 5 hours a day but 5 hours of intensive telephone work.

My friend and stockbroker Tom Jandt used to make up to 500 calls per day. He lives in California. He started at 6 am calling the East Coast early in the morning and eventually moved across the whole country until he reached Pacific Time. In the evenings we called Hawaii and this way he covered several time zones in one day.

His efforts had paid off. He was able to get many big clients and because of his hard work he was able to retire in his early thirties.

There is not really a limit to how much anyone can raise per month. Some people raise $100,000 with a few clients and some can raise several hundred thousand per month because they target higher net worth individuals.

If you raise less than $50,000 per month, then you are either doing something wrong or you are lazy or afraid of rejection. $100,000 should really be a minimum goal that can be achieved with making lots of calls.

> Go BIG or go home. Be hard working and diligent. Make hundreds of calls each day. What do you have to lose?

If you have the right contacts, you can raise millions. If you have a sales organization, you can also raise a lot more for your projects compared to being alone. When I had a sales organization in Zurich, we raised between $1 million to $2 million every single month.

Some sales people that I know have raised $5 million or even $10 million from a single client.

> With the right project and the right contacts anything is possible.

It takes courage to ask for bigger numbers. Some of my friends say that the minimum investment is $250,000 and that they usually have clients with one million or more invested. They do this to intimidate the client and to get him to invest a higher number than what he is used to.

If you ask a client for $50,000 and he has it, then $50,000 is no hurdle. But if you knew that he had more money, he would have invested $100,000 easily, too. That's why you must do your homework and start with big numbers to find out where it starts to hurt.

Some people invest $5000 and some $100,000. It all depends on the quality of your leads.

You can either pay yourself a fixed salary from the company or get a percentage of the money raised. If you raise $1 million and your commission is 10%, then you make $100,000.

Lesson 2: The 4 levels (people) of raising money

> **Level 1:** Marketing person / Cold Caller
> **Level 2:** Private Equity Broker / Sales Person I – Opener
> **Level 3:** Private Equity Broker / Sales Person II – Loader
> **Level 4:** Private Equity Entrepreneur – Dealmaker and initiator

There are four different people or levels involved when raising money. Four different people can do each level or all four can be done by one person alone.

Level 1: Marketing person / Cold Caller

The first level is the marketing person or cold caller. Typically, a marketing person has a random list of doctors; business owners or another specific group and they start doing the cold calls.

The job of the marketing person is the most important one. The longer he or she can talk to a client, the better. A person who simply accepts the materials but who is not really interested is not a good lead. A good lead has been informed and made curious.

Level 2: Private Equity Broker / Sales Person I – Opener

An opener is a person who gets the client to invest a first small amount – just so he is in the deal. This amount could be $2000, $5000 or $10,000. The idea is to get the client's initial trust so that he can be loaded later on.

Level 3: Private Equity Broker / Sales Person II – Loader

A loader only calls existing clients and gets them to increase their investment. A loader typically comes with some good news or a story that he can still get shares for the old price.

I have seen people increase their investment from $5000 to a total of $100,000 by reinvesting 4 or 5 more times.

One client invested $2000 initially and then ended up investing $500,000 in total.

Level 4: Private Equity Entrepreneur – Dealmaker and initiator

The last stage is to start your own company and take it public in the stock market. You raise money yourself from investors but you also have others help you to raise money. Being in control of a deal is the best place to be in but it also comes with a lot of responsibly. You need to make sure that the deal gets funded, that the company goes public and that the projects will succeed.

Sometimes a person has to do all 4 levels by himself. This happens typically in the beginning. But some sales teams are organized in such a way that even the most experienced sales person does the initial marketing calls.

Lesson 3: Finding names, leads and research

No phone calls = no leads = no sales

Generating leads and sales is your number one task as a private equity entrepreneur. If you want to raise $3 million in 12 months, then you must raise $250,000 per month. This means that you will need at least 5 clients each month. In order to do that you must generate a lot of leads and follow up with them.

Finding the right names is key. You can go online, buy lists of business owners or use the telephone directory.

A typical investor profile looks like this:

- Age group: 40 to 65 (Young people typically don't have as much money saved.)
- Business owners with at least 20 employees
- Highly paid professionals like doctors, lawyers or architects
- Men (95% of all clients are male.)
- Is willing to take more risk
- Already has a portfolio of stocks and other investments

You can also buy a business directory that has valuable marketing information. Typically, you will see the number of employees, yearly sales, industry, contact information including emails and phone numbers of the CEO.

It makes sense to invest into those kinds of business directories because it fits your target investor profile.

Sometimes ONE CUSTOMER can change everything.

There will always be a surprise if you contact enough people. Often your best customers come from the least expected sources.

If you make 100 calls per day and get 5 to 10 good leads, then you can sell your way into financial independence. You need to make sure you talk to enough people each day to have the odds in your favor.

Business is a numbers game and if you contact enough potential clients, you will get lucky and get a big one once in a while. When I first started out, my first two clients invested $5500 and $11,000. But the third one invested $160,000. With this one client alone I was able to kick start the company.

When it comes to research you could also think outside of the box and not just focus on your own country.

Here are some interesting facts:

- 1/3 of all the money in the world lies in Switzerland
- Germany is doing well economically in Europe and there is a lot of money
- China is going to be the new super power – lots of money from China goes into USA
- Don't waste your time with Dubai or Saudi Arabia – it takes years or the right contact
- USA – lots of people got burnt. Sometimes it is better to look for other options.
- Personal contacts are often better than cold calls. If you already have a relationship of trust, then it is easier to raise money.

Lesson 4: Developing leads through a marketing person

> Cold calling potential prospects can be frustrating and hard but it is essential in closing potential customers.

If you don't want to call 100 clients each day yourself, you could hire a few marketing people and build a small call center. I once opened a small call center where I hired 5 women who made about 100 calls each day during 5 hours from Monday to Friday. They would do the cold calling and generate each day about 5 good leads each. So basically, they got the 95 "no's" and the 5 "yes".

But then you can follow up with the 5 leads yourself because you know that those will already be people who have received some basic information from your company and who are generally speaking interested in your products. The second call is going to be much easier and friendlier.

If you have a team of 5 marketing people who generate 25 new good leads each day and you follow up on those leads because you are the best sales person, then making sales is really easy.

If you hire one marketing assistant and that person makes 100 calls per day, then the math looks like this:

100 calls per day
95 people say no
5 new good leads generated

5 hours telephone time x $10/hour = $50
5 days per week = $250 per week
4 weeks = **$1000 salary for your marketing assistant**
(plus % of your sales)

5 leads x 5 days x 4 weeks = 100 good leads generated in one month

100 leads = 5 clients (for example)

Let's say that you have 100 good quality leads each month and you are able to generate 5 clients. Depending on your product and your price structure you might make $1000 per client. Let's say you make $5000 in commissions. Now you simply deduct the $1000 salary that you have to pay your marketing assistant and you will end up with $4000 for yourself.

Maybe you want to give your marketing assistant an incentive by giving him or her a percentage of your closed deals but that is up to you.

If you study this example and then scale it to 5 or even 10 marketing people, you can generate a lot more sales.

This example is not just theory but I actually did it in real life and it worked. I was able to find 5 women who wanted to work part time because most of them had kids and needed flexibility. At the same time they were happy to have a job on the side and 5 hours per day was manageable.

> Statistics show that women around the age of 45 with a British accent have the highest success rate on the phone when first taking to a client.

Lesson 5: Methods to raise money

1. On the phone
2. In Person (face-to-face)
3. Presentation in a hotel
4. Third party intermediary (financial advisor who already has clients)

In the end the best way is to sit face-to-face with a client. But if that's not possible then you must convince him on the phone.

The main reason why people invest is because they trust you. The second reason is that they are greedy (they want to find a hot tip and get something for nothing).

In order to raise lots of money you must become an expert in sales and communication. Often, financial knowledge or product specific knowledge is secondary. If you can convince a client and get him to trust you, then the product doesn't really matter.

As a financial advisor you make the suggestions like a doctor would prescribe medications. You don't question it. Often, sales people talk hours on end about life in general and spend only 5 minutes on the product itself. Once you have established a good relationship with a client, he will do whatever you suggest.

Win the person first and don't start arguing about the details of the product.

In the past, we held a presentation once a month for potential and existing shareholders in a hotel. Usually, about 15 to 20 people would show up and we would raise between $200,000 and $300,000 from one presentation alone. Sometimes a client just needs to see that others have invested, too. It is often the deciding factor to see the management team and a technical person (in our case the geologist) talk about the project and the company.

Another great way is to use intermediaries. An intermediary is a financial advisor who already has lots of clients and manages their money. I used to have about 20 individual financial advisors who worked on commission selling my product to their clients. I typically paid them a 10% commission in cash and 5% in stocks if they brought more than $100,000 in total.

Sometimes ONE INTERMEDIARY can change everything.

There is one intermediary in Germany who committed to raise $5 million for one of our projects. Another intermediary is connected to 15 other financial advisors and they can raise a lot of money combined. Sometimes finding the one right contact / intermediary can make all the difference.

Lesson 6: First conversation with sales person

> Never attempt to sell on the first call.
> Focus on information gathering.

After a marketing person has sent out the initial information package about the company, a sales person follows up with the client.

If the marketing person did his job right, then the sales person should have some basic information about the client. He should know whether or not he has invested into a similar deal before, where he has his investment portfolio and if $50,000 to $100,000 is a possibility for the client.

Since there is no trust yet, the first job of the sales person is to introduce himself. The best way to do this is by **positioning**. The client must feel like the sales person is a real specialist who deals with millions of dollars on a regular basis and the client should be happy to even be able to talk to him.

The job of the sales person is to **position himself as a specialist in high finance**. Just like a doctor, he is a professional. He is not a sales person who has to beg for the business. Once you understand this distinction, the way you talk to clients changes and the way they see you as well. You need to come across as a real expert in investments.

It is often unrealistic to close a deal on the first call. So the goal is not to close but to build trust and to send another document like a more detailed business plan or a project report to the client. It will give the sales person a reason to call again. The goal in the first call is to start developing a relationship. The longer the conversation is, the better.

> Typically, it takes 3 to 4 conversations until a client is ready to invest.

Most people start a conversation like this:

"I am not sure if you can remember me but we have spoken about one year ago and I offered you something good but at the time you were not interested. The

deal back then went through the roof and now I am offering you something even more interesting."

Most say this even if they have never even spoken to the client before.

Lesson 7: Second call with a sales person

The goal of the second call is to sell the product. This conversation is the actual sales pitch. You have to explain the product and explain why the client must invest now.

There are 3 very important things to consider in this conversation:

1. Make it scarce / special
2. Price increase
3. Make it urgent / set a time limit

<u>Make it scarce / special (not everybody can have it)</u>

Mr. Client, normally I offer these kinds of investments only to my clients who already have more than one million invested with me. It is only for accredited investors, which means that you have to have a net worth of at least one million dollars or a household income of $300,000 per year in order to qualify. There are only a small number of people that I am allowed to include in this offer. I would like to include you in this group but the minimum investment from your end has to be at least $50,000.

<u>Price increase</u>

We are currently in a private placement round of $0.50 per share and this financing round is going to end by the end of this week. Next week we will be in a new round and the price will be $0.80 per share.

Make it scarce (take it away)

The demand for this investment is huge and we are 10 brokers selling this deal to our clients. It sells like hot cakes. If you don't act soon, I cannot guarantee that you will be able to get any shares at all.

Make it urgent / set a time limit

If you don't want to lose this opportunity then you must act in the next 48 hours or else the opportunity will be gone. At least sign the contract now so that I can reserve the shares for you.

Lesson 8: Closing the deal

> It's not about "**deserve**" – it's what you **believe**.
> (From movie "Wonder Woman")

Closing is not something that everybody is capable of doing. The main goal is to get the client to invest at all even if it is just a small amount at first.

You could say something like: *I understand that you cannot trust me 100% at this point in time. That's why I only want 5% of your trust or $5000. The other 95% of your trust I still have to earn.*

Once the client has invested in the deal, he has given you some trust and he believes in the deal or the story. That is great news because it is much easier afterwards to convince him to reinvest some more (loading the client).

You can also say something like this: *Mr. Client, I am interested in a long-term relationship with you. I just want to win you as a client so that I can offer you a lot more interesting deals in the future and make lots of money just like my other happy clients. Please just invest a small amount like $10,000 so that you are one of my clients and then I can show you what else the world of IPOs has to offer.*

Picking the number

If you start out with the number $250,000 that you ask him to invest, chances are that he will not yet be ready to invest that amount. But he might agree to invest $100,000 instead. If you start with $100,000, he might end up doing only $50,000.

> The average amount was $55,000 per investor.

I have had investors who invested $5000 and I have had investors that invested $500,000.

When the investor asks what the minimum investment sum is, that's when you have a buying signal.

Lesson 9: Getting better at communicating – learning and improving

> If you just communicate, you can get by. But if you communicate skillfully, you can work miracles. (Jim Rohn)

My former sales manager Yves was a great sales person. He could turn anyone who said "no" into a "yes" after just 10 minutes of talking to him.

Yves was 28 years old at the time, skinny, had yellow teeth and was constantly drunk or on cocaine. You could not have put him in front of a client back then. His appearance was simply not professional looking enough. But nothing or no one could match his communicational skills on the phone. He talked to CEOs and millionaires and made them feel grateful for even talking to him. He was simply the best. In his first year working for me he earned over $500,000.

Amar (or "Hammer" like we used to call him) was a 23-year-old Serbian who was also a great sales person. He lied about his age and pretended to be in his mid 40s. His clients were all rich entrepreneurs and CEOs in their 50s and 60s.

But you don't have to pretend to be someone you are not. If you are professional and learn how to talk to investors, you will be successful.

> A bird sitting on a tree is never afraid of the branch breaking because its trust is not in the branch but in its own wings.

In order to raise more money and therefore make more money, you must constantly get better at communication and sales. The more you learn, the more you earn.

The best way to learn is to sit next to other successful sales people in the office and listen to their sales pitches. A sales team can also provide a healthy sense of competition, which will drive you to do better. It is hard to get better by yourself alone in your own office with no one around.

Lesson 10: Having a bad day

> No matter what yesterday was like, birds always start the new day with a song.

One bad day is not the end of the story. It happens to everyone. The best thing you can do when everything goes wrong and everybody says "no" on the phone is to call it a day. Sometimes you need to take a break and do something for yourself instead. You could go for a nice dinner or watch a movie.

It usually destroys more potentially good contacts if you try to call them when you are in a bad mood. Your negative energy will come across in your voice and you will lose some good contacts like that. It is better to call them when you are in a better mental state.

My business partner Christian makes very few calls. But when he is in the right mood, he closes 100% of his deals. He always makes sure that he is in a good mental state and has the right energy before he calls his clients. He knows that it is pointless to call a client if his energy is not right. He is always well prepared before a call and knows exactly what to say. He is never impulsive or acts in the moment.

Other people are the complete opposite. Adrian who also raised millions in the past, hears something motivational and then he immediately calls a client with his excitement.

> Pick up the phone and start dialing. Do this every day for several hours and you will eventually be successful again. (Bernhard Fanger)

I was once down and out and lost all hope. Then I went for lunch with my old friend Bernhard. Bernhard had just raised $8 million in 6 months for a new water project. I told him that I was not doing well and he said that the only way to get back on your feet is to go back to basics. You need to pick up the phone and talk to people. You need to do this every day and eventually you will close some deals again.

Even though I was looking for a different answer, it turned out that he was right. In the end the only thing that counts are results. You don't need a new strategy or a new product. You just need to continue making phone calls and talking to potential investors. Eventually, you will find an investor again and feel good about yourself. In the end it is all a mental game. If you believe in yourself and have high levels of self-confidence, then you will do well provided you are a good communicator.

Lesson 11: Self-discipline

> Success will come when you develop absolute certainty in yourself, your dream and your ability to make it real.

Intentions or knowledge is nothing if you have no self-control. Intentions are good but without action your intentions are worthless.

Doubt is only removed by action. If you are not working, then that's when doubt comes in.

The problem starts when you stop doing things like talking to customers, etc. When you are no longer selling is when doubt creeps in. If you stop talking to clients, making phone calls or initiating marketing activities, you start to doubt your whole strategy and business.

> Doubt kills more dreams than anything else. The only way to remove doubt is to take action, which means calling up clients.

If you talk to clients every day, you feel like you are in control of your destiny. If you "delegate" the money raising to someone else and they don't perform, then you will get disappointed and feel like your fate is in someone else's hands.

> Work until your bank account looks like a phone number.

Lesson 12: Money raising strategies and ideas

> One good idea can save you 10 years of hard work.

Let's assume that you want to raise $1.2 million in one year. In that case you will have to raise $100,000 per month. What kinds of strategies could work?

<u>Strategy 1:</u>

- 1 marketing person makes 100 calls per day and generates 5 leads each day
- 5 leads x 5 days x 4 weeks = 100 leads per month

- 1 sales person follows up and closes 4 clients
- 4 clients = $100,000

Strategy 2:

- Cheap office in Eastern Europe (or other Third World Country)
- $300 to $400 base salary per person
- 5 marketing people
- 500 leads per month
- 2 sales people close 8 clients and raise $200,000 per month

Strategy 3:

- Office in Switzerland, Germany (or other country with wealthier people)
- $2500 base salary plus commission per person for 3 months
- 5 people get hired
- All 5 people do marketing and sales at the same time
- $200,000 per month

Strategy 4:

- Contact all old investors from previous deals
- 2 sales people contact them all
- The power of the second voice (2nd sales person) will help to close the deal
- $100,000 starting capital for new team and office will be raised

Strategy 5:

- Ad on Facebook for $50 per day
- Clients can download a free PDF for free
- Example: "8 mistakes that investors make…"
- Client has to give name and phone number in return
- Sales person follows up with a call

Strategy 6:

- Get a list of people who bought a health insurance lately
- Talk to clients for about the health insurance and then switch the conversation to investments

Strategy 7:

- Meet with financial advisors in person
- Present the project
- Pay a 10% commission to financial advisors for raising money
- Clients start with a small investment of $10,000 and then a sales person can load them later on

Strategy 8:

- Buy names and lists of potential investors
- Only contact people who are already interested to invest money

Strategy 9:

- Generate brand new leads by researching names on the Internet
- Try to contact people who have never been contacted or burnt before

Strategy 10:

- Rent a big office with space for 20 people
- Start with 5 to 10 people
- Start aggressively with contacting hundreds of people each day
- Hire aggressively to build a sales team of 20 people
- Have a great sales manager who is like a drill sergeant

Lesson 13: Likeability and trust versus product

One of the biggest mistakes that new sales people make is to talk too much about the product. If you don't have a good relationship with the client established first, then talking about the product will only bring objections.

The first step is to create a relationship where the client likes you and starts to trust you. You can't establish that unless you talk about other things than the product. In fact, I know lots of sales people who talk an hour about life and everything else and then in the end spend 5 minutes explaining the product.

If the client trusts you, he will accept whatever you tell him. But if there is no trust, then he will question every single detail and give you lots of objections.

You need to win the person first before you can sell him a product.

Lesson 14: Marketing materials

In general, I have lots of great marketing material to describe the product. This is what I usually have:

- 2 pager – summary
- 10 page brochure (Corporate Summary)
- PPT – Power Point Presentation
- Geological report
- PPM – Private Placement Memorandum (= legal prospectus)
- SSA – Share Subscription Agreement (= contract to buy shares)
- Business Plan (50 to 60 pages long)

If I send the whole package, I know that 95% of all clients never read it because it is too overwhelming.

Therefore, it is usually best to only send the 2-pager or the corporate summary initially. When I follow up with a second phone call, I can always send more information afterwards. This also gives me a reason to call him again.

The idea is to make him curious without giving away too much information. The main goal is to establish a good relationship with the client and then I can argue about the product later. If I have to discuss the pros and cons of the product without having a basic relationship, I usually lose.

Lesson 15: Objections

If you have a good relationship with the client first, then there shouldn't be any objections. It is like the relationship between a doctor and patient. If the doctor prescribes a medication, the patient accepts it without questioning the doctor. The same should be true for you as a financial advisor. If you recommend a stock, then the client should not question your choice. You can tell the client that you did your research and that you believe that this is a great stock. Since you are the specialist and he is your client, he has to follow your advice.

Of course, there are some general objections that some clients have. Usually, they have to do with **a lack of trust or fear**.

Your goal has to be to get the client to invest into deal even if it is a small amount at first. Once he is in the deal, he has given you his initial trust and then loading the client (= getting him to invest more later) is easier.

When a client is invested, he typically doesn't want to lose his investment and will continue to invest.

Lesson 16: Business is a numbers game

> I don't believe in the term "bad economy". That's an excuse. There is always someone out there who has money and who is willing to invest. (Thomas Horvat)

Business or sales is just like math. You success is measurable. Everything is a numbers game. The more people you can contact the more sales you will make.

There is really only one rule: The more people you talk to, the more prospects you will get and this will improve the **probability** to make a sale.

Everything is based on the law of cause and effect. The more causes that you set by calling more people, making more appointments, the more deals can you close. The busy and active sales people will always outperform the lazy ones – no matter the difference in their skill set.

The only person standing in your way might be yourself. If you are not lazy or afraid of rejection, there is no limit to what you can achieve.

<u>The sales funnel</u>

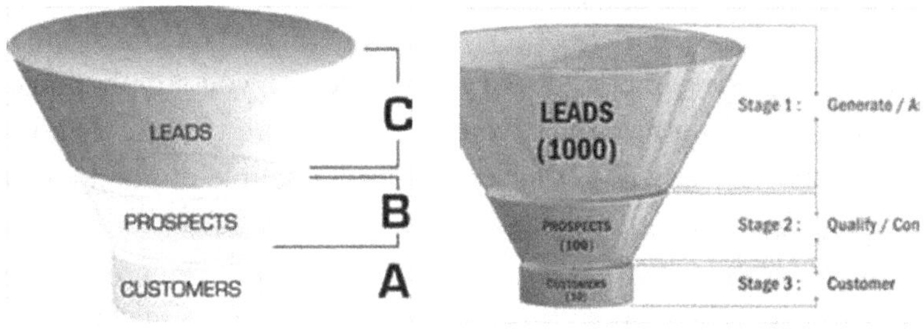

Sales are contingent upon the attitude of the salesman – not the attitude of the prospect. The economy can be bad and you can still find investors that will invest in your deal.

You have to get to a point in your life where your mood is no longer affected by the opinions of insignificant others. You are the master of your own destiny.

Lesson 17: Working hard

Nothing will work unless you do. If things don't seem to work, then you must examine whether or not you are really putting in the hours and necessary amount of calls to customers.

Sometimes the reason why you are failing is because you are simply not working enough hours trying to get customers. Maybe you are working 10 hours a day but 8 hours are spent in the office doing other things like administration, organization but NOT actively selling.

You need to be actively and constantly selling a product every single day.

Working = selling = making money = living your dream

This means making 100 phone calls every single day. It means spending 80% of your time on income generating activities like sales, marketing and dealing with clients.

It means that if you don't set enough meetings with clients in your calendar every single week (at least 10 to 15) face-to-face meetings every single week, then you are not doing enough.

Sometimes a business model doesn't work because you simply don't talk to enough clients in a month. If you talked to more clients, then by the law of probability you will get lucky and find a couple of good clients to generate enough sales.

Some people don't have enough LEADS to contact. And maybe then you need to focus your time and energy on creating and finding many new leads.

Lesson 18: Face your fears

Once you become fearless, life becomes limitless.

What you are afraid to do is a clear indicator of the next thing you need to do. Everything you want is on the other side of fear.

To achieve your wildest dreams: you have to walk through your greatest fears. But what does that mean for most people? Fear of rejection and fear of failure!

Basically, it means dealing with people and asking for a sale. Most people are afraid to go out there and make business happen. But in order to get ahead you mustn't be afraid. You must be active and fearless. You must be able to ask anyone anything. You must be able to call up 100 clients each day and ask for a sale. You must be courageous and ask anyone anything.

The fears you don't face become your regrets. So just be brave today. Act so that you won't have any regrets later on. If you give up today, you will never know if you could have made it.

Every day you have a new chance to make things happen. One day you win, one day you lose. But if you don't give up, you can't lose. Success is not final and failure is not fatal. It is the courage to continue that counts.

Fear comes from uncertainty. We can eliminate the fear when we act despite the fear. Fear is a liar. Don't allow it to steal your dreams.

For some people making phone calls is painful. They suffer and try to avoid talking to clients like the plague. No one likes pain or suffering. In fact, we all try to avoid it. But when it comes to success, it is not possible to achieve anything worthwhile without pain.

Being self-disciplined is painful. Working long hours and dealing with problems is painful. Overcoming fear is painful emotionally.

But all these things are the price that you need to pay for success. It is not possible to achieve success without facing pain and dealing with fears.

On the other hand, failing to act or dealing with difficult situations not makes you feel paralyzed and means suffering. Lots of people "suffer" because they try to avoid certain situations. They rather avoid pain and conform to a life of suffering and mediocrity rather than dealing with the problems head on.

You see, constantly fighting for survival is hard. It is harder than dealing with a difficult problem or dealing with fear. In the long run it is much harder to live a life where you never achieve anything and constantly worry about money and stress over little things.

Pain is necessary but **suffering is a choice**.

You don't need to suffer. You need to face your fears. But you can't be free from pain or problems in life. Difficult situations are a part of life. You can't avoid it. But you can actively do something. You can call up clients and make your life better.

Sometimes you don't realize the weight of something you have been carrying until you feel the weight of its release. Sometimes you realize that you suffering was not really necessary and that you could have simply done the things that you needed to do in order to have the life that you deserve!

From now on decide not to be afraid of anyone or anything anymore. Decide to face all your problems and difficult people head on. Once you do that, life will never be the same.

Lesson 19: Proximity is power – working in a team

Proximity is power – surround yourself with more successful sales people and have their successful energy rub off on you.

Create the right circumstances for yourself. My friend Adrian is a person who needs to be in a team to be successful. Nothing is worse for him that to be making phone calls all by himself. If he is surrounded by others who are also calling clients, then he develops a healthy sense for competition.

Sometimes the only reason why you are not getting ahead is because you are in the wrong environment and have the wrong circumstances. In that case you must change your environment. Create an ideal work place for you. Make sure that you are surrounded by other successful people who motivate you.

Maybe you are surrounded by toxic people, have the wrong contacts, use an old system or you simply are in the wrong profession using your weaknesses and that is why you are not getting further in life.

You can only do well if you use your best talents and strengths and if the circumstances are good. This means that you might have to change something in your life. You might have to get rid of some people, change jobs, move to a new city or use different leads.

Change is painful. But nothing is as painful as staying somewhere you don't belong.

The only person who can make those changes is you. You are responsible for everything in your life. If the circumstances are not good, then you must change them. No one else can do this for you.

Lesson 20: Thinking bigger

> Big results require big ambitions.

You can earn a million dollars if you raise enough money or you can build a multi-million dollar company. You can achieve huge success if you just raise enough money and are the founder level of a new company.

> So many of us choose our paths out of fear
> disguised as practicality. (Jim Carrey)

So many people have achieved success before you. There are thousands of companies out there with people who started with nothing in the beginning.

Once you understand the power of Private Equity and money raising, you can turn any idea into reality because you have the funds available to do it.

This also means that you must open yourself up and change your thinking. You must start to think in bigger dimensions and get away from the average way of thinking. You must think how to create a company that is worth several hundred million dollars in the stock market. You must see yourself as the CEO with a large share position and being a multi-millionaire.

You need to show the Universe that you are not afraid of big numbers.

Once you change your thinking, you will change the way you talk to clients. You will start to pick different clients and you will open yourself up for getting more funds.

Believe in yourself, your idea and your ability to make it happen. Don't let small minds convince you that your dreams are too big.

The Universe cannot play a bigger game until you do. Don't be surprised how quickly the Universe will move with you once you have decided.

The difference between where you are now and where you want to be is your mindset.

You attract what you believe you deserve.

Raising millions of dollars is possible. It is always possible and in any economy. A business partner of mine said it well. He said: We will raise the $6 million that we need for our current project. Either we will raise it in 6 months or in 5 years. But we will not stop until we have the funds together.

Optimism is a happiness magnet. If you stay positive, good things and good people will be drawn to you.

Your biggest enemy is fear and self-doubt. It is that little voice inside of you that creeps up and gives you doubt. And doubt paralyzes you.

You need to decide to become absolutely the best in your chosen field. And once you have made the decision to get to the top, you can't ever doubt yourself. You need to fully go for it and believe in yourself.

> There are no unreasonable goals – only unreasonable deadlines.

Focus on financing the project and making the company successful. Don't put yourself under pressure because of an unreasonable timeline. It is better to wait another 6, 12 or 18 months and make the deal successful than to feel pressured because of time.

One of my big mistakes was to do the IPO too early. The company wasn't ready and there were not yet real assets in the company. Don't make the same mistake. Take your time. Manage expectations with your investors. It will make your life so much easier.

Lesson 21: Dress for success and get into shape

No matter what level of business you're in, it's important to dress for the client you want, rather than the client you have. There's this idea of working from home in PJs. Usually, this is not a good idea.

The most successful people get up early and dress like they're off for a day at the office, and it's reflected in their attitude.

> When you look good, you feel good and you're more confident, too.

If you are overweight, then your starting point should be to get into shape first. Go on a diet and exercise plan for 3 months and get fit.

Most people underestimate what the positive effect of "feeling good about yourself" has on your success, level of self-confidence and overall positive energy level. Make sure you eat lots of healthy foods and exercise.

In order to be successful in business, you need to be feeling good about yourself and be in good physical condition. But also your clothes matter. If you wear an expensive suit and feel like a million dollars or the CEO of a corporation, then you will have a different energy, too. This energy can be heard through the phone and when people meet you they will feel it.

Feeling strong and self-confident is so important. People follow winners.

Lesson 22: Make your investors happy

> A satisfied customer is the best business strategy of all. (Michael Leboeuf)

When we did our first deal and all of our investors made money, we were surprised to see that 80% of all investors reinvested immediately into our second deal. Some of them called up, sent us and email and one even told us with a fax that he wanted to participate in the second deal. It was so much easier than the first time around.

If you make your investors happy, you will have their trust and you can use them over and over again. That's when Private Equity becomes really fun.

Your goal should be to build a database of investors and use them to invest into several deals.

You don't always have to double and triple their investment. Sometimes they are happy if you make them 10% or 20% as long as you don't lose their money.

On the other hand, if you screw up your deal and investors lose money, they will punish you legally and damage your reputation to such a point that it will be almost impossible to do business again in the future.

> You are only as good as your last deal.

You can have 10 great deals and then 1 bad deal and people will only remember the last deal where you lost their money. That's why you must always plan in such a way that you make sure that your investors make money even if it means that you won't.

Getting started

Start now.
Start where you are and with what you have.
Start with fear.
Start with pain.
Start with doubt.
Start with hands shaking.
Start with voice trembling.
Start and don't stop.
Just...start!

CHAPTER 5

HOW TO RAISE $1 MILLION IN 12 MONTHS

The $100 Million Dollar Secret

> You must learn to trust that there is a future waiting for you that is beyond what you might be able to grasp at this present moment.

There are a total of 46.8 million **millionaires** worldwide at the beginning of the year 2020, and they collectively own approximately $158.3 trillion.

In the 33rd annual Forbes list of the world's billionaires, the list included **2,153 billionaires** with a total net wealth of $8.7 trillion.

There are millions of millionaires in the world and the number is increasing with each year. The only question that you should ask yourself, is why you are not one of them yet?

How did those people become millionaires or even billionaires? Did they have a great 9 to 5 job that paid them really well? Most definitely not!

They are all business owners and **own shares of their own public company**. No one becomes a billionaire by simply earning a salary from a job each year. People become wealthy by owning a significant share position in a company that is listed in the stock market.

But how did they start out? How do you become a multi millionaire?

They all started with a business idea. Then they incorporated a corporation, issued shares for themselves and raised money from investors. Eventually, they took the company public in the stock market and it was valued a several hundred millions of dollar.

Why you should raise money from investors

You are about to go from just functioning in life to flourishing.

If you don't want to have a 9 to 5 job and work for someone else, then you need to start your own business.

If you want to take control over your life and financial situation, then there is really no alternative.

74% of all self-made millionaires started their own business. Only about 10% climbed the corporate ladder, 10% are doctors, lawyers or other specialists, 5% are salespeople and only 1% are lottery winners, musicians, actors or other famous people.

If you can't sing, dance or act exceptionally well, then your best bet is to **start your own business** if you want to become financially independent.

Ideally, you want to build a business that you enjoy and that will make you lots of money.

But starting your own business can be difficult in the beginning – especially if you lack money to get started.

Instead of trying to "just make it or to get barely by", you can focus your time and energy on **raising money first**, so that you will have enough money to operate your business later.

This will ensure that you make enough money and can live comfortably. It will also ensure that your idea or project gets the funding that it requires in order to become a success.

Use the right vehicle for success

> A corporation is the greatest invention of our time.

Someone has an idea and through a corporation this idea will take on a life on its own.

The cool thing about founding a company is that you give life to something that was simply a piece of paper and you put value into it.

Nobody has become rich by having a job or an income. The way that people became multi-millionaires is by **owning a big share position** in a company.

No one is really smarter or better than you. Successful people simply are using the Private Equity strategy to make more money than you.

Most people use **common thinking** and that's why they have a **common life**.

The specific knowledge that you can obtain by understanding corporations, Private Equity and the going public process can generate millions of dollars for you. You can make money beyond a normal scope if you know how to do it. The cool thing is that those are all skills that can be learned.

So the plan is to build a company, sell shares to investors and raise money for the company, go public and then sell some of your shares in the stock market and become rich in the process.

Why should you listen to me?

> I raised $40 million in 2.5 years from 500 investors and my company was valued at over $300 million in the stock market.

If I have done it, so can you.

If you want to learn the real secret of business success in the stock market, then you should learn it from someone who has actually done it. Not from someone who writes books about success but has never actually tasted success like I have.

When my first company was trading, the initial private placement price for investors was $0.27, the first listed price was $0.80 and the highest price was $3.50 per share. If you had invested your money at $0.27, then you would have made 12 times your investment.

Over 50 million shares exchanged hands in the first year and the average trading price was around $1.50.

My personal net worth was over $123 million in stocks, $1.3 million in cash, I owned a house for $1.5 million, rented a luxury apartment for $10,000 per month, owned two Porsche Cayenne and my monthly income was over $100,000 per month.

I had 65 people working for me in total in my organization. I managed about 10 different companies; I had a total of 25 gold exploration projects, 10 geologists and several other projects in the natural resource sector.

I took several companies public and over the course of 3 years I spent over $1.4 million in legal fees to my securities lawyer.

Life was great. I took vacations to Dubai, where I stayed at the only 7 star hotel in the world and I had everything a man could dream of.

How did I do it exactly?

> No dream is too big with the right attitude and work ethic.

It's not easy. If it were easy, everyone would be able to do it. But even though it is not easy, it is very possible. Lots of other people have done it, too. And if they did it, so can you.

All you need is the right knowledge, strategy and desire to do it. The main key in my opinion is the word "clarity". The more clear you are in regards to what you would like to achieve, the faster you will get there.

Make no mistake – there is a lot of rejection and possibly ridicule involved. But once you have reached a certain milestone, people will take you seriously.

I remember when we first did our presentations in Zurich and 9 out of 10 people laughed at us. But eventually we started raising more and more money and in the end even the press started to write about us in a favorable way.

You will need the following pieces for your plan:

- Share structure with private placements
- IPO Plan
- Business Development Plan for your operations
- Money raising strategy
- A good team of people you can trust (Don't ever trust anyone with the accounts, that will always stay in your control. Whoever controls the money, controls the company.)
- A system to generate leads for potential investors

The timeframe can be anywhere between 12 and 24 months to take your company public and raise the necessary funds.

What's the secret?

> With clarity and focus you can achieve anything that you put your mind into.

The most important thing is: CLARITY. You need to have a clear goal and a clear plan. You need to **start with the ideal end result first** and then work your way backwards from there.

It all starts with the share structure and the private placement financing rounds.

Example:

Let's say you have a corporation where you have **100 million shares authorized**.

You can technically issue up to 100 million shares. Out of those shares, you want to issue **20 million for yourself** and your key management members.

The remaining **80 million shares will be for investors.**

Share structure

Total shares authorized	100 million
Key people / management	20 million
Investors	80 million

Private placement rounds

1st round:	\$0.25 - \$250'000 – 1 million shares issued
2nd round:	\$0.50 - \$500'000 – 1 million shares issued
3rd round:	\$0.75 - \$750'000 – 1 million shares issued

First price / IPO $1.00

Total shares issued and outstanding after financing rounds from investors: 3 million
Total shares including management and key people: 20 million
Total shares issued and outstanding: 23 million

Future valuation

23 million shares x \$1.00 per share = \$23 million market capitalization

How did I raise millions of dollars?

> Focus all your time and energy into one thing and you will be successful.
> (Dorian Yates, 6 time Mr. Olympia)

When I started I had asked my friend Bruno if he wanted to join my company. Since Bruno was a "fallen angel" at the time, meaning that at one point in his life he used to be a successful banker but now he was over $300,000 in debt and completely lost.

But Bruno knew a lot of people in the financial industry in Zurich. He was a happy and positive person and simply started to contact his network of contacts.

In the first month we got only two clients: One with $5500 and one with $11,000. The following month we raised zero. At that point I started to question the whole thing and almost gave up. But because I wasn't alone and Bruno was optimistic, we decided to continue. In the third month we got lucky. We raised $165,000 from a small gold fund in Liechtenstein.

This money helped us to fly to Mexico and buy 3 projects. Also, we were able to improve our marketing materials due to the new funds.

Things started to improve from there. Before we knew it, we had 3 new sales people, which turned into 25 people just three months later.

One initial geologist turned into 10 geologists and 1 project turned into a total of 25 projects.

Eventually, and because of the large sales force and our positive business development, we raised between $1 and $2 million per month.

Once a month I also organized a presentation in a hotel where about 10 to 20 prospects attended. Each time we raised between $200,000 and $300,000 from a presentation alone.

Start small – finish big

> Starbucks Founder Howard Schultz spoke to
> 252 people and only 12 invested.
> 240 people rejected him.

You need to start somewhere. You need to start small and probably just by yourself.

But you need to learn and grow each day. You need to improve your company and raise more and more money.

It is not easy by any means but it is possible if you stay positive, learn and constantly improve things.

<u>Here is quick overview on how you could start:</u>

Step 1: You do 100 marketing calls per day by yourself
Step 2: You hire 2 marketing people and they do 100 marketing calls each. Your job is to follow up and do sales.
Step 3: You hire 5 marketing people and you do sales
Step 4: You add sales people to your team
Step 5: You have independent sales people and your own sales organization

<u>If you start with zero contacts and no money, this is how you could do it:</u>

Phase 1: Start with your family and friends (if you have no other contacts or lists)
Phase 2: Build a small marketing team (3 to 5 people) and raise money yourself
Phase 3: Build a sales team of 5 to 10 people
Phase 4: Online marketing to generate leads
Phase 5: Institutional investors once your company is public

<u>Business development (Project or product)</u>

- Acquire a project with an option

- Pay for the project
- Do the work on the project
- Proof of concept / prototype
- Acquire more projects or expand
- Improve management team and add specialists

IPO preparations while raising money

- At least 35 shareholders
- S-1 Registration Statement SEC
- Audited financial statements
- Securities lawyer
- Market Maker – FINRA File 15c2-11 Form

Things must be done parallel at the same time. You must develop your company and do the necessary steps to go public at the same time. The going public process takes between 9 and 12 months. The development of your company might take longer. But there is no rush to go public. Just raise money every month and wait as long as necessary until you are ready.

Strategy

Hope is not a strategy.

Wishing and hoping is not a strategy. Thinking of all the reasons why you can't succeed is not a strategy. Waiting for that perfect moment is not a strategy. Those are all excuses. You have to make moves.

Strategy

1. Define the share structure
2. Get a project
3. Define Private Placements
4. Set a goal to raise $1 million in 12 months
5. Take company public
6. Raise money from institutional clients

Remember that the main goal initially is to raise the money. The money comes only from one source: people (investors). Investors only come from leads that you have generated and therefore you must focus on generating new potential leads and you must focus 80% of your time on sales (making presentations, calling people, etc.)

Your daily goals in the beginning when you are starting out by yourself:

1. Define your **ideal customer**
2. **Make a list** (research from the phonebook, Internet, yellow pages, clubs, etc.)
3. **Buy a list** ($1 per lead from a list broker)
4. **Hire 2 cold callers** (pay them $10 per hour plus commission) – they should each make 100 phone calls and generate 10 new leads each day
5. **Make 100 phones calls yourself each day** – generate 5 to 10 new leads each day
6. **Follow up with a second phone call** and try to sell your deal – in the mornings generate 10 new leads and in the afternoons start selling and closing deals
7. **Raise $50,000 to $100,000 per month all by yourself** in the first 3 months and use that money to hire 2 marketing people (cold caller)
8. Continue to raise money in the first 12 months by using **80% of your time and energy on sales (**direct contact with investors, personal meetings, phone calls, presentations, etc.)
9. **Establish relationships with financial advisors and intermediaries** who will help you to raise the money from their client base.
10. **Build a sales team / office for the sole purpose of raising money** (selling shares of your company) besides the actual operations of the business

How to raise $1 million in 12 months

> There are people less qualified than you doing the things you want to do, simply because they decide to believe in themselves. Period. (Denzel Washington)

Imagine being able to raise $1 million in 12 months. What could you accomplish with $1 million in the bank?

If you are starting out with an idea and you are all by yourself, then you can make it happen, too. All it takes is a plan and a lot of daily self-discipline.

Once you have raised the first $1 million by yourself, you can use the money to attract more money, more salespeople, improve the company and even buy a publicly listed shell to go public.

Here is a possible breakdown of this goal:

- 10 months (July and December excluded due to holidays, etc.)
- $1 million / 10 months = $100,000 per month

$100'000 per month

- $10'000 from 10 clients
- $25,000 from 4 clients
- $50,000 from 2 clients
- $100,000 from 1 client
- A combination of different amounts

Weekly goal: 1 to 2 new clients / investors
Lead generation: 100 new leads per week

> If the plan doesn't work, change the plan, not the goal. (Brian Tracy)

I used to raise $100,000 per month by myself, while I was running the company and leading over 60 people at the same time.

I did lots of presentations in front of investors, met wealthy individuals and motivated my sales teams to raise money.

I was on a roll back then and because I was so clear and focused, I closed every single person I came in contact with. I was really convincing because I knew exactly what each step involved.

Generating Leads

Who is your ideal investor? Where do you find him or her?

> It doesn't matter how good your ad is. If you are targeting the wrong people, it won't work. Just try selling dog toys to someone who doesn't own a dog…it's hard.

The main thing is **targeting**. You need to have the right contacts to people who match your ideal target market profile. You life will be easier if you approach the right people. And if you approach the wrong people, life will be very frustrating.

You need to call 100 people each day and at least 5 to 10 potential investors need to be open to receive your company information.

Those people need to be open, willing to listen and have the ability to invest at least $10,000.

The first call is a marketing call. The goal is to send out the information and make the client curious. You also want to find out some basic information about the client to see if he is a potential investor or not.

<u>Ideal client</u>

- Male
- Age: 40 to 70 years old
- Business owner
- Management of company

- Independent specialist like doctor, lawyer, etc.
- Income higher than $100,000 per year
- Home owner

The perfect list is a list of past investors from a different deal. People who are willing to send money over the phone are the best candidates.

If you don't have a list like that, then you want to make phone calls to people who are close to your target group. For example: you could call 100 doctors. A doctor has the money to invest. It might be hard to get them on the phone at times, but they are great clients.

In general, it doesn't really matter which profession you choose to call. Sometimes a group like famers for example, might have the surprising ability to invest a lot of money.

Your goal is always to start with an amount like $10,000 to $20,000 first. Later on you could ask them again and "load the client" to a total of $100,000.

This business is a numbers game and the more people you can contact, the more money you will raise.

In this business you the following **3 things** in order to be successful in raising money:

1. The right contacts, names or lists
2. A talent for sales
3. Working hard and consistently every single day (Numbers game)

$100 Million business secret

> The secret of happiness is freedom. The secret of freedom is courage. (Thucydides)

How do you create a $100 million company in the stock market?

Let's look at the formula:

(Shares issued and outstanding)	x	(share price)	= market capitalization

50 million shares	x $2.00	= $100 million market capitalization
25 million shares	x $4.00	= $100 million market capitalization
10 million shares	x $10.00	= $100 million market capitalization
100 million shares	x $1.00	= $100 million market capitalization

Now let's look at the share price:

(Annual Earnings)	x	(P/E ratio)	= market capitalization

$5 million	x	20	= $100 million market capitalization
$10 million	x	10	= $100 million market capitalization
$4 million	x	25	= $100 million market capitalization

The P/E ratio (price per earnings ratio) is dependent on the industry. Old economy has typically a factor of 10. The average P/E ratio is 15. Modern technology has a ratio of 25. Some hyped up industries that are new and upcoming can have a ratio of 1000. It all depends on the current market.

The only question is now how you can generate for example $5 million per year in earnings with your projects to justify a market capitalization of $100 million.

What do you need to do in regards to business development? How can you use the money that you have received from investors and create an annual profit with it?

Institutional investors

You cannot expect that an institutional investor like a bank, a mutual fund or an investment company is going to invest into a brand new company.

Most institutional investors need to have a listed trading symbol of a company so that they can buy shares so that at a later stage, they are able to sell their position with a profit. They can only buy a listed company because it has a real value in their books.

It is a waste of time to try to solicit money from institutional investors if you are still a private company. They will all tell you to come back at a later stage when you are further ahead.

That's why you need to make it your goal to **raise the first one or two million dollars yourself from private investors**. Once you have the first million or two, you can either take your company public or buy a company shell that is already listed and use the money to start your operations.

Once you have done the groundwork, which means that you have purchased your first project and made it a success, then you can ask an institutional investor for money.

An institutional investor will give you money to expand your existing company. But you need to prove and show that you were able to do the first project without their help.

There are two main factors:

1. **Proof of concept:** You were able to put a project into production
2. **Proof of management**: You were able to raise money, use it wisely and create a successful prototype.

> Raise the first couple million dollars yourself and then get an additional $10 million from an institutional investor.

Leadership skills and building a team

> You can't do it alone. You will need other people.

You need to become a charismatic leader. Here is why:

- You need to be able to win people for your cause / mission
- You need to be able to sell yourself
- You need to be able to sell your ideas
- You need to be able to sell your company and its projects
- You need to attract good people who will work for you
- You need to able to influence other people
- You need to develop communication and sales skills
- You need to know all the techniques and tricks in order to raise money from investors

A leader has a clear vision and can motivate other people to follow him. You can't be the only one who will profit in the end. You need to make sure that your people will also make money and own shares of the company. You need to have them on board because they believe in you and your ability to make it happen.

That's why **you must lead by example**. You must be convinced of your vision for the company and **you must become the best salesperson**. You must be really qualified to talk about your projects and how you are going to turn them into a success. Your knowledge about the industry and how you will move forward must be exemplary.

As the CEO you must have all the pieces of the puzzle together and understand how they work together. But you will also need specialists (e.g. geologist, scientist, etc.) who are professionals in their field.

Having a partner who is good at sales, finance or operations is a good idea, too. Your team must consist of a group of people who are all really good in their individual field.

You must know exactly what the plan is and execute it precisely. You must know what the **IPO plan**, the **plan for the projects** and the **plan for the money raising**.

Making money while you raise money

> Success is 20% skills and 80% strategy. (Jim Rohn)

Let's say that you want to raise $1 million in 12 months. You could pay yourself a 10% commission and earn $100,000 in the first year while the rest, 90% or $900,000 will go into the company.

Summary

- Raise $1 million in 12 months
- 100k personal income
- 900k goes into project, admin, etc.

If you are not doing well and you are suffering, then there is no company. You also need to get paid.

Some people decide not to take out a salary until the company makes a profit. But I think that it the wrong approach. You can't function if you go broke hoping for a future that might take longer than expected.

I used to pay myself $10,000 per month, regardless of the amount that I raised. Sometimes I raised $1 million a month, sometimes less. It is "noble" not to rob the company of its funds but if it means that you are broke and unhappy during the process, then it's not worth it in my opinion.

Some people take a small salary and hope that their stocks will be worth a lot in the future. That's also a possible strategy. You have to make that decision for yourself.

You can make money before the company goes public, at the IPO and after, too.

Make an offer that they can't refuse

> Deliver what you would buy if the circumstances were reversed. (Charlie Munger)

When you create your financing offer and potential exit strategy for your investors, always ask yourself if you would invest into your company if the circumstances were reversed. Is your offer attractive? How could you make it even more attractive? What kind of information would you want to see if you were on the other side?

When I typically create a new company, I offer shares at around $0.50 per share. The exit should be at least $1.00 but $1.50 is even better. If an investor invests into the company and the company goes public, he will have about three times of what he had invested.

The mid-term outlook should be at $2 or $3 per share and the long-term potential of the company should be at least $5 to $10.

If someone invested $10,000 at $0.50 per share, then there should be that potential or future possibility that the shares could be $10 or even $20 worth if the company did well.

A person doesn't invest into those kinds of deals for safety or moderate returns. Either it will be a hit or a flop. That's why this is risk capital. If he wants safety, then he should invest into government bonds.

> 20% return per year is not trustworthy for most people. But once you mention 1000%, they will turn off their brains and invest.

Your deal must be exciting. People will either lose their investment or make 10 times of what they invested. You must sell them the vision and the future potential. The potential rewards must far outweigh the risks.

When you start out, the company is still somewhat empty and with little valuation. You must have the excitement and the ability to communicate how the future valuation could look like if you executed the business plan perfectly.

You need to sell the deal, you need to sell yourself and exaggerate a future that does not yet exist. Your goal is to turn your vision into reality. Your fire and excitement will motivate investors to trust you.

Be brave enough to suck at something new

No one ever got a private jet living in a comfort zone.

You need to do the things that are uncomfortable: contacting clients, making phone calls, asking for an investment, etc.

In fact, you should become really comfortable doing those things that are uncomfortable for other people.

You need to be able to deal with rude people, deal with rejection and people who ridicule you at times. But that is the price that you need to pay. You need to focus 80% of your time on talking to investors: either on the phone or in person.

You need to become a great sales person. It is not talent that determines who will become a great sales person but skill. And sales skills are all learnable. Sometimes it's not about who has more talent. It's about who is hungrier.

In the end everyone is a salesperson. No matter what you do in life.

In this case you **sell yourself, your dream and your company**. You sell shares of a company that is still somewhat empty and only has a vision. You sell the intangible future.

Closing deals and becoming successful

Mindset is what separates the best from the rest.

Change your schedule and your environment if you have to. Don't let your surroundings and circumstances be the reason why you didn't achieve your goal.

The most important thing in reaching the goal of raising money is the mental side. Your mental attitude must be strong and clear. It is all in your head. The difference between winning and losing is your mindset.

You will need:

1. Clarity
2. Courage
3. Self-confidence
4. Momentum (= little successes each day)

Each day you need to have a little success, a closed deal, a positive conversation, a new potential project, etc. Each day something needs to happen that is positive.

Every morning you should define your goals again. You need to be crystal clear about your daily goals. Make a list of 5 things that you need to do each day and then work concentrated on those 5 things.

Typical goals could be:

- Send out the information package to 10 new potential investors
- Follow up with 10 clients who have received the information package a few days ago
- Close one deal for $10,000
- Close one deal for $5,000

The next investor is only one phone call away. (Julian Poehlmann)

Do you suffer from FEAR OF REJECTION BY INVESTORS?

What we FEAR doing most is usually what we most NEED to do.

Sit down ask yourself what you truly want from life and map it out. You can't advance in the right direction if you don't know where you are headed.

Success

1. Decide what you want
2. Write it down
3. Set a deadline
4. Make a list of what you have to do
5. Prioritize your list and create a plan of action
6. Take action

Remember: Slow progress is still progress. Just keep moving forward. Do something each day that brings you closer to your goals.

Don't wait for someone to help. Help yourself. In the end hard work always wins.

The biggest challenge will be conquering your fears of rejection and failure. You must keep contacting 100 new people each day and stay positive. You must continue to improve yourself and your company. If you don't give up, you will succeed eventually.

Make it happen. Shock everyone.

Beyond normal

If you limit your choice only to what seems possible or reasonable, you disconnect yourself from what you truly want, and all that is left is a compromise.

You just need to get started and set yourself up the right way so that you can legally attract investors. You start with small amounts and you keep growing the company.

Once you have made the decision to think big, the Universe will conspire on your behalf. You cannot imagine at this point what lies ahead for you.

I have had phone calls with financial groups that fund companies that are in the oil business and they start their financing at $100 million and go up to $500 million if they like the deal.

You could be meeting a rich oil billionaire from Dubai who likes you and wants to invest into your deal.

When I went to London for a meeting I was offered $1.5 million from a small mutual fund if they had a personal guarantee. They only did that because the company was listed at that point.

I made a deal with a gold fund in Liechtenstein to give them $2 million for the conservative fund from regular investors if they then used that money to invest into my company who was still private at that time.

There are so many thing possible if you put yourself in the right position first. Only once you are in that position you will find out what those opportunities are.

> Doing the best at this moment puts you in
> the best place for the next moment.
> (Oprah Winfrey)

When I was invited a go to my friends villa in Mallorca, Spain I met one of my old financial advisor friends. His name was Michael Forster. While we are all sitting at the pool and enjoying the sun, I pitched the deal to my friend David who ended up investing $100,000 for himself and $100,000 from his brother Javier.

But Michael was also listening and asking questions. I didn't pay too much attention to it at the time but one week later he met me back in my office in Switzerland and handed me over signed contracts from his clients in excess of $500,000.

Within a week, I received so much money for my company and once you have this money at your disposal, many options become all of a sudden available.

Starting out...

Your 9 to 5 pays the bills. You 6 – 12 builds the empire.

LACK of money (not money itself) is the root of all evil. If you don't make it your number one priority, you will never have it.

Here is what I recommend:

- **Sales and communication skills:** Learn absolutely everything about this topic and become very good at it.
- **Project:** Find and acquire a project that has a huge upside potential, even though it might be not much initially.
- **Sales team / Office:** Get an office that has a potential for 5 to 10 people (desks). Once you have the office, people will come.
- **Operations:** Keep your operations separate from the sales team.
- **IPO and legal:** Get a securities lawyer. This is your most important person initially.

Reverse gap comparison

When you play the comparison game, you will always lose.

If you compare yourself to where you want to be in the future, you feel like you are always behind. But if you compare yourself where you are today with where you were 3 years ago, you feel gratefulness. If you constantly feel like you are behind and trying to catch up, you will feel demotivated.

Don't compare yourself with other people or companies unless it fuels to your motivation. Make a plan and follow it regardless of where you are today.

The problem with a lot of people is that once they get rejected, their self-confidence gets shattered in an instant because they don't have an abundance mindset. If you know that no matter how many times you will get rejected, you tell yourself that tomorrow you will find 10 other people who will invest, you realize that you always have an abundance of possibilities. One bad day or moment shouldn't matter. The world is full of people who have no idea on how to invest their money. You will always find someone who is willing to risk his money by investing in your company.

> Life is too short to be living somebody else's dream. (Hugh Hefner)

CHAPTER 6

SALES TECHNIQUES, PSYCHOLOGY AND STRATEGIES

How to do you sell stocks over the phone?

It is similar to selling in person but you have to focus on developing TRUST. You have to **focus on the relationship first** before you present the product.

Selling is a learnable skill. Raising money on the phone is also learnable. This program will teach you what you can say and how to say it.

Like everything in life, practice makes perfect. You should read everything several times and repeat it often so that it flows and becomes second nature.

The best way to practice is to make calls with real people. The more people you talk to, the easier it will get.

What do you say in the first call?

- *Hello, my name is .... I would like to talk to Mr. John Smith.*
- *I am not sure if you remember me but we have spoken about 6 months ago.*
- *Back then I wanted to recommend an investment to you. The investment has tripled in the meantime but you weren't interested at the time.*
- *Today, I am calling you with an even better opportunity.*

- *It's about a new gold company that will go public in the stock market in the next few months.*
- *The company just finished its first round of financing for $5 million and now is offering its second round of financing.*
- *The company has three different private placement rounds before its IPO for $0.50, $0.75 and $1.00 and it will get listed at around $1.50 per share.*
- *I would like to send you some information about this deal by email so you can have a look at it and decide whether this is something that you might be interested in. Does that sound fair?*
- *What is your email address?*
- *Do you have any experience with pre-IPO stocks?*
- *Are you currently invested in the stock market?*
- *If you like what I have to offer, would you be able to invest between $50,000 and $100,000?*
- *No? How much could you invest?*
- *Great, then I will send you the information and I will give you a call back in a couple of days to see if you have any questions.*

What is the goal of the first call?

1. You don't have to convince him to invest. Your main goal is to send out the information package.
2. You need to qualify your investor. Does he have the ability to invest and how much?
3. Focus on likeability and trust. Focus on developing a positive relationship.

Second phone call: Positioning yourself and your company as an expert

- *Hello, Mr. Smith. Did you receive the information that I have emailed you? Did you have a chance to read it?*
- *Before we get into that, I would like to introduce myself properly. I work for the company IFS. Our company has been in the market since 1995 and we have raised over $1 billion from investors and for projects. We*

have over 22'000 satisfied customers and we took about 150 companies public in the stock market.

- *Personally, I have been a financial advisor for more than 25 years and I have personally consulted over 3000 clients. I have 12 finance diplomas and I am registered with FINRA as an official stockbroker here in the US.*
- *Most of my clients have been working with me for many years and they are in the 7-digit range when it comes to their net worth. So typically, the average investor has more than $1 million invested with me.*
- *My goal is to develop a long-term relationship with you as well and hopefully also grow your net worth past the million-dollar range.*
- *How does that sound, Mr. Smith?*

The reason for positioning

- You need to position yourself as THE expert in the field of IPOs.
- People like to deal with the best.
- You also need to differentiate yourself from being a regular "sales person" and position yourself as the financial expert. (Just like a doctor)
- He must be glad to be on the phone with you and not the other way around.
- Mention lots of numbers and size. This creates TRUST.
- The main goal is to develop TRUST and confidence.

Let's talk about the client

- Ask lots of questions about the client.
- Show a lot of interest in what he does professionally and privately.
- The goal is to talk about HIS INTERESTS so that he will LIKE YOU.
- Some advisors talk one hour about some random topic and then spend 5 minutes on the actual deal.
- Remember: LIKEABILITY AND TRUST always comes first before you can talk about the product.

Talk about the deal

- If you have done your job well building trust, then there should not be any objections.
- You are the expert and your expert advice should not be questioned. You wouldn't question your doctor either if he prescribes you some medication.
- The main thing at this point is that you focus on three things:

1. Make it rare
2. Price increase
3. Time limit

Make it rare

- Hot deal – tell him how "hot" this deal currently is
- Not everybody can get in – you need to be an accredited investor
- We have only a limited amount of shares available
- Lots of other brokers wanted this deal but only we got it.
- His bank will never offer him an IPO like this.
- It is super special. It's a rare opportunity.
- A deal like this comes along only every 10 years.

Price increase

- The first round of financing at $0.50 is already over. Now we are in the second round of financing, which is at $0.75.
- But if you let me know right now, I still might be able to get you a certain amount of shares for $0.50.
- Next week, the price will definitely increase and then you will have to pay more.

Time limit

- We have to act fast – otherwise this opportunity is gone.
- Sense of urgency – if you send me the contract today (or at the latest by tomorrow), then I can still reserve the amount of shares.
- Next Monday, the shares will be gone because they are oversubscribed. A big German investment fund wants to buy all the shares for $15 million.
- That's why we need to act now. Please send me the contract today so that I can reserve the shares.
- I also need the payment immediately. By when can I expect a confirmation of the transfer?

Sales is a numbers game

> Inaction breeds doubt and fear – Action breads confidence and courage.

If you make 10 phone calls and get 10 rejections, it is easy to give up and believe that the whole process doesn't work.

But in order to succeed, you need to make 100 phone calls per day and out of those calls, 90 people will say no and 10 people will be open to receive your marketing package.

The only way to conquer doubt and fear is to be active. Never be lazy. Work the numbers. Do the 100 calls and don't stop until you have done them all.

You could also focus on getting 10 people who say yes and maybe then you only need to make 50 calls in order to achieve this goal.

You just have to create enough leads of potential investors each day so that you can constantly sell. You should close a deal every single day.

Creating a deficit (making him aware of a problem)

An investor will not invest with you if he thinks that his personal financial situation is great the way it is. You need to show him that he could do better and that he is actually missing out and losing money if he doesn't change certain things.

You need to create a deficit by making him aware of a problem.

You could say that your investors are all millionaires (in the 7-digit range) and that you can help him to get there, too.

You could say that your investors have doubled their money each year (made at least 100% on average) and that on some deals, you were able to generate 500% or even 1000%.

He needs to feel like you could offer him things that his regular banker cannot offer.

You could also say:

- *How much was your performance with your local bank? 7%*
- *That's nice if you want to grow your wealth slowly. But if you want to double or triple your money each year, then you should really check out our IPOs.*

People will think that 30% or 40% is not realistic. But they will turn off their brains if you mention 1000%.

Everyone wants to get rich quickly. Everyone wants to find this one deal that turns him or her into a millionaire without working for it. This idea that a deal like that exists, is in everyone's head.

The most curious animal in the world is not the cat. It's the human.

Many others have done it, too

You need to give him a good feeling that he is not alone. You need to let him know that many others have also done the same investment.

People are scared of being ridiculed by their friends. If you can show him that he is not the only one, then he is more likely to do it, too.

Professionalism

- Confuse him with financial terms, share structures for 1 minute. This will "show" the investor that you are competent even if he doesn't understand what you were just saying. The main goal is to build trust and credibility.
- Position yourself better than you actually are. You can mention facts and numbers that he can't actually double check.
- Not everybody can do it (only 35 non-accredited investors in 6 months). Tell him that only people with a net worth of $1 million or an annual income of $200,000 or $300,000 per family can legally invest into such a deal. But you will make an exception in his case.

Don't say which product it is in the first call

- Introduce yourself as the specialist who deals with multi million dollar clients and institutional investors
- Tell him that you get special packages
- Usually you are starting with an investment from $500,000 or more.
- You are holding back from giving away the actual product in the first call to make him curious. You just say that you have something special but you need to check a couple of things first before you can reveal to him what the product is.
- You are waiting for another client to release the information first before you can offer him this deal.

- The goal of the first call is to make him curious and to find out whether or not he is open to invest.
- The goal is to make him excited and to find out how much money he actually could invest.
- Based on the information that you gather in the first couple of calls, you can put together a proposal that he can't refuse because he already told you all the things that he is expecting.

Start with higher numbers

> If you want a kitten, start out by asking for a horse. (Naomi, 15 years old)

If the client asks what the minimum investment is and you tell him that it is $10,000, then you have lost.

You need to first know what kind of client you are dealing with. You need to know how much money he has and how much he could invest. If you only ask for $10,000 but he could have easily invested $100,000, then you leave all this potential on the table.

This is what you could say:

- *I have three types of clients. The first group, the bigger investor, invests about $250,000 or more. The second group, invests anywhere from $100,000 to $200,000 and the smaller investors invest less than $50,000 per investment. In which group are you Mr. Client?*

Since he doesn't want to look bad or cheap, he will always say a higher number, even though it wasn't his original intention.

You could also say something like this:

- *I typically start with a smaller investment of $250,000 with a new client and build it up from there.*

- *Since all of my clients are in the 7-digit range, it is my goal to bring you there as well.*
- *What amount could you invest today? Is this the maximum amount? I have an option to double your investment in the next 3 months but we need to act now before this opportunity is gone.*

Only sell one product at a time – not two...

> If you confuse people, you lose people. Marie Forleo

It is better to focus on one product than to offer two or more products at the same time. People will easily get confused and then they have too many open questions and won't be able to make a decision.

Be very clear and specific about each step in the sales process. Make sure that you have no open questions left unanswered.

If he is unsure about the amount and says that he wants to think about the number, then don't leave him alone with it. Help him and make the decision together.

Here is an example:

- Client says: *I am not sure how much I should invest. Anywhere between $20,000 and $40,000. But please let me think about it.*
- You say: *Mr. Client, let's talk about this now. If you invested, $40,000, what would be the problem? Is the amount too much? Do you have other plans with the money?*
- *If you invested $20,000, would you feel comfortable? Or could you invest even more?*
- *Why don't me choose a number in the middle? Why don't we choose $30,000? Would that number work? Yes.*

It's important that he can choose a number that he feels comfortable with. The main thing is that he will invest in the first place. You can always call him back a few weeks later and "load" the client (= increase the investment amount).

Once he is in the deal, he trusts you and the company. Once he is in the deal, he doesn't want to lose any money and he will do whatever you will recommend.

The main goal is to eliminate any questions or uncertainties that he might have. Go through each step and make sure that each step is very clear for the client. Get a "yes" for each step so that he doesn't have any objections or says "I need think about it" anymore.

Close one deal per day

$10,000 per day x 20 days = $200,000 per month

If you work 10 hours per day and generate 10 good leads per day (1 new lead per hour), then you will have one potential client per day.

If a client invests a minimum of $10,000, then you should have about $200,000 per month (20 working days per month) in raised capital.

This sounds great in theory but in reality, you will probably about 25 to 30 leads to close one client.

So the more leads you create per day, the better are you chances of closing one deal per day. This should really be your goal. You should focus on finding at least one client each day that will invest $10,000. There is always one person out there who can invest $10,000. Out of 100 people one person will always say yes.

You should focus on lead generation and marketing, too. You need to create a system of several people who will help you to generate leads each day.

Your job is to follow up with all these leads and close a deal per day.

How to succeed in this business

Making phone calls by yourself is possible but it is a lot more difficult if you are by yourself, alone, home and in your pajamas.

Most people will only do well if they are in a group of people at an office making those kinds of calls.

> Shared pain is half the pain – shared pleasure is double the pleasure. (German saying)

It is easier to rent an office and hire 5 marketing people who will do the first call.

Objections

If you have a good relationship with the client first, then there shouldn't be any objections. It is like the relationship between a doctor and patient. If the doctor prescribes a medication, the patient accepts it without questioning the doctor.

The same should be true for you as a financial advisor. If you recommend a stock, then the client should not question your choice. You can tell the client that you did your research and that you believe that this is a great stock. Since you are the specialist and he is your client, he has to follow your advice.

Of course, there are some general objections that some clients have. Usually, they have to do with a lack of trust or fear.

Your goal has to be to get the client to invest into deal even if it is a small amount at first.

Once he is in the deal, he has given you his initial trust and then loading the client (= getting him to invest more later) is easier. When a client is invested, he typically doesn't want to lose his investment and will continue to invest.

Building trust over the phone

- Call several times (the more often you talk to him, the higher the level of trust)
- Be available when the client calls
- Respond quickly and call back immediately
- Position yourself as an expert
- Talk about lots of facts and numbers
- Be self-confident and convinced of your product

The first step is to create a relationship where **the client likes you** and starts to trust you. You can't establish that unless you talk about other things than the product.

In fact, I know lots of sales people who **talk an hour about life and everything else** and then in the end spend 5 minutes explaining the product.

If the client trusts you, he will accept whatever you tell him. But if there is no trust, then he will question every single detail and give you lots of objections.

Second call with a sales person

The goal of the second call is to sell the product.

This conversation is the actual sales pitch. You have to explain the product and explain why the client must invest now.

There are 3 very important things to consider in this conversation:

1. <u>Make it scarce / special (not everybody can have it, take it away from the client)</u>

"Mr. Client, normally I offer these kinds of investments only to my clients who already have more than one million invested with me. It is only for accredited investors, which means that you have to have a net worth of at least one million dollars or a household income of $300,000 per year in order to qualify. There are only a small number of people that I am allowed to include in this offer. I would like to include you in this group but the minimum investment from your end has to be at least $50,000."

"The demand for this investment is huge and we are 10 brokers selling this deal to our clients. It sells like hot cakes. If you don't act soon, I cannot guarantee that you will be able to get any shares at all."

2. Price increase

"We are currently in a private placement round of $0.50 per share and this financing round is going to end by the end of this week. Next week we will be in a new round and the price will be $0.80 per share."

3. Make it urgent / set a time limit

"If you don't want to lose this opportunity then you must act in the next 48 hours or else the opportunity will be gone. At least sign the contract now so that I can reserve the shares for you."

Make yourself more important than you actually are

People like to deal with a specialist or with the best. You need to give him the feeling that you are exactly that.

Often, the broker mentions how he travels the world and meets important clients who invest millions.

It is all a big show but the client thinks that he is in good hands.

Some loaders have the assistant call the client first and announce him the following way:

- *Mr. Client, I have some good news for you. I was able to have Mr. Meier look at your file.*
- *Mr. Meier is an absolute specialist who only deals with clients who invest $10 million or more at a time. He is a very important person and normally doesn't deal with regular clients.*
- *He doesn't have a lot of time and he told me that he would give you a call in the next 30 minutes.*
- *If he decides to call you, then you can consider yourself lucky. He is really the best and most important person in our company.*

The assistant is building up the loader / broker. She is preparing the client so that he will have immediate respect from the loader.

It is all a game of course but the client will feel like he got a special treatment and he will not question anything that the broker says.

Just go for it

Yesterday you said tomorrow…just do it!

Objections

Client: ***I need to think about it.***

Broker: *What exactly do you need to think about?*
The exact amount? The deal itself?
Is there anything else that you didn't mention before?
Just tell me openly and maybe I can help you.
What is the exact problem? Let's figure it out together.

Client: ***I am not sure if I should invest $10,000 or $20,000.***
Let me think about it.

Broker: *Let's figure it out together. Tell me your thoughts. Is 20k too much?*
What is holding you back from investing 20k?

Would you feel more comfortable to invest 10k at first?
What about 15k?

Client: ***I need to ask my wife first.***
Broker: *Of course, I can understand that.*
Who makes most investment related decisions in your family?
Do you have to ask your wife each time you make a trade?
Why do you think you need to involve her?
Why don't you surprise her with a new car or a new house when you have doubled your money with this deal?

Client: ***I am buying a house at the moment. I can't invest any money now.***
Broker: *Do you invest absolutely everything to the last penny into the house? No.*
Don't you think you should also have some regular investments anyway?
Don't you think that doubling your money in a short period of time would give you some extra cash for your house in case you needed it?

Client: ***I think it is too risky for me.***
Broker: *If you invest now at the lowest possible price, pre-IPO, and with the company having already done the SEC filing and proven reserves, there is virtually no risk. The main reason why you should do this deal is because you already have all kinds of other conservative investments but they don't give you the performance that you need.*

Client: ***I don't know you or your firm well enough.***
Broker: *That's why we are only starting with a small amount to begin with. I want you to make money on this first deal so that you will see what I am capable of doing for you in the future. Just give me 5% of your trust and I will have to earn the other 95%.*

Client: ***I don't like sending money to a different country.***

Broker: *The biggest IPOs in the world happen in America (Europe, etc.). That's why the company will be listed there. The company will also a do a co-listing in Frankfurt, Germany as well as in New York.*

Client: ***I already have a stockbroker.***

Broker: *That's great. I don't want to replace him. I just have additional products that he currently can't offer.*

Client: ***My banker / my accountant / tax expert says no to this deal.***

Broker: *Your tax expert has to say no. That is his job. He doesn't want to be responsible if you lose money. He might be an expert in his field but he is no expert in IPOs.*

Client: ***I have lost money before.***

Broker: *I am sorry to hear that. But in our case this is a whole different situation.*

Client: ***I need to wait 3 months.***

Broker: *I can't guarantee the price of $0.50 in 3 months. It will be too late. If you want to double your money, you need to act now.*

Client: ***I am happy with my performance from my banker.***

Broker: *That's great. How much annual performance do you have each year? 7%*

I don't want you to get rid of your banker. But with us you can double or triple your investments. Why don't you try it out and see what I can do for you?

Client: ***I don't want to be stuck with the investment for too long.***

Broker: *An average investment into stocks should ideally be between 5 to 10 years. But in our case it will only be 1 to 2 years.*

Client: ***I have never heard of your company. It is too small.***

Broker: *We don't advertise. Our company only deals with high finance and high net worth individuals. Typically, people with $10 million or more invest into our deals. Those people belong to a special group of individuals and companies that don't look for ads in the paper.*

Client: ***I have read something negative about your company on the Internet.***

Broker: *That comment is not about us. Whoever wrote this is probably a competitor. We have over 22'000 satisfied customers and manage over $1 billion in assets and we have been around since 1995. In today's age of the Internet, you will always find haters on the Internet. But that doesn't mean that it is the truth.*

Client: ***I don't have time to talk right now.***

Broker: *I need to talk to you for about 5 or 10 minutes. It is very urgent. When can you talk today? I promise you that you won't regret it.*

CHAPTER 7

HOW TO BUILD A SALES ORGANIZATION

Still broke?

So you didn't win the lottery...now what???

I guess the second best way to get money is to **start your own business**. Running a business means selling a product or service to customers. You can sell products online, in person, in a store or over the phone. But you must focus your time and energy on **sales and marketing activities** if you want to make money.

As a new business owner you will have a lot of responsibilities but the main key to success is to focus on generating new customers. It can be quite overwhelming if you try to do everything by yourself. That's why one of the best ways to generate sales is with a sales and marketing call center.

A sales team gives you the necessary **leverage and sales power** to get ahead faster than just doing it by yourself.

The sales team can either sell your company's products or **sell shares of your company** (and raise capital for your company). Either way, you need to start a sales organization if you want to make money and make your business successful.

> A hungry stomach, an empty pocket and a broken heart can teach the best lessons of life and give you real motivation to improve yourself.

My former sales organizations

Over the course of my career I have built several sales teams and organizations. Some were extremely successful and we raised between $1 and $2 million each month from private investors.

Other sales teams were not doing so well but they provided me with valuable lessons about how to build and lead a sales team.

Here is a quick list of some of the sales teams that I started or was involved in:

- Team in Zurich - 25 people - $25 million in 2 years
- AWD Europe - 75 sales people - $400 million in 6 years (all insurance and investment products)
- MAN Investments UK – 8 sales people - $600 million in 1.5 years (institutional clients like banks, etc.)
- Team in Switzerland– 2 people - $500,000 in 1 year
- Team in Switzerland – 20 people - $5 million in 5 years
- Hemis (Independent intermediaries) - $5 million in 2.5 years
- Hemis Group - $5 million directly from clients
- Team in Macedonia- $50,000 in 6 months
- Team in Serbia - $2 million in 3 years
- Team in California – 5 marketing women - $200,000 in 1 year
- US Broker dealer – 15 brokers - $200,000 in 1 year (failure)
- Individual independent sales people and brokers - $1.5 million in 5 years

Being a Private Equity Entrepreneur

> All men are created equal. After that it is up to you.

Have you ever thought how people back in the day had much easier or better circumstances? I often thought that if I knew what I now know and were able to raise money in the 80s and 90s I would have made millions more.

Do you know when the best time was to plant a tree? It was 20 years ago. Do you know the second best time? It is today!

Even if times are tougher today than they were 20 years ago, there is still so much opportunity to raise money for your projects and ideas. You can always find people to invest into your company and make your dreams come true – no matter what the economy does.

You can achieve anything in this business if you are self-disciplined and not lazy.

Once you have realized what kind of potential this knowledge has, the world is going to be yours! Let nothing stop you. Live your dream. Start a sales team and start raising money for your dream.

> There will always be clients who will invest into an idea and there is money out there like there is sand on the beach.

Raising money from private investors with a call center

> Ambition without action is fantasy.

Even though you can create a call center for almost any product, I am going to focus this program on **how to raise money from private investors and sell stocks over the phone**.

Some people also call this a "Boiler Room", which can have a negative association or might even be illegal in some countries.

But with anything in life you need to do business with integrity and ethics if you want to be successful. Otherwise success is short-lived. You can legally sell shares of your company to private investors in the US if you are a director of the company.

If your call center consists of marketing people who "prepare" the clients and then a representative or director of the company actually then sells the shares, then you can do it legally.

In any case, I would consult with a lawyer to make sure that you are doing it the right way in your country.

Why should you have a sales team?

10 average sales people sell more than 1 great sales person.

There are two main ways to raise money from private investors:

1. You are operating by yourself and you have a lot of high net worth individuals.
2. You have a sales team and get lots of smaller investors but a larger total amount.

My friend Oskar, who learned the business from me, is successfully selling shares of a pharmaceutical company in Switzerland. He has raised millions of dollars for this one company alone over the last few years.

When he does cold calls, he told me that out of 10 calls, 7 people tell him to "f@#k off" and 3 people are open to receive his information package / email.

Out of about 30 information packages that he sends out by email, he usually generates 1 big client per month who invests between $100,000 and $250,000. His commission is 20%.

Often, he tells me, he hates his job, but because he makes so much money, he won't stop because he doesn't have an alternative that pays that well.

His strategy is very simple but effective. He only operates in Switzerland and in or around the city of Zurich. The pharmaceutical company has a laboratory in the city and he invites the clients to meet him there with the company's main scientist. Once the see the lab and the scientist, all objections are gone and the investors have immediate trust in the project.

By yourself or a team?

> Having a sales team means **leverage**. If you have leverage, you can accomplish a lot more than if you are just by yourself.

But not everyone is a team player or team leader. Some people have a difficult character and are better off selling on their own. Alex, a former business partner of mine, had a difficult time attracting and keeping sales people. He was an excellent sales person on his own. But when it came to building a team, he could not keep anyone long-term. His personality was very focused on details and he questioned everything, which made him very professional. But when it comes to leading a sales team, you must be more open and flexible because you are often dealing with a lot of "wild people". Not everyone will succeed as a team leader and you must ask yourself if you are suited for this kind of job or better off alone dealing with clients directly.

The cost of a small call center

If you don't want to call 100 clients each day, you could hire a few marketing people and build a small call center. I once opened a small call center where I hired 5 women who made about 100 calls each day during 5 hours from Monday to Friday. They would do the cold calling and generate each day about 5 good leads each. So basically, they got rejected 95 times a day and generated 5 new leads.

But afterwards you can follow up with the 5 leads yourself because you know that those people will already have received some basic information from your company and who are generally speaking interested in your products. The second call is going to be much easier and friendlier.

If you have a team of 5 marketing people who generate 25 new good leads each day and you follow up on those leads because you are the best sales person, then generating sales is really easy.

It's not what you pay a man, but what he costs you that counts. Will Rogers

If you hire one marketing assistant and that person makes 100 calls per day, then the math looks like this:

100 calls per day
95 people say no
5 new leads generated

5 hours telephone time x $10/hour = $50
5 days per week = $250 per week
4 weeks = **$1000 salary for your marketing assistant**
(plus % of your sales)

5 leads x 5 days x 4 weeks = 100 good leads generated in one month

100 leads = 5 clients (for example)

Let's say that you have 100 good quality leads each month and you are able to generate 5 clients. Depending on your product and your price structure you might make $1000 per client. Let's say you make $5000 in commissions. Now you simply deduct the $1000 salary that you have to pay your marketing assistant and you will end up with $4000 for yourself.

Maybe you want to give your marketing assistant an incentive by giving him or her a percentage of your closed deals but that is up to you.

If you study this example and then scale it to 5 or even 10 marketing people, you can generate a lot more sales.

This example is not just theory but I actually did it in real life and it worked. I was able to find 5 women who wanted to work part time because most of them had kids and needed flexibility. At the same time they were happy to have a job on the side and 5 hours per day was manageable.

Additional costs are rent, phones, Internet, general office expenses and maybe even a secretary or assistant.

In the end, most of the expenses are somewhat irrelevant if you have the ability to raise enough money each month. It is better to invest enough money into a team and an office so that you generate plenty of leads.

Cheap office or prestigious address?

> With today's technology, the Internet and smart phones you can operate this business from anywhere in the world.

Some of my sales teams were in Eastern Europe due to the low employee costs per month. A sales person in Switzerland would cost me at least $3000 to $5000 per month and a sales person in Serbia would only be about $350 to $400 per month.

In Serbia, the sales people were former immigrants who lived in Germany for 10 years or more and spoke perfect German. But their families decided to return to their home country. The living expenses in Serbia are much lower than in Western Europe and when they called clients in Germany with their perfect German accents, then they were able to work from Serbia and earn their money there.

When I started my sales organization in Zurich/Switzerland, our expenses were huge. We rented an office on Löwenstrasse in Zurich. This is the second best or prestigious street in downtown Zurich. The 4th floor of this office cost $14,000 per month and it looked great.

We started with about 10 sales people and immediately had huge success. Raising money was much easier because once we told the clients where our address was, there was an level immediate of trust from the clients. Also, the sales people were proud to work at such a prestigious address and you could hear it in their voices when talking to clients. Automatically, we easily raised the difference in cost that a much cheaper office would have cost us. If we invited a client to our office, then making a sale was easy because the client was immediately impressed with our office.

After a couple of months we decided to add the second floor in the same building. This was another expense of $12,000 per month. The team grew to 25 people and we started raising between one and two million dollars per month. All the expenses with 3 secretaries, physical mail, etc. ended up being over $100,000 per month but it was all worth it.

> If you have a crappy office space, the people's
> motivation is low to work there.
> And it will show in having lower sales.

One of my offices in California was really outdated and with old carpets. I would have never dared to bring any clients into that office. And at the same time, the team was not successful due to a poor motivational environment.

Step 1: Get an office first and the people will follow

If your goal is to start a sales team, then you need to **have an office first**. Most people make the mistake that they want to get the sales people first and then look for an office.

I have tried both approaches in the past and **when I only had an idea but no office, no one really committed to join my team.**

> If you build it, they will come.
> (From the movie "Field of Dreams" with Kevin Costner)

So your first step is the office. When you get started, I suggest you start with at least 5 desks or working spaces. The office in itself should have potential for at least 10 people so that you can grow.

It is important to have at least 5 people in the beginning so that there is a positive working mood. If everyone is on the phone, there is a feeling of success and it motivates everyone around.

If you only have one or two people and one is not very motivated, it will negatively influence the other person.

> A positive mood and good working environment
> is a key factor for success.

In the beginning **you absolutely must be involved in sales and being a role model**. If you don't do that, people won't follow you and won't take you and your orders seriously. You can't expect others to do what you are not willing to do yourself.

Step 2: Interviews and ads to hire people

In the past I ran a cheap online ad on Craigslist that said "Private Equity Broker Trainee Program". I emphasized that there is a **base salary plus commission**.

This is important because most people don't like to work solely on commission. You might miss out on some great people if they don't even apply.

Sometimes paying a base salary seems like a big expense. And if you pay it to the wrong person, you will get upset. But paying a base salary to the right person is totally worth it. Sometimes the only way to attract good sales people is by supporting them financially in the beginning. But if you don't pay any base salaries, then it will be much harder and slower to build a successful team.

I typically have one Power Point Presentation about the company and the job description for my interview. I also explain how much they can potentially earn if they do well.

Since this is a sales job where people have to make at least 100 phone calls per day and get 95 times rejected, I emphasize this point after I talked about how much they can earn. I basically sell them on the fact that the job is going to be hard and that they will get lots of "no's" so that they don't get frustrated later on.

Even though they only make little money if the performance is low, I try to motivate them with big numbers in case they do well. But sometimes they need some basic security to be able to function.

Typically, all new sales people start as a marketing person doing lots of phone calls and generating leads for more experienced sales people.

Normally, you only have to run one or two ads to get the initial 5 people. Afterwards most people are friends of your employees and the team grows from referrals.

Most sales people know other sales people who could join the team.

Step 3: Marketing, Opening, Loading

There are 3 types of roles:

1. Marketing
2. Opener
3. Loader

A marketing person makes 100 cold calls and the goal is to find 5 people who agree to receive the marketing materials.

An opener is a sales person who will take over in the second call and initially sell the investment to the client. The amount that first gets invested is typically low (for example $5000 or $10,000) because there is not so much trust yet.

A loader is a more experienced sales person who takes over the client from the opener. Normally, a loader will get the investor to invest $50,000 or $100,000. Since the client is already in the deal and doesn't want to lose what he has already invested, it is usually easier to convince him to invest more.

If you have a team of 10 people, then you should have about 6 marketing people, 3 openers and 1 closer. Some teams rotate their roles and do all three steps.

Step 4: $10 per hour base salary

Typically, I pay $10 per hour in the US plus a commission based on closed deals for a marketing person.

Since the job in a call center can be quite challenging at times and no one can really work 8 to 10 hours efficiently, I only expect someone to work for 5 hours per day.

5 hours proved to be a perfect amount of time because people still work efficiently and don't get drained too much. At the same time I expect that a marketing person generates at least 5 new leads per day. Some people can easily generate 10 or 15 per day if they are in a good mood or have a good list.

A part-time job like this is also ideal for single mothers or married women with children who want to earn some extra money on the side. Since most jobs are not flexible for mothers with children, you can offer different working times during the day available as long as they work for 5 hours. Another good options are students that go to University. Their schedule is often flexible and they can work part-time.

When I ran my office in California and targeted German clients, some of my German speaking marketing women even came very early due to the time difference with Europe. I had expected them to work from 6 am to 11 am every day. Some women preferred to work from midnight to 5 am and some from 4 am to 9 am depending on their life and commitments.

Most of the time a 5-hour work day is an ideal time frame since a lot of moms who want to make some money on the side without neglecting their children.

Cost of a marketing person

5 hours x $10 per hour = $50 per day
$50 per day x 5 days per week = $250 per week
$250 per week x 4 weeks = $1,000 per month

Expectations from marketing person per day:

100 calls per day
95 people say "no interest"
5 people receive info package = 5 leads per day

5 leads x 5 days = 25 leads per week
25 leads x 4 weeks = 100 leads per month

One person costs me $1,000 per month but generates 100 new leads.

Closing

100 leads per month
80 people have no interest after all or are not qualified
20 people – second and third phone call
4 closed deals

Money raised: **$50,000 to $100,000**

If only 2 leads get generated per day, then the entire calculation goes out the window. Also, if the 5 leads turn out to be weak leads, then it doesn't make sense, either. Therefore, it is crucial that the office manager makes sure that the numbers get achieved every single day.

Business is a numbers game.

If you don't put into the hours and manpower to generate enough leads, you can't generate new sales.

Step 5: Commission and salaries

Typically, a marketing person has a salary. In America I paid them $10 per hour and if they worked 5 hours per day, then their monthly base salary was $1000.

In Serbia the base salary was around $350 per month per person.

Since it is important to create **well-prepared leads** so that it is easier to close the deal for the sales person, I also paid an additional 2.5% commission for every sale made later on by a sales person.

Example: a marketing person creates a lead and the sales person closes the client with a $100,000 deal, then the marketing person gets an additional $2500 on top of the base salary of $1000. This is a total compensation of $3500. $3500 is a great salary for a part-time job and is ideal for women who want to have their own money on the side.

Sales people usually have a higher commission. Typically, it is between 10-15%. An opener typically gets 8% and a closer 12%. The sales manager gets between 3-5% of the overall sales result.

If the sales person is an independent sales person who has his own office and expenses, then the commission can be higher.

A total commission structure for a sales organization should never be more than 30%, though. The most important thing is to finance the project and make sure that company will be successful.

Just remember that the main goal is to raise money for the company. This initial capital is the most expensive capital for any new start-up company. You can pay a 5% commission and let 95% of the money go into the company but the problem is that most sales people won't be motivated by that. It is better to pay a sales organization 30% and only have 70% of the money go into the project but then raise millions of dollars instead.

5% of zero is still zero. But 70% of a million dollars is $700,000.

As long as you make sure that the company gets enough money and the project gets financed, I would advise you to pay higher commissions instead of lower ones. If you want your deal to succeed, then you should be smart about it and pay your sales people well.

Step 6: Sales manager

The sales manager is key. He needs to be like a military drill sergeant.

The most important person in the beginning is your sales manager.

A sales manager needs to be able to teach others how to close deals on the phone and he must also make sure that the minimum requirements are achieved.

It is better to find a sales manager in the beginning than to turn your best sales person into a sales manager after a while. If 5 people start out and then you turn your best person into the sales manager, he will automatically produce less and he will not necessarily have the respect from his peers.

A great sales manager is the most important factor when running a call center. He will be the deciding factor between failure and success.

Sales Manager to new employee: *"I am not your friend. If you want a friend, get a dog. You will hate me but I will help you to make lots of money if you do what I tell you."*

Typically, a sales manager gets a percentage of the overall sales result of the team.

Step 7: Telephone systems, computers and VOIP

In the old days we used to have a huge telephone bill every month. But since the age of the Internet, things are a lot cheaper.

It is crucial that you have the absolute best and most reliable Internet connection if you choose to use a VOIP (Voice-over IP) telephone system. You will also need special VOIP telephones.

Depending on your location you should get phone numbers from different countries to help with certain clients and to achieve a **perception of a global presence**.

Each person should have a computer but you need to make sure that you control things like Facebook and YouTube. Often people avoid talking to clients and spend hours on social media.

Some call centers only have a phone and **physical lead cards** on the table to make sure that people actually have enough calling time and don't waste it on surfing the Internet. I don't think that this is necessary because sometimes they need to research a client or find phone numbers online. Also, if your VOIP system is run through a computer, then you must have a computer on each desk.

In the US it has become increasingly difficult to make cold calls due to caller ID and due to the fact that too many sales calls are bothering people. Often, people don't even answer their phones anymore if they don't know who is calling.

This situation is much better in Europe. The market there is much better and people answer their phones. You can still engage in a conversation or at least talk to them. Also, people in Europe have a landline and a cell phone. All the landlines can be found online in the electronic phone book and you can target any group, profession or location.

You might want to consider choosing a certain country because some countries have not yet been "destroyed" by people selling bad investments over the phone.

In general, it is always best to have a reference when you call. If you have an existing contact, a list of past shareholders or a person who inquired about your company on the Internet, then you will have it easier to talk to them.

Step 8: Generating quality leads

If you can't generate **leads**, you can't generate **sales**.

How do you generate high quality leads for your business? Obviously, the more leads you have the better are your chances to generate customers.

In my opinion there are a few ways to generate leads:

1. Marketing sales team / call center
2. Online strategy – a client requests a free PDF report about your topic and you follow up with a phone call
3. Lists of existing shareholders from a different deal or old clients
4. Referrals from existing clients
5. A financial advisor or professional who already has a lot of clients who trust him
6. Buying leads from a list broker

Having the right kind of leads can make all the difference. You can have people who are interested in your product but **have no ability to make a large investment**. So therefore you should focus on people who actually have money like business owners, doctors or self-employed specialists.

When it comes to Private Equity investments you also want people who don't have too much of a financial background as clients. Because of the nature of these stocks and the inherent risk, a normal financial advisor would never recommend those types of investments to his clients. But because people are greedy and believe that they can multiply their money with a hot stock tip like yours, they will believe almost anything that you tell them.

Interestingly, sometimes people like butchers or farmers are the best clients. They have money from their business but no idea about stocks.

> The best leads are people who have already invested once into a similar Private Equity deal in the past.

If you are able to get **old shareholder lists**, then you hit the jackpot. Those are the best names. We have had clients that invest $100,000 in every deal that comes along, lose every time and still continue to invest into the same bad kind of deals.

> Once a gambler – always a gambler!

Interestingly, you can also promise a 50% return and people will say that you are making false claims but when you talk about 1000% returns or more, their brain will stop working and their greed will take over.

You can also **buy leads** but typically it is better to have lists of business owners and then use your own marketing team to generate new leads.

A good lead will not just accept the information package but will also answer some basic questions like:

- Are you currently invested in the stock market?
- Have you ever invested into a pre-IPO stock before?
- Are you interested in the topic of________(oil, gold, biotech, etc.)?
- Do you have the ability to invest money now (do you have liquid assets of more than $10,000?)
- Are you able and willing to invest anywhere between $50,000 and $100,000 if you like the deal?

The marketing person must inform the potential client and make him **curious**. He also must know that a sales person will give him a call in a few days.

A bad lead is someone who simply accepts the info package but then there is no real conversation afterwards. A really bad deal is when the person sends the material to the secretary and has never even spoken to the potential client.

The better a person is prepared for the second call (= sales call with sales person), the higher the chance of success.

In general, it takes several conversations with a sales person until the clients has enough trust to send money. Often, simply talking about life in general is often more effective than discussing the investment.

Step 9: Paying commissions to an intermediary

What is an intermediary? An intermediary is an independent financial advisor who sells third party products.

In Switzerland there are a lot of **independent financial advisors** who manage $100 million or more with a couple of hundred clients.

Typically, these financial advisors have a basic investment strategy where they invest some parts into more conservative investments, some balanced and some more dynamic securities. Such an advisor once approached me and he told me that 5% of the overall investment portfolio would go into risky investment like for example "private shares of a pre-IPO company". So basically he didn't care if the client lost money or not because it was only 5% of the portfolio. But if he won, it would be an extra bonus for the overall performance.

In the US financial advisors cannot be independent. They need to be employed by a broker dealer and be licensed. They cannot freely choose their deals. The compliance officer of the broker dealer (Series 24) has to first approve the deal otherwise the financial advisor (who has a Series 7) is legally not allowed to sell it.

In some countries like for example Switzerland, financial advisors only need to be part of a self-regulatory organization against money laundering and they can be independent.

Often, financial advisors also manage so called "**family offices**" where they deal with all the investment decisions, taxes and estates of a few rich families.

So if you can manage to convince an independent financial advisor of your company and agree to pay him a commission, then you can easily end up with several hundred thousand of dollars from one contact alone. If a financial advisor manages several hundred million dollars and decides to put a few "more risk-adverse" clients into your deal, then you could end up with $500,000 very quickly.

You need to understand that a financial advisor is also motivated by commission and making money for himself. Typically, he gets 1% or 2% for recommending a stock to a client. If they can sell a mutual fund, it can be up to 5%. But if you offer him a commission agreement that pays 10% cash and 5% in stocks for himself, then he will have a big motivation to convince his own clients to invest into your company.

I was once in Mallorca, Spain on holidays at a friend's villa. As I was sitting at the pool, Michael Forster, who happened to be an independent financial advisor, kept asking me questions about my company Hemis Corporation. I didn't think much of it as it was a casual conversation. The following week when I was back home, I was surprised to see that he had brought me deals in excess of $500,000 from his clients and all that in just one week!

The interesting part is also that Michael was part of a church where people already trusted him. So when he brought me all these clients, they were all not just his existing clients but also people who went to church with him every Sunday.

> Developing **trust** takes time. Find people who already have clients that trust them.

Another independent financial advisor was called Domeniconi. He was Italian and his clients could not speak German. But because they trusted him, he brought us about 20 clients in the course of a year.

Another sales person of our organization was originally from Hungary. He brought us about a million dollars worth of investments from clients from Hungary.

All you need is **the right contact** or one financial advisor. This contact already has clients and they trust him. This is one of the quickest ways to raise money from private investors. All you have to do is to convince one person.

> Find an independent financial advisor can immediately raise several hundred thousands of dollars from his existing clients.

Step 10: Sales scripts, training and internal education

> Nobody is a natural. You work hard to get good and work to get better. (Karate saying)

A new sales person must master three main topics:

1. Sales skills
2. Product knowledge (the actual deal that you are selling)
3. General financial knowledge (especially about Private Equity, stocks and IPOs)

In order to succeed in this business, you must become really good on the phone when talking to clients. It doesn't matter how much you actually know about finance. What matters most is your ability to talk to the client and develop trust. Your sales skills are much more important than your technical knowledge.

Since you are only selling shares, the amount of financial knowledge that you must have is somewhat limited and it is learnable for almost anyone.

It is very important that you train your people and teach them not just sales skills but also additional knowledge about the products, your industry as well as basic financial knowledge.

Hire character – Train skill.

I have seen average people with no prior financial education become great in this business. But I have had also people with amazing resumes who have done very poorly. The attitude and character of a person is much more important than his background.

And then there is also **"the fear of cold calling"** for a lot of people. In order to succeed, you must become so comfortable on the phone that it will actually turn into a **strength.**

Instead of trying to solve problems with logic, the first thing you should do is making peace with your biggest fears when calling up new clients.

Step 11: Minimum requirements

Lack of self-discipline is the main reason for failure. (Jürgen Höller)

You could also say that "laziness" is the main reason for failure. But in my opinion there are no lazy people – only people with no compelling goals. If you have exciting goals and you can face your fears, then the self-discipline will come automatically.

In this business you need to be able to deal with rejection every day and it takes a strong personality to stay self-disciplined. Therefore you must have a good REASON and know WHY you want the make so much money. Otherwise you will fail for sure and not do as many calls as you should.

Most people "suffer" in this business because they are simply not doing enough calls. And then it is like a downward spiral. Combine it with alcohol and drugs and you can set your watch until you hit rock bottom.

Most people do better if a strict sales manager is leading them. This will ensure that they put in the effort and do enough calls each day.

For your calculation as a sales organization you need to set some **minimum requirements** for your marketing and sales people. Otherwise you will pay your team and don't make any profit until you run out of money yourself.

> Clarity leads to power and power is the
> ability to do or act. (T. Harv Eker)

Examples:

Marketing person: **100 calls** per day and at least **5 info packages** sent out

Sales person 1: Follow up **25 leads** per day and have **5 good conversations**
Sales person 2: Raise at least $20,000 per month
Sales person 3: Raise at least $100,000 per month

You need to **make activities measurable** and you must **control** them – otherwise nothing will happen.

If someone doesn't fulfill the minimum requirements on a consistent basis, then they need to leave the organization. They will only cost you money and influence the other sales people negatively (with their lack of success and negative words due to lack of money).

Your people need to have some **sales super stars** in the office so that they get inspired and can see that it is possible to make lots of money. They need a role model. If you don't have those people yet, then **you must be that role model by brining in money from your own clients.** It is all about respect. You can't get respect from your sales people if they don't think that you have greatness in you.

This business is a numbers game and it is always possible to raise money from private investors. If you are unsuccessful, then the only reason was because you didn't do enough – period.

Step 12: Marketing people and sales people

> *"I buy distressed people. That's what I do."* (Alexander Sascha Baldi)

There are a lot of so-called "fallen angels" out there. Fallen angels are distressed people who struggle financially and have a low self-confidence but who used to be very successful and knowledgeable in one area. If you can get a fallen angel and help him in a moment of need, you will have found a valuable asset for your organization.

Where do you find sales people? Since this job is a very challenging job because you have to make 100 calls and get 95 rejections per day, no "normal" person would voluntarily do it. The main reason why people are in this business is the ability to make so much money.

> Often, the only way to start is with people who are either extremely money hungry or who have a lot of financial pressure.

In a regular job you can't make $20,000, $30,000 or even $50,000 per month but in this job you can. That's the bait.

Often, you have to pay them a fixed monthly salary of about $1000 to $2000 so that they will be able to come. You should only pay the salary for the first 3 months and if they don't succeed after that, then it is an unnecessary expense.

At first, you should run an ad and hire some marketing people. Every sales person has to start in marketing so that they know how to generate leads. Once someone gets better on the phone, you can move him or her into a sales position.

Step 13: Close deals and make money

> In the end all that counts is making money. Sometimes all it takes is ONE GOOD CLIENT per month.

Therefore it is important that you have great leads and contact that are not just willing but also with actual money to invest.

One of my partners only deals with people who invest between $100,000 and $500,000. He specifically looks for older business owners with lots of employees who can easily invest $250,000.

But depending on your cost and commission structure, you can do well with 3 or 4 clients who invest $10,000 each.

In the end you don't just want to survive but you want to fund your project so that it has a chance to become a success.

One sure way to find big clients is simply by being very active and contacting lots of potential investors. You never know who has money and you will get a few surprises if you don't try. Often, people regular people with regular jobs (like farmers or butchers for example) can invest $500,000 and you would have never guessed it.

You should look for people who are between 40 and 70 because they usually have enough savings.

Step 14: Regular motivation – 1 night out per month

> Once a month take the entire team out for an event like bowling or something similar. That's where you build team spirit.

I can't stress this enough. Your team will be like a family. The sales people will party together and spend their commissions to have fun.

If you are always in the office and you have a bad mood without any fun, then you will eventually lose all your people.

This job is so special and emotional that people will bond very well together. The interesting thing about this industry is that once people have been a part of it, they will not leave the industry but only change companies.

In Zurich, there are about five big Private Equity companies. The sales people always seem to rotate from one company to another. But because they make more money in this industry and they are with people who enjoy success, money and partying, it is hard to leave this life behind and go work in a regular job with a regular salary.

Most sales people have no University education or a prior well-paid job. If they made $5,000 in a regular job before they came into this industry and then all of a sudden earn $20,000 per month, then it is very difficult for them to ever consider going back to a regular job.

Step 15: Control

As a leader you must control your people – especially in this business. If people have to make 100 calls per day and get constant rejection, then they often try to avoid making calls altogether by surfing the Internet or not having enough telephone time.

> The more disciplined your sales room is, the more results are produced.

I have also created a **Rules Manual** for my sales organizations where I outline some basic expectations and minimum requirements. The very first day when someone new starts they must read this manual and also sign off on it in the employment contract.

It basically states the "**no-nos**" and what ideally is expected of a new person. It also sets the tone for how you want to run your team.

The experience that I made is that you must have absolute control over the numbers and activities or else you won't succeed in this business. You cannot be lazy about controlling your people and making sure that enough calls are being made.

Step 16: Wild and crazy horses (sales stars and losers)

> **Extreme success** results from am **extreme personality**. (Mark Zuckerberg)

Guys who are raising a million dollars per month are typically extreme people with big egos.

Maybe you have seen the movie "The Wolf of Wall Street". In this movie you can see how many of the young sales guys make a lot of money and spend it excessively on drugs, girls, expensive cars and clothes. The truth is that this movie is not exaggerated at all and that most Private Equity sales teams are acting in very similar manner. When young men make lots of money, things can get out of control.

As a sales manager or owner of such a team, you must be able to control those "wild horses". Obviously, you need to be a lot more open and flexible in your leadership style than if you had regular employees.

The problem with this industry is that it also attracts the "bad crowd". I know many sales organizations that operate completely illegally. They use fake names, only keep phone numbers for 3 months and delete them afterwards and their "deals" don't even exist.

Often, they sell shares of Facebook or Ferrari (international brand names) but in the end the money ends up in an account in a foreign country and the sales person has disappeared.

Some people even fake documents from companies to convince clients. There was once a company who claimed to be taken over by the oil giant Shell and they proved it with a fake written confirmation from Shell.

Others promise a huge payout for a small investment but the payout never actually happens.

A guy named Goran ran an organization with 150 people in Belgrade, Serbia. Over the years he raised over 80 million Euros. Obviously, Interpol is looking for him now.

It is easy to get tempted to bend the rules. My advice to you is this: **Have ironclad contracts, make sure you have a great accountant and do everything by the book.** Always assume that in the end the deal goes bad and that there is an investigation against you and your company. With that in mind, you should prepare your contracts and the money-flow so that nothing can happen to you.

Even though I had the best intentions when I ran Hemis, in the end $40 million from 500 investors were lost. I did everything by the book and there were **zero** lawsuits or legal investigations against me.

Step 18: Hire more people – up to 25 people

> Sales people bring other sales people and
> the team grows automatically.

When you start out, you should have at least 5 people. After a month you will lose 1 or 2 people and add two more. It is a natural process to go through many sales people and lose some. Unfortunately, not everyone is suited for this kind of job and often people give up because they can't deal with rejection.

The key for growth is to **keep hiring aggressively**. You need to **grow your team quickly**. Your goal should be to go from 5 people to 10 people within 2 months; and then after to 20 people one month later.

You will finance the cost of hiring new people with the first sales that the team generates. In the beginning you must invest into your team and grow it fast. If you fail to do this, you will have a mediocre producing group of people who will all quit after 3 months. The people must feel that the organization is rapidly expanding and that more and more sales are being produced.

You also need to have a career path planned for your best sales people. You should motivate them with a second office, become team leader or even part of the management team if they continue to do well. They all need a vision for the future. And it is your job to give it to them.

Interestingly, out of 25 sales people, you will always have 5 people who raise $200,000 or more, 15 people raise about $50,000 and 5 people don't raise anything. But the 5 who don't raise anything are always different 5 people than the previous month.

If we have to think anyway, why not think POSITIV?

When I started with my organization in Zurich, I was looking for a new apartment in the city. I found an amazing penthouse apartment on the top of the hill overlooking the entire city with all the luxury that you can imagine for $10,000 per month.

Even though I already made about $20,000 per month, I hesitated for a moment. But then I said to myself that if I didn't believe in myself and my ability to grow the team, that I might as well give up altogether. So I decided to rent the apartment and gave a clear sign to the Universe that I wasn't afraid of big numbers. Guess what happened? My income went to over $100,000 per month shortly after.

Sometimes you need to give a clear signal to the Universe that your intention is to move forward in a big way and you must do something that supports your attitude. Renting this apartment was my way of believing in myself.

Step 19: Being a leader of a sales organization

> Got to look successful to be successful.
> (Saul Goodman – Breaking Bad Character)

You can't motivate money-hungry ego driven sales people if you act like a poor person. You can't drive an old, crappy car and expect that people will follow you.

Your appearance must say "money". You should have an expensive suit, an expensive watch and your dress code should have a couple of details that stand out like special cufflinks or your initials on your shirt pocket.

Back in the day I only wore tailor-made suits and all my shirts and jackets had my initials on them. My ties matched my cufflinks and also my handkerchief. I looked like a million dollars and I also had it. People can feel that.

I drove a Porsche Cayenne and I only ate at the best restaurants in town. Even though it cost me a lot of money, it was well invested because my sales people wanted to have the lifestyle that I was living and they worked harder.

But at the same time I also felt better about myself. I felt super successful and invincible. And because of my attitude and energy **I was also the best sales person**. I ran the company and on the side I raised more money than my average sales people. I was only dealing with big important clients and they always had a lot of money to invest.

> Clothes have a big influence on how you feel and act.

Clothes can communicate things like "seriousness" or "sporty". It also has a big influence on your self-confidence. If a woman is constantly pulling down her skirt or a man is rearranging his pants, it appears that this person is unsure and feels uncomfortable. Always wear clothes that sit well and feel well. You should also like yourself in your clothes. This will make you feel better and you will appear more **self-confident**.

Being a leader also means that people need to respect you. Therefore **you are not allowed to have crazy, wild parties or nights out with the sales people.** You must always keep your composure and be professional. The only time you should go out and have fun is with your most trusted key people or friends who have nothing to do with your company.

Step 20: Your database of contacts and clients / CRM

> Your list of clients is as valuable as gold – because people who invest into pre-IPO stocks will do it again (even if they lost money before).

Customer relationship management (**CRM**) is a term that refers to practices, strategies and technologies that companies use to manage and analyze customer interactions and data throughout the customer lifecycle.

Having the right software is important in this business. Over the course of a year you contact thousands of people and create leads of people who could become clients at a later point in time. You must be organized and use a software to manage your contacts.

Personally, I like an online software called Highrise HQ (www.highrisehq.com). It is easy and simple to use for the often not-so-computer-nerdy sales people. And it helps you to keep all your contacts in one place.

Sales people often steal contacts and lists when they change companies. That's why you must be in control and make sure that this doesn't happen. With Highrise they can only access their own leads.

A lot of leaders prefer **physical paper cards** that go in a box. Those cards can't be electronically transferred or stolen. Often the only person who has all the contacts is the personal secretary of the leader.

Step 21: How to make $100,000 per month with your sales organization

> Money affirmation: There is plenty of money in the Universe and there is plenty for me.

Business is a numbers game and if you contact a lot of clients, you will get lucky. If you are self-disciplined and you have the right system, then there is nothing that you can't achieve.

You need at least 10 to 20 sales people to really excel financially. You need to work hard and have good people, too. **Success alone (without other people) is not possible.**

Great success only comes with a team of good people. This also means that you must take good care of your key people and pay them well so that they will stay with you. (In case of doubt: always be generous with your people!)

> Write it down on **real paper** with a **real pencil**. And watch **things get real**.
> (Erykah Badu)

My goal was to make at least $100,000 per month and I made it happen on a consistent basis for about two years. This was only possible with the sales power that a money raising sales organization can provide. But you cannot delude yourself into success. You must plan it and be very clear about every step of the way.

There are only two possible outcomes: You are doing exceptionally well or things are at their worst ever. There is nothing in between.

You are only as good as your last deal.

Step 22: Global organization

The ultimate goal of a **Private Equity Entrepreneur** is to have a global organization.

When I was the head of the Hemis Group I had several sales teams in Switzerland, projects in Mexico, USA, Canada and Peru. Some of my key people were in Vancouver, Canada and some were in Las Vegas, Nevada. We even started a team in Manila, the Philippines at one point.

If you can build sales teams who raise money from different countries or regions in the world and they are all working towards the same goal, then you will become one of the big players.

With the Hemis Group we had about 60 people all over the world. My recent project has people in Switzerland, the UK, USA, Serbia and even the Far East.

From a friend of mine I heard of a sales team in Bali with 50 people who call clients in Australia. If they sell your product, then you can easily raise a million dollars per month from that organization alone. Getting a contact like that is like finding gold.

The other day I was approached by an old contact of mine who has a sales team of 26 German speaking sales people in Kosovo. Get them on board and you have it made.

My point is that you should try to find **existing sales organizations** that can help you to raise money for your company. They might be more expensive, meaning you have to pay more percentages, but they can make a huge difference.

If you know some people in a specific region that you trust and that could be your key person, it would make sense to invest into those people.

Example: you can't speak French but you know someone who lives in Paris and who could start a team there with your help. This person would mainly target French-speaking clients. Why not?

Act now!

> Never allow waiting to become a habit.
> Live your dreams and take risks.
> Life is happening now.

Times are changing and right now you still have an opportunity to start a sales organization. Start now and don't procrastinate!

If you are struggling to raise money, then take my advice and start a sales team. You need to focus your time and energy on talking to as many clients as possible. You need to be aggressively marketing to potential investors. And you can do it better with 10 people than just by yourself.

> If you are NOT getting the results you want, you don't need to do another VISION board. You need to FOCUS on getting things done. (Raul Villacis)

CHAPTER 8

MARKETING FOR PRIVATE EQUITY

No leads = no clients = no company.

There are two parts to marketing when it comes to Private Equity:

1. The marketing materials
2. Generating leads of potential investors

Let's talk first about the marketing materials. Here is a list of the things that you should create:

Marketing materials

- 2-Pager
- Brochure
- Power Point Presentation
- Website
- Newsletter
- Business Plan

Other documents

- PPM (Private Placement Memorandum)
- SSA (Share Subscription Agreement)
- Share certificate (Design)

Due diligence package

- Special report (e.g. geological report, study, analysis, etc.)
- Share structure in detail
- Financial statements
- Contracts for projects
- CVs for key members and management
- Independent analysis or report from 3rd party about company / stock

Newsletters

- Monthly or quarterly newsletter (about 2 to 3 pages long)

Create the basic marketing materials

> The most important person in your team is the designer. You need impressive marketing materials that look professional if you want to succeed in this business.

Next to impeccable looking marketing materials you will need **great content**. The key is to have financial terms in your material as well as easy to understand texts that explain what your company does so that **regular people will be motivated to invest** into your deal.

You designer is one of the most important people in your organization. Having great looking marketing materials is the foundation for your success. On the other hand, poor looking materials can be the reason why people are reluctant to invest into your company.

You need impressive marketing materials that look professional if you want to succeed in this business.

You can have a weak or empty company with little assets but if your marketing materials look great, then you have a chance to raise money from investors.

On the other hand if you have poor looking marketing materials but a great company, it makes it harder to convince people to invest.

What goes out to clients, matters. Everything must be perfect. Every detail counts. The difference between winning and losing lies in the details.

Having good-looking marketing materials is key. If it can impress investors, then it makes your job to convince them a lot easier.

Often, good marketing materials can make up for a company that is still young and that has flaws.

Years ago I was lucky to find Mariano Duyos (www.marianoduyos.com), a designer from Argentina. He has helped me to create numerous brochures and marketing materials that made my success even possible. Without him, I would have been lost. Having a great designer makes all the difference in the world.

You should create at least the following marketing material for your potential investors:

1. 2-Pager (Summary about the company, details about the private placement)
2. Corporate Summary or brochure (Colorful marketing brochure about the company)
3. Business Plan (numbers, details, strategy, EBITDA projection)
4. PPT (Power Point Presentation)
5. 10 reasons to invest into *ABC* – 10 reasons to invest into *this industry* (e.g. oil)

Freelancers / Online workers

You can also use an online service like for example Upwork (www.upwork.com) to get your materials created. Some people are great at copy writing; some at web design and others can create great logos and brochures.

You don't need to become an expert in Photoshop all of a sudden. Let others do help you with that. **Become an expert in sales** instead so that you can pay for all those experts!

Creating all the necessary legal materials

<u>You also need to create the following things:</u>

1. SSA – Share subscription agreement
2. PPM – Private Placement Memorandum
3. Form D – SEC Filing and registration / Announcement to raise capital
4. Accounting – Financial Statements / do not mix personal and business
5. Proper contracts for projects
6. Management agreements (for you and your officers)
7. Consulting agreements

Your legal documents are also important. They also required to be designed professionally. The better they look, the trust worthier they come across.

General advice

1. **Professionalism:** Make it look bigger than it actually is. Since you are just starting out, you need to look like you don't need the money and are already advanced as a company. The investor must get the feeling like he gets a chance to be part of something big.
2. **Keep the FAQs simple and easy to understand:** Put yourself in the shoes of a new investor who is not a financial specialist. Answer all his basic questions in an easy to understand manner.
3. **Include the share structure:** The main idea is to show a few financial or technical things. Even though your investor might not understand everything, he must get the feeling that everything is well organized and calculated.
4. **Management team – hire experts:** It is always good to have one or two real specialist like a PhD or a geologist who is an expert in his

field. You need to show credibility in your team. It is sometimes easier to convince people to join your advisory board rather than to become a director of the company.

5. **Project report – just option or LOI is ok:** Even if you have not yet started or completed your project, you should create a technical report based on your business. Use lots of technical information, graphs, pictures, etc. to give the impression that your project is advanced.
6. **No more questions left open**: The goal of your marketing and duc diligence package is to make sure that all questions are answered. Often, people hesitate if they feel like the whole thing is a "black box" and they can't see all the details.
7. **Be positive about the future:** Your outlook must be positive and you should give an example of someone investing $10,000 in the first round of financing and what it could turn into in the future.

> Comparing yourself to others is the thief of joy. The problem is that you compare your chapter 1 with someone else's chapter 20.

Investor Relations, news releases or 8-Ks

> Just like someone can destroy your deal and reputation online, it is also possible for you to post extremely positive things about your own company.

There is no Internet police who checks if all your statements are real. But people will not invest into your company if they read something negative about you even though it is not true.

Create a positive online image. Post positive articles every week and make your company stand out.

> Don't give up just because of what someone said about you or your company.

You can use top media outlets that will let you post an article about your company, process or industry for a fee. One of my former business partners used to post things on N-TV, Handelsblatt and other outlets in Germany. Those names are a great reputation and you can use those links in your marketing efforts with your clients to gain more credibility and trust. This makes it a lot easier to sell.

Another thing that you can do is an 8-K filing with the SEC. You can post a news release and then have it disseminated through several financial online channels. If your company is public, your 8-K filings are automatically linked to your trading symbol.

Raising money over the phone with a marketing team

> You don't have to be great at something to start. But you have to start to be great at something.

If you have a marketing team of 5 people who will each make 100 cold calls each day and generate 5 good quality leads (95 of the people say no and 5 people say yes), then you will have 25 good leads each day. This is 125 leads per week or 500 leads per month.

In general, the people call up a person and send them some general information about the company or the deal. They prequalify the client so that the sales person who calls afterwards knows that this person could be a potential client who shows a general interest in the product.

If you call 100 quality leads, you must assume that 80% of them will fall off and that you can only continue to work with 20 of them. Those 20 leads are open to talk and you can have a third or fourth conversation with them.

Out of those 20 people, you have to assume once again that 80% won't buy your product and that in the end you will get 4 clients.

So out of 100 good quality leads, you will get 4 clients.

If the average initial investment is $10,000 per client, then you will raise $40,000 in total.

Your marketing team can be in a low cost country where salaries are cheaper. If you pay $500 per person per month, then your marketing expenses are $2500.

Cold calls (marketing calls) per day	100
NOs	95
Leads	5
Monday to Friday	25 Leads
1 month	100 Leads
80% say no in second call	20 Leads left
80% say no in third call	16 Leads left
Clients	4
2000 cold calls = 100 Leads = 20 good ones = 4 clients	

1 marketing person – 100 leads per month – 4 clients
5 marketing people – 500 leads per month – 20 clients
10 marketing people – 1000 leads per month – 40 clients

The right office environment

> I don't believe in self-discipline. I believe in the right environment. (Dan Lok)

This job is not an easy one. One of the hardest things is to make cold calls all by yourself. It gets even worse if you have to do it alone and from home in your pajamas. I have been in this business for more than 20 years and I don't know of anyone who has successfully been able to work from home doing marketing cold calls on his own on a consistent basis. It just doesn't work.

The reason for this is the loneliness and the frustration from the constant rejection.

It is much easier to be in an office environment where others share your fate. You will need other people around you if you are making marketing phone calls.

Ideally, you want to create an office where you have a marketing department where about 4 or 5 people make the initial phone calls and a sales room where the more experienced sales people close deals.

A motivating office environment is key to the success of your sales organization. It needs to be positive, have lots of encouragement, a kitchen with food and drinks and a good team leader.

Focus

1. Marketing team that generates new leads every day
2. Gathering good contacts and lists
3. Having a couple of really good sales people
4. Office – the right environment is key for success
5. Good product to sell
6. Online strategy as an additional way to generate leads

> Nothing will replace the telephone and a personal conversation with a client when it comes to investing into a private equity deal.

Generating new leads

> When it comes to marketing to find investors, use a strategy that is proven to work – even if it is a more difficult approach like for example cold calling.

There are four ways how you can generate leads for potential investors. In general, the best way to convince is person is face-to-face. The second best is on the phone.

1. Make calls yourself
2. Marketing team
3. Online strategy
4. List broker, existing lists, clients, former investors, referrals, etc.

If you are alone, then you have to be in charge of raising money first. In that case you have to make 100 cold calls. You can use the telephone book, yellow pages or make your own list. Your goal is to generate 5 to 10 leads per day where you are able to send the initial information package to the client and get him interested in the deal.

The second method is to hire 2, 5 or 10 marketing people who generate leads for you to follow up. If you hire 5 people and they make 100 cold calls each and generate 5x 5 leads per day, then you will have 25 leads per day to follow up with. This method is usually much easier and better because you already know that the person showed some initial interest and is open to talk to you.

The third option is to run an ad online. If a person clicks on your ad, he gets redirected to a landing page and in exchange for his telephone number and email, you will give him a report about investing. Your job is then to follow up with a call after that person has read the report and try to sell him the shares.

The fourth option is to buy leads from a list broker. A professional marketing company can sell you a lead for $5 to $100 per lead. These lists can be really good because you have the perfect target group of people who have the right age, income and who are interested in investing. But be careful that you don't buy a list where 5 other companies have called them.

There are five ways how you can generate leads to get potential investors.

In general, the best way to convince is person is face-to-face. The second best is on the phone. Since you don't always have the opportunity to meet in person, you will probably conduct 90% of your business over the phone. That's why **you must become a master on the phone** and have the right leads so that you can increase your chances to close a deal.

In order to find investors, you need to have a clear strategy.

The Nr. 1 question in marketing

Ask yourself the following question: Who is your ideal customer?

<u>Answer</u>

- Male
- Age between 40 and 70 years old
- Manager, self-employed, businessman, professional
- Income over $100,000 per year
- Home owner

Numbers game: How many people will you call per day? What are your sales numbers?

- 100 calls per day
- 95 people say no or are not interested
- 5 people agree to receive the information package
- Ideally, you want to get 10 leads per day but 5 leads are the minimum

Product / USP (Unique Selling Proposition): Why should they buy from you right now?

- Upcoming IPO
- Cheap price at $0.50 per share – later it will be $1.00 at IPO (100% return)
- Great company with long-term growth potential
- Exit in 1 to 2 years (short-term investment)

Make phone calls yourself

> This business is a numbers game.

If you are alone, then you have to be in charge of raising money first. In that case you have to make 100 cold calls. You can use the telephone book, yellow pages or make your own list. Your goal is to generate 5 to 10 leads per day where you are able to send the initial information package to the client and get him interested in the deal.

- 100 calls
- 95 no
- 5 leads (minimum) but goal is 10 leads per day

If possible, set up a personal meeting once a person has received your information. Your closing rate will be much higher if you can meet someone in person.

> Success is doing ordinary things extraordinarily well. (Jim Rohn)

Marketing sales team

The second method is to hire 2, 5 or 10 marketing people who generate leads for you to follow up. If you hire 5 people and they make 100 cold calls each and generate 5x 5 leads per day, then you will have 25 leads per day to follow up with. This method is usually much easier and better because you already know that the person showed some initial interest and is open to talk to you.

- 5 marketing people
- $10 per hour base salary
- Pay them an additional 5% in commission for every deal that you close
- 5 hours per day x $10 x 5 days x 4 weeks = $1,000 per person
- 5 people x $1000 base salary = $5,000 per month

- Your goal has to be to close enough clients to pay for the salaries
- 5 people x 5 days x 4 weeks x 5 leads = 500 new leads per month

> I never dreamed about success. I worked for it. (Estee Lauder)

Online strategy with landing page and free PDF

> If you confuse people, you lose people.

The third option is to run an ad online. If a person clicks on your ad, he gets redirected to a landing page and in exchange for his telephone number and email; you will give him a report about investing. Your job is then to follow up with a call after that person has read the report and try to sell him the shares.

Your message needs to be clear and easy to understand. Also, don't give your client a choice. He must follow the steps (fill out form) and submit it.

Referrals, lists, former investors, etc.

> Former investors are more likely to invest again than new ones.

In general, the best list consists of former investors. These are people who already once invested into a private placement and bought shares elsewhere. Most of these people are risk-takers and somewhat naïve or greedy.

People want something for nothing and they want it quickly. When it comes to investing, most people have an unrealistic idea for the timeline. Nevertheless, you can use this to your advantage.

It is interesting to see how many people who have lost money before in a different deal are willing to risk it all again.

Buy leads from a list broker for $1 to $100 per lead

> You can buy leads but often it is just as easy to create them yourself with a mini call center.

The fifth option is to buy leads from a list broker. A professional marketing company can sell you a lead for $1 to $100 per lead. These lists can be really good because you have the perfect target group of people who have the right age, income and who are interested in investing. But be careful that you don't buy a list where 5 other companies have called them.

Some leads are very expensive and cost $100. But you will only need to close one of those to make a profit. I worked with an organization that bought leads for about $100,000 per month but raised over $1 million per month from investors.

It is easy to close those deals because the client requested information about investments and he has the ability to invest.

You can consider doing things like this once you have more money. In the beginning you have to create the leads yourself.

Marketing goals

- Send out 10 docs (documentation) per day
- Minimum: 5 docs, good day = 15 to 20 also possible
- Quality must be good (no secretaries, must show interest, must be open, must have money to invest)
- Customer must be informed in general and must know what it is all about.
- The main objective is that he accepts the documents, knows that it is about an investment and that he is basically open to invest.
- He must have the ability (money) to invest otherwise it makes no sense.

- The customer does not yet have to be convinced of the investment. That's the job of the sales person.
- He has to be made curious.
- He must be open to have a second conversation.

Internet leads – PDF about your industry or investing

If your audience isn't listening…it's not their fault. It's yours.

Step 1: You run a Facebook AD, Google Ad or YouTube Ad (grabbing their attention)

Step 2: Client gets on a landing page

- You offer a free brochure / PDF about investing in general or about investing into your industry
- In exchange you will receive his email address and / or phone number

Step 3: You follow up with a phone call and sell him the shares over the phone

<u>Possible titles:</u>

- The 7 mistakes that investors make
- How to avoid the 7 mistakes that investors make
- How to invest into the stock market from 2020 to 2025 to make more money
- How to invest into gold and other precious metals
- Double your money this year with IPOs

Curiosity kills the cat (human).

Online strategy or call center?

You have to start somewhere.

Cold calling is a difficult way to generate clients. This is especially true for the USA. It is very difficult to find client that way. In Germany on the other hand, cold calling is still very doable. Depending on where you are located in the world, it might be a good or a bad strategy.

In the end, you still need to speak to an investor either in person or on the phone. So the phone cannot be replaced.

But if you have figured out a way to generate leads of people who are interested in your topic, then it is much easier to call them up later.

I personally don't make any marketing cold calls but only people who have already received the information package and are open to talk. The hard work I leave to a team of marketing cold callers who are typically located in a second or third world country and who cost less.

For example: I used to have a marketing call center in Serbia. The people who worked for me used to live in Germany and spoke perfect German. They called with a German number and called up clients in Germany. This way, the client was unaware of where the call was coming from. But the advantage for me was that I only had to pay about 300 to 400 Euros per person per month and they generated about 5 to 10 leads per day.

This is actually a great way to do business. You hire 5 marketing people and your cost per month is about $2000. If you get a couple of hundred leads per month, you only have to close at least one deal for $10,000 (which is a small deal anyway) to be profitable.

Ideally, you also want to hire a few sales people who will do the selling for you. You pay them between 10% and 20% in commission and you will have created a business system that automatically brings in money for your company.

Position yourself as THE expert

> Life's barely long enough to get good at one thing. So be careful what you get good at. (Matthew McConaughey)

If you know my background, then you know that I am actually a financial expert. I have many years of experience. But in order to succeed in this business, you don't necessarily need this. You just have to position yourself as an expert and be seen as one.

I usually start the conversation about high finance and how I am an expert in this industry. I want him to give me the same respect that he gives a doctor. I consider myself to be a "doctor of finance".

Here is an example of how you could do it:

- *Mr. Smith, I wanted to introduce myself to you. I have been in the financial industry for more than 22 years. I have an MBA and I am a licensed stockbroker. I have over 3000 clients all over the world and I have raised over $400 million from investors for private and public companies. Most of my clients have invested more than $1 million with me but the average person is in the 6-digit range.*

You are positioning yourself as a financial specialist. You are not just like another telemarketer calling him. You are like a "financial doctor" and he should be grateful to even to be able to talk to you.

This switches the entire viewpoint from "I want to sell you something to you should be glad to talk to me." You become the consultant rather than the sales person.

Go for it

> You can achieve any goal if your goal is clear and you persist long enough.

In the end it all comes down to picking up the phone and calling up enough people. This business is a numbers game. People fail in this business because they don't call enough people and then they start to doubt the market, the product and themselves.

But this is not you. You can do this. Focus on the numbers and take out the emotions. Just talk to enough people and success is yours!

CHAPTER 9

PRIVATE EQUITY BROKER TRAINING PROGRAM

Only you can change your life. You have the power to create a better life for yourself. You can learn everything about raising money from investors, go to work and build a company that eventually goes public and becomes a multi-million dollar company. All the tools and knowledge are in this program. All you have to do is to apply it.

This knowledge is my gift to the world. It is my gift to the new entrepreneur who is struggling today but wants to create a better life for himself and his family.

> If you want to break the chains of **suffering and mediocrity**, you must be **willing to pay the price.**

Part 1: Marketing (initial phone call and sending out information about the deal)

The sales process of raising money from private investors

Step 1: Initial marketing call or cold call (The goal is to be able to send out information about the deal and to get the person curious.)

Step 2: Sales call from a Private Equity Broker (The goal is to sell the deal and get the person motivated to invest into the company.)

Step 3: Closing the deal (Often it is required to talk three or four times to a client before he will invest. The goal is to get him to invest an initial amount.)

Step 4: Loading the client (Once a client has invested, he typically will invest a second or even a third time.)

Script for initial marketing call

- *Hello, my name is Norman Meier. Can I please talk to Mr. John Smith? Speaking.*
- *Mr. Smith, I am not sure if you remember me but we spoke about 6 months ago. I tried to offer you an interesting deal but at that time you were not interested.*
- *No, I don't remember you. What is it about?*
- *I am calling from the company ABC Energy, a new and upcoming oil company. Our company is about to go public in the stock market and we are currently doing a pre-IPO private placement. We are offering our investors to buy the shares at $0.50 per share and the initial price when the company is listed and trading will be at about $1.50 per share.*
- *Basically, all I would like to do today is to send you some general information about our company so that you can decide for yourself whether or not this is an interesting investment opportunity for you. Does that sound like a fair proposal? Yes.*
- *Great, then I am happy to send you the information. What is your email address? john.smith@mail.com*
- *Before I send you the information by email I would like to ask you a few questions.*

1. *Are you currently invested in the market?*
2. *Have ever invested into an IPO before?*
3. *How aware or familiar are you when it comes to the topic of oil and it's long-term potential?*

4. *Assuming you like the offer, would you be willing to invest anywhere between $50,000 and $100,000?*

- *Thank you very much for your time. An experienced broker will call you in the next few days and will answer any questions that you might have. Goodbye.*

Generating new leads

There are five ways how you can generate leads to get potential investors.

In general, the best way to convince is person is face-to-face. The second best is on the phone. Since you don't always have the opportunity to meet in person, you will probably conduct 90% of your business over the phone. That's why **you must become a master on the phone** and have the right leads so that you can increase your chances to close a deal.

In order to find investors, you need to have a clear strategy.

> The reason why entrepreneurs are struggling is because they use **hope** as a **strategy.**

Who is your ideal customer? (Nr. 1 marketing question)

Ask yourself the following question: Who is your ideal customer?

- Male
- Age between 40 and 70 years old
- Manager, self-employed, businessman, professional
- Income over $100,000 per year
- Home owner

Numbers game: How many will you call per day? What are your sales numbers?

- 100 calls per day
- 95 people say no or are not interested
- 5 people agree to receive the information package
- Ideally, you want to get 10 leads per day but 5 leads are the minimum

Product / USP (Unique Selling Proposition): Why should they buy from you right now?

- Upcoming IPO
- Cheap price at $0.50 per share – later it will be $1.00 at IPO (100% return)
- Great company with long-term growth potential
- Exit in 1 to 2 years (short-term investment)

Generate leads – path 1: Make phone calls yourself

> In order to make it in this business, you need a clear **strategy and system**. This business is a numbers game.

If you are alone, then you have to be in charge of raising money first. In that case you have to make 100 cold calls. You can use the telephone book, yellow pages or make your own list. Your goal is to generate 5 to 10 leads per day where you are able to send the initial information package to the client and get him interested in the deal.

- 100 calls
- 95 no
- 5 leads (minimum) but goal is 10 leads per day

If possible, set up a personal meeting once a person has received your information. Your closing rate will be much higher if you can meet someone in person.

> It is enough if **only one person** believes in you – even if this person is **yourself.**

Generate leads – path 2: Marketing sales team

The second method is to hire 2, 5 or 10 marketing people who generate leads for you to follow up. If you hire 5 people and they make 100 cold calls each and generate 5x 5 leads per day, then you will have 25 leads per day to follow up with. This method is usually much easier and better because you already know that the person showed some initial interest and is open to talk to you.

- 5 marketing people
- $10 per hour base salary
- Pay them an additional 5% in commission for every deal that you close
- 5 hours per day x $10 x 5 days x 4 weeks = $1,000 per person
- 5 people x $1000 base salary = $5,000 per month
- Your goal has to be to close enough clients to pay for the salaries
- 5 people x 5 days x 4 weeks x 5 leads = 500 new leads per month

> Despite the Internet it is still the best way to get clients through the telephone. However, it is much easier if you don't have to make the cold call yourself.

Generate leads – path 3: Online strategy with landing page and free PDF

> Use online marketing to generate leads. Use the telephone to follow up.

The third option is to run an ad online. If a person clicks on your ad, he gets redirected to a landing page and in exchange for his telephone number and email; you will give him a report about investing. Your job is then to follow up with a call after that person has read the report and try to sell him the shares.

Generate leads – path 4: Referrals, lists, former investors, etc.

In general, the best list consists of former investors. These are people who already once invested into a private placement and bought shares elsewhere. Most of these people are risk-takers and somewhat naïve or greedy.

> Remember this about your clients: *"Once a gambler – always a gambler!"*

People want something for nothing and they want it quickly. When it comes to investing, most people have an unrealistic idea for the timeline. Nevertheless, you can use this to your advantage.

It is interesting to see how many people who have lost money before in a different deal are willing to risk it all again.

Generate leads – path 5: Buy leads from a list broker for $1 to $100 per lead

The fifth option is to buy leads from a list broker. A professional marketing company can sell you a lead for $1 to $100 per lead. These lists can be really good because you have the perfect target group of people who have the right age, income and who are interested in investing. But be careful that you don't buy a list where 5 other companies have called them.

Some leads are very expensive and cost $100. But you will only need to close one of those to make a profit. I worked with an organization that bought leads for about $100,000 per month but raised over $1 million per month from investors.

It is easy to close those deals because the client requested information about investments and he has the ability to invest.

You can consider doing things like this once you have more money. In the beginning you have to create the leads yourself.

Marketing goals

- Send out 10 docs (documentation) per day
- Minimum: 5 docs, good day = 15 to 20 also possible
- Quality must be good (no secretaries, must show interest, must be open, must have money to invest)
- Customer must be informed in general and must know what it is all about.
- The main objective is that he accepts the documents, knows that it is about an investment and that he is basically open to invest.
- He must have the ability (money) to invest otherwise it makes no sense.
- The customer does not yet have to be convinced of the investment. That's the job of the sales person.
- He has to be made curious.
- He must be open to have a second conversation.

> What is the goal of the first conversation? Being able to send him the documentation!
> You don't have to convince the customer to invest.

Important questions

1. Is he generally speaking open?
2. Does he have money to invest?
3. How much money can he invest? (10k to 20k / 50k to 100k / more?)
4. Does he have experience with investments?
5. Does he have experience with pre-IPO stocks or IPOs?

Awareness when it comes to the topic of oil (example)

- Oil is a basic human need.
- Millions of cars, planes, factories, plastic is made from oil
- 50% of the oil has been found worldwide - at some point it's done
- China and India have more and more people and need more and more oil
- It takes at least 1 generation for alternative energy methods to replace oil
- There is now a rising trend over the next 5 to 10 years, where the price of oil will rise
- Gasoline at the gas station is becoming more and more expensive

Personal attitude on the phone

Smile and dial.

- Always stay positive
- Smile
- Focus on the relationship rather than the product
- Give praise and recognition
- Create trust and confidence
- Enthusiasm: if you don't have the fire in yourself, you cannot expect it to transfer the spark of excitement to others.

LTNP

LTNP = LIKEABILITY before TRUST before NEED before PRICE

This is the basic rule when it comes to sales in general. You cannot sell to a person who doesn't like you, doesn't trust you and doesn't see a need to do business with you. Once you have covered the first three points (Like, trust, need) then and only then you can proceed with the product or price.

- **Likeability** = Focus on the relationship. If he doesn't like you, he won't do business with you.
- **Trust** = If the customer doesn't trust you, he will not do business with you.
- **Need or Benefit** = The customer must recognize a need or a benefit for himself otherwise he will not do it. The best way to make him aware of a need is to make him aware of a problem first so that he has a motivation to invest.
  (Example: The money in the bank generates only a 1% return. Inflation is 3% so he is losing money by not investing. With us he can double his investment.)
- **Price or product** = The customer is willing to buy only when likeability, trust and need have been covered first.

Answers to objections from the marketing call

- *That's a good question (praise and recognition)... the best thing is to look at the information that I will send you and then talk to the financial expert who will call you in a few days. I'm sure he can help you and answer your questions.*
- *That's why I suggest you take a look at the documents so that you can decide whether or not this is interesting for you. Does that sound fair? (He has to say yes to this question)*
- *I can understand that well...(expression of understanding)*
- *If I were your shoes, I would probably react similar at first...(expression of understanding)*
- *Just read it through. You can still decide later if this is for you or not. Is that a fair proposal? (He has to say yes to this question)*
- *The financial expert will contact you by phone next week to answer any questions you may have.*

Initial public offering

- *IPO: from $0.50 now to $1.50 IPO (300% possible)*
- *Oil topic: oil will rise in the long term*

- *There is currently a boom for the next 5 years, and then it is over. You must act now.*
- *Saudi Aramco, the world's largest oil company, goes public next year. This will generate a hype for oil companies in the market.*
- *This IPO will be bigger than Facebook, etc. It will be the biggest IPO in history. What do you think happens to the companies that are also in the oil sector? Their stock will rise, too!*
- **Make the product "scarce"** (*There are only a small number of pre-IPO shares left at $0.50)*
- **Threaten a price increase** (*the price will go up next week*)
- *The first round of financing has already been completed. We are already in the 2nd round. But I can still give you shares for the lower price if you act now.*
- *If you're lucky, you'll get a few more for the lower prize. But you must act now.*
- **Time limit:** *You need to act in the next 24 hours or the opportunity is gone.*
- *Mr. Smith will contact you in the next 2 days.*

The job of marketing agent is critical to your success

- The better the preparation is made, the greater the likelihood that the salesperson will succeed.

Good questions

- *Assuming that you like the investment, would you be willing to invest?*
- *How much exactly could you invest?*
- Customer says: *"I have to look at the deal first before I can make a decision"*
- *Of course, I can understand that well. But if you really, really liked it, how much would you be willing to invest?* (Get a commitment now and get a specific number)

Do not send documents if ...

- Send documents to the secretary - that does not help. Only talk to decision makers.
- He has no interest and you send him the documents anyway. That is a waste of time. This is a bad lead for the sales person and only creates unnecessary frustration.
- If you are in a bad mood while making phone calls, take a break. Only call if you are in a positive mood.
- If he's skeptical, that's ok. But he must be willing to talk and still be open in general to consider the investment.

Colombo technique (TV series)

Just like in the TV series when the conversation has ended and everything has been talked about, the detective asks one last question. This question is usually the most important question.

- *Just one last question ... If you really like the project, would you be able to invest between 50k and 100k?* (Feel him out where his limit is)
- *You can already look forward to talking to our specialist / broker.*

Most people will be surprise to hear that a client is able to willing to invest $100k. If you had not asked this question, you might only get about $10,000 in the first investment. This question is key.

Marketing is a numbers game

- 50 to 100 calls will generate 5 to 10 leads per day
- 80% rejection - that's normal.
- Do not lose heart. Many people earn a lot of money this way. It works when you talk to enough people.
- There is always a surprise with a very potential customer. But you only get that if you make many calls.

Possible introduction

- We talked to each other briefly about 12 months ago. I had offered you an interesting product then, but then you were not interested.

Bad leads / do not send an information package

- The worst thing for a broker is when he gets bad leads.
- Please send only good and interested contacts.
- The client has to be willing to talk.
- The client must have money to invest.
- The client must know what the conversation is about.
- Make the client curious.
- Someone who is open but has no money is also a waste of time.
- If someone is extremely negative, threatening or being from the press, don't send anything and end the conversation quickly.

Checklist

- ☐ Email address? ____________________
- ☐ Mobile number ____________________
- ☐ When available (time and number)? ____________________
- ☐ How much could he invest? ____________________
- ☐ Experience with stocks? ____________________
- ☐ Already bought pre-market shares? ____________________
- ☐ Other things (hobbies, personal information, etc.)? ___________
- ☐ Mood? Was he nice, open or critical, etc.? ________________

Part 2: Sales

Sales process

Once the client has received the information package, a sales person will follow up with a second call. The goals of the second call after the initial marketing call are as follows:

1. Introduce yourself and **position yourself as the expert**
2. Develop **likeability and trust**
3. Sell the product and **tell the story** about the deal
4. **Create awareness** for a problem or a specific topic (e.g. banks pay low interest, oil is currently in a huge upwards spiral or trend, etc.)
5. **Get him excited and curious**

It is not typical that you can close a deal after just one conversation. It usually takes 2 or 3 conversations before he is willing to invest. 80% of the people will need a bit more trust and time. 20% of the people you can close now.

You can get rid of 80% of the leads that you talk to. The goal is to identify the ones that you can continue to talk to and who are willing to invest.

You can disqualify the prospect – not the other way around.

You can disqualify 8 leads out of 10 people from the second call and continue to talk to 2 leads (those will most likely become clients).

If you talk to 10 people per day, you will get 2 really hot potential clients.

What to say…

- *Mr. Smith, have you read the documents that my assistant has sent you?*
- **Yes or no – it doesn't matter. Tell the story again anyway.**

Position yourself as THE expert

- *Mr. Smith, I wanted to introduce myself to you. I have been in the financial industry for more than 22 years. I have an MBA and I am a licensed stockbroker. I have over 3000 clients all over the world and I have raised over $400 million from investors for private and public companies. Most of my clients have invested more than $1 million with me but the average person is in the 6-digit range.*

You are positioning yourself as a financial specialist. You are not just like another telemarketer calling him. You are like a "financial doctor" and he should be grateful to even to be able to talk to you.

This switches the entire viewpoint from "I want to sell you something to you should be glad to talk to me." You become the consultant rather than the sales person.

Positioning yourself a specialist in high finance

- *I am an expert in high finance. Mr. Smith, do you know what high finance is exactly? (No)*
- *If you bring your hard earned money to the bank. How much interest will you get in return? (1% or 2%)*
- *What does the bank do with your money? (Loans, they invest it, etc.)*
- *How much money does the bank make on average? (8% to 15%)*
- *Do you find this fair? (No)*
- *You see, Mr. Smith, high finance is cutting out the middleman, the bank, and then investing directly into projects that generate such a good return.*

Why this deal?

- *Mr. Smith, I have seen many different opportunities come and go. But this deal is without a doubt the best deal I have personally seen in my career in the last 10 years. It is such a great opportunity that I can't even believe it myself.*
- *If you invest at $0.50 per share, the company goes public at $1.50, you will already have tripled your investment. But based on the business plan, it is expected that the share price will go up to $5 in the mid-term but over $10 in the long-term.*

You are selling a pre-IPO deal. This is a very young company that compared to big companies, is still very fragile. In order for any normal person to invest into such a deal, **you must talk about the future potential**. You must talk about how he can double, triple and quadruple his money.

People will dismiss a return of 20% per year but they will believe you that they can make 1000%.

Most people turn off their brains when you talk about how much money they could make. Their sense of **greed** will take over. Most people want to find this special investment that makes them rich over night. Obviously, this doesn't exist but you must make them believe that it could be possible with your deal.

The deal is as good as financed (with an institutional investor)

- *Mr. Smith, We currently have 3 pre-IPO financing rounds. The first round of financing is at $0.50, the second round is at $0.75 and the third round is at $1.00. All three rounds are $5 million each or $15 million in total.*
- *We are currently in negotiations with a big investment firm from Germany. This is an institutional investor who believes in our company so much that they want to buy all three rounds for $15 million. This would guarantee that our projects will be successful and that our stock will go through the roof.*
- *We will most likely come to an agreement with this big investor by the end of the month. And then no one will be able to get any more shares at this low price of $0.50.*
- *Ideally, we would like to have a broad variety of many smaller shareholders so that we are not dependent on one big investor alone. Currently, we have about 75 private investors in this deal. You could also profit from this low price of $0.50 but you must act before it is too late and no more shares are available.*
- *This institutional investor alone will "guarantee" the success of this stock.*

Objections from investors

The client says:

- *I am not interested*
- *I have no money*

- *To risky*
- I have to think about it.
- Let me get back to you.
- Etc.

You answer:

- What would it take for us to do business **today**?

Find out what the real objections are.

- *Dear Mr. Prospect, I hear this a lot. Do you really have to think about it or is this just a polite way for you to tell me that you don't want to do it?*
- *Was it the terms?*
- *Was it the price? Would a payment plan help?*
- *Was it the XYZ?*

Once you cut through the BS you can find out what the real reason is why the prospect doesn't want to buy today. And then you can help him to solve the problem right now.

Following up

As I have mentioned earlier, you might not be able to close a deal after one conversation alone. That's why it would be good to schedule another call and time with the client.

Ideally, you should send him another document (e.g. a geological report, a more detailed summary, etc.) and then have a reason to call again.

> If you cannot close a deal, do not end the conversation. Plan a date and time to follow up again with the prospect. (Brian Tracy)

A relationship takes time and you must focus on developing trust. It is ok to **call several times about little details** just so that the client gets used to you.

I would also advise that you **DON'T say this**: "*Oh, Mr. Smith, take all the time you need. The shares will be waiting for you whenever you are ready.*"

Instead say: "*Let me check with headquarters how many shares and at what exact price are still available. You should know that we are 10 stockbrokers here and those shares sell really fast. They are selling faster than hot cakes.*"

The shares must be made **scarce.** If something is scarce, it will be more valuable. If everybody can get it, then it has no value.

Reservation of shares

- *Mr. Smith, let me call you back in 5 minutes. I will check with the headquarters if and how many shares are still available.*
- ...After 5 minutes
- *I just talked to the head of finance. I was able to reserve 2 packages for you. One package is for $20,000 or 40,000 shares and the other one for $35,000 or 70,000 shares.*
- Another option could be: *I have 80,000 shares available at $0.50. This is $40,000. How much of that would you like to get?*

Get a commitment

- *Ok, I will reserve these shares for you now.*
- *I can only hold this reservation for 48 hours. You must send me the contract and the confirmation of the transfer as soon as you can. When exactly can I expect it?*

The 3 most important factors

1. Scarcity
2. Threaten a price increase
3. Time pressure / limit

Openings can be small to get him in the deal

The main goal is to get the person to invest the first time and to believe in the deal. Even if he only invests $5,000 or $10,000 at first, this is good news.

Some people want to see if the transaction goes smoothly and how the service is afterwards. Once a client has invested, a more experienced loader (sales person) can call the client and get him to invest more money.

Some clients can be loaded several times and will invest substantially more than their initial investment.

The power of the second voice

Sometimes you will run into a client who is hesitant. Often, it is a matter of lack of trust. That's where the power of the voice comes into play.

I have used this technique many times. A colleague of yours will also call the client. He will pretend to be from the accounting department. He will just follow up with the reservation and wants to know where the client stands.

A second voice will often create more trust. It shows the client that there is an organization behind a company and it is not just a scammer calling.

Another great way to start a new call is for the assistant to give him a call first. The assistant will **build up** the sales person as this really important broker who will take out extra time out of his busy schedule to call the client.

By preparing and positioning the broker accordingly, the client has more respect and is more likely to invest a larger amount.

Cool things to say to a client

- *Please only give me **5% (or $5,000) of your trust now**. I will have to work for the remaining 95%.*
- *If you don't have lots of money, you have to take lots of risk and speculate. Once you are in the same league as my clients, you no longer have to take risks.*
- ***We are not a Casino** and hope for red or black. We work with proper analysis and proof.*
- *You might risk a few dollars. I, on the other hand, **will risk my entire career** and reputation.*
- *Is there a sign at your door that says: **"Closed because of wealth?"***
- *Guaranteed is only death. I don't have a crystal ball that tells me the future. But based on my experience, this is as good as it gets.*
- *Do you have to work hard for your money? Why don't you let your money work hard for you for once?*
- *I am always just one phone call away.*
- *If you buy a BMW today for $40,000 and you know that the same car will cost $60,000 in a few days, you won't wait until then, either.*
- *My job is to determine the **best entry point** and the **best exit point** for your investments.*
- *The Universe has given us all the signs. Now we must act.*
- *I will not only give you 100% of my commitment but 200%.*
- *I have never played **Russian roulette** in the stock market. And I don't intend to do it here, either.*
- *It's like diving into a pool. You jump in and get out quickly.*
- *If you own bonds, you will sleep well. But if you own stocks, you will live well.*
- *You should not chase money. You must embrace it.*
- *Often it is better to think a couple hours about money than working an entire month for it.*
- *All my clients are invested with **7-digits** with me.*
- *I only chose the best of the best as products. Only those will be offered to my clients.*
- *I can only hand you the **golden spoon**. You must swallow the food yourself.*
- *How do you want to reach your destination? In a **Rolls Royce** or an old piece of crap car?*

- ***The money lies in the streets.*** *All you have to do is to pick it up.*
- *It is like* ***dating****. In order to get love, you must go on a first date. The same is true here. You must do a first deal with me to experience the love later on.*
- *I hope you have truly understood the* ***magic and scope*** *of this kind of investment. Nothing has more potential than this.*
- *We are currently in a* ***really special market situation****. We have to take advantage of it. This doesn't happen very often.*
- *Why don't we start with* ***a little taste of what the future can hold for you****? Let's start small with $10,000.*
- *You don't like that I am calling you on the phone? What do you prefer?* ***Smoke signals?*** *This is the way this business is done.*

Part 3: Private Equity knowledge

Please read and study all NMI Private Equity related brochures:

- Basics about Private Equity
- Basics about Public companies
- Business Development for public companies
- Stock Promotion and Marketing
- Private Equity Business System
- Private Equity Glossary
- Workbook (The $100 million blueprint)
- How to become a millionaire with your company and PE
- How to turn an idea into a listed company
- Brochure: Money Raising Masterclass
- Brochure: How to build a sales organization
- Marketing for Private Equity
- Brochure: Sales Psychology and techniques to raise capital
- The business of finding investors
- ABC Corporation – PPM (Private Placement Memorandum) Example
- ABC Corporation – Consulting Agreement Example
- ABC Corporation – Management Agreement Example
- ABC Corporation – Business Plan Example
- ABC Corporation – Financial Statements Example

- ABC Corporation – International connections and list of contacts
- ABC Corporation – IPO Plan
- ABC Corporation – Share structure example
- ABC Corporation – SEC Filing (steps explained Form ID and Form D)
- ABC Corporation – SSA (Share subscription agreement) example

Please watch the following Private Equity movies either on YouTube or with the file:

- The $100 million blueprint - www.normanmeier.com
- How to become a millionaire or billionaire with your company - www.normanmeier.com
- How to create a $100 million company - www.normanmeier.com
- Stock promotion and business development - www.normanmeier.com
- Private Equity Presentation Example - Investing into a gold company
- How to raise money from private investors
- Finding investors and raising money
- Making money with your corporation
- Setting goals for the company and yourself

Part 4: Financial knowledge

- Please read the brochure "Investing simplified".
- Learn the basics about stocks
- Open up an online trading account and learn how to make basic trades
- Consider studying the book to pass the Series 7

Please watch the following movies about investing either on YouTube or with the file:

- Financial Planning - www.normanmeier.com
- Basic investments and strategies - www.normanmeier.com
- Online trading accounts - www.normanmeier.com

- Real Estate, oil and gold - www.normanmeier.com
- Technical analysis and buying signals - www.normanmeier.com
- Markets - www.normanmeier.com
- Hedge funds and futures - www.normanmeier.com
- Options - www.normanmeier.com
- Money management - www.normanmeier.com
- Protecting your position and research - www.normanmeier.com

Part 5: Private Equity Broker Trainee (3 months)

Private Equity Test, product and industry knowledge

- Study everything about your product and industry
- Pass the Private Equity Test and review the answers
- Pass the test about natural resources and geology
- Pass the oil test
- Pass the test about alternative energy

Diploma: Private Equity Specialist

- After successful completion of all test a new trainee will receive a diploma.

Nach bestandender Prüfung erhält der Teilnehmer ein Diplom von der Swiss Management Academy mit dem Titel „Private Equity Specialist".

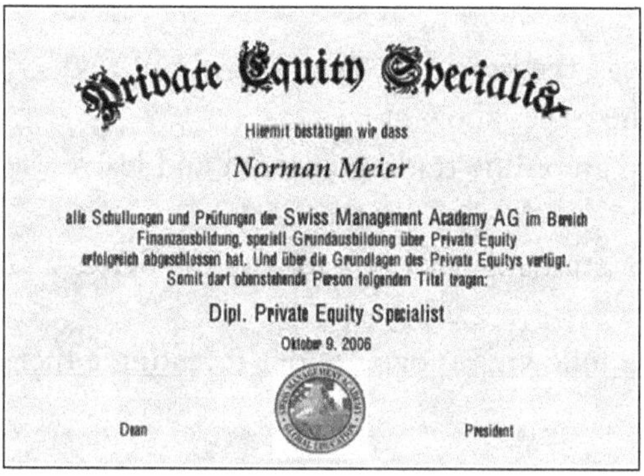
Private Equity Specialist

Hiermit bestätigen wir dass

Norman Meier

alle Schullungen und Prüfungen der Swiss Management Academy AG im Bereich Finanzausbildung, speziell Grundausbildung über Private Equity erfolgreich abgeschlossen hat. Und über die Grundlagen des Private Equitys verfügt. Somit darf obenstehende Person folgenden Titel tragen:

Dipl. Private Equity Specialist

Oktober 9. 2006

Dean President

- **Marketing and Lead Generation:** The new trainee must learn how to generate new leads. It is expected that a new trainee will generate at least 5 new leads per day. Ideally, 10 new leads per day are the goal.

- **Sales, Openings and Loadings:** The goal for someone new is to learn how to close a deal on the phone. In the first 3 months the goal is to close a few clients (openings, smaller amounts). The trainee will still need help from a more experienced sales person.
- **Test Private Equity:** The main test to get the basic knowledge is the Private Equity test.
- Test geology, energy, gold and oil: Depending on the product and industry, a separate test is necessary to learn the basics about the topic.
- **Basic financial knowledge about stocks:** The trainee must have a basic understanding of stocks and the stock market. This knowledge can be learned by studying the first few chapters of the Series 7 book and through practical examples in the market.
- **Sales Training:** A big part of being successful in this business is the ability to sell over the phone. An extensive sales training is necessary to learn all the skills to sell stocks to private investors.
- **Apprenticeship (3-month training):** In the first 3 months the goal is to learn everything about Private Equity, the sales process, the product and the industry. The main goal is to generate new leads, close a few deals and pass all the tests.
- **Sales Organization:** After successful completion of the first three months, the trainee will receive a permanent job as a Private Equity Broker and will raise money every month for the sales organization while earning commissions.
- **Intermediaries:** The goal is also to build a network of new intermediaries so that new clients and money will come from that network.

PART 2

ENTREPRENEURSHIP

CHAPTER 10

JUST OVER BROKE?

> I told my boss three companies were after me and I needed a raise to stay at my present job. He asked which three companies were interested. I said: gas, electric and cable!

Warning: Scam Alert!

Millions of people worldwide have fallen for the "40-40-40 scam"! The "40-40-40 scam" is where you make someone else rich by working 40+ hours a week for 40 years, and try to retire on 40% of what you couldn't afford to live off in the first place! It is also commonly known as: "A JOB".

The rat race

> You were born to do more than just go to work, pay bills and die.

Our parents' generation was told to do well in school so that they can get a well-paid job. After the Second World War, the economy needed to be rebuilt and many new companies grew out of that time.

The first world took advantage of cheap production of the third world and things were booming in the late 1900s. But in the new millennium things have changed.

People got stuck in the rat race paying for bills just to maintain their current lifestyle and things have gotten harder for many people.

Doing well in school and getting a good job simply isn't working anymore. You have to do more. Times have changed again.

In order to do well in the 21st century you must start your own business if you want to be financially successful. And since we are now in the information age you need to incorporate the Internet in your strategy.

There are many new and unbelievable stories about the new Internet millionaires. Regular people who have harnessed the power and the leverage of the Internet have changed become the new super rich.

Lack of money is the problem

Many couples fight over money. Lack of money and the financial pressure are the number one reason for divorce and marital problems.

Lack of money creates more worry and fear. People get physically six and because they are lacking money. A doctor once said that the main cause of illness is "the cancer of the wallet".

The old ways of thinking

Old way: Job = security = good life New way: Your own business = great lifestyle = good life

Many people are stuck because they still use "old techniques and principles" that have worked 20 or 30 years ago.

But gradually people have lost more and more sales and money because they are still mentally stuck doing the same things that they used to do.

If you don't realize that times have changed you will become a relict. You will go down with all the others who are still stubborn about how business is "supposed to work".

You can be one of the new winners of this time if you can adapt to change and realize that how money is made is different than before.

Disadvantages of having a job

Joke:

The owner of the company where I work pulled up in his brand new BMW this morning.
Employee: *Wow, that's a really nice car boss!*
Boss: *Let me tell you something: If you set goals, work hard, and act determined, I could get an even better one next year!*

Disadvantage 1: Getting paid by the hour

Selling your own time will never make you rich.

If you have a job you are by contract required to work 40 hours per week for an hourly rate. This is the maximum amount of money that you can make.

If you work 8 hours per day and you make $15 per hour, then you have two options to increase your salary:

1. You can work overtime (=more hours)
2. You can get an increase per hour (=getting a raise)

But the problem is that there is a limit to the amount of hours that you can work in a day. You can maybe work 10 or 12 hours but eventually there is a limit.

You can do well in your job and because your boss appreciates your extra effort he will pay you a few dollars more.

In the end, there is a limit to the amount that you can earn and it is not the best system to become financially independent.

> By working faithfully eight hours a day you may eventually get to be boss and work twelve hours a day. (Robert Frost)

Disadvantage 2: No real security

People used to talk about "job security". But job security is a myth. You can lose your job within 2 weeks in America. If your company is in trouble, you make a mistake or you have a low performance, you will be out of a job.

Having a job is risky because you are NOT in control of your destiny. Someone else decides whether to keep you or to fire you.

If you are self-employed on the other hand and generate income from your own efforts, no one can fire you. The market can't fire you.

Disadvantage 3: You make someone else rich instead of you

> If you have to work hard anyway in life, you should work hard on your own business and eventually get rich.

If you don't work for yourself, you are working for someone else's goals. You will help someone else to make more money.

If you give your time in exchange for money, you have **no leverage** to make more money.

Disadvantage 4: No freedom, no holidays

You can't just NOT show up for work if you don't feel like it. And you can't travel the world for months on end and work from your laptop if you have a job.

A job usually ties you to a location like an office. But if you have an online business, you are free to work from anywhere in the world.

You can make your own hours and work during the night if you are a night owl. You can use the freedom and flexibility to be there for your kids or enjoy your hobbies.

<u>Disadvantage 5:</u> Boss tells you what to do

> The only time some people work like a horse
> is when the boss rides them.
> Gabriel Heatter

If you worked for yourself, you are in charge of your fate and there is no limit to what you can earn.

People want to be in charge of their own fate and they want to make their own decisions. It can feel very degrading if you have a boss who tells you what to do all the time and "bosses" you around.

> I was well motivated. What I wanted to do was work for myself.
> I had twenty-two jobs before I started my business at the age of
> twenty-three and I didn't want one more boss telling me what
> to do. So I was motivated simply because I didn't want a boss.
> Barbara Corcoran

"Advantages" of having a job

Having a job is not a bad thing in general. Having a job for a few years, earning some money and learning about business is good thing. But having a job for **40 years** is BAD!

Never having the courage to break out the cycle of being an employee is a bad thing. Unless of course, you never have the ambition to amount to anything special in life and achieve financial independence. In that case, stop reading right here. I wish you all the best. But if you want more, then please continue.

> The only person who can give you security is you!

Job security is a myth. In order to have "job security" is to continuously learning and improving yourself so you don't become obsolete and your services and you contribution is something that people pay money for.

But there are also a few things that a job is good for. It can help you to get prepared to become a great entrepreneur.

Here is how:

1. The average entrepreneur worked for 10 years in a specific field or industry before he or she started his or her own business.
2. The average entrepreneur knows everything about his or her industry and is able to identify an opportunity in that field.
3. A job can be springboard for your future career as an entrepreneur. You will learn business skills, your market, how to deal with employees, how an organization is structured, etc.
4. A consistent paycheck can give you the temporary security to build your own business during your free time.
5. You can learn how an organization is support to be run so that you will have an example for your future company.

Having a job is nothing bad. But it is not supposed to be the long-term solution for financial success.

The 3 vehicles

> You can get there with your bicycle or in
> your Ferrari. The choice is yours.

In order to achieve financial success, you need to think outside the box. You need to become aware that there are more options to you available than simply looking for a "better job".

There are four ways or vehicles how you can make money:

Vehicle 1: Job
Vehicle 2: Self-employed professional (you create sales yourself)
Vehicle 3: Entrepreneur (operation makes money without you constantly being there)

You can compare it like driving in a vehicle: You can use your bicycle, a regular car or a Ferrari. How do you think you can get fastest from A to B?

Do the math

Even though the numbers vary from industry to industry, the average salary of all occupations in America was $47,230.

If you were an executive who spent 20 years or more working on his career, the average salary of managers is $112,490.

Many people who left their regular jobs and started their own business earn **several hundred thousand dollars and more.**

Why would you waste 40 years in a job and not get paid what you could earn?

The victim mentality trap

> To perform with greatness, you must understand
> who you are in this world.

The number one reason is fear. The second reason is lack of knowledge. The third reason is "tradition". It simply doesn't occur to some people to start their own business because their parents did the same.

The next reason is no clarity in regards to what they want and who they are.

Many people also feel like they have no other choice and they are victims of their circumstances.

But you always have a choice in life. You are not a prisoner of your own life because you made some bad choices in the past. If you created a lot of debt or financial liabilities and the only way to pay for them is by working in a job that you hate, then your life seems to be an unhappy one.

Stop playing the victim and by giving all of your power away!

There are other options available to you. You just have to become aware of them. Staying in a job that makes you unhappy is not the solution.

Getting awareness

Transform disappointments into successes.

Humans will only make major changes when a situation becomes so bad that they no longer accept it. It is when they break out of their comfort zone.

Gain some power back today!

The first step is to gain awareness that you have MANY OTHER OPTIONS available to make money. You don't have to stay in a job or situation that kills your spirit.

Make a list of all the skills and talents that you have. Then brainstorm what kind of industries you could work in.

Get rid of your job and build a successful business

> Don't let someone who gave up on his or her dreams talk you out of YOURS.

This is your life and you should be happy. Work is a major part of your life. Everyone has to work. All the millionaire and billionaires also work all the time. No one stops working because they have enough money. Money can make your life easier and more comfortable but we all need a mission in our lives. We all have a purpose.

What is your purpose in life? How could you live a life that you enjoy while making money at the same time?

This life is not a test or a preparation for something else. This is your time. Live your life now!

The Internet has changed everything

> I can learn about any topic like for example: rocket science. My parents didn't have that opportunity growing up. There is so much opportunity out there but people are still blind.

Is there something better out there for you? Of course there is! Everything and anything is out there waiting for you to be discovered.

There are thousands of options available to you to make money. The world has opened up and everything is available to you. You just need to find it and then make a decision.

> The Internet has changed the economy. It has changed how people make money. It is a new age! The rules have changed.

Money = value for someone else

MONEY is an EXCHANGE of VALUE. In order to make money you need to provide a value for others. The more VALUE your bring the MORE MONEY you will make.

Therefore you need to find or develop a product or a service that is of value to others and that they are willing to pay money for.

Once you have created your product (= prototype) you need to duplicate it, use leverage (= Internet) and use sales and marketing to sell it.

Using leverage

Using leverage can make all the difference. Archimedes who lived 287 to 212 before Christ said: *Give me a lever that is long enough and a place to stand on and I will move the entire world.*

All successful entrepreneurs use some form of leverage in their business. Leverage is the crucial factor that sets apart normal businesses from very successful ones.

I have put together a list of ten forms of leverage:

1. **Other people:** If you want to grow, you can't do everything by yourself. You will need employees that will do the work for you. Hiring people is the first form of leverage. Having a job means you are the leverage for someone else.
2. **More stores or branches:** The more sales channels that a business has, the more sales it will have. Ten stores will produce more sales than just one store.
3. **Other people's money:** This can come from banks or investors. The more money you have the faster you can expand and grow. The faster you will make more money again.
4. **The knowledge of other people:** You can't know everything. Certain specific information can ensure that you are getting ahead

quicker and better. By hiring experts you have an advantage over your competition.

5. **The Internet:** If you offer your products 24 hours a day 365 days a year to be purchased online, you can potentially make more sales than if you only did it the conventional way. The speed and the amount of people that you can reach within seconds has changed the way business works.
6. **Cooperation with other companies:** If you are trying to find new clients you might consider sharing your client list with another company and vice versa.
7. **Sales teams or organizations:** Having your own sales group might increase your sales power enormously. Instead of you trying to get clients all by yourself, ten sales people for example will get ten times more clients.
8. **The right list or target group:** If you are looking for a specific target group of customers, you can also buy or rent a list from a list broker. Sometimes having the right group will lead to increase your success dramatically. If you have to eliminate the first hundred people that are not suitable for your product, you might lose a lot of time finding the right clients.
9. **Capital markets:** Using the possibilities that the financial markets offer can be a huge leverage. Having more money means that you can execute your plans faster and better. Getting a loan or investors is leverage.
10. **Financial professionals or firms:** Knowing the right person can be great leverage. Sometimes one person is the reason why you can get a big contract or access to money.

There are also other forms of leverage: talents of other people, contacts, credibility, resources, technologies, software, famous people, reputation, and production without having to pay first, and so on.

> If you are not using leverage, you don't earn as much money as you could. An employee uses no leverage.

The turning point: The steps for lasting CHANGE

We don't grow when things are easy. We grow when we face challenges.

Many people resist change but change is necessary if you want to improve your situation. I have put together a list of 12 steps that will help you to create lasting change.

Step 1: Awareness

Awareness is always the first step for anything that requires change. You need to be aware that your previous mental attitude has brought you to where you are today. In order to move forward and into a new and better direction you need to **change your mental mindset.**

You need to overcome self-doubt and fear. You must follow your heart, not give up and overcome obstacles.

Success is all in your **mind** and it starts with your **mental attitude.**

Step 2: Self-discovery

You can only excel and be wildly successful if you **use your talents and skills**. You cannot be successful in an area where you have weaknesses. You can't be good at everything. You will never be successful in an area where you don't have talents or strengths.

The first step here is to find yourself. What are your main **skills, talents and strengths**?

Make a list of all the areas and skills where you posses the biggest amounts of strengths and knowledge.

Step 3: Self-confidence

Believing in yourself is key in becoming successful. You need to have a high level of self-confidence to be successful.

You need to develop courage, have a good self-image of yourself, believe in your abilities, have conviction and make decisions.

Self-confidence and mental strength is foundation for success in anything that you do. Fear and lack of self-confidence is what is holding you back.

Step 4: Use the right vehicle

You simply cannot be wildly successful if you have a job. You need to "change the vehicle" (from job to your own business). You need to make the transition from having a job to being an entrepreneur by starting your own business (the right vehicle).

Step 5: Change your habits

Your daily habits have brought you to exactly this point in your life. In order to change your life you need to change your habits.

You need to **stop doing certain things** and **start doing new things**.

For example: Stop watching TV and spending time with people who "waste" your time.

New habits: self-discipline, work more hours, exercising, reading, learning, and building your business.

It is important how you manage your time and what activities you do.

Step 6: Use leverage

The key to success in business is leverage. You need to use the **right tools** and the **right strategy** to get ahead faster and better.

The Internet, money, knowledge, contacts and other things will help you to get ahead in business.

Step 7: Clarity

You cannot hit a target that you cannot see. You need to get absolute clarity in regards to your goals.

Clarity means: developing ideas in detail, setting goals, crystal clear planning, plan of action, strategy and defining milestones.

Step 8: Business ideas

In order to create business so that you can make money you need to find a **product or service**. This means that you need to create something that is **value for others**.

How can you create a product or service creates value for someone and that people are willing to pay money for?

Step 9: Improve your skills

But in order to get ahead personally, you also need to work on yourself.

Besides learning about "Personal Development" products, I would also recommend reading books about business and marketing, learning about your field / industry, improving your communication and sales skills and getting better in your areas of strength.

Success is a series of little improvements and steps that you do on a daily basis. The number one reason why you are not yet where you could be is because you are lacking some knowledge.

You need to educate yourself continuously in order to get better. This means that you should learn everything about business, sales, marketing and online strategies.

People who are the best at what they do are avid readers and learn something new every day to improve their knowledge and skills.

Make a pact with yourself to constantly improve your skills by continuous learning.

Step 10: Sales and Marketing

Sales and marketing are the foundation for any business transaction and therefore money in your life.

You should focus on improving your knowledge and skills in sales and marketing.

No matter what your company does or what business you are in, sales and marketing are the main factors for success.

Step 11: Body

As a human being you have "Body-mind-soul connection".

In order to be successful and happy you need to make sure you are healthy so that you can function well.

Physical exercise, nutrition, lifestyle and spiritual connection are the basis for a good life.

Step 12: Happiness

People who have a purpose in life tend to be happier. Your family, your relationships, the quality of your life, piece of mind, making a contribution and making an impact in the world and other people's lives are key pillars of your life and happiness.

Basically, it is the reason WHY you do the things you do and it is your driving force.

> Take some alone time and empty pad of paper. Go to a quiet place for a couple of days and rewrite your life.

Life as an entrepreneur

> If you think running your own business is tough…try going back and getting a job working for someone else…(Brad Sugars)

If you feel that your life as an entrepreneur is hard then try going back to work as an employee once you experienced that kind of freedom!

Being an entrepreneur can be great but it also comes with a price. Buy paying that price is much easier than having to feel like a slave every day doing a job that you don't like.

If you currently have a job but you are unhappy with it, then you must break free from that life.

> The most important thing when making the transition is to focus on **activities that generate income** and not on activities that are task-oriented just to keep busy!

The number one reason why people become entrepreneurs is because of the freedom that they gain from it. But it is only the freedom to choose your own hours. You still have to work regardless!

The second reason is the potential to earn more money. If you structure your business the right way, you can earn much more than an employee.

The third reason is to be your own boss and making your own decisions. Some people are simply not "wired" to take orders (like myself).

The fourth reason why people go into business for themselves is to do something that they love. But remember: 80% is what you love, 20% is still stuff that you have to do. But that is still better than hating 80% and liking 20%.

And the fifth reason is that people want to make an impact in the world. What does your heart yearn for?

Definition of success

> Success is liking yourself, liking what you do, and liking how you do it. (Maya Angelou)

Your personal goals define if you are successful or not. But in my opinion, you are successful if you can support your current lifestyle doing what you love. If you can at least generate enough money every month to pay for your main expenses then you can consider yourself to be one of the lucky ones.

You can always grow and expand. But being able to support yourself with your own business is the first step and it has power. It means that you have the power to make things happen on your own.

If your monthly expenses are $5000 and you can create a business that generates that, then you are financially independent from a job.

It is great to want millions and you can get them later. But your first milestone should be to generate enough income to cover your monthly expenses.

John Reese, the Internet marketing guru, says that if you can at least generate $1 in profit with your system, then you have it made. All you have to do afterwards is to duplicate and expand your efforts. But if you main concept is working, then you are on the right track.

So start with that in mind before you target the millions. It seems very doable and encouraging. Live by the motto: Start small and finish big!

This is your life – go get them Tiger!

> Life is like a tennis game. You can still win the game – no matter what score says.

You can be behind 0-6, 0-6, 0-5 and 0-40 in a tennis game and still win the game. The same is true for life. You might have made bad choice, be already in your second half of life or not where you want to be.

But as long as you are breathing, you can still change your life. You can still win the game of life – just like in tennis!

There is a book called "Late bloomers". It contains stories of many famous people throughout history. Many of them found their calling in their second half of their lives.

People like Louise Hay, Colonel Sanders, Stephen Covey, Miguel Cervantes, Coco Chanel, Ferdinand von Zeppelin, Paul Cezanne, Harry S. Truman and Charles Darwin became successful and famous later in life.

Your past is not your future. You can change at any time. You can still have everything you ever wanted.

Can you really be wildly successful if you are fat and overweight?

I really don't want to insult anyone with my next question. My next question is a little bit provocative. But...

> Can you really perform at your best if you feel fat, sluggish and have low physical energy?

Do you think you can reach maximum performance in business and life if you are overweight, feel tired all the time and have low physical and mental energy?

Be completely honest with yourself.

Of course you can have a certain degree of success but you will not achieve maximum results if you are in poor physical condition.

A healthy mind can only exist in a healthy body. Even the old Greeks knew that principle.

In the end what really counts is your **energy level**. You will need physical, mental and emotional energy to perform at your best. And it all starts with your body.

That is why you must first (or at least parallel to everything else) focus on getting fit and healthy. This means two things: Diet and exercise.

Your diet needs to help you to have more energy and to lose excess weight.

Exercise will help you to increase your energy level and to develop the same traits and habits necessary that business success requires: Self-discipline, stamina, being goal-oriented, following through, etc.

Getting fit and healthy is the starting point for your business success.

The greatest single cause of failure is fear and a poor self-image.

I remember personally that I was at the height of my personal financial success AFTER I had become into the best shape of my life. I had just finished two bodybuilding competitions and only 2 ½ years later I became a self-made millionaire.

Things started to get worse in business when I gained 60 pounds afterwards and moved to the land of unlimited food consumption (= America).

And things started to improve again when I started to exercise and go on a diet. Do you see the connection?

The starting point

> Actual statement from Donald Trump: *"Things have not been easy for me. I started out with a small loan of a million dollars from my father..."*

And you thought you had it bad...ha,ha,...

Take some time and think about your life and your goals. You need to get clarity in regards to your goals and your future.

The starting point is to **decide** what you want. Manifestation starts with your thoughts. The second step is to **write down** your thoughts into a plan. The third step is to take action and do something every day.

If I had a job I would think about starting my own business and brainstorm for as long as it took to find the perfect idea for you. It has to fit your personality, skills and strengths.

Working on your ideas and developing a plan is one part. Parallel to that you should focus on continuous learning and getting physically and mentally stronger so that you are ready for future challenges.

Remember: Success is all in your mind and a stronger mind comes from a stronger body.

Four simple steps to get started in business

From a practical point of view, there are four steps that you need to be aware of. If you decide to start your own business, then you will need customers. In today's day and age, customers are online.

<u>Step 1: Go to where the money/traffic already is (= Google and Facebook)</u>

This is where you should start to advertise your new products. Google gets 3.5 Billion searches EVERY SINGLE DAY. Facebook has 936 Million users EVERY SINGLE DAY.

Step 2: Don't reinvent the wheel

Copy a person who is already successful. Success is based on modeling other successful people. You can put your own twist on it to make it special or your product. But you will get rich by modeling other people and strategies.

Step 3: The power of your own power

Even though you might not have had the success you wanted up until now, you can change that at any time and start new.

You are not happy with something in your life. The only question is if you are going to do something about it or not.

The only person who can create changes is you. No one will do it for you.

Step 4: Be willing to do what others are not willing to do

Winners do what losers aren't willing to do.

You need to be willing to work hard, pull all-nighter if necessary, and change your daily habits if you want greatness.

Failure is not an option for you. If you don't give up and keep learning you will find a way to create a better life for you.

CHAPTER 11

ENTREPRENEURSHIP: RAISE MONEY TO START YOUR BUSINESS

> It's time to start living the life you have imagined.

Give yourself permission to live a big life. Become who you were meant to be – Stop playing small. You were meant for greater things.

You can continue to live and work in mediocrity for the next 40 years or break out of the masses and become something special and greater.

Do you want to change the world? Do you want to become a successful businessperson? Do you want to build a multi million-dollar company and be proud of your accomplishment?

I am going to share my business model for financing any company with you. When I started with my first company in 2005, I was able to raise $40 million from 500 investors in a matter of 2.5 years and create a publicly listed company with market capitalization of $300 million.

The company was called Hemis Corporation and it was a gold exploration company. It had gold projects in Mexico and the US. I was the main shareholder with a net worth of over $123 million and my monthly income at the time was over $100,000. I had over 60 people working for me and I owned a new $1.5 million house, drove a Porsche and I lived in a luxury apartment overlooking the city that cost me $10,000 per month.

How was I able to create such a company and live such a lavish lifestyle?

I had a dream of being a successful entrepreneur and becoming a self-made millionaire. Then I started my first corporation and decided to raise money from investors. I didn't know exactly what I was doing at first but I knew I wanted to create something big. The main thing was having the courage to have a big vision. You need to think big and just go for it. I believe that having a driving force and fire inside of you was the key to my success.

> Show the Universe that you are not afraid of big numbers. Have a bold vision.

Start your own business

> It doesn't matter if you flip burgers, bricks or houses. Just don't sit on your ass all day flipping channels. Hustle. (Denzel Washington)

If you are broke, depressed and unhappy because you are stuck in a job, then it is time to change your life.

You will never achieve financial independence as an employee. It just doesn't work. It is the wrong strategy. Saving money every month won't make you rich. You need to start your own business, go out there and take a risk. Otherwise things will never dramatically improve.

If you are not getting ahead in your own business, then it is time to focus on sales and marketing to change your outcome.

The keys to success in business are:

1. **Clarity** (detailed goals)
2. **Sales power** (your ability to communicate and close deals)
3. **Marketing** (generating leads)
4. **Products** (first product and real moneymaker)
5. **Action** (talk to 100 clients each day)

You need to be **very clear** in regards to what you want to achieve. You need to set very clear goals and develop a plan or strategy.

The main keys to succeeding in business are **sales and marketing**. You need to **generate leads** and then be able to **close those clients with your sales ability**.

Everything is a numbers game and the more leads you generate, the more opportunities you have to close a client.

You need to define what products you can sell and how much they cost. Typically, it is better to create a product that generates $2000, $3000 or $5000 in profit rather than selling a product for less than $100. Whatever product or service you are selling must have the potential to make you at least $100,000 in sales per month.

But the most important thing is that you **take massive action**. What do I mean by that? It means working at least **10 hours per day** and spending **80% of that time on trying to close sales and talking to customers.** Without self-discipline success is impossible. Period.

Not sure what to do? No clarity? Get clarity first and then act!

Life won't give you what you deserve. It will give you what you demand from it. Get clear about what it is you want and have the courage to bring it into existence.

> The key to success is to start before you are ready. (Marie Forleo)

It is never the right time and you will never be 100% ready. But that also means that right now (today!) is the right time to get started.

I once started with a diet. I really wasn't mentally ready to "suffer" but I started anyway. I lost 10 pounds in 5 days and just kept going even though I didn't feel like I was ready yet to begin my diet.

The secret to success is "Just do it". Get clarity and get started. No matter where you are today. The same is true for anything in life.

> I had to make you uncomfortable, otherwise you never would have moved. – Universe

Mr. Olympia – Dorian Yates

In an interview people have asked six Mr. Olympia Bodybuilding Champion Dorian Yates what the secret to his success was.

He said that the principles were the same for bodybuilding as well as for success in business.

When people tell him that they want to become a millionaire, he asks them the following question:

- *"How are you going to get there?"*

He is basically saying that you need a roadmap or a plan. Just like you would need a map if you wanted to go from Berlin to Rome.

Dorian Yates was known for his attention to detail and planning when it came to nutrition and training. He wrote down every single weight, food and number in a journal. He planned absolutely every step of the way. He left nothing to chance.

The same is true for financial success.

Most people are unrealistic dreamers without an actual plan. But if you want to become a millionaire with your business, you first need a realistic plan or a roadmap.

This program should help you to create such a plan. Success takes time and hard work. Don't be fooled by people on social media who seem to do better than you.

> Don't let the Internet rush you. No one is posting their failures.

Business model / system / proof of concept

In order to get started you will need a **product or service to sell.**

Your business should not just be a business that makes $50,000 or $100,000 per year. It should be a business that makes at least $1 million per year but should ideally be a business that has a multi-million dollar potential.

You need probably not just one product but several products that you can sell. But one of them is the big money maker.

But you need to start somewhere with your first product. What does your business model look like? How do you make money? How could you make money?

The first step is to find something that works. This is called "**Proof of concept**". Once you have something that works, you can copy your system and do it in a different location. Once that works you can multiply and expand it.

The actual plan

> An idiot with a plan can beat a genius without a plan. (Warren Buffet)

If I start a company, I usually make a plan like this:

1. Define Industry (e.g. natural resources like gold, oil, etc.)
2. Acquire a project (e.g. gold mine property) – I get an inexpensive option first
3. Incorporate a new corporation in the US
4. Create the marketing materials

5. Raise money from investors by selling shares of my company (European investors)
6. Use the money to develop the project
7. Take the company public in the stock market (IPO)
8. Create a valuable company with a solid share price and market capitalization
9. Get more money from institutional investors to make the company bigger
10. Sell some of the shares in the market and turn stocks into cash

The basic idea is to find **a project that has a multi-million dollar potential** and to raise the money from private investors to fund it.

In general, I need to **raise the first $1 million in the first 12 months** from private investors.

I will use some of the money to live, some to develop the project and some for the legal cost of the IPO.

<u>Example: $1 million raised from private investors</u>

$100,000	Personal salary or commission
$200,000	IPO cost
$500,000	Project cost
$100,000	Expenses like office, administration, etc.
<u>$100,000</u>	Capital reserves
$1 million	

In order to raise **$1 million in 12 months** from private investors, I need to raise at least **$100,000 per month in 10 months** (excluding summer holidays and Christmas break).

<u>How do you raise $100,000 per month?</u>

You need to talk to lots of different potential investors.

You could…

- Get 1 investor with $100,000
- Get 2 investors with $50,000
- Get 4 investors with $25,000
- Get 10 investors with $10,000
- Get 20 investors with $5,000
- Get mix thereof

In order to find private investors, **you first need to generate leads of potential investors** that you can talk to.

You get leads online by **placing an ad that leads to a landing page** and then follow up with the prospect or you can put together a small mini **marketing call center of 5 people** who do nothing but cold calls each day.

The goal of the marketing call center is to generate new leads of potential investors each day. Each cold caller has to do **at least 100 calls per day and generate at least 5 good quality leads** of potential investors.

The next step is for an experienced sales person or broker to follow up and to try to sell the investment.

If you have a team of 5 marketing people, you should generate at least **25 new leads each day or 125 leads per week or 500 leads per month.**

The goal is to generate at least **$100,000 per month** in raised capital from investors.

> Use the resources available to take command
> of your life. Focus on what you want.
> The Universe favors boldness. You have the
> ability to manifest something big.
> Be courageous enough to define that goal.

Setting up your office and getting started

> If you cannot do great things, do small things in a great way.

In order for you to raise $100,000 per month, you don't need a large team. You can start with 3 or 4 people. 2 people are responsible for marketing calls and 2 people (including you) sell the shares to the investors.

When I started with my very first office, I hired a girl for a 50% position. Her name was Laura and she took care of all my administrational needs. Because I needed to pay her at the end of the month and I was freed up from doing anything office or paperwork related, I had no more excuses but to sell. I focused all my time on talking to investors. And because I did that, I succeeded. I raised enough money to pay her salary and things started to take off from there.

When I started my sales organization in Zurich, we also started out with 3 sales people. I had the office manager; the sales team leader and a marketing cold caller. We started with a small team of 3 people and within one month we were 10 people. Two months later the team grew to 25 people. Each sales person had a friend that they brought and we grew really quickly.

The result was that we raised between $1 million and $2 million each month.

> Once you have the office – the sales people will follow.

The main thing is to have an office first and set up working spots. Once you are prepared, the sales people will come really fast.

When I started my office in California, I hired 5 marketing sales people within 1 week because everything was already set up.

You don't need a lot to get started. Start with a few people and then grow the team. Get

Get an assistant even if it is only for 50%. Have no excuses for the administrational part – leave it to your assistant. This was a game changer for me.

You are in charge of sales. You are responsible for making sales in the beginning.

Work 5 days per week and spend 10 hours per day on talking to customers.

Ways to raise money

Everyone wants to eat but few are willing to hunt. (Wolf)

If it were necessary, you could do it all by yourself. You could do 100 cold calls per day by yourself by using the phone book. You would create 5 new good leads and get rejected 95 times.

Of course this is very frustrating and lots of energy gets lost but it is possible if you have no other choice.

Maybe you need to do something like this in the very beginning or during a time when you lost all your money and have to start over.

100 calls per day
90 "bad" calls
10 "positive calls"
2 really good leads
10 good leads per week = 2 closed deals per week
5 clients per month
$50,000 raised

Everything is a numbers game! Stay positive, work hard and make it happen.

Just remember that the founder of Starbucks, Howard D. Schulz, had to talk to over **250 different people** just to get **12 investors** when he first started. This also means that he got **rejected about 240 times** before he got the initial capital to make this dream come true. We all know how big Starbucks has become.

Ideally, you want to build a team of sales people who will do the selling with you. If you have the ability to rent an office and hire 5 marketing people who will make the cold calls and create 5 leads each per day, then you can follow up with 25 people yourself and sell your deal.

Once you have reached that level, you can turn some of your people into sales people and eventually you will end up with a team of about 25 people. In that case you no longer have to do any kind of selling and you can focus on developing your company.

One of the best ways to get investors is by having intermediaries. These are financial advisors who already have clients and will refer them to you by getting a 10-15% commission of all monies raised.

And finally you can contact investment firms and mutual funds and get a few million dollars at a time.

The 4 levels of raising money

1. **YOU:** You sell directly to clients
2. **YOUR SALES PEOPLE**: Your own team of sales people who sell
3. **3RD PARTIES**: Intermediaries and other people with existing clientele sell for you
4. **INSTITUTIONAL INVESTORS:** Mutual funds, professional investment companies, etc. who can invest millions at a time

Increase…

1. Number of clients
2. Number of sales people
3. Number of intermediaries (financial advisors)
4. Talk to more investment firms, mutual funds, etc.

New markets

One of my friends did a private placement and took a company public. The financing was for $60 million. **$55 million of that money came from China**.

If you have a contact in a different country, region or market, things could really change for the better. Maybe focus your time and energy on finding those kinds of contacts. Every one of us knows someone who knows someone. Make a list of all your contacts and think outside of the box.

Fight every day to earn $5000

20 days per month x $5000 per day = $100,000 per month

You have 10 hours of working time per day available to close a deal. The goal has to be to close **one deal per day** where you make $5000 or raise $5000 from an investor.

Either your product or service costs $5000 or you sell shares to an investor who invests at least $5000 (or even $10,000) per day.

If you work Monday to Friday excluding the weekend and holidays, you should have at least 20 net working days per month. Typically, a regular month has an average of 22 days per month.

The main thing is that you have enough leads to call or contact. If you call enough potential clients or have enough meetings per day to **close one deal of $5000**, then you will have either earned or raised $100,000 per month.

If you do this consistently, you will have $1.2 million per year. You can comfortably live off $200,000 and use the $1 million to invest into your project.

Focus on generating enough quality leads. Also, you need to talk to enough people in the 10-hour window and be selling all the time.

> Luck is what you have left after you give 100 percent. (Langston Coleman)

You will find that you will get lucky, too. One day you will not close any deals but on other days you will close a deal for $50,000 or even $100,000.

But this only works, if you work. This means putting in the time on the telephone to sell.

> If you give up at the first sign of struggle you are not ready to be successful.

Employees don't cost you money - they actually make you money

> The right employee will make you money - not cost you money.

Don't think how much they will cost you but rather how much money they will make you.

An employee should make you $5000 per month (for example) and not just cost you $2000 per month. The more employees you have, the more money you make.

Your goal has to be to build a sales team of at least 25 people. You should start with about 5 and increase it to 10 in about 3 months. From there the goal has to be 25 employees.

You need to have the leverage and sales power of 25 people to bring in enough money each month. This is the most important strategic decision you will ever make to turn your sales from small amounts to big amounts.

Marketing = Lead generation

Most people fail in business for one big reason: poor marketing! (T. Harv Eker)

If you had enough leads to talk to every day, would you be able to close deals and make sales? Of course you would! This is the easy part. The more challenging part is to find the people that are open to talk to you and who fit your client profile.

In order to succeed in business, you must become a master in marketing. Marketing cannot be delegated. It is the job of the boss or CEO. It is your job and that's why you must learn absolutely everything about it.

Structure equals success. (Christian Zimmermann)

The right set up with marketing, sales and employees is the key to any success in business. The entire process must be structured efficiently so that there is a **daily flow of new leads and new sales.**

Marketing is always a two-step process. The first step is to generate a lead of a person who is generally speaking interested in what you have to offer. Here is what you should consider:

<u>Generating leads and sales over the phone</u>

- Non-threatening first contact
- Free or inexpensive product to try out
- Receiving general information about the product or company
- Huge benefits for the client

Once you have a lead, the job of the sales person takes over. The first contact has to be non-binding and non-threatening. You simply send him some general information.

The actual sales call however that follows needs to focus on the closing a deal. In every new relationship you need to first focus on developing rapport and trust.

Optimize your work environment

> You won't be at your best in the wrong environment.

You can't become successful in your pajamas and a messy environment at home alone and talk about money and success. You need to improve your environment. You need to surround yourself with people who are motivated. You need to get dressed in a business suit and feel successful.

Your environment is so important. The energy from which you operate is key. If you have negative people in your environment, then you need to get rid of them. If you don't feel good or proud of what you do and how you to it, then you must change something.

You need to create a place where you like to be and where you can attract success.

If you work in a "shithole of an office" and you are ashamed of working there, then move into a better office. The shift in your attitude will justify the extra cost.

> If you hate the work you are doing and are just turning up so that you can survive, then it is not going to create **energy that attracts abundance**.

If what you do makes your soul smile, then the joy that you radiate will attract good things back to you. Attracting abundance has to start inside you.

Gratitude is a key factor in creating abundance. Be grateful for what you have today and you will attract more of the good things in your life.

Have you ever thought about the fact that it costs absolutely nothing to feel wealthy? How would you feel if you won the lottery tomorrow? Would there be a massive shift in your energy? If so, you still have a lot of room to bridge the gap between where you are today and where you ideally want to be financially.

Your bank account should not be determining how you feel about your financial state. You have the capacity to increase your energy, to connect and align it where your true desire lies.

> If you want to become king, you have to act
> and feel like a king already today.

Money raising

> If your idea is good, the money will come.

Raise the first $1 million and prove that you can make good business decisions. This is called "**Proof of management**". You have proven that you are capable of receiving money and make a project profitable. Now that you have proven this, you can be trusted with more money to do it again.

In order to have the working capital to make your underlying business a success, you should consider raising money from private investors by selling shares of your company.

You could in fact focus in the first year on nothing else but on raising money so that you can later on fund your projects.

You could raise $1 million in the first 12 months. You could pay yourself a salary of $100,000 in the first year and then use the $900,000 to make your business successful.

If you bought an oil field and spent $500,000 on drilling for oil, you could potentially generate a producing oil well that generates 100 barrels per day.

The $400,000 that are left over you could use for expansion or taking your company public in the stock market.

100 barrels of oil per day at a price of $70 could generate a gross income of $2.5 million per year for the next 20 years.

Phase 1: Raise $1 million from private investors for your business idea
(Only focus on money raising)

Phase 2: Put your business idea into action and make your company successful
(Focus on business development)

Phase 3: Take your company public in the stock market
(Get more funding to expand)

Example oil and gold companies

Say this out loud: "*Today is the last day of my business struggles.*"

I have created many companies in the past. Some were successful and some didn't do well.

The process is always the same. I first choose an industry like oil, gold or similar. Then I acquire a project by either getting an option or by buying the exploration rights of a piece of land.

The next step is the incorporation in either Nevada or Wyoming. I use these states because they are very flexible. Then I open up a corporate bank account and do the initial filings with the SEC to start the money raising process.

Then I create the marketing materials first. Even though I might not yet own the actual projects, I will secure them and pay for them later with the money that I am going to raise.

Basically, I don't have to start with much money at all. All I do is incorporating a new company and creating professional looking marketing materials.

And because I have done this process many times before and I have all the necessary legal documents from the past, all I do is "copy – paste".

The main key to your long-term success is of course the right deal, project or product. But initially, you don't need anything substantial to get started. A contract, an option or a plan is enough to motivate people to invest.

Everything has to be legal, of course. But as long as investors are aware of the risk and you do everything by the book, you are fine.

Real entrepreneurs don't wait for permission from anyone or anything.

Wisdumb...(or something like it)

Your excuses are lies.

An excuse is a way of promising ourselves we will have the same issue again.

In order to grow, you must be willing to expose your weaknesses. You can only move forward if you are **brutally honest with yourself** and have a **realistic plan of action**.

The main problem is however that most people feel like a victim of their circumstances. They feel like they have no other options. But once you have discovered your own light, you can snatch your power back and the game will change.

Don't give up trying to do what you really want to do in life. Where there is love and inspiration, you can't go wrong. Don't downgrade your dream to match your reality. Upgrade your faith to match your destiny.

All you need to do is having a better strategy. You need a better plan and you need to focus on marketing and sales. These are all skills and tools that can be learned.

Ideally, you want to create a business where you have some profound knowledge or where you have a passion.

> You are who you are and you can't change but you don't have to change, either. It's in your DNA. And it is good who you are. Don't try to be someone you are not.
> (A message in a dream I had)

If you are not doing what you love, you are wasting your time.

Hustle = talking to lots of different people and trying to sell them a something

> Progress = Happiness

Sell something every day. Your goal has to be to **close a deal every single day**. You need to hustle every day and talk to many different potential clients. At the very least you need to send out a new contract to a client every single day.

If you do this consistently for 20 days and each day you send out an offer for $5000, you will generate $100,000 each month.

Every day is a new opportunity and **you need to create the opportunities**. If you have a constant flow of new leads, you should be able to generate a daily flow of new sales.

> *"I wish someone would save me…"*

No one is coming to the rescue! You need to save yourself!

It is the hard truth about making your dreams come true. No one will do it for you.

Don't wait to get hired by someone else. Don't think that someone will discover how great you are and give you a chance. Things don't work this way when it comes to success. People will only give you an opportunity if you do your part first. You need to be proactive and take action first. You need to create a new company, system or business that will attract others – not the other way around. You need to position yourself so that others want to get involved with you when you already have some success.

Be bold and go out there. Start something new. Create your own opportunity and save yourself.

It's better to cross the line and suffer the consequences than to just stare at that line for the rest of your life. Take a risk. This is your life. Either it will work or it won't. But you will never know if you don't try.

Wealth is not about having a lot of money. It's about having a lot of options. The only person who can give you these options is YOU.

> When you think everything is someone else's fault, you will suffer a lot. When you realize that everything springs from yourself, you will learn both peace and joy. (Dalai Lama)

Business relationships and employees

> Ignoring red flags because you want to see the good in people will cost you later.

The most important factor in creating a successful business is your relationships: your business partners, your employees, your clients and your closest friends.

If you have friends with questionable characters and integrity, your life will be more challenging. If you have great business partners, your life will be easier.

Remember that the little things count. If you have a problem with someone who owes you $50, then you will have issues when it comes to $500,000. Don't ignore red flags. Look out for people who talk well and promise you the world but don't act accordingly.

I have met many "parasites" that promised me the world but fell short and left me with unpaid bills hanging later on. Today I can easily spot these people and I stay away from them like the plaque. But when I was younger I trusted the wrong people and lost lots of money by supporting these parasites.

> A man that chases women will run out of money. But a man that chases money will never run out of women.

The same is true for people who are candy to your eyes can be poison to your hearts. Looks can be deceiving. Many men got financially screwed because they turned off their brains and only looked at the face and body of a woman.

A person becomes 10 times more attractive not because of their looks but by their acts of kindness, love, respect, honesty and loyalty they show. Try to look beyond the outside and "see" with your heart.

Always trust your gut. Your brain can be fooled and your heart is an idiot but your gut doesn't lie. If something doesn't feel right, it usually isn't right.

> Evaluate the people in your life: Then promote, demote or terminate. You are the CEO of your life.

Be also careful what you tell people. A friend today could be an enemy tomorrow.

Encourage your employees

> A lot of people have gone further than they thought they could because someone else thought they could. (Zig Ziglar)

Your employees are the most important people in your business life. You need to make sure that you take great care of them. Their emotional well-being is most important in my opinion.

I used to work with lots of great sales people who performed well but were not necessarily good people with integrity.

It's funny how your quality of life improves dramatically when you surround yourself with good, intelligent, kind-hearted, positive and loving people.

All business skills are learnable and people with a positive attitude will always do well eventually. That's why it is important to look at the character and heart of the people who you want to hire.

The quality of people you work with cannot be underestimated. You need good people especially when things get difficult.

> If speaking kindly to plants helps them grow, imagine what speaking kindly to humans can do.

Increase your energy level

The key to manifesting quickly is to have very high energy levels. And the easiest way to increase them is through **physical exercise**. Choose a fun activity and it becomes a reward.

You attract what you are and not what you want. If you feel fit and powerful, you will become more and more powerful in all other areas of your life, too – especially in business and your relationships.

Just like you brush your teeth every day, you should work out every day. Going to the gym or doing some other physical exercise should be treated just as important if not more important as a business appointment. You can't cancel it. It is a necessary part of your success.

Eating a healthy diet is the next important factor. If you feel good physically, you will perform better. Your food and digestion play a huge role.

Every time I drink a green juice with celery, spinach and other vegetables, my energy level goes up.

Every time I eat McDonald's I feel like I need to take a break and rest.

> It's not fat that makes you fat. It is sugar.
> I have finally realized that I need to treat
> sugar the same way I treat heroin.
> It's a no go. I am an addict.

Embrace challenges with open arms

> The most important spiritual growth doesn't happen when you are meditating or on a Yoga mat. It happens in the middle of a conflict, when you are frustrated, angry or scared and you are doing the same old thing, and then suddenly realize that you have a choice to do it differently.

Choose to be happy because it is good for your health. Nothing is worth diminishing your health. Nothing is worth poisoning yourself into stress, anxiety and fear.

Don't wait to be rich to be happy. Happiness is free. Decide to be happy today. Be happy right now. You don't need a reason. You should be happy just because you are alive.

All you can control is yourself and having a positive attitude.

Choose to be positive in every situation – no matter how difficult it may seem. The decision alone to stay positive will very often change the outcome.

Look at life's challenges like a game. You are here to win the game of life. You are given several tasks and challenges and the better you perform, the better your life will be.

Always remember this: Bad times don't last. After a difficult day, there will always be a better day. Take each day and do your best. Don't lose your head when things are tough. Stay positive.

> A great attitude becomes a great day, which becomes a great month, which becomes a great year, which becomes a great life.

Create a vision (3 to 5 years from now)

> 10x goals

Let's say your current goal is to make $100,000 a year. Take your current goal and multiply it by 10.

How does it feel?

Does it scare you? Does it create resistance inside of you? Are you coming up with reasons why it won't work?

Just remember that there are thousands of other people out there who make at least $1 million per year consistently.

Why should you not do the same? Are you not deserving of success?

Take a good look at all the emotions that come up. Write down your thoughts, fears and concerns and try to brainstorm ways how to overcome them.

Once you define something on paper with clarity, the fear or uncertainty will go away.

Your life does not get better by chance. It gets better by change.

Look for an opportunity. Anything is possible for those with a dream, a plan and the will to make it happen.

Ask yourself the following questions:

- What is my life going to look like?
- What are the milestones on my way to the vision?
- Am I heading in the right direction or do I need to change my approach?
- Is my happiness based on my long-term vision or my on short-term goals / outcome?

If you constantly feel bad by not reaching your goals and you start to set lower goals but it is not empowering. You need a vision instead – not just goals. Goals are milestones on the way to reaching your vision. Your vision is the thing that should motivate you – not your goals.

Your vision is not static. It is a living breathing, changing organism. Look at your vision and look out for opportunities that you can incorporate into your success.

Don't be emotionally invested into your short-term goals because you might not exactly reach your goals. Instead be emotionally invested in your vision.

My personal business vision

- **Successful international Private Equity Firm** with offices and sales teams all over the world who are raising money for projects who will go public. Making over $100 million with my public company through share ownership and making a consistent income of $200,000 per month from my sales organizations.

- Making income from oil projects, etc. that are based on a commodity
- Having a diversified investment portfolio
- Owning several homes and real estate all over the world
- Having a successful online business that focuses on personal and business development
- Being the CEO and president of a public company
- Traveling the world for business
- Being in great shape and competing one more time in a bodybuilding competition
- Having a happy family and loving relationship
- Taking care of my children financially

It's never too late to be whoever you want to be. I hope your live a life you are proud of, and if you find that you are not, I hope you have the strength to start over.
(F. Scott Fitzgerald)

A year ago...

- You started **working out** … now you love your body
- You **launched your podcast** ... Now people are tuned in.
- You **started your business** … now you out-earn your 9-5.
- You **asked** that special person **out** … now you are in love.

Nah, this **didn't** happen… You were **afraid** to take that **first step**…

Or were you?

Go out there and make it happen!

CHAPTER 12

HOW TO BECOME A SUCCESSFUL BUSINESSPERSON

The need for freedom

> Those who do not have goals are doomed
> forever to work for those who do.
> Brian Tracy

When I was 20 years old I started working on straight commission. At that time I made $10,000 per month, which was a lot of money for someone at my age.

My whole life, expect one time, I have been self-employed or an entrepreneur. That one time when I was employed, I was working for MAN Investments, a hedge fund company. I made $160,000 per year and I was never unhappier in my life. Those 1.5 years were torture for me because I felt like I was not free.

I even started to do the opposite of what I was told to do because I just couldn't handle having a boss. I realized that the only way for me to be completely happy was to be my own boss or someone else's boss.

I wanted to become a millionaire and I knew that this was not possible with a regular job. So it was clear to me that I needed to become an entrepreneur if I ever wanted to amount to anything in life.

What does it mean to be an entrepreneur?

<u>Success</u>
Myth: Fame, cars, mansions, women, possessions
Reality: Family, meaning, purpose, accomplishment, quality

Did I have all the toys and attention? Yes, for a while. I made over $100,000 per month, rented a penthouse apartment overlooking the city for $10,000 per month, owned two Porsches, owned a big house and spent money like there was no tomorrow.

It was fun for a while but it wasn't the answer to true happiness.

Most millionaires are married, have children, focus on work and have a vision rather than chasing money. The vision of what your business will look like in the future becomes the most important driving force. Money is important but it is a by-product of your success. The reason for being in business is to pursue a specific vision – something that gives you purpose. The vision is much more important than money.

Freedom to be yourself

The most important kind of freedom is to be what you really are.
Jim Morrison

One of my main motivations was freedom. I wanted the freedom to work when I wanted or to take the day off. I wanted to have the freedom to take $5000 and book a flight around the globe at any given moment. I wanted to be free in choosing my type of business and what made me most fulfilled.

A lot of people walk around in self-made prisons; with the key held by strangers from they seek validation and approval. They are too afraid to speak their mind, and too afraid to give themselves permission to live like they so desperately want to, they live and die by the opinions of others. That's exactly what I didn't want. I wanted to live my life on my terms.

When we are living to please others we are starting to feel stressed and get depressed. The most important thing in life is to be yourself and to live the life that you want to live. And this is mostly only possible as an entrepreneur with your own business and ideas. Besides all that, no one can fire you from your own business.

> Most unhappiness is caused by a lack of clear
> meaning and purpose in your life.
> (Brian Tracy)

Become all you can be

The best way to create a bright future is to have **a powerful and positive vision** of it. Once your **vision is clear**, the energy of the Universe will begin to align with your vision. Create a vision, hold onto the vision, put your efforts towards the vision and in short time that vision will become your reality. I am encouraging you to **take action** in order to **bring your vision to reality.**

> Sometimes all you need is a break alone in a
> beautiful place to figure everything out.

A dark past doesn't disqualify you from a bright future. So start over. Set new goals and create a vision that works for you. Maybe you were chasing the wrong vision in the past or didn't have a vision in the first place.

Remember: You can be, have or do anything in this life that you desire. But you need to decide what that means for you. Everything is available in this world. Money is available like sand on the beach. But you must decide to get it. Life is like a buffet. There are so many different options to choose from. You can't have **everything** but you can have **anything** you like. But must make a decision. You must set a goal and make a plan to get it.

Being unrealistic is a matter of opinion

> Miracles are normal. Jake Ducey

Many want to point out "reality" to you. They say "face the facts" and only look at "what is". If you are able to see only "what is", the by the Law of Attraction, you will only create more "what is". You must put your thoughts beyond "what is" in order to attract something that is different.

> Stay away from negative people. They have a problem for every solution.

I think that being realistic and having common sense at the same time are important traits to have. However, be careful of being cynical because you failed in the past. You need to keep your big goals and have daily realistic goals that make sense. But keep your big vision alive at all times.

Being positive and optimistic

> Optimism is a happiness magnet. If you stay positive, good things and good people will be drawn to you. (Mary Lou Retton)

Every day you have the choice to think positively or negatively. Thinking negatively will make you feel bad and quite honestly it won't help you to achieve your goals.

It is so easy and simple to choose to think positive. So why not do it? There is no downside to it. If you are positive and optimistic you will start to believe in yourself that you can achieve any goal.

If you are you self-confident and positive, then you can do, have or be anything you like in this life.

> You have to brainwash yourself before the world does.

Listen to motivational speakers on YouTube while you work out. Your subconscious mind will take in everything anyway. Listen to audio programs in your car on your way to work. Go to seminars and get inspired.

Read your goals out lout every single day. Say things like: *I have a million dollars* or *I own a 4000-foot house*. Say your goals as if you already achieved them in the present tense.

Smiling and laughing is also hugely important. If a problem arises, laugh it off. Don't take problems too seriously and then they will go away quicker.

> Use your smile to change the world. Don't
> let the world change your smile.

No one ever injured their eyesight by looking on the bright side. So be positive and optimistic and always expect the best possible outcome.

Develop mental strength and power

Before I became a self-made millionaire my goal was to become the person who could earn $100,000 per month. I knew that I had to change as a person. I had to become more focused, more self-disciplined, better organized and mentally stronger.

The main factor though was **clarity.** I would say that having crystal clear goals was the main factor for my success. I knew exactly what I wanted to achieve and what I needed to do. **Clarity** gives you that mental power that you need to accomplish your goals.

Another factor is your **physical fitness**. Before I became a millionaire I went through a 16-week preparation to do a bodybuilding show. Your body was nothing to do with how well you do in business per say but it provides you with the same qualities necessary like being self-disciplined, working through pain, not giving up, etc.

Peace of mind

If it costs you your peace, it is too expensive.

There is a big difference between something "*being difficult*" and "*not having peace of mind*". Having peace of mind should be your most important principle. If a situation feels wrong, get out. If a person gives you the wrong vibes, get rid of him or her.

I was once in a dilemma. I could have made a lot of money with a particular person / organization but every time I thought about it, it felt wrong. My intuition told me that it was not a good situation to be in. It turned out that this organization was doing things illegally and the financial authorities were onto them.

I was walking away from a lot of money but at the same time I could have eventually been in a situation that would have been far worse. It felt good to say "no" to this organization. I knew I didn't want to lose my peace of mind because the way I was doing things in my business were good.

If you are working on something that is in a grey area legally speaking and it makes you feel uneasy, then you should do something different.

You will only succeed at something if you feel good about what you do and about yourself. You need to be able to feel proud without screwing people over. You need to be 100% honest and have integrity when it comes to your business. There is no two ways about it.

The secret of my success

> The secret of happiness is freedom; the secret of freedom is courage. (Thucydides)

1. **Courage to ask** anyone anything
2. **Courage to start** my own business
3. **Courage to dream** big and to have a big vision
4. Superior **sales and communication skills**
5. A **business system** that generates money
6. **Leverage** with employees (sales team)
7. **Leverage with Private Equity** and financial knowledge
8. Being very, very clear about my business goals (**clarity)**
9. **Self-confidence** and mental strength through fitness and bodybuilding
10. The **desire** to rise above the masses and not to be average anymore
11. High levels of **energy** with a healthy and fit lifestyle
12. Being **competent, logical, smart and using common sense**
13. Always **acting from the heart** and with **love** and the best intentions
14. Being 100% **honest and have integrity** with myself and the people I deal with
15. **Encourage others and motivate them** to be more successful

When I reached my goal of making $100,000 per month and becoming a millionaire, I decided to get a tattoo on my spine. It is three Chinese symbols that say: **Courage, self-confidence and freedom.**

I decided to get this tattoo so that I would never forget what the most important factors for success were in my life.

Besides that I think that it looks pretty cool, it is on my spine where the character lies. If you have a strong character, you have a strong spine. Meaning you stay true to your values and you are honest.

I really think that losing my fear and having the courage to ask people to join my team was a big factor in my success. When others feel that you have no fear and that you have a big vision, people will automatically follow you because they like to follow strong people.

Most of us are paralyzed by fear and don't dare to have a big vision. That's why they never achieve anything great in life. But once you lose that fear and courageously focus on your clear vision, things will take off like never before.

My vehicle was Private Equity or selling shares to investors and raising money for my businesses. In my opinion, a corporation is the greatest invention of our time. If you feed your ideas with money, then they can grow and become a reality.

Business partners

> Surround yourself with people who push you to do and be better. No drama or negativity. Just higher goals, motivation and positive energy. No jealousy or hate. Just bringing out the absolute best in each other.

Nothing is worse than having people who cheat you and put you down. It can kill all of your motivation.

Make sue that you develop the kind of character traits as a business person that is 100% reliable and dependable. Someone who people love to do business with.

Always create a win-win situation. Otherwise you will do business exactly one time and no more.

> If you have a reputation to be cheap or difficult to negotiate with, nobody wants to do business with you.

The right business partners can make all the difference. Having the wrong business partners is a nightmare and usually the end of your business dreams.

The power of the Internet

Your customer is online...are you?

Your business strategy must include the Internet. The power of the Internet is undeniable. It can give you the necessary leverage that you need to make it as an entrepreneur.

Starting an online business

1. Choose your niche
2. Setup, website, funnel, automation
3. Create high quality content
4. Advertising
5. **Focus on content not money**
6. Grow audience
7. Create products that make money
8. Create a system

If you decide to start an online business besides other businesses, then you should have a clear plan and focus. In this time and age it would be a sin not to start an online business. It is the coolest thing during this lifetime.

So take your passion and turn it into products and sell it online. Don't worry about what negative people have to say about your business. There are thousands of people who will appreciate what you have to sell.

Even at your best, someone will have something negative to say. Pursue greatness anyway. (Sylvester Stallone)

The most important thing is to focus on **quality content** when you publish YouTube videos for example. Your **message and the quality** is what will make you successful.

Quality of your products

> Don't settle.
> Don't finish crappy books.
> If you don't like the menu, leave the restaurant.
> If you are not on the right path, get off it.
> Chris Brogan

Studies have shown over and over again that companies with superior products outperform companies with poor quality products.

When it comes to your business and its products you should only create the best possible products. If your products are of high quality and if they fill a need, then they will sell if the price is right.

If you have to do something anyway, then you might as well do it well.

Planning work and life one year ahead

> 1 year = 10 working months / 1 month = 20 working days

One of the most effective ways to plan your business and life is to plan one year in advance.

In December, between Christmas and New Year's, when you typically set new goals for the year, you should plan the entire year in advance and write all your most important appointments in a calendar / diary.

I would typically start with your holidays. Plan 6 weeks of holidays and about 4 longer weekends into your schedule.

Typically, the last two weeks of December and the first two weeks in January are when most people are away or not working. That means also that your customers are hard to reach.

The second time is during the summer. Typically, mid July to mid August is a dead time in Europe. Everybody is on holidays. Doing effective business or finding clients is more difficult during that time. That's why I would plan my holidays also during those weeks.

Even though a year has 12 months and you should set your yearly goals as if you only had 10 months.

Example: Let's say you want to reach $100,000 in sales per month. Your yearly goal would be $1.2 million but because you "loose 2 months" during summer and New Year's, your realistic goal should be $1 million (10 months x $100,000).

The same applies for a month. If you want to make $100,000 per month, then you cannot divide $100,000 by 30 or 31 because you typically don't work on weekends.

That's why you should realistically only calculate with **20 or 22 working days per month**. If you want to make $100,000 per month, you need to make $5,000 per day for 20 days and focus on $5,000 rather than $3,333.

A year has 365 days but because of sick days, unforeseen circumstances, lost days, family events, public holidays, weekends, etc. you can really only work on about **200 full working days per year.**

Now of course you can work on more days and be more effective. But for a realistic goal setting plan that you can achieve, you should plan with 240 days and try to reach your goals during those days.

Life often gets in our way when we try to achieve a goal. That's a normal part of life. Family, distractions, sickness, unforeseen things, etc. get in the way.

> Many people give up on their goals because they plan unrealistically.

You need to stay motivated and have momentum when it comes to achieving your goals. **If you constantly feel like you are falling behind, it will discourage you** and eventually you will give up.

In general, you should plan about 70% of your schedule in advance and be flexible about the rest.

$5,000 per day x 20 days = $100,000 per month

> The first step before anybody else in the world
> believes it, is you have to believe it.
> (Will Smith)

Make earning **$100,000 per month** your new goal. It forces you to think outside of the box and you can't have a regular job and earn that kind of money. The only way you can do it is as an entrepreneur or in sales.

I did it and it changed my life. This goal was a really awesome motivator because it forced me to think outside of the box and the normal options.

A typical month has about 22 working days (Monday to Friday). If you make it your target to earn **$5,000 per day** then you will achieve that goal. For simple math reasons, let's just say 20 days per month. Maybe you take two days off or have other commitments.

Here are some ideas:

1. Your commission per deal is $5,000. You must close one deal that pays you that kind of commission.
2. You charge $5,000 per consulting client. You have to sign up one new client per day.
3. You sell products online and generate sales that net a profit of $5,000 per day. For example: 5 products at $1,000 each.
4. You find an investor each day that invests $50,000 and you earn $5,000 (10%) in commissions.

5. You sell products to Europe that you import from China for $200,000 per month, sell them and half is your profit.

You have to be creative and do lots of brainstorming if you want to achieve that goal. It forces you to think differently than a regular person. You need to come up with different options like "*getting a better job*" or "*getting promoted*". Ideally, come up with 20 different ways or solutions to earn $100,000 per month. Often, the last two options when you had to be most creative in your thinking because the obvious solutions were already written down, will provide you with a new breakthrough idea.

Personally, I have set a new goal for myself. Instead of becoming the person who can earn $100,000 per month, I have decided to double that target. So in 20 days I have to earn $10,000 per day in order to make $200,000 per month.

One way is to grow my sales organization so that it raises $100,000 per day and if my commission is 10%, then I would earn $10,000 per day. Back in the day I used to raise between $1 and $2 million per month. So I know for a fact that this is possible. But there are also other ways to reach that goal. The first step is to brainstorm ways and then believe that I can make it happen.

Other things than money – your character and behavior

> Every morning a new day is starting that
> can change everything in life.

10 things that require **0% Talent** but will get you **100% Respect:**

1. Being on time
2. Being prepared
3. Listening
4. Work ethic
5. Effort

6. Positive attitude
7. Integrity
8. Being 100% reliable and dependable
9. Doing extra or additional things
10. Responding or acting quickly

In my opinion, the most important factors are to **be fast when it comes to acting, honest and 100% reliable.**

In the past there was a time when I used to be slow when it came to paying commissions to my sales people. This created a lot of problems and I eventually lost a lot of people unnecessarily. They chose other companies over mine because of it.

Then I made the conscious decision to become the person who pays everyone the fastest. The minute a client would transfer the money into the account, I would immediately initiate a wire transfer to my sales person to receive his commission. I developed a reputation to be quick and 100% reliable, which ended up being an important part in my success.

Your reputation to be fast, professional and 100% dependable is more important than the product that you sell.

> If you have the **right behavior**, you will **attract better quality people** who will open up new doors and opportunities for you.

Sometimes all it takes in life is to meet the right person at the right time and then your life will change for the better. But you will never impress that person if your behavior is sloppy, disorganized or unreliable.

Sales and marketing

> If I could teach my children only one thing, it would be the skill of marketing. With this one skill, they will be successful at anything in life.

Business is selling a product to a customer in order to make money. Making money means being successful.

The better you are at sales, the better your business will be. The more money you make, the more success you have.

The foundation of business success is sales and marketing. That's why should become an expert in both those fields. Read all the books, take all the courses and learn from the best.

If you read **10 books on sales, marketing or business in a year**, you will see how your business will take off.

You need to work on yourself and continuously learn and motivate yourself.

> Income does not far exceed personal development. (Jim Rohn)

When you work out at the gym always listen to inspirational or motivational material. If you just read 3 books on any subject will have 90% more knowledge than the average person.

Companies, accounts and legal structures

Once you make money, you need to protect yourself. Success also comes with people who are envious or people who want to take it away from you. That's why you should set yourself up with several companies, accounts, and legal structures in several different countries.

Your life can change from one day to the next if the tax authorities decide to freeze your accounts from whatever reason. I have had banks close my accounts because they suspected a transaction to be fraudulent even though it wasn't. But in a situation like that you need options. You can't only rely on one bank and account.

I have had many advantages because I had accounts in the USA, in Switzerland, the UK and in offshore countries. I was able to move money from one country to the next without paying taxes or with being exposed to risk.

I strongly suggest for you to protect yourself and your money with different bank accounts and corporations that are in different countries.

When I set up my stock marketing promotion plan, I owned 17 companies in the Marshall Islands with 17 different directors and had accounts in Liechtenstein. Each company held a couple of million shares of the deal that I was promoting. This enabled me to stay hidden from the public and a company could sell shares without me officially having to file an insider SEC 8-K report.

Turning an idea into reality with Private Equity

Become a millionaire with your own company through Private Equity

If you understand how to raise money for your ideas, then anything is possible in this life for you. The trick is to understand that each business is a corporation with shares. In order to finance your ideas, you need capital. And you can get the capital by selling shares to investors who believe in your idea. Once you understand how this process works, you can organize the money and try out any business idea that you have.

The cool thing is that you don't even have to invest your own money (if you have any). Most people don't have any money but just a dream. I believe that all business dreams are doable. You just need to convince enough people to give you money and motivate them with returns. That's why learning about Private Equity and public companies is so important.

Once you learn about the principles of Private Equity and how you can create the right share structure so that investors are motivated to invest, there is nothing that you cannot do.

The business of Private Equity gives me the freedom to work when I want and from where I want. I can work from anywhere in the world. As I am writing these pages, I am in Northern Ireland where my wife was born. It always was her dream to live here for a while and because of my independence and flexibility, we have been here for the last 2 years. Of course, we are planning to go back to America but there is no pressure or stress to do it because of what of Internet and technology these days. I can reach investors, sales people or financial advisors by phone or Skype and it really doesn't matter anymore where I am located in the world.

Build a sales team or have intermediaries

Another important factor for success is **leverage.** If you have a sales team of 10 people who sell your products to clients, then they will achieve a better result than you just by yourself ever could.

Intermediaries are another important group. An intermediary is an independent financial advisor or group. If I pay a commission to financial advisors who already have several hundred clients and manage already millions of dollars, then it is much easier and quicker to raise capital for my companies. Their clients already trust them and I don't have to convince them or gain their trust.

We are currently talking to a group that would guarantee between $1.2 and $1.5 million per month in new investments.

This **one contact alone** could finance my entire deal and I don't ever have to talk to one single investor myself. That's why you should contact as many different people as possible. You never know which contact will be the jackpot.

> Your association determines your destination. This is why you must choose your relationships wisely. (Joel Brown)

Having the right people as your business partners is key. If you have average people around you, then your results will be average or low. If you work with great people, then you will do much better and this kind of momentum will motivate you even more.

Self-discipline

> Discipline is my best friend.
> Gisele Bundchen

It is not possible to be successful without self-discipline – no matter what you do or in what field or industry you are in.

Success and self-discipline go hand in hand. **The average working time for an entrepreneur is 59 hours per week**. If you are only working 8 hours a day you better have a rich uncle.

Self-discipline means to work all the time whether you feel like it or not. You have to train your mind to be stronger than your emotions. Otherwise you will lose every single time.

> You will never always be motivated. That's why you have to learn to be disciplined.

The best way for me to be disciplined is to create my own rules. Let's take personal fitness for example. I have decided to go to the gym every single morning whether I feel like it or not. There is no two ways about it. I don't have the option not to go. I know that if I go and work out, the result is better than if I don't work out.

When it comes to working, you need to create a schedule that you stick to. You need to plan your activities and keep your own promises and appointments. When I have to call clients from 2 to 4 pm in order to set new client appointments, then I will use that time to make phone calls and not schedule anything else (not even a client). I create rules for myself and stick to them.

Every day I set 5 goals for the day and the day isn't over until those 5 goals have been crossed off my list.

> Don't go back to your old ways. Toxic habits, people and energy always try to come back when you are doing better. Stay on track and stay focused.

Affirmations, goals, meditation and your dream journal

In order to get more clarity, I write into my daily journal. I write my goals, ideas and plans into it. It is a summary of my thoughts and best ideas.

It is important to understand that you are a spiritual being and that you can attract and manifest anything into your life. That's why you have to set goals, dwell on them and do affirmations so that your subconscious mind will help you to turn them into reality.

All successful people dream, set goals and meditate on them. The more you dream and imagine your goals, the more likely you will attract the people, money and circumstances into your life to make them happen.

Life is not what it seems. Your thoughts are real and have power. That's why you must focus on positive outcomes and use the power of affirmations, suggestion and meditation to help you achieve your goals.

> Quantum Physics teaches us that everything we thought was physical is not physical. (Bruce H. Lipton)

Once you understand that your thoughts have the power to bring things into reality, then you should focus on your goals on a daily basis.

Being an entrepreneur

> Find 3 hobbies you love: One to make money, one to keep in shape and one to be creative.

I chose the following things in my life:

Money:	Private Equity Business
Shape:	Bodybuilding – working out every morning
Creative:	normanmeier.com – writing brochures and posting videos on YouTube

Being in shape is the starting point for success in business. You need to have discipline, set goals, control your progress and put in the work – just like in any other business. The mental and emotional strength that you gain from working out is the key for success in business. They go hand in hand. You will only excel in your field if you have the physical power, too.

All my knowledge and lessons are in my NMI (Norman Meier International) programs. It helps me to get clarity myself and the lessons should encourage others to do well. It gives me the balance that I need to be creative in my life.

Creating a legacy

> Skepticism and doubt kills dreams.

We all came here with a certain set of skills and talents. If you find out who you really are and what makes you unique, then you must have the courage to pursue your true calling in life – otherwise you will never be truly happy.

Results happen over time – not overnight. Work hard, stay consistent and be patient. Don't let fear and doubts hold you back. Just keep going confidently in the direction of your goals!

CHAPTER 13

BUSINESS IS A NUMBERS GAME

Business is simple

Question: What is the purpose of a business? Answer: to create a customer (Peter Drucker)

In general, business is very simple. There are only 3 main steps involved:

1. Create a quality product or service
2. Sell it at an affordable price
3. Deliver it in a quality way

Money only comes from one source = other people (= customers)

Business or "making money" comes from selling a product or service to a customer. The more customers you have, the more money you make.

Therefore you must become great at sales and marketing. You should learn absolutely everything about those topics.

Obviously, you need a quality product that people want but then the next step is your process.

How exactly do you create leads that will turn into customers?

What products are you selling at what exact price?

How do you deliver your products?

How to make $1 million per year

SELL A $200 PRODUCT TO 5000 PEOPLE
SELL A $500 PRODUCT TO 2000 PEOPLE
SELL A $1,000 PRODUCT TO 1000 PEOPLE
SELL A $2,000 PRODUCT TO 500 PEOPLE
SELL A $5,000 PRODUCT TO 200 PEOPLE

5000 PEOPLE PAY $17/MONTH, FOR 12 MONTHS
2000 PEOPLE PAY $42/MONTH, FOR 12 MONTHS
1000 PEOPLE PAY $83/MONTH, FOR 12 MONTHS
500 PEOPLE PAY $167/MONTH, FOR 12 MONTHS
250 PEOPLE PAY $333/MONTH, FOR 12 MONTHS

If you want to make a million dollars, you need to know how many customers you will need to achieve that goal. Depending on your product price, you will know what your goal in regards to the amount of customers is.

Once you have clarity it is much easier to plan the necessary activities to guarantee that number. When you break it down into numbers, you will get more clarity and it will become easier to achieve.

How to make $100,000 per year

SELL A $200 PRODUCT TO 500 PEOPLE
SELL A $500 PRODUCT TO 200 PEOPLE
SELL A $1,000 PRODUCT TO 100 PEOPLE
SELL A $2,000 PRODUCT TO 50 PEOPLE
SELL A $5,000 PRODUCT TO 20 PEOPLE

500 PEOPLE PAY $17/MONTH, FOR 12 MONTHS
200 PEOPLE PAY $42/MONTH, FOR 12 MONTHS
100 PEOPLE PAY $83/MONTH, FOR 12 MONTHS
50 PEOPLE PAY $167/MONTH, FOR 12 MONTHS
25 PEOPLE PAY $333/MONTH, FOR 12 MONTHS

Most people would already be happy to simply make $100,000 per year with their business so that they can survive and pay their bills.

Once you break it down to that level, it seems very doable and takes away the mystery of creating a six-figure income.

It is actually very encouraging to look at these numbers. It seems that almost anyone can do it if you make sure that you do the right things first.

How much does your product cost? ________________
How many clients do you need in 12 months? ________________
How many clients do you need in one year? ________________

Tip 1: Break down yearly goals into daily goals

$100 per day = $30,000 per year
$200 per day = $70,000 per year
$300 per day = $100,000 per year
$500 per day = $180,000 per year
$1,000 per day = $360,000 per year
$3,000 per day = $1,000,000 per year

If you want to make $100,000 per year, then you should focus your activities on making $300 per day. $300 per day seems very realistic and doable. It could be the equivalent of one sale (depending on your product).

Breaking down a larger goal into a daily goal will show you what kind of activities you need to do in order to achieve your goal.

If you want to make one sale or $300 per day, maybe this translates into having 10 sales calls with clients in a day. By making sure that you do the right kind of activities on a regular basis, you can ensure the achievement of your overall, big goal.

Business (sales) is like math – success is measurable

5 out of 4 people struggle with Math. (ha,ha...)

Everything is a numbers game. The more people you can contact the more sales you will make.

When it comes to financial success in sales you need to realize that everything is a numbers game. There is really only one rule: The more people you talk to, the more prospects you will get and this will improve the **probability** to make a sale.

Everything is based on the law of cause and effect. The more causes that you set by calling more people, making more appointments, the more deals can you close. The busy and active sales people will always outperform the lazy ones – no matter the difference in their skill set.

If you want to earn a certain amount of money in a year, you must break it down to a monthly average amount. If you want to earn $300,000 per year, you must earn $25,000 per month on average. If you can sell on 25 days of the month, you must make at least $1000 in commission per day. If you can make $500 in commissions per closed deal, you have to close two deals per day on average.

This is your basic goal setting calculation of what you want to achieve.

But now you must know your actual numbers from your activities. What are you numbers or quotas in each area?

If your closing rate is 50%, then you must have 4 sales opportunities with clients each day. If you know that 20% will move, change or cancel the appointment, then you must set 5 new appointments each day.

Depending on the quality of your contacts and by having the perfect target group, your numbers might increase dramatically.

Basically, success in sales is predictable. It is like math. You can calculate it. All you need to self-discipline to ensure that you do the right activities.

> Everything is based on numbers and the amount and quality of your contacts.

The law of probability

> In order to change or improve something you must analyze your numbers and figure out what could be done to improve each area.

Selling a product or service has a lot to do with the law of probability. Whatever it is that you sell, it is always a numbers game. That means that you might have to offer your product or service to many potential clients in order to make a sale.

So the more people you talk to, the more sales you will make. You can literally calculate how much money you want to make. Selling is just like math.

If it doesn't sell, it isn't creative or appealing enough and you must change the product. But once you have a product that actually sells, then there is always a certain percentage of people who will buy your products.

The sales funnel

Try to think in numbers when it comes to your business. You need to be able to calculate the number of efforts it takes in order to achieve an end result.

You might have to talk to 1000 people first before you can make a sale. There is always somebody who will buy your product. The only question is which sales channels work better and what you can do to improve the individual steps in your sales process to get better numbers. The more people that come into contact with your product or service, the more sales you will have in the end. This is the law of probability.

The founder of Starbucks had spoken to over 256 people about investing into his business. Only 12 people ended up doing it. He was rejected over 240 times but his persistence paid off in the end.

So if your product can be sold and the result is in reasonable proportion to the efforts that you have to put forth, it is only a matter of the amount of acquisition efforts that you have to do in order to be successful.

> The only person standing in your way might be yourself. If you are not lazy or afraid of rejection, there is no limit to what you can achieve.

The psychology of the sales funnel might be tricky. You might have spoken to 50 people on the phone and gotten rejected each time and therefore you conclude that no one wants to buy your product. Often people give up way too easily and early because they are afraid of rejection and they don't see the bigger picture. The truth is that they simply haven't spoken to enough people to make that assessment or they are using the wrong technique to go about their business.

What is your target / goal? (Amount of clients) ________________
How much money does that translate into? ________________
How many people do you have to talk or contact? ________________

How many new leads do you need to generate each month to reach your target?

> Sales are contingent upon the attitude of the salesman - not the attitude of the prospect. W. Clement Stone

Tip 2: Sales statistics – the real numbers before you can close

> Failure is not the opposite of success. It is part of success.

48% of sales people never follow up with a prospect
25% of sales people make a second contact and stop
12% of sales people only make three contacts and stop
10% of sales people make more than three contacts

2% of sales are made on the **first** contact
3% of sales are made on the **second** contact
5% of sales are made on the **third** contact
10% of sales are made on the **fourth** contact
80% of sales are made on the **fifth to twelfth** contact

(Source: National Sales Executive Association)

Statistics show that it takes up to 8 times until a person who comes into contact with your company buys from you.

When you create leads online, people are always skeptical at first. But if you keep contacting them by sending emails over a long period of time, they will eventually start to trust you and then buy from you.

Some people are also in a bad mood or not in a happy buying mood when you first contact them. But if you catch them on a better day, they might decide to buy. Sometimes all it takes is the right moment.

And finally, some sales people can be so persistent and annoying that the clients finally gives in and buys the product because he doesn't want to be bothered anymore.

Tip 3: Sales scripts and online marketing psychology

You can contact 1000 clients and maybe one client will buy your products but if you want to achieve success faster, then you must also work on your skills and improve your numbers. You must work on your sales script and the sales process. You must increase your closing rate and the numbers of leads that you can convert to customers. You must increase the average number or amount of sales per client. You must improve all the numbers during the entire process.

If you have the right sales script that works well, then you have a version that you can use over and over again.

That is why I want to encourage you to learn and study absolutely everything about sales, marketing, human behavior, communication and psychology. Once you can identify why humans buy products and how they buy them, then you can adjust your strategy online or in person.

Tip 4: Putting in the hours

> Nothing will work unless you do. (Maya Angelou)

If things don't seem to work, then you must examine whether or not you are really putting in the hours and necessary amount of calls to customers.

Sometimes the reason why you are failing is because you are simply not working enough hours trying to get customers. Maybe you are working 10 hours a day but 8 hours are spent in the office doing other things like administration, organization but NOT actively selling.

You need to be actively and constantly selling a product every single day.

Working = selling = making money = being successful

This means making 100 phone calls every single day. It means spending 80% of your time on income generating activities like sales, marketing and dealing with clients.

It means that if you don't set enough meetings with clients in your calendar every single week (at least 10 to 15) face-to-face meetings every single week, then you are not doing enough.

Sometimes a business model doesn't work because you simply don't talk to enough clients in a month. If you talked to more clients, then by the law of probability you will get lucky and find a couple of good clients to generate enough sales.

Some people don't have enough LEADS to contact. And maybe then you need to focus your time and energy on creating and finding many new leads.

Tip 5: Telephone book, door-to-door, do whatever it takes

Self-discipline equals freedom.

Most people are afraid of contacting clients. They are afraid of rejection and of failure. Those two reasons are so strong and dominant in some people that they will do whatever it takes to avoid it. They rather "suffer" and do nothing than to call up clients.

But in order to generate sales and make money there are no two ways about it. You must deal with clients.

Imagine the following situation: Imagine that someone that you love is dying and needs an operation. You need to organize $50,000 in 30 days to pay for the operation and if you don't do it, that person will die. Imagine that this person is your mother, your father, your spouse or even your own child.

Here is the question:

Would you be able to save that person? Would you be able under these extreme circumstances to make all the necessary sales to generate enough money to come up with the commission of $50,000? Would you go crazy asking every single person you come across making a sale with you? Would you work hours on end and talk to enough people to see whether or not they will buy your products? Would you use the telephone book if necessary or go door-to-door if you had no leads? Would you do whatever it takes to save that person's life?

The answer: Of course you would!

But why don't you do it today? Why are you not working like crazy generating $50,000? The answer or the reason is because **you are afraid** and because **you don't have enough compelling goals.**

Selling is a skill set that anyone can learn. It is literally possible for almost anyone to generate sales. Technically speaking there are no excuses.

So ask yourself what you need to change within you and your internal motivation to make it happen. What kind of fears are you still struggling with and why?

Sometimes all it takes is writing down the numbers, making a plan of action and then following through without question.

Why don't you decide today to call up at least 100 clients each day (Monday through Friday = 500 per week) or 2000 clients per month?

Do you think that once you **actually have made 2000 phone calls** that a few clients will stick? You bet!

Tip 6: Don't give up when things get difficult

> Nothing worth having comes easy. You gotta work for it.
> (Karina Elle – Fitness / Bikini World Champion)

With anything in life whether it is getting into shape or making money, you have to work for it. Success is simple in theory but it is not easy. Putting in the effort and the hours is the price that you have to pay for success.

People often give up way too quickly and easily when things get difficult. Just ask yourself the following question: Are there other people in this industry that are successfully selling the same products like you and they are successful doing it? And if the answer is yes, then you must continue. You must find out what they are doing right and then adjust your strategy. If it is possible or doable for others, then it is possible and doable for you, too.

There are certain laws like the law of cause and effect, for example. If you do the same things like other successful people, you must achieve the same results.

In every industry there are sales superstars making a million dollars per year. If you are struggling today, then you are either not doing enough or you are doing something wrong.

If you find out what you need to change and then do it and never, ever give up, then you can't help but being successful as well.

Always do your best. What you plant now, you will harvest later.

Tip 7: Client segmentation

We used to categorize our clients into A-clients, B-clients and C-clients.

A-clients have the highest income and they are the best clients and they will give you the highest amount of sales and commissions.

B-clients are good and solid and you can work well with them but they are not rich.

C-clients are bad clients. They have little money and you can't make a high commission with them.

The more A and B-clients you have, the better. People who mostly have C-clients have poor sales results.

Now here is the interesting part.

> It takes exactly the same amount of time and effort to deal with an A-client as it takes with a C-client.

So why not focus only on A-clients?

And here is the second epiphany for you: A-clients know other A-clients that you can get referred to. B-clients know B and C-clients BUT c-clients only know other C-clients or even D-clients.

Once you are in the wrong circle it is hard to get out of it. So focus your efforts on the right group. But this also means that you must be absolutely professional so that you can handle the big clients.

> A-clients know other A-clients.
> B-clients know other B-clients.
> C-clients know other C-clients and D-clients.

In general, you must differentiate between A, B and C clients. A-clients have the biggest potential, B-clients are average and C-clients are below average.

The more A and B clients you have the more sales you generate. The more you deal with people from this segment, the more referrals and other clients will also come from the same segment.

Once you realize this fact, the faster you will change your focus.

You could also do your own segmentation of your clients. This could be based on income:

A-clients = Income over $100,000 per year
B-clients = Income between $50,000 and $100,000 per year
C-clients = Income below $50,000 per year

Some people give up their sales job because they spend too much time in the C-segment. It is hard to fight for every little commission and you get a lot of "sorry, I can't afford your product" objections.

Maybe the only thing you need to change your motivation is to change your client segment.

Realistically, you can't only have A-clients. It will always be a mix. Most new sales people start with the C-clients because they need to make their experiences first.

But you should also realize that it takes exactly the same amount of time and effort to deal with an A-client than with a C-client.

Some sales people are very particular about this. They refuse to deal with anybody who is not an A-client. And if you are consistent with this approach, you will do much better. If you see yourself as an expert who solely deals with the best people, your whole approach changes from being an annoying high-pressure sales person to a professional consultant and expert.

The 80/20-rule is applicable in almost every area of selling. You can use it to analyze your clients and their potential, your own sales activities and your earning ability.

Ask yourself which 20% of your time and energy will yield 80% of the result. Which activities do you need to do more of so that you can excel in your overall sales result? If you realize that prospecting will give you 80% of your results, then you should do more prospecting. If you realize that A-clients will give you 80% of your results, then you should focus on more A-clients.

Tip 8: Generating quality leads

How do you generate high quality leads for your business? Obviously, the more leads you have the better are your chances to generate customers.

In my opinion there are three main ways:

1. Marketing sales team / call center
2. Online strategy – free report
3. Lists

Marketing sales team / call center

If you don't want to call 100 clients each day yourself, you could hire a few marketing people and build a small call center. I once opened a small call center where I hired 5 women who made about 100 calls each day during 5 hours from Monday to Friday. They would do the cold calling and generate each day about 5 good leads each. So basically, they got the 95 "no's" and the 5 "yes".

But then you can follow up with the 5 leads yourself because you know that those will already be people who have received some basic information from your company and who are generally speaking interested in your products. The second call is going to be much easier and friendlicr.

If you have a team of 5 marketing people who generate 25 new good leads each day and you follow up on those leads because you are the best sales person, then making business happen is really easy.

Online strategy

A new way of getting new leads is to first run an online ad on Facebook for example. You offer some free interesting information or a free PDF report. If you are in finance, you could say something like:

- "Stock market outlook 2020 to 2025"
- "The eight most common mistakes that investors make"
- "How to generate a monthly income with stocks and options"

Once the person clicks on your ad, the get to a landing page and then they have to give you their name, email and phone number. In return they will be able to download the free PDF report. But once they have done this, you can follow up with a call a few days later. You will have a reason to call or follow up because this person has requested information from you. When you call that person, it is not a cold call because he already knows your company and he is generally speaking already interested in your topic.

Lists

There are a number of list brokers around that you can contact and buy leads from. Remember the rule: Who is your ideal customer? Once you have clearly defined your ideal customer based on his income level, interests, sex, age group, etc. you can get leads from a list broker that have exactly the profile that you want.

Once you start calling up clients from a list of people who clearly fit your profile because they have shown a certain interest in a topic in the past, etc. you have exactly the right names to target. Your life as a sales person becomes much easier because you don't have to weed out the bad names.

Tip 9: Start a small call center

Bait first

Another way to generate leads is by offering a free product as an opening product. It is possible that this initial free product doesn't have much to do with your actual end product that you intend to sell but it is a free gift from your company that will give you a reason to follow up someone. But once you talk to someone and there is a reason why you are speaking to them, then you can later follow up with the real product or moneymaker.

The cost of a small call center

> It's not what you pay a man, but what he costs you that counts. Will Rogers

If you hire one marketing assistant and that person makes 100 calls per day, then the math looks like this:

100 calls per day
95 people say no
5 new good leads generated

5 hours telephone time x $10/hour = $50
5 days per week = $250 per week
4 weeks = **$1000 salary for your marketing assistant**
(plus % of your sales)

5 leads x 5 days x 4 weeks = 100 good leads generated in one month

100 leads = 5 clients (for example)

Let's say that you have 100 good quality leads each month and you are able to generate 5 clients. Depending on your product and your price structure you might make $1000 per client. Let's say you make $5000 in commissions. Now you simply deduct the $1000 salary that you have to pay your marketing assistant and you will end up with $4000 for yourself.

Maybe you want to give your marketing assistant an incentive by giving him or her a percentage of your closed deals but that is up to you.

If you study this example and then scale it to 5 or even 10 marketing people, you can generate a lot more sales.

This example is not just theory but I actually did it in real life and it worked. I was able to find 5 women who wanted to work part time because most of them had kids and needed flexibility. At the same time they were happy to have a job on the side and 5 hours per day was manageable.

Tip 10: Consistency versus getting a "lucky break"

Warren Buffet didn't become a billionaire until he was in his fifties.

When you take a look at the development of Warren Buffett's net worth, you will see that it took him a long time to become the richest man in the world. The first 40 years he was consistently working on growing his wealth.

When it comes to sales and business success consistency is key. It is a long-term development of consistent sales results and increasing them every year.

People who get one of two big clients and then quit are not successful for long. Your strategy must be long-term oriented and over time things will eventually get huge.

Give yourself time and build a long-term strategy. Most strategies or businesses are not financially interesting the first few years but after a long time they become great.

Example 1: If you want to become a stockbroker, the first 3 years are hard. You need to first find clients and build up your assets under management. In the first 3 years you will not make a lot of money. But once you have build up a certain number of clients over a few years and maybe have $100 million under management you can make $1 million per year.

Example 2: Incorporations. There is a company in Nevada that does incorporations as a business service. They charge a few hundred dollars for the incorporation and then about $100 per year to maintain the annual registered agent service. The company has been around 10 years and over those 10 years they were able to incorporate 10,000 companies. $100 per year doesn't seem like much at first but once you have built up 10,000 companies, then this is an annual income of $1 million. With new companies and other services they generate another $1 million and the overall business makes about $2 million per year. The owner of this company has 7 employees and he pays them about $30,000 per year each. They manage everything without him and he lives in California. The first few years it was not possible to survive but over time with more and more repeat customers, the owner was able to generate enough sales to make a lot of money.

> Profit in business comes from repeat customers, customers that boast about your project or service, and that bring friends with them. A satisfied customer is the best business strategy of all.

Tip 11: Start your own business from home (or in your garage)

> Apple, Google, Amazon, Harley, Disney and Mattel all started out in a garage.

The numbers are also important when it comes to cost and expenses. You don't always need an actual office where you pay thousands of dollars each month. Some of the greatest companies were started in a garage or from home.

Today, with the Internet and technology this is true more than ever.

Personally, I have done the same. At one point my three girls were all still very young (all under the age of 5 years old) and my wife needed my help and support. It was easier for me to work from home and not lose time with a long commute. That is when I transformed half of the garage into a functional office and decided to work from home. I generated millions of dollars working from my garage and if you ever had a Skype call with me, you would not have been able to tell the difference between a "real office" and my "garage office".

Tip 12: The cash flow quadrant principle

> I'd rather hustle 24/7 than slave 9 to 5.

4 ways to produce income:

E – Employee
You have a job
No leverage
The amount of work determines your income
95% of population
You give your own time in exchange for money

S – Self-employed
You own a job
No leverage
95% of population
You give your own time in exchange for money

B – Business Owner
You own a system
Leverage
Income does not depend on active work
5% of population
Your employees work for your business system

I – Investor
You own investments
Leverage
Income does not depend on active work
5% of population
Your money works for you

Most people are only familiar with being an employee or self-employed. This is the way that 95% of the people have been conditioned or taught.

> If you do what everyone else is doing, you will get what everyone else has: nothing.

That is why you should focus your time and energy on building your own business system if you want to be more successful than 95% of the people.

Tip 13: Wannapreneur versus entrepreneur

> "I don't know yet how but I will achieve it." is the motto of the typical entrepreneur.

Entrepreneur:

Today:	new idea
One month from now:	business started

Wannapreneur:

Today:	new idea
One month from now:	new idea (still not taken action)

Habits of entrepreneurs

- Create a daily routine
- The mornings is the most important time of the day
- Workout
- Meditation
- Get up early and start working before everyone else starts
- Focus on income generating meetings – plan appointments with clients
- Tracking the progress by keeping track of the numbers
- Encourage and motivate team members
- Focus each day for one specific task or business activity
- Learning and reading

The difference between a real entrepreneur and a wannapreneur is **taking action**. It doesn't matter whether or not your plan or idea is perfect or perfectly executed but it is better to take action than not to take any action at all.

The key is to improve things along the way but getting started is often the main difference between being successful and unsuccessful. Especially in the beginning you will need **momentum and small successes** to keep you going.

Tip 14: Millionaire or Nillionaire?

Nillionaire (= “someone having little or no money”)

Stage 1: Nillionaire
Stage 2: Millionaire
Stage 3: Billionaire

Maybe today you are a nillionaire and not a millionaire. But that doesn’t matter. Every millionaire started as a nillionaire.

Everyone who is making $1 million per year started making $50,000 per year. But it is the steps and the development in between that eventually lead to that goal.

No one becomes a millionaire or a billionaire overnight. It is always a process and it takes time. Maybe today you are at an early point in your development but you have greatness within you to become a millionaire. All you have to do is **stick with it until you have made it.**

The price for freedom is making sales.

Things take time and it is always a long-term process. Sometimes all it takes it to stay in your chosen field long enough and not giving up. If you have invested a lot of time and effort in a particular field then it might be best to stay in that field so that you can reap the benefits of your long-term work and investment.

A goal is a dream with a deadline. Napoleon Hill

It is also important to differentiate between goals versus dreams. A dream without devotion is a fantasy not a reality. A goal is measurable and has a time line.

I want to encourage you to dream big and have big goals / numbers. But turning this dream into a reality requires you to look at it from a very practical, analytical point of view. You need to try to define your dream into numbers and tangible goals. You need to define it in a more practical manner. You need mini-goals, a plan of action, milestones and timelines for its achievement.

You need to take out the "romantic part" of the dream and translate it into numbers and facts. You can still feel and enjoy your dream when you have achieved it but getting there realistically requires a more analytical kind of thinking.

Tip 15: Start small – finish big: Leverage with a sales organization

> Coca-Cola sold only 9 bottles in its first year. Today, more than 1.7 billion servings are sold in a single day.

You cannot become really truly successful all by yourself. You can't become a millionaire all by yourself. That is not possible. There are always other people involved. You will need employees and contractors. Great things in business are never done by one person – they're always done by a team of people.

Most of all, you will need leverage. You need other people who will help you to achieve your goals. You will need people who will help you to sell more of your products because you alone can't sell enough to make it really big.

Therefore you must think bigger and differently. You must consider starting a sales team or have a plan for affiliates or intermediaries.

10 average people will always sell more than one person – even if that one person is the best sales person.

If you want to become rich, you will need to make people rich, too. You will have to provide opportunities for your business partners as well. You can't become successful all by yourself and expect the others to do the work.

> You cannot isolate yourself into prosperity. Bryant McGill

In order to create enough leverage and to hire a few sales people, consider thinking outside of the box. Why don't you hire a small team in a different country? I used to have sales teams in Eastern Europe. Instead of paying my employees in Switzerland $5000 per month, I hired German speaking sales people in Serbia and Macedonia for $350 per month. They grew up in Germany or Switzerland and spoke the language perfectly but then moved back to their original country with their families. But a salary of $350 in Serbia can be enough to survive there.

Another way could be to hire people online in the Philippines or in India for that matter. Those people also speak English.

In general, I would start with renting some office space and put in 5 to 10 working spaces. Get a VOIP telephone system and start with a couple people first and generate new leads for yourself. As you figure things out, increase the number of people and generate a bigger call center.

> If you can't do great things, do small things in a great way.

Tip 16: Job = Just over broke = dream killer

> It is not Monday that is shit – it is your job!

Why do people go to a job? Well the obvious answer is to make money or to earn a living. But the problem is that you will eventually get complacent and fall into a rhythm like most people and end up in the rat race.

You will lose track of why you go to work in the first place. You will get used to working for someone else you don't see any other options to earn money in a different way.

My advice to you is this: Make a monthly budget of all your main expenses. Let's assume that you will need $5000 every month to survive. Instead of finding a job that will give you this kind of income, you should focus on time and energy on creating a job for yourself by selling a product or service. Your first goal is to create your own business that will at least replace your income needs of $5000 and free you from having a regular job.

There is power in making things happen on your own. You don't have to make millions but at least shoot for making $5000 in a first phase. The goal is simply to free you from the bond and time requirements that a job will bring.

You can sell a product over the phone, start an online business or provide a service locally so that you get out of the typical rat race dilemma.

Freedom doesn't mean that I can do what I want when I want. It means that I can stop doing certain things.

Once you are free and independent, you will start to think bigger and you will have the time and energy to focus on building a big business.

Staying in a job that takes up most of your time and life is a dream killer and it will rob you of the power and energy that you will need to create your own business.

Tip 17: No excuses ever

Success is your own damn fault!
(Larry Winget)

There are no excuses. You are no longer allowed to make any kind of excuses or give explanations why you didn't achieve success.

You either do it or you don't do it. But don't ever complain or make excuses. If you don't achieve your goals then you have to adjust your actions. In most cases you are probably not selling enough products to clients. It is as simple as that.

You can either complain or act. But you can't do both. When things don't work out, change your actions. But complaining and worrying will not help.

> We don't grow when things are easy.
> We grow when we face challenges.

Success is really simple but it is not easy. The price for success is dealing with uncomfortable things. It means working more hours, dealing with clients, selling a product, dealing with rejection, dealing with failure, dealing with fear and overcoming obstacles.

But once you have figured it out, life will never be the same. Life will be 100 times better. But it is the price that you will have to pay in advance before you can reap life's rewards.

Success is hard and painful but being broke is also hard. Unfortunately, you must choose between one of the two.

> Becoming rich is hard. Staying broke is
> hard. Chose your kind of "hard".

Tip 18: Think outside of the box

> Common thinking will only you get you
> a common life. Bryant McGill

You can't become financially independent with a regular 9 to 5 job. You will need a different strategy.

There was once a man who got himself in debt for more than $1.5 million. Three years later he had $2 million in the bank. How did he get himself out of this situation? His answer: *"I could not look for a regular 9 to 5 job to solve my problems. I had to think bigger and outside of the normal options."*

Most people will only try to look for a better job or try to get promoted. They don't dare to think differently.

Here are some alternative ideas:

1. Start your own business (import a product from a foreign country and sell it here)
2. Become a professional investor (trade stocks, options and futures)
3. Start an online business (sell a thousand products for $1000 and make $1 million in 6 months)
4. Make a big transaction happen between two parties (e.g. company and VC firm) – get finder's fee for several hundred thousand dollars
5. Buy a big piece of real estate, turn it around and sell it to another party for more money
6. Raise $10 million for a pharmaceutical start-up company and get 10% commission (=$1 million for you)
7. Produce cheap products in China or India and sell them to a big company in the US (toys, plastic items, clothes, etc.)
8. Buy foreclosed homes, fix them up and sell them for more money (sell 10 homes in a year and sell them for at least $100,000 a piece more)
9. Invent a new gadget and get it financed for millions through private investors or through a venture capital firm (get a patent first and then own shares in your company)
10. Buy a piece of land and drill for oil (find a larger deposit and produce 100 barrels of oil per day at $100 per barrel for the next 20 years)
11. Buy a piece of land and find a gold deposit (e.g. 500,000 ounces of gold at $1200 per ounce = $700 million)

12. Partner up with a biotechnology student at the research center at your local University and patent a new cure or medication – develop it further, raise money and sell it to a pharmaceutical giant for $500 million
13. Start a loan or mortgage company – process thousands of mortgages online and find a special financing partner / bank who is likely to approve most applications
14. Invest into commodities market – find out insider information and use it to your advantage
15. Become a sports agent, find new talent and sell the contracts for millions to a major sports team
16. Export a local US product to Europe and sell it there for more money – get the rights for an existing company and become the new representative for the country by simply asking for it
17. Secure a contract in a third world country (maybe somewhere in Africa) with the government and offer it to a company who wants to do business there (for drilling rights, etc.)
18. Go to Africa, find diamonds and sell them in Amsterdam in the market
19. Go to Russia or somewhere else in Asia and find a rare precious mineral or natural resource and become the owner of that project / company – make deals with the local government and foreign companies
20. Develop an environment-cleaning up device and sell it to a country – get the funding from politicians

I was simply brainstorming 20 ideas other than getting a regular job. And my guess is that if you put one of these into action that you could make way more money than with a regular job. Just think differently. Think outside of the normal options!

> The secret of business is to know something that nobody else knows. Aristotle Onassis

No one said that it was easy. But it is possible. Others have done it, too. Just be creative and don't be scared of big numbers.

> If you do what you have always done, you will get what you have always gotten.
> Anthony Robbins

Tip 19: Getting started and momentum

> The secret to getting ahead is getting started. Mark Twain

You don't have to be great to start but you have to start to be great. Getting started even if it is not perfect at first is the key to success.

I think a simple rule of business is, if you do the things that are easier first, then you can actually make a lot of progress.

I have a friend who is very successful in business, and his motto is, *"Don't do what you can't do. Do what only you can do."* First of all, you have to know what your specific, unique gift is and then you do that.

If you decide to start an online business, you need to build a list of names. You will need to build an email list. How do you start?

The answer is easy. Start with a simple ad and a newsletter. Generate 30 new subscribers each day. In one month you will have 900 names and in one year you will have 10,800 names on your list.

Do something every single day to grow your list. Post a daily video on YouTube, run a small ad or write a blog. Every successful online marketer had to start somewhere. You need to start today so that in one year you will have 10,000 names. Maybe your goal is 1 million names. Well, get to 100,000 next and so on. Buy lists, exchange lists with other companies or people. Be creative and do what needs to be done.

> The first step is that you have to say that you can. Will Smith

Do something you love and the money will follow. Get a good start and get momentum in the beginning. Sooner or later, those who win are those who think they can.

> Success is nothing more than a few simple disciplines practiced every day. Jim Rohn

There are no secrets to success. It is the result of preparation, hard work, and learning from failure.

Tip 20: Build an online business – become an expert in online marketing

> Everything I learned in college can now be found for free on the Internet.

Today we live in the absolute best time to make money. There are countless new opportunities available to you and technology and the Internet has opened up and connected the world in a way that has never been there in history.

You can learn absolutely everything for free on the Internet. Everything is available to you. You can find out just about everything. You can learn about rocket science or any other topic that you like.

It is really unbelievable.

Today, you can send out one email to 100,000 people at the same time in a matter of seconds. You can make money online 24/7. You can record a sales presentation once and have it automatically played to thousands of potential customers all over the world at the same time.

There are countless examples of the new Internet marketers who made millions online without any overhead and in a very short period of time.

Frank Kern made $18 million in 24 hours. John Reese made $1 million in one hour or Jeff Walker's product launch formula generated over $500 million in sales for other people (his students).

Right now, we have a huge opportunity and I don't know for how many years this will still be the case. The Internet is not yet regulated and anyone can pretty much do anything. The market and the options to do business are still endless.

Don't waste any more time and learn absolutely everything that you can about Internet marketing. Learn what you need to learn and feed your brain with positive messages and knowledge from other successful people.

> Try, try, try, and keep on trying is the rule that must be followed to become an expert in anything. W. Clement Stone

Tip 21: Follow your heart and choose something you love doing

> People rarely succeed unless they have fun in what they are doing. Andrew Carnegie

Interestingly, most successful people didn't make money for the sake or sole purpose of making money. They started a business because they loved a certain topic or industry. They got passionate about a certain topic and developed a product or service.

> Disneyland is a work of love. We didn't go into Disneyland just with the idea of making money. Walt Disney

And that is also where you should start. Pick something that you love. Pick an area that you could commit to for the next 20 years if necessary. Don't just do it for the money. Do something that you believe it or that you like.

The reason is because things will get though. Things will get difficult and at times you want to give up. If the topic sucks and it was just to make money, you will give up for sure. But if it is something that you are passionate about, then you will continue.

> I would rather die of passion than of boredom. Vincent Van Gogh

Tip 22: Dream big and develop a vision for your life: Start your own business and live your dream

> What you want in life will not come to you if
> you are sitting on your ass waiting for it.
> Raul Villacis

Ten years from now, make sure you can say that you chose your life. You didn't settle for it. You are far smarter than you can ever imagine. Your mind is a creative muscle but it only develops with use. Don't settle for a regular job because of "security". Live your life and make something great happen. Build a multi million-dollar business! Develop a vision for your life.

> You can be young without money, but you can't
> be old without it. Tennesse Williams

This is your life and you have 40 years of working time available. It is ok if you spent the first 10 or 20 years working for someone else learning about business and about your industry but now you must make the switch and start your own business.

Develop a new vision and don't be afraid of big numbers. Remember: there are no unrealistic goals – only unrealistic timelines for their achievement.

You can be, do or have anything in this life if you decide to get it. Everything is available to you but you must work for it. As long as you don't give up, there is nothing that you can't achieve if you set your mind to it.

Live life as if everything is rigged in your favor. Rumi

You only have control over 3 things in your life: the thoughts you think, the images you visualize and the actions you take. Dwell on your goals every day and do something small every single day towards the achievement of your goals. Your speed doesn't matter. The main thing is that you are moving forward.

CHAPTER 14

SUCCESS SIMPLIFIED

> In 1995 I had $7 in my pocket and knew two things: I'm broke as hell and one day I won't be. ("The Rock" – Dwayne Johnson)

Every big accomplishment starts with a dream. A dream that lights up your heart and fuels your desire.

The world is such a big place and it is full of opportunities. The main problem in life is not lack of motivation but rather to decide exactly what you want and then go for it. Most people have no idea what they really want and because of that they never accomplish anything out of the ordinary.

But success is possible for almost anyone these days. The world has changed and the technological advances and the Internet have made it possible for anyone to achieve great success.

Step 1: Turning a dream into a goal

> You can't win if you don't begin.
> (Robin Sharma)

The first step to accomplish any dream is to turn it into a **measurable goal**. You need to decide exactly to the last detail what it is that you want to achieve.

The challenge is to take a dream or wish and then to define it. What does it mean if you say that you want to be successful? What kind of business do you want to start? What kind of house do you want to buy? How much money do you have to earn? Why do you even want to achieve your goal in the first place?

Let's say that you want to become rich. But what does that mean exactly? If you simply want "more money" then it could mean that you would be happy with $50,000 more? Or do you want $10 million? Without a proper definition, you will never achieve anything. That is why you must first get **clarity**. Define and decide exactly what you want. You can't hit a target that you can't see.

Step 2: Quantify your goal

A goal without a plan is just a wish. (Antoine de Saint-Exupéry)

Most dreams stay dreams because they never get quantified. You need to **take the romantic part out of the dream** and try to **define it as a doable task**.

Then you must develop an action plan. Basically, you break down your goal into smaller mini-goals, steps or milestones. Once you have made a plan you must have deadlines or timelines for their achievement. This is your way of controlling whether you are on track or not.

Goal – Plan – Activities – Control

It sounds very simple and in reality it is. The main problem is that most people don't have unrealistic goals but rather **unrealistic deadlines** and no control. People get distracted or give up too easily and that's why they don't achieve their goals.

But a study from Harvard has shown that 97% of all people never actually write down their goals and only 3% do so. And it is the 3% that end up achieving their goals.

Therefore, write down your goals, make a plan and define with absolute clarity what you want and need to do. Failing to do this will almost certainly lead to not achieving your goals.

Step 3: Create a product – do what you love

> When you do what you love, you have PURPOSE. When you share it with others, you have MEANING.

Making money comes from **selling a product to a customer**. That is why you must first create a product or service.

Since you are going to spend a lot of time building your business, you should choose something that you love and where you can **use your strengths**.

If you start with something that you don't really like and only do it for the money, you will eventually give up when things get tough or difficult. And that is going to happen sooner or later in any business or undertaking.

> Success is not the key to happiness. Happiness is the key to success. If you love what you are doing, you will be successful. (Albert Schweitzer)

If you ask people what is most important in life, they will usually say "to be happy". So if you are doing something that makes you happy and at the same time you make money with it, then it is a win-win.

I think it is much more important that you chose something that you love and that makes you happy rather than only money. If you do it well, then the money will come, too.

Always remember: If you are not excited about it, it's not the right path. How you make your money is more important than how much money you make.

> You will never find peace of mind until you
> listen to your heart. (George Michael)

Step 4: Sales every day

Making money means selling. You must be selling a product to a customer every single day to move forward. It is the only way.

You can sell in person, on the phone, over the Internet, in your store or in any other way but you must be selling a product every single day.

In simple words: If you are selling daily, you will be successful and move forward. If you don't sell, you are failing.

> Doubt is only removed by action.
> If you are not working, then that's when doubt comes in.
> (Conor McGregor)

The problem starts when you stop doing things like talking to customers, etc. When you are no longer selling is when doubt creeps in. If you stop talking to clients, making phone calls or initiating marketing activities, you start to doubt your whole strategy and business.

Doubt kills more dreams than anything else. The only way to remove doubt is to take action.

Step 5: Get clarity

> As soon as you truly commit to making something happen, the "how" will reveal itself. (Tony Robbins)

You can't hit a target that you can't see. The same is true for your goals. It is nice to dream but without **crystal clear clarity** you won't achieve anything.

That's why the first step to achieving anything is to define your goals in detail. And I mean in detail! There were many reasons for my personal success but one of the main ones was definitely "having clarity".

> People are not lazy. They simply have goals that don't inspire them. (Tony Robbins)

Once you have your goal you need to know **the reasons WHY** you want to achieve your goal. Goals are great but reasons are stronger. If you have a goal without the motivation and the driving force to achieve it, you won't fully pursue it.

Step 6: Think outside the normal options

> If we demand one dollar from life, then life will punish us with one dollar.

Life is too short not to be important. I had achieved my success because I set huge goals. But my goals were unrealistic and way too big for me at the time. But I grew into my goals. Don't be afraid to think bigger.

Being an entrepreneur can be very difficult at times. But then again, so is being a regular employee. If you want to achieve success out of the ordinary, you can't do it with a regular 9 to 5 job. It is not possible.

> You have to think anyway, so why not think big?
> (Donald Trump)

But if you set goals, then you might as well set big goals because you have to work anyway. If you decide to earn a normal income like everybody else, then the struggle of being an entrepreneur is not worth it. But if you decide to make millions, then your only option is to think differently than 95% of the people. You must look for other options and business opportunities to make it happen.

We all work about 45 years from the age of 20 to 65. What you do in those 45 years is up to you. But working in a slave like environment that doesn't fulfill you and that will leave you with a regular income is probably not what you were born to do. Don't be afraid to fully embrace your destiny and start a business with your talents and strengths.

> Entrepreneurship is the key to wealth,
> security and impacting the world.
> (Robert Kiyosaki)

Step 7: Don't reinvent the wheel (10% better)

Everything has already been invented. Every business opportunity that you believe to be unique or special is already out there in some form. It can actually be quite discouraging when you Google your idea and find 1000 other companies just like it.

> Somewhere someone is looking for exactly what you have to offer.

Don't worry about whether or not your idea already exists. You came into this world with a specific set of talents and strengths and you must do what you can do best. The world is big enough for your products and services and you don't need to reinvent the wheel and try to come up with something that has never been there before.

All you can do is to be yourself and then create a product or service that has your ideas in it. If you create a special product that is about 10% different from the current other products, then you are doing well.

Step 8: How to find clients

Advertise on social media and Google (that's where people are today)

Selling a product or service and making money means **sales and marketing**. You need to find customers and sell them a product. But where are the customers these days? The answer: **On the Internet and social media!**

That is where you must advertise and do your marketing. The world has changed and traditional marketing has moved from print ads and TV commercials to online advertising. Therefore you should study everything about online marketing and how to best position your products online.

You should run ads on Facebook, Google, YouTube and on similar popular online forms. Your goal should be to learn absolutely everything about this topic and become a specialist. Read books, go to seminars, buy courses, test ads and eventually you will figure out how to make money online and build a business for the future.

Step 9: Stay true to yourself

No one is you and that is your power.

Be yourself no matter what. Some will adore you and some will hate everything about you. But who cares? It's your life. Make the most out of it.

The world is such a big place and there are all kinds of personalities in it. But if you try to change or conform to someone that you are not, then you will never fully be happy or successful.

If you are different from most people, a bit weird or even strange in some way, then you should embrace it. Whatever makes you, you, is who you should be. Your personality and whatever makes you special is what makes you different from the rest. If you are going to be weird, be confident about it.

> Stay with one thing long enough until you become the best at it and your tribe will find you. (Joel Brown)

You don't need the whole world to love you or to approve of you. You will never be popular with everyone – so just be yourself. The right kind of people will appreciate you for who you are.

In order to have a successful business you need maybe a few hundred clients at most. With the connectivity of the Internet, your kind of people will find you and that's who your clients will be.

Don't worry about criticism and people who don't like you. There will be enough other people who will absolutely love what you do if you create a quality product that adds value to people's lives in some way.

Step 10: Work longer (10-12 hours)

> There is no elevator to success. You have to take the stairs. (Zig Ziglar)

Success is like an iceberg. People only see the result (or 10%) like your big house, your nice cars, your money, etc.

But in reality, the 90% that no one sees are things like overcoming obstacles, disappointments, hard work, taking huge risks, late nights, struggles, self-discipline, courage, dealing with fear and doubt, criticism, adversity, sacrifices, rejection and personal failures.

Anyone who has success had to work hard for it. There is a price for success and **it must be paid in full and in advance before** you can reap the benefits. Unfortunately, that's the truth – whether you like it or not.

Success is not possible by chance or without any effort. No one simply just got lucky or it didn't happen by accident, either.

That's why should never be envious of someone who is more successful than you because you know that that person had to work hard to get where he is. You should rather try to learn something from that person and find out how they achieved success.

In order to make more money, you must be able to deal with more difficult challenges. The more difficult the problems are, the more money you will make. So don't condemn difficult situations. Embrace them and grow stronger with them. If your life just got harder, it means that you just leveled up.

While one person hesitates because he feels inferior, the other is busy making mistakes and becoming superior. Working hard and long hours is the price for success and the price for getting better. Making mistakes is also part of that.

Nothing worthwhile is easy to achieve.

> Have you ever seen a Lamborghini television commercial? It doesn't exist because the people who buy them aren't sitting around watching TV.

Step 11: Leverage

> The difference between an entrepreneur who is struggling and one who is doing well is usually leverage.

Leverage is something that will help to generate a lot more clients or sales. There are many different forms of leverage. Let me give you a few examples for leverage:

1. **Internet:** Leads and sales are generated 24/7 through the Internet. If it is just you and you have to call up clients yourself and try to make sales at the same time, you might be struggling. But if you have a system that generates good quality leads online, then generating sales is much easier.
2. **The right leads / list:** Maybe you are trying to make sales using the phone book or the yellow pages and you constantly get rejected. Making cold calls in that case is hard and frustrating work. But if you have the right list, then making those calls might be 100 times easier. If you have a list with exactly the right target group and people who have bought something similar in the past, then working with that particular list can make all the difference.
3. **The right contacts:** In order to sell larger quantities of your product, maybe all it takes is the right distributor or contact. Having the right contact can change everything.
4. **Sales people**: 10 average sales people sell more than 1 great person. Having a sales team can change everything.
5. **More locations / stores**: If you have one store, your sales and profit are limited to that one location. But if you have a system and expand to 10 locations, then you have more sales and earning power.
6. **Money**: Having external influx of capital can help you to expand your business faster. If you had $2 million that you get from a private equity company or from private investors, you can build a business that grows much faster and better.
7. **Software / tools**: Having the right kind of software or tools can help you identify the right clients or business opportunities. Technology can help you to save time and energy.
8. **Famous people**: If you can win a famous person for your cause, people automatically associate your company with that person and trust you immediately.
9. **Cheap production**: If you find a way to produce your products for example in a third world country for a fraction of the price, it can give you an enormous competitive advantage.

10. **Other companies**: Other companies don't necessarily have to be your competition. If you can strike a deal with your competitor and exchange client lists or combine products, it can boost both of your sales at the same time.

Leverage can give you the competitive advantage to succeed in business. One good idea is all you need to improve your business model.

Step 12: Habits

> Change your life today. Don't gamble on the future, act now, without delay.
> (Bradley Martin, Bodybuilder)

You will never change your life until you change something you do on a **daily basis**. The secret of your success is found in your **daily routine**.

Even if you are not great today, you need to keep doing your best at this moment. Once you do that you put yourself in the best position for the next moment.

Sometimes you have to do what you have to do until you can do what you want to do.

You need to accept responsibility for your life. Realize that it is only you who will get you where you want to go and no one else.

> We don't have to be smarter than the rest – we just have to be more disciplined than the rest. (Warren Buffett)

Self-discipline leads to freedom. Being active and following a plan with lots of income generating activities will go a long way even if you don't have immediate success. In the long run self-discipline will always win.

Make sure that your daily plan and activities help you to achieve your goals.

Step 13: Adding value to other people's lives

Since you need to sell a product or service to clients in order to make money and to be successful, you need to be aware that people are only willing to spend money if the product that they buy **adds value to their lives** in some way.

So in effect, the first question must be: "How can I add value to someone's life? How can I make someone's life better?"

You won't sell anything to anybody if you don't have their best interest at heart. The product that you create and sell must somehow improve someone's life or add value in some way.

So think about it and brainstorm ideas. How can you add more value than the competition in your chosen field? What can you offer that makes it hard for someone to refuse your products? What makes your product or service **unique** so that the customer will preferably chose your company over another?

Step 14: Momentum

> The start is what stops most people.

Sometimes there is no next time, no time outs, no second chances. Sometimes it's now or never. What are you waiting for? This is your life and you need to make it happen now.

Momentum is a key factor for initial success. If you have little successes in the beginning, you keep going. You can build on small successes and it is your driving force to continue.

It is better to get started even if you don't have everything 100% figured out.

> It's the "maybes" that will kill you.

Doubt is what holds most people back from a life of greatness. And doubt creeps in when you are lacking self-confidence.

Sometimes you just need to have the motto "just do it" from Nike. Either it will work or it won't. But you can't be hesitant and always wonder whether you would have made it or not.

> Do not let what you cannot do interfere with what you can do. (John Wooden)

Things will never be perfect in the beginning and you can't expect it to be the case, either. In the beginning, the most important thing is momentum. Things need to keep moving forward. You need little successes and you need a positive development of your business venture.

One of my favorite quotes goes like this: "Do what you can today with what you have."

Better tools will come once you have more success or money. But don't do it because you believe that without it being perfect, you can't have success.

Step 15: Dress for success and get into shape

No matter what level of business you're in, it's important to dress for the client you want, rather than the client you have. There's this idea of working from home in PJs. Usually, this is not a good idea.

The most successful people get up early and dress like they're off for a day at the office, and it's reflected in their attitude.

> When you look good, you feel good and you're more confident, too.

If you are overweight, then your starting point should be to get into shape first. Go on a diet and exercise plan for 3 months and get fit.

Most people underestimate what the positive effect of "feeling good about yourself" has on your success, level of self-confidence and overall positive energy level.

Kai Greene, one of the best bodybuilders in the world, said the following thing:

"When I was a young man I remember being told that the guy that goes to the gym is the guy that is concerned with the physical and the man that goes to college is a man that is concerned with the development of his mind. I struggled with this as a young man because I realized that THEY ARE NOT SEPARATE. To identify myself as a thinking being is to identify myself as a bodybuilder. My body becomes a physical manifestation of my thoughts. My power is not my body. My power is my mind."

In order to be successful in business, you need to be feeling good about yourself and be in good physical condition.

Step 16: Self-confidence

> You've always had the power my dear; you just had to learn it for yourself.
> (The Wizard of Oz)

Your biggest enemy is fear and self-doubt. It is that little voice inside of you that creeps up and gives you doubt. And doubt paralyzcs you.

The only way that you can really become successful is with your strengths. You can't build a successful life based on your weaknesses. But once you start comparing yourself and your strengths to others, it is easy to get discouraged and to believe that you are not good enough.

> If you do not see yourself as a winner, you cannot perform as a winner.
> (Zig Ziglar)

The foundation of success is high levels of self-confidence. But you can only believe in yourself if you work on your strengths and talents and keep improving them. Believe and act as if it were impossible to fail.

You need to decide to become absolutely the best in your chosen field. And once you have made the decision to get to the top, you can't ever doubt yourself. You need to fully go for it and believe in yourself.

Learn also about the **impostor syndrome**. Many professionals will at some point experience a psychological phenomenon known as imposter syndrome, complete with feelings of inadequacy and a fear that everything accomplished to date has been through sheer luck. To overcome this, learn to internalize accomplishments. Peer groups are a great place to talk it out and build confidence.

> Your self-confidence needs to be rooted in who you are completely outside of your success in business.

Step 17: Dealing with problems or difficult situations

> When we face our problems, they disappear.
> (Carlos Slim, richest man in Mexico)

Nothing worth having in this life comes easy. Creating a successful business is not easy and you will be faced with many challenges and problems before you make any money.

But you must realize that problems are a normal part of business and of life. We all have to deal with problems and the bigger the problem is, the more money we can make.

Obstacles can't stop you. Problems can't stop you. Most of all, other people can't stop you. Only you can stop you.

Problems are uncomfortable and hard. But avoiding them doesn't make them go away. Often, we get paralyzed because of fear. But what we fear doing most is usually what we most need to do.

> If you are overwhelmed by the size of a problem,
> break it down into smaller pieces.
> (Chuck Close)

The trick or solution is to objectively look at any problem and then break it down into smaller, manageable tasks. Make a to-do list.

When people get overwhelmed with too many problems at once, they usually don't do anything because it is too much to handle. In that case simply focus on one problem at a time or one problem per day. After one week or one month, your situation will already look much better.

Your ability to deal with problems or difficult situation will determine your income level. So don't condemn difficult situations – embrace them and grow.

Step 18: Find yourself and your business idea

> If you haven't found it yet, keep looking. (Steve Jobs)

Your big opportunity may be right where you are now. Typically, the things that you are already doing and that you are interested will give you a pretty good idea where to look.

There will be a time in life when all your instincts will tell you to do something, something that defies logic, upsets your plans, and may seems crazy to others. When that happens, it is a sign and you must follow your intuition. Ignore the odds and just go for it.

> There is no passion to be found in settling for a life that is less than the one you are capable of living. (Nelson Mandela)

Once you start understanding yourself, once you start executing on who you actually are versus who you wish you were, things start to change very quickly. Often people are living in a dream world and because of it, they fail to take the necessary action today.

It is important that you **find yourself** first. **Know who you are and what you are really good at**. And then make a plan and build your business based on your **talents and strengths.**

If you can't do great things, then do small things in a great way. Eventually things will take off.

Listen to your own voice and soul. Too many people listen to the noise of the world instead of themselves. Deep down you know what you should be doing.

> You are not too old and it is not too late.
> (Rainer Maria Rilke – 1875 – 1926)

Remember your light has the ability to light others. Ignite the world. Life is about moments: Don't wait for them, create them.

Step 19: Marketing

You need to create a system to generate new leads constantly. That's why your marketing process is so important. You need to create business system that makes sense and will provide you with a constant flow of opportunities.

But marketing alone won't help you if your product is of low quality. You also need a **high quality product.** Otherwise your marketing efforts will be short-lived and you won't be successful in the long run.

The best way to learn more about marketing is to become a client yourself and then **reverse engineer their marketing strategy**. Find out where they advertised, how they got potential clients in the door and what upsells they offer in the end. Maybe the initial offer is a low-priced offer and the real moneymaker comes later in the cycle.

> Copy successful marketing strategies – to earn more, you must learn more.

You must study all the successful companies and how they market their products. You must become a specialist in marketing.

Remember that you need a cheaper priced product first to gain trust. Once you have a client relationship established, you can offer more and more expensive products later.

Step 20: Create the right circumstances for yourself

> When a flower doesn't bloom you fix the environment in which it grows, not the flower.

Even Albert Einstein once said that if you judge a fish by his ability to climb a tree, it will always think that it is stupid.

Sometimes the only reason why you are not getting ahead is because you are in the wrong environment and have the wrong circumstances.

Maybe you are surrounded by toxic people, have the wrong contacts, use an old system or you simply are in the wrong profession using your weaknesses and that is why you are not getting further in life.

You can only do well if you use your best talents and strengths and if the circumstances are good. This means that you might have to change something in your life. You might have to get rid of some people, change jobs, move to a new city or use different leads.

Change is painful. But nothing is as painful as staying somewhere you don't belong.

> If you are born poor its not your mistake, But if
> you die poor its your mistake. (Bill Gates)

The only person who can make those changes is you. You are responsible for everything in your life. If the circumstances are not good, then you must change them. No one else can do this for you.

Step 21: Develop a vision

> A man doesn't die when his heart stops beating.
> He dies when he loses his dream.
> (Raul Villacis)

The tragedy in life is not failing to reach your goals. The tragedy in life is having no goals to reach.

I believe that goals should never be easy. They should force you to work even if you are uncomfortable at the time.

If you limit your choices only to what seems possible or reasonable, you will not strive for what you really want. You will only go for what is a compromise. Those half-hearted goals will not give you the spirit and power to accomplish anything great that you are capable of.

> Have big dreams. You will grow into them.

Be somebody nobody though you could be. No dream is too big with the right attitude and work ethic.

Maybe your vision is to build a successful business and make at least one million dollars per year. Your starting point in that case is goal setting and to get clarity.

> I want to see what happens if I don't give up.

Step 22: Setting business goals

> Those who do not have goals are doomed forever to work for those who do.

Focus on daily activities

$100 per day = $30,000 per year
$200 per day = $70,000 per year
$300 per day = $100,000 per year
$500 per day = $180,000 per year
$1,000 per day = $360,000 per year
$3,000 per day = $1,000,000 per year

How to make a million

Sell a $200 product to 5,000 people
Sell a $500 product to 2,000 people
Sell a $1,000 product to 1,000 people
Sell a $2,000 product to 500 people
Sell a $5,000 product to 200 people

Monthly subscription = $1 million per year

5,000 people pay $17 per month for 12 months
2,000 people pay $42 per month for 12 months
1,000 people pay $83 per month for 12 months
500 people pay $167 per month for 12 months
250 people pay $333 per month for 12 months

You need to set goals for yourself and for your business if you want to get ahead in this life. Take a good look at these numbers and decide which ones make sense to you.

> How long are you going to wait before you
> demand the best for yourself?
> (Epictetus)

You are the only one who can change your life. No one else can do it for you. And no one is coming for the rescue.

CHAPTER 15

BUSINESS SYSTEMS

> If you don't find a way to make money while you sleep,
> you will work until you die. (Warren Buffet)

This program is for all those people who know deep inside that they are capable of so much more but haven't found the right path yet.

Sometimes finding the right path means **finding or creating the right system** to get ahead. You probably have already found your true calling but the way you execute it or make money is not satisfying enough. Maybe all you need is the right business approach or business system.

Often, it comes down to sales and marketing. Other times it is the **right set up, strategy or leverage** that can help you to reach more clients and make more sales.

In the end you need more clients so you make more money. You get more clients from more leads and from effective marketing strategies.

Passive Income

> The day you plant the seed is not the day you eat the fruit. Be patient.

Most people misunderstand passive income. It's not making lots of money without putting any effort into it. It's about putting in 100% at the beginning and collecting the fruits afterwards without you having to take further action.

You can compare it to a planting a tree. The fruits will eventually grow without you taking further action. It happens automatically (passive) but you have to plant the tree **first**. You have to water it, etc. You had to **do the work in advance** before you could reap its benefits.

Hustling versus automatic income

Chronic stress makes you physically and mentally tired.

You can't work all the time and function at 100%. You need to **automate the process** so that you can make money without having to hustle all the time.

The reason why most sales people burn out is because they have to constantly do cold calling and start new every month new with zero sales.

It's ok to hustle in the beginning to get things going. But eventually **you will need a proper system** so that you don't have to hustle anymore.

When you are young, you have a lot more energy and you are willing to do whatever it takes because you are somewhat naïve. Being inexperienced or naïve can be a good thing because you keep going despite difficulties when you start out. But after years of trying to get clients you will eventually get tired and your energy level will go down.

Once you hit a certain age, have a wife and kids, a mortgage to pay and lots of other responsibilities, it is easy to burn out. The price that you will have to pay and the amount of energy that it takes to start out and conquer your field are huge. Not everyone is willing to go through this ordeal anymore once you hit a certain age.

Some people will *burn out* and others will *bore-out* (= unproductive). Doing the same thing over and over for many years can be boring and will steal your joy and energy, too.

That's why **you must develop business systems** that will help you to generate automatic income, sales or leads.

We used to do a lot of cold calling to generate leads. But this process was very tiring and frustrating. One day I met a person who was in the same business like me (Private Equity / selling shares over phone). He paid a marketing agency about $100,000 per month to get leads online of people who showed an active interest in investing into stocks. The leads were easy to close and he generated sales of about $1 million per month for his organization. Instead of trying to convince clients to invest, he chose to work with clients who already wanted to invest and wanted a consultation. This small but critical difference made his business success so much easier.

Sometimes all it takes to be successful is **a small but critical change** and then things go smoothly. You might be doing 90% right but still be stuck.

Applying the right strategy can save you 10 years in your career.

New strategies for a new age

The Internet has changed the world. It has changed business. It has changed how people and companies make money. The entire buying process has changed.

In the past people went to a store to look for a certain product or they got a call from a salesperson who sold them a product.

Today, people go first on the Internet to get information. Then, they either order the product online or go to the store where they can buy the product.

Cold calling has become increasingly difficult because of caller ID and too many sales people trying to sell you products. People have become annoyed with the constant attack.

Marketing has also changed. In the old days, people watched TV commercials, read ads in a magazine or newspaper or got something in the mail.

But today people record TV shows so that they can fast forward through the commercials and all unnecessary mail goes straight to the garbage bin.

Today, 95% of marketing happens online. There are ads on Facebook, on YouTube, etc. and if you want to look up something you will see all the ads.

Because the selling and buying process has changed, some of the old professions are dying out and with it some old school sales people.

Some people are still living in the past and after years of working hard in a certain profession; it gets increasingly harder to sell and to generate money. People try harder to make money but they get less and less results. Then they start to doubt themselves and fall into a depression because they can't reach their goals anymore.

But the problem is not that you have gotten worse. The strategies have changed.

> You should not doubt YOURSELF. You need to doubt your STRATEGY.

In the past you used a certain strategy to generate business. But this strategy is now obsolete but you just haven't figured that part out. It has nothing to do with you or your own worth.

You need to let go of old strategies or ways to be successful because they don't work anymore in today's world.

This is very hard for some people to understand and that is why they fall into a hole.

> Remember when your grandparent refused to use a computer to write a letter? They still believed in the old typewriter. Well, it is the same thing with you today but it is even more extreme.

You can't survive if you don't harness the power of the Internet, smartphones or social media.

The sooner you realize that it's never going to go back to the way it was, the sooner you can move on.

What you need in your life might be simply a **new strategy**. Maybe that is the **real problem** and you doubted yourself and your abilities for no reason.

You need to realize that there are 3.5 billion Google searches each day and 1 billion people go on Facebook. **So that is where people are today. That is where your customers are. That is where you can make money.** That is where you must be if you want to achieve your personal and financial goals.

We are in the information age and we are in a new area. This means change but also opportunity. Most people are still stuck in the past but if you realize that you can harness the power and leverage of the Internet for you, you can emerge as one of the new winners.

My suggestion to you is this: learn absolutely everything about "Online Marketing", sales psychology, Internet business success, etc. if you want to succeed in the new world.

Sales and marketing is key to every business success. But sales and marketing methods have changed. They are mostly online now.

Don't be a dinosaur...if you want to survive and thrive in the new age.

Live your own dream – but how exactly?

First of all, you need to break free from the masses. You need to get out of the rat race. You need to free yourself from having a regular 9 to 5 job.

Basically, you need to **start your own business** and get rid of your 9 to 5 job. You can't achieve financial independence as an employee.

The next step is **clarity.** You need to be absolutely **clear about your goals**. You need to know exactly what you want to achieve in your business. You will not reach your goals without clarity. If you don't know what you want, you don't know what you need to do to get it.

> If you can't put your idea on paper, your idea is not going to work.
> Lee Iacocca

That´s why it is key to create a **business plan**.

Focus on your ideal future

You can't hit a target that you can't see. You first need to set a goal and know exactly what you ideally would like to achieve. You need to start with the end goal in mind and then work your way backwards.

Be bold and plan big. Once you have your ideal company, an ideal model 5 years in the future, then figure out what needs to be done.

> Your energy will go where your focus goes.

How many employees will you have? How much revenue or sales will the company have per year? What will you stand for? What will be your main product or message to the world?

Assuming you could wave a magic wand, what will your company look like 5 years from now?

The ABCs of making money

> Do you want to get rich? Then solve problems for other people.

1. Product
2. Marketing – Leads
3. Sales – customers
4. System
5. Leverage

Become a specialist in your field

You need to become really good at what you do in order to make money and to be successful. This applies to any field or profession. If you are an accountant, you must become really good at it so that you can get a good reputation and get more clients.

1. Choose a field
2. Become really in your field
3. Create a product, program or system
4. Sell your system with leverage
5. Automate the process

Creating a product

You need something to sell in order to make money. You need to **create a product or a service** that people are willing to pay money for. In general, you try to solve a problem for someone.

> In order to make lots of money, you need to
> **sell it to many people** to get rich.

You should have a number of products. Usually, you start with an inexpensive product and then develop several products that are more and more expensive.

Product 1: $20 to $100
Product 2: $500
Product 3: $2000
Product 4: $5000
Product 5: $10,000

Most new clients will start with a cheaper product first and as they get to know you and your company, they will trust you more. Eventually, you will be able to sell them a more expensive product where your profit margins are higher. Often, it is not likely that you can start with a product that costs $10,000. That requires a past buying experience and trust. That's why you must start with a cheaper product in your chain of products.

Another possible strategy is to start with a free product:

Product 1: Free
Product 2: $297
Product 3: $1000
Product 4: $5000
Product 5: $10,000

Create a prototype and duplicate it

> As soon as you have found something that works, you need to focus your energy on duplicating it.

You need to develop one product that sells. Or you need to develop one strategy that works and then you need to duplicate it.

Typically, you need to come up with a product or prototype that people want and that you can sell. Creating that first product is one of the most important steps. Once you have seen that it works, then all you need to do is to sell to it more people on a bigger scale.

There are many ways to use leverage. Leverage can be the Internet, other people's time, other people's money, distribution channels, etc.

In order to sell your products to many people you need to incorporate leverage in your business. You cannot just open up a local store and hope that you will have lots of revenue. You need to use leverage to expose your products to a bigger audience.

For example: You are a specialist in nutrition and fitness and you have a YouTube channel with lots of subscribers. You will need to create a product like for example a protein powder or a multi vitamin that can be sold as well. Your free information is great but in the end you also need a product to sell. Being on YouTube and educating people is your leverage to sell your product to more people.

Quality product

The designer Tom Ford doesn't believe in marketing. He doesn't believe that a cheap, poorly produced product with extensive marketing can outsell a high quality product that gets word-of-mouth advertising.

He is a firm believer in creating products with the highest quality. And because they are so high quality, that is why they sell. Trying to push a poor product with lots of marketing is pointless in his opinion.

You still need to do marketing and have a system but every successful brand or product is superior because it has a higher quality than a cheaper priced or produced product. If you want long-term success, you are better off creating a high quality product even if that means that it is more expensive.

> Your business system will only work if you have a high quality product that gives lots of value to people's lives.

Creating a system

The system is the success. Not one person alone. That's why you need to automate the process. You need to take yourself out of the process.

You can't generate millions of dollars by working alone and hustling clients all by yourself. It is not possible. **You need to create a business system that generates leads, sales and clients.**

How will you generate leads?
Do you require sales people?
How and where do you produce your products?
How can you increase sales?

> You need to create a system that does most of the things automatically without your involvement.

Potentiation – Success on steroids

> 2019: lemons
> 2020: lemonade
> 2021: lemonade stand

If you sell a product on your own, then you are self-employed. You are not an entrepreneur. You have created yourself a job. If you stop working, then your income will also stop.

A true entrepreneur will create a business system that will automate the selling process. Your job is to create that system or company. Your job is not to work as an employee of that system. Your job is to expand it, improve it and duplicate it.

McDonald's uses a franchise system to duplicate its locations. Maybe you could do the same in your industry. You need one system, one company or one location that works successfully and then your job is to think about how you can open up more locations or make contracts with other people so that they can sell your products, too.

Delegate the work

You need employees. You can't conquer the world alone.

You need to see yourself as the entrepreneur or the business creator that sets up the system. You need to try to exclude yourself from the sales process. For that, you need to hire sales people who will do the work for you.

Your job as the business owner is to create a business system that runs without your involvement. Of course, you need to first set it up, create the products and the processes. But once it is up and running, you need to focus your time and energy on expanding the system by finding more sales channels, doing more advertising, opening up more branches or locations and improving the overall quality.

You need to either have sales people, employees or a process in place that excludes your from directly dealing with clients. If you have to do all the selling, then you didn't create a business system but you rather created yourself a sales position or job.

True entrepreneurship is building a business system that runs without you. Your job is to control the employees and the work that they do.

Building a sales team

In order to build a successful company you need a sales team.

If you have sales channels that sell your products for a commission, then you are lucky. But the problem is that a sales organization can decide to sell a different product and drop you as a client. That is why I suggest that you build a sales team within your own company that you control and pay.

You can start out with a small team of five people and then slowly increase it to 10. If you pay a commission and have a sales manager who can run the team, then your costs will not be too high.

10 sales people sell more than 1 person.

The lifeblood of any company is sales. Without sales, there is no company. That is why building a sales team is a key factor for your success.

Marketing – generate leads

Without leads there is no revenue. As simple as that.

The most important factor is to generate leads through your marketing efforts. Without leads, there are no clients and without clients there is no revenue.

Your marketing efforts need to be tested and budgeted. You need to do marketing online or use a call center to generate leads.

When it comes to marketing you must know your numbers. Typically, you will have a sales funnel where 1000 people show interest or fill out your landing page form. 100 become potential leads and 10 people actually become clients.

But you also need to know how much money you need to invest into marketing each month to generate the 1000 contacts that go into your funnel.

In the end, once you have found a way that works and know how much money you need to allocate each month for marketing and advertising, then all you need to do is to leverage the amount if you want to increase your sales.

Write a book as a basis for your business model

> There comes a point in your life when you need to stop reading other people's books and write your own. (Albert Einstein)

The main idea of writing a book is not to get rich by writing a best selling book. The goal is to **use the book as a marketing tool** to sell a higher priced product later on in your marketing process.

Top Internet marketers give away the physical book for free but the client only has to pay for shipping (usually about $7). The reason why the client has to pay for the shipping is to make sure that he is a real buyer and is willing to use his credit card. A lead who is willing to spend money is also willing to pay for a more expensive product later. Someone who only wants something for free will not buy anything later on and is therefore a bad lead.

If you give away your book / knowledge for free the client has an opportunity to make a first experience with you. After reading the book, they want to know more or use your services. It is a great way to build trust and to establish who a potential client will be in the future.

Business System Idea 1: Raising money over the phone with a marketing team

If you have a marketing team of 5 people who will each make 100 cold calls each day and generate 5 good quality leads (95 of the people say no and 5 people say yes), then you will have 25 good leads each day. This is 125 leads per week or 500 leads per month.

In general, the people call up a person and send them some general information about the company or the deal. They prequalify the client so that the sales person who calls afterwards knows that this person could be a potential client who shows a general interest in the product.

If you call 100 quality leads, you must assume that 80% of them will fall off and that you can only continue to work with 20 of them. Those 20 leads are open to talk and you can have a third or fourth conversation with them.

Out of those 20 people, you have to assume once again that 80% won't buy your product and that in the end you will get 4 clients.

So out of 100 good quality leads, you will get 4 clients.

If the average initial investment is $10,000 per client, then you will raise $40,000 in total.

Your marketing team can be in a low cost country where salaries are cheaper. If you pay $500 per person per month, then your marketing expenses are $2500.

Cold calls (marketing calls) per day	100
NOs	95
Leads	5
Monday to Friday	25 Leads
1 month	100 Leads
80% say no in second call	20 Leads left
80% say no in third call	16 Leads left
Clients	4
2000 cold calls = 100 Leads = 20 good ones = 4 clients	

1 marketing person – 100 leads per month – 4 clients
5 marketing people – 500 leads per month – 20 clients
10 marketing people – 1000 leads per month – 40 clients

Business System Idea 2: Internet leads

Step 1: You run a Facebook AD, Google Ad or YouTube Ad

Step 2: You use a funnel (e.g. clickfunnels)

- Client gets on a landing page
- You give a free product, video or brochure
- In exchange you will receive his email address and / or phone number

Step 3: You follow up with email marketing
Step 4: You sell him a product online

Advantages: The people who are interested in your topic contact you
Disadvantages: Costs money for ads

Business System Idea 3: High ticket products

Step 1: You run a Facebook AD
Step 2: You use a funnel (e.g. clickfunnels)

- You give a free product, video or brochure
- In exchange you will receive his email address and / or phone number

Step 3: The client must **fill out a questionnaire to qualify** for your service
Step 4: You follow up with the client by calling him
Step 5: You sell him a high-ticket product (e.g. $3000 to $5000) in person on the phone
Step 6: You hire someone else to sell the product and pay your sales person a commission

Advantages: The people who are interested in your topic contact you + you get a lot of detailed information about the client that you can use to sell him a product or service
Disadvantages: Costs money for ads

Business System Idea 4: Recorded webinar

Step 1: You run a online AD
Step 2: You use a funnel (e.g. clickfunnels)

- You give a free product, video or brochure
- In exchange you will receive his email address and / or phone number

Step 3: The client watches your 1-hour sales presentation that you have recorded and plays 24/7 all over the world
Step 4: You sell a product online and automatically for $500 to $2000

Assets that make people rich – most important income streams

Assets make you rich – liabilities make you poor.

1. Businesses
2. Real Estate (e.g. rental income)
3. Investments (e.g. stocks)
4. Commodities (e.g. oil)

Instead of leasing a sports car to impress random people, you should invest your money into assets that can eventually generate an income. These assets are businesses, real estate, stocks and commodities.

Your goal should be to create several streams of income. Here are some ideas or examples:

1. **Online business:** you create an online store and sell things 24/7
2. Buying a house and renting it out: **collecting rent** (or covering mortgage payments and value will increase over time)
3. Build an **investment portfolio** – your wealth grows over time
4. You own an **oil well** and you get a monthly income from the sale of the oil

5. Business – **owning a restaurant** – someone else runs it for you
6. **Business – Co-owner / investor** – someone else runs the company and pays you part of the profits
7. **Real Estate** – buy low, fix up, sell higher
8. **Having a sales team** – a sales team sells products over the phone and generates sales and profits for you.
9. Consumer product – **people order a recurring product** from you once they have become customers
10. **Dividend income** – income from stocks
11. **Royalty income** – income from others using your idea
12. **Investments**: Covered calls – generate a monthly income with stocks that you already own by selling calls into the market
13. **Investments:** Dividends
14. **Investments:** Mutual fund – your money grows over time without your involvement
15. **Give away a free book** – customer pays $7 for shipping – once he has read the book and is convinced – he will order your product or services
16. **Hire 2 marketing people** to do cold calls and generate leads – they generate 100 leads per month for you and a sales person who works for you closes the deal almost automatically
17. **Create an online sales funnel** and sell your products online automatically without your constant involvement. Once you have set up everything and made all the videos and online sales presentations, you will generate sales every day from your sales process.
18. **Free seminar** – sell a course after people have been to your free 90-minute seminar that costs several thousand dollars. In the future have other people do the free seminar for you.
19. **SamCart online 1 page store** – Instead of creating a website, etc. you can use a one page store to sell a product. Have someone do your ads every week from upwork.com
20. **Run ad in magazine** – people call in – you set up a consultation – you close 50% over the phone

What is financial freedom?

Financial freedom is having enough monthly income from your business systems or investments to cover your monthly expenses. An income from an automatic source is also called passive income.

> Your goal should be to create several income streams from business systems that will cover your monthly expenses and give you the freedom to build more businesses.

But how much money do you really need? Is it $1million? $10 million? $100 million?

People want money and time. Not just money. That's why building several income streams will give you the freedom and time to do what you want to do.

A lot of famous founders of big companies stay on as a Chairman of the Board but select another person to be the CEO or president of the company. The CEO or president then can run the day-to-day operations and the Chairman of the Board who is typically also the biggest shareholder can influence the overall direction of the company but has the freedom and time to do something else.

If you are the main shareholder of a company and you own preferred shares with a special right to receive dividends, then you can get an income from dividends simply by owning shares. This is also a type of passive, automatic income. So when you build your own company, think long-term. Issue yourself enough shares that will eventually pay you a dividend once the earnings are high enough.

The law of attraction

> Just because you can't see oxygen, you don't dismiss it as fantasy. The same is true for the law of attraction.

A dog can hear a dog whistle but you can't. But the sound is still there. The same is true for gravity. Gravity is invisible but it is still there.

There are billion things that we block out but that doesn't mean that they are not there.

When it comes to the law of attraction, which is a mental law, it is just as real as a physical law. When you dwell and focus on what you want and act as if you already have it in your life, it will eventually manifest into reality.

When it comes to building a business system that generates a monthly income for you, you should also take 5-10 minutes per day and dream about your goal. Imagine how it will feel when you generate an income from several businesses.

How to disappoint people and live your life

> Don't let ordinary people tell you that you
> can't live an extraordinary life.

When I first started planning my companies, my initial idea was to create 4 income streams of $8000 each. When I showed it to one of my old friends, he told me that it was impossible and that I was totally unrealistic.

But I knew deep in my heart that I was going to do it. I ended up creating more than 4 income streams. I created 5 companies that paid me $10,000 per month and 3 sales organizations where I had a percentage of the overall sales. I ended up with more than $100,000 per month because of my model of creating several income streams for myself.

Some things are simply out of the reality for certain people. They can't imagine that something like this could be possible or realistic.

If you don't fit into the general way of how you are supposed to live your life, it is difficult for other people to understand and accept it. I am not saying that you should ignore common sense and make bad decisions. But once you have understood that you could have a better life doing things a little bit differently than the average person, you can never go back and accept a regular, boring life of having a 9 to 5 job.

If you want $1 million, shoot for $10 million not $1 million.

Start today to build several businesses

No matter where you are today in life, you need to start somewhere. You should let the past be and think about how you can create several streams of income from businesses and investments going forward.

You should probably start with the end goal in mind and write down how your ideal future should look like.

Start with the first step today and never give up! I wish you all the best!

CHAPTER 16

THE POWER OF YOUR OWN POWER

Be aware of your personal power – other things than money

> Don't underestimate the power of your vision to change the world. (Leroy Hood)

If you lack money and you think that you cannot start a new business until you have money, then you are holding yourself back because of a false belief.

You don't always need a lot of money to get started. And you don't always need your own money, either. You have assets other than money. Most people underestimate those assets.

> You have ideas, time, skill, energy, knowledge, contacts and talent.

If you have a clear idea of what you want to achieve you will find that the money will come your way sooner or later. If the idea is good, the money will follow.

You also don't need success gurus or teachers. You have everything inside of you and you need to unlock this power inside of yourself. Most success teachers will motivate you and encourage you to dream big. That is great but no one really tells you how to achieve your goals. Success teachers don't teach you to make baby steps first and focus on simply daily tasks. But that is what you need to do.

There is no secret to success. There is no secret formula or club. You need to simply set a goal, make a plan by breaking it down into little steps and then go to work.

If there were a secret it would be this: You and your belief in yourself is the secret to success. If you were aware of your own power and capabilities, you would not be lacking self-confidence. If you lose your fear, you can accomplish anything in this life.

All the power you need already lies within you, not in outside circumstances. Don't give away your power to circumstances like luck, magic tools or other people. Everything you need to know and have is already inside of you.

> The real source of power is you!

All the real power is already within you and not anywhere on the outside. You are the master of your own circumstances. You don't really need anything to ignite your own power. All you need is to do is trust that you have the power, and then you will succeed.

Face your fears

> Self-doubt and fear are the only things that are holding you back from a life of greatness.

Most people are paralyzed because of fear. The two most common fears are the fear of rejection and the fear of failure.

But there are also other fears like for example the fear of success, fear of confrontation or the fear of not being deserving enough, etc.

You must realize that 95% of all of your fears and concerns **will never actually take place**. Fear is not real. Anthony Robbins even said that fear is F=False E=Evidence A= Appearing R=Real.

It's interesting to note that **the majority of the most common fears are not innate**; meaning that we have learned to have these fears. Which means the good news is that we can learn unlearn them.

One of my favorite quotes by E. E. Eddison is: "He without fear is king of the world!" Think about that quote for a moment. What would you be able to do if you had no fear at all?

In order to get rid of fear you must do the very things that you fear. You must exercise courage. The more often you do it, the quicker you will lose your fear.

Typically, being aware what you are (an unlimited spiritual being) and what you are actually afraid of is the first step of losing your fear. Often, people are afraid of things like calling up clients or public speaking but in reality those things can't hurt or kill you. So basically, nothing can happen to you. The worst that could happen is that you get ridiculed or you get rejection. But is that really the end of the world?

Think more about the things that could go right
than the things that could go wrong.

By not taking action because of fear we will not gain anything. Taking action despite fear will bring some results. It is better than NO result.

Developing courage is like a muscle. The more often that you exercise courage, the stronger it will get. Courage is not the absence of fear. It is the ability to face it, overcome it and finish your job.

Everyone has fear. That is normal. You cannot have courage without the absence of fear. Otherwise you are simply reckless or a lunatic. But you must learn to judge every situation that you are in. Are you afraid because you feel uncomfortable or is there real danger?

Remember: in order to be a real man or woman you must not be afraid of anything or anybody. In my opinion, a real mature man or woman should be able to face anything. Otherwise you are simply a coward who will never amount to anything.

Fear is your biggest challenge in life. Master it and you will master life and business once and for all.

Mentally and physically strong = financial success

> The secret to success is high levels of self-confidence, clarity, courage and determination.

Money is power. Money is freedom. Money can solve a lot of problems. That is why you need to have money in your life.

But money is a result of your mental state. It doesn't define you. It is the logical consequence of your mental attitude that leads to results.

You can only attract more money into your life if you are mentally strong. That is the only way.

This also means that you must be self-disciplined, focused, physically strong and determined.

By physically strong I mean that you should exercise to the best of your abilities every day. Some people prefer running, some like the gym, and some like Yoga. Whatever it is your mental state will only be at its best if you are physically fit.

> "Mens sana in corpore sano" – translation from Latin: "A sound mind in a sound body."

If you are not financially doing well today then **that should be your starting point. Get fit first.** Go on a 3-month diet and work out every day. You will see how everything around you will improve. Your business life will improve as well as your personal relationships.

The positive effect on your life is unbelievable. Most people totally underestimate how much a physical transformation can change their life. It will have a positive effect on your health, energy level, attractiveness, mental power, happiness, love life, future outlook, money, business, relationships and positivity.

A lot of successful people are former professional sportsmen or people who did really well in a particular sport. The reason for this is that it requires the same traits as business success. The traits are being goal-oriented, planning, fighting when things get hard, being determined, self-disciplined, not giving up, etc.

If you have kids encourage them to do sports. It is the best teacher for business later in life.

No one is better or smarter than you

> Never underestimate the capacity of another human being to have exactly the same shortcomings you have. (Leigh Steinberg)

Don't get intimidated by other people. Other people are not better or smarter than you. They might have had a better strategy or a better role model but rest assured that they also had to fight for their success.

They have simply found a better or smarter way or method to be successful. But as a person they have the same emotions, fears, concerns and motivations as you.

You job is to learn the strategies that work and that will help you to be more successful. If you do the same things that other successful people have done, you will get the same results.

Maybe you need to develop a certain personality trait like self-discipline or self-confidence to get ahead. Maybe you are using an old strategy that is no longer effective in the current market.

One of the lessons that I remember from my karate teacher is this:

"When you go into a fight, just remember that the other person is just as afraid as you are. But if you are afraid, you will not perform well and give your best. So lose that fear. On the other hand if you are intimidating to the other person because you are so self-confident, he will become more scared and then he will not perform well, which is to your advantage. In any case, don't ever be scared."

He also told me to make a strong power noise or yell before I got into the fight. This would not only intimidate the other person but also give me additional courage and power. Most fights were decided before the fight even started.

Don't ever be afraid or intimidated by other people. If they are acting arrogant, it doesn't mean that they are better than you. Either they are rude or they don't feel the need to please everybody. Being somewhat arrogant helps some people to improve their levels of self-confidence.

I think that you should become aware of your own power and know how good you are in your field. This will give you the confidence that you need. Always treat others with respect but don't worry too much about how they act. Just don't lose your power because someone wants to make you feel inferior.

Associate with sheep and you will become one yourself

The quality of **people that you associate with on a regular basis** determines your personal success.

Interestingly, we all want to **live up to the expectations of our peer group**. One of our biggest fears is not being able to live up to it.

We spend most of our lives trying to please other people. We bend our beliefs, our rules and our desires so we can feel accepted by our peer group.

If you **take a look at your closest five relationships** you will see you have similar lifestyles, similar economic status, similar hobbies, religious beliefs and similar attitudes.

You automatically become whom you spend most of your time with.

But in order to succeed you must **stand out from the crowd** and have the courage to go into a new direction or to set a new trend. That is the moment when people will follow you.

You probably have stayed with the same peer group for too long and that is why you haven't progressed. It is time to associate with new and more successful people. You need to find people who are at a similar successful level or better than you.

People who are more successful than you are the only ones who can really give you the right kind of advice because they have gone before you and they don't look up to you. They will tell you what you need to hear. People who admire you will never tell you what you need to hear.

You need to have people around you who have had similar success like you and who are able to give you a better perspective when things get difficult.

You should also be around people who don't want anything from you and who are not afraid to call you out on your BS.

The power of proximity means that you have people in your group who are just as "bad ass" as you and who will inspire you to do better. So chose your people well and form new bonds.

> If you are surrounded by sheep, you will not become a sheep.
> You will become a PUSSY! (Raul Villacis)

Always maintain a positive attitude – no matter what

> Thoughts have power; thoughts are energy. And you can make your world or break it by your own thinking. (Susan L. Taylor)

Is the glass half full of half empty? This old test was used to see if someone was thinking positively or negatively. But what if you said that the glass was completely full? Technically, it has 50% water and 50% air. Therefore it is 100% full.

You can always find something positive even when things appear to be negative. Being able to maintain a positive attitude will go a long way. You should develop the mindset that **everything is an opportunity to learn. Nothing is really negative**. There are no negative events. There are only events and it is up to us to give those events a meaning. This meaning can be positive or negative.

But because you cannot change the event anymore you should learn to develop a positive mindset for everything that happens to you.

"Oh well, this just happened and I can't change it anymore anyway. But what can I learn from this situation?" This should be your new attitude if you don't already have it.

Always stay positive. Always stay optimistic. You will get out of a seemingly negative place much faster if you adjust your attitude. If you drag yourself down, you will not only lower your mood but also your own energy level and all of a sudden things will get even worse.

Try to have "fun" in life – no matter what happens to you. Always look on the bright side. Laugh at people or situations even if they appear to be a problem. By taking a problem with humor or lightheartedness you will diffuse the seriousness of the situation.

You need to protect your own energy and enthusiasm so that you can perform at your best level. If you feel negative, down and depressed you won't be able to overcome anything easily.

> Nothing has meaning in this world until we give it meaning.

But one small positive thought in the morning can change your whole day.

Only you can make yourself happy or unhappy

> No one is in control of your happiness but you; therefore, you have the power to change anything about yourself or your life that you want to change. (Barbara de Angelis)

The biggest mistake that I used to make is to blame my wife for my unhappiness. If she didn't do what I needed from her, then I would feel unhappy. It got so bad that I made my entire happiness dependent on her and her mood.

But as I became wiser I realized that this was a recipe for disaster and unhappiness. It was also not fair to her.

I had to learn that the only person that is responsible for my happiness is ME and no one else. I learned that happiness is a decision. It is a state of mind and not dependent on a person or a situation.

If you feel unhappy then it is your personal choice. You can be happy RIGHT NOW no matter what the circumstances are.

Most people say or think that need to achieve a certain goal in order to be happy and in the meantime they have to suffer and be unhappy because they haven't achieved the goal yet. But this is not necessary and also destructive behavior. Be happy now and still work on your goal.

> Alcohol doesn't get rid of worries and sorrow but neither does milk.

Some people use external things to improve their state or level of happiness. These are things like alcohol, drugs, and food, shopping or gambling. But those things will not make you happy in the long run. They will only temporarily improve your emotional state but they do more damage in the long run.

The best strategy is to be happy now. It is your choice and your decision. It doesn't matter what your current circumstances are. Be grateful and happy today. Things will change for the better around you once you decide to be happy no matter what.

Dreaming is powerful

> To accomplish great things, we must not only act, but also dream; not only plan, but also believe. (Anatole France)

The Universe is an interesting place. Everything starts with a thought or a dream. Everything that was once small and is now big started with a person having an idea, a thought or a dream.

Thoughts and dreams are very powerful and they are the essence of creation. They are the beginning point of creating anything in this world.

Your intention is also important. If you have the intention to make something happen, you will activate the cosmic energies.

I want to encourage you to dream every day for 5 to 10 minutes. Think about what you would like to have, do or be. Dwell on your goals and imagine every little detail. See yourself as if you have already achieved your goals.

In the summer of 2004 I was on a vacation in Malta with my wife and son. I remember how I was sitting at the pool and I made a list of 10 goals.

When I got back home I put the list away and two years later I accidentally found the list in one of my drawers. To my surprise I could cross off seven out of the ten things from my list and the remaining three things were almost achieved, too.

This list was an easy list to accomplish. Those goals were big goals. One goal was for example to have 100 employees and I had about 60 at the time.

But I had an epiphany in this moment. I realized how powerful goal setting and dreaming really is. It will change your life and everything in it if you dream big.

> You can design and create, and build the most wonderful place in the world. But it takes people to make the dream a reality. (Walt Disney)

I want to encourage you to make your own list of the 10 most important goals in your life. And then go to work.

The first step is to dream. The second step is to WRITE IT DOWN. The third step is to do ONE thing like making a phone call, sending a message or inquiring about something. That is the starting point of every great accomplishment.

The crucial thing is **writing it down** because otherwise your thoughts can easily be lost or forgotten. The act of taking a thought and **putting it on paper** is the first step to manifesting it into the real world. You take the thought from the spiritual world (or the world of thought) and you put it into the physical world (where you want it).

Maslow Theory of Human Motivation

In 1943 Abraham Maslow published a paper in which he explained the theory of human motivation.

Maslow used the terms "physiological", "safety", "belongingness" and "love", "esteem", "self-actualization", and "self-transcendence" to describe the pattern that human motivations generally move through.

Maslow's hierarchy of needs is often portrayed in the shape of a pyramid with the largest, most fundamental levels of needs at the bottom and the need for self-actualization at the top.

The most fundamental and basic four layers of the pyramid contain what Maslow called "deficiency needs": esteem, friendship and love, security, and physical needs. If these deficiency needs are not met – with the exception of the most fundamental (physiological) need – there may not be a physical indication, but the individual will feel anxious and tense. Maslow's theory suggests that the most basic level of needs must be met before the individual will strongly desire (or focus motivation upon) the secondary or higher level needs.

Basically, if your physiological needs like food or shelter are not met, there is no point in talking about achieving big goals and realizing your dreams. **You need to first have a roof over your head and food in your stomach before you can think of other things.**

The next level describes things like safety, which means personal security, financial security, health and well-being. If you constantly have to worry about your income or your personal safety, you will not have the focus and attention that you need to accomplish great things in your life.

Without going into every detail about his theory you should take from this that you need to first take care of some basic needs before you can fulfill your dreams.

The theory also suggests that every one of us wants to eventually fulfill ourselves and become great or special in one area. Once you have achieved a certain amount of success in your life it is normal that you want to fulfill yourself and go even higher, leave a legacy or do the one thing that you always felt you needed to do in your heart.

Fulfilling your true destiny is part of self-realization. Eventually each one of us will develop the need to fulfill our greatest destiny and become all we can be.

Understanding this pyramid will help you to understand more about yourself and other people.

Self-Actualization: Pursuit of inner talent, creativity, fulfillment
Self-esteem: Achievement, recognition, mastery, respect
Belonging / Love: Friends, family, spouse, love
Safety: Security, stability, freedom of fear
Physiological: Food, water, shelter, warmth

The great truths in life are simple – Life is not complicated

Sometimes life appears to be difficult and things that used to be easy are hard now. Some people are looking for the perfect way or the perfect strategy to be successful and they get caught up in complicated messages or methods.

But often we forget that some things are very simple in life. We don't need gurus or a secret knowledge to succeed. All it takes is common sense and basic logic.

A lot of things are NOT complicated at all. **They might not always be EASY and they might take TIME and some people confuse them with being difficult.**

But the great truths in life are simple. Losing weight is simple. Making money is simple. Being a successful is simple.

We are in the information age and the Internet has too much information available and it is easy to get confused.

This program is supposed to remind you how simple the most important things in life really are. It should encourage you to get back to basics and do the things that you want in life.

False belief 1: I can't lose weight...

Some people say things like...

- "I can't lose weight."
- "I have a slow metabolism."
- "I have tried all the diets."
- "I have heavy bones."

All BS.

> You can't get fat from breathing in air. What you put into your mouth is what goes into your body. There is no two ways about it.

There are a hundred different health and nutrition experts with a hundred different strategies and of course it is easy to get confused. Some people teach you to eat asparagus to lose weight while others tell you to try the grapefruit diet.

But when it comes to losing weight, there are only three truths:

1. Your body burns a certain amount of calories per day to maintain the body heat, blood flow and other functions. This is on average **2500 calories per day for a man** and **2000 calories per day for a woman**. If you put more calories into your body you will gain weight and if you reduce the calorie intake you will lose weight.
2. You need to **exercise** to support weight loss. You will burn additional calories but you will also increase your metabolism by building muscle and increase the ability to burn more calories.
3. Eat more protein and less carbs. Excess carbs will be turned into fat. Your body will get rid of excess protein. If you eat NO CARBS for 3 months you will get into a state called "ketosis" where your body MUST take the fat from your storage for energy because he

can't convert the food into energy. This is THE FASTEST and MOST EFFECTIVE WAY to lose weight.

> Losing weight is not rocket science at all. Everyone can do it. You have made bad choices in the past and all you have to do is making better choices.

Some people think they need a special trainer who puts together a special scientific diet and plans a workout that is based particularly to your body type. All BS.

Maybe all you need is a drill sergeant who yells at you: "RUN!!!" and you should EAT HALF of what you normally eat. After 3 months you are going to be fit.

Whether you believe it or not but if you run 5 miles every single day for 3 months you will be in good shape. There is no question about that. Think about it for a moment.

Lose weight and get into shape:

1. Work out every day for one hour
2. Eat half of what you normally eat
3. Reduce your carbs (especially after 5 pm)

False belief 2: I am struggling with money…

> If you don't have any money then you don't have a money problem. You have an attitude problem. (Larry Winget)

You have a problem with something else. You might have a self-discipline problem or a strategy problem or an integrity problem, etc.

But money will always come as a result of doing the right things first.

First of all, most people DON'T WORK ENOUGH. If you want to get ahead financially and become a millionaire one day, you MUST work NO LESS THAN 10 to 12 HOURS per day. Otherwise it is not possible.

Secondly, you cannot achieve financial greatness by having a regular job. That is the wrong strategy. You should either be SELF-EMPLOYED or an ENTREPRENEUR.

Third, you need to be ACTIVELY SELLING A PRODUCT. Maybe you need to make 100 phone calls every day or conduct 20 meetings per week. But without an active and aggressive sales strategy you will never achieve anything.

Fourth, maybe you are using the wrong approach or marketing tactics. Figure out what OTHER SUCCESSFUL PEOPLE DO and then COPY their strategies.

Fifth, you need to BECOME A SPECIALIST or very, very good at what you do. Therefore you should pick a field or an industry where you have some natural talents and knowledge about it. Decide to become the best in your field.

False belief 3: I can't get along with other people...

In general, communication will always help. Communication is the answer to problems in relationships between people. If your relationship with your business partner or your partner at home is bad, then you must communicate better.

Love is always the answer. Often people get into conflicts with others because of silly issues like jealousy, envy or misunderstandings.

People are often too proud to admit when they are wrong and because of that they destroy relationships with others.

All people have weak moments from time to time and no one is perfect. Not even you! Therefore, forgive easily and admit mistakes quickly.

Act with LOVE in whatever you do. Act with the BEST INTENSIONS and everything will work out fine.

In the end, **your life is a reflection of the qualities of the relationships that you have**. Family matters and love are the most important things in life. You will never be truly happy if you distance yourself from other people.

If you want more love in your life then you first must give more love. It is as simple as that.

False belief 4: I can't find a partner to love...

Women:
Factor number one for a man is physical attraction. If you are overweight, you must lose weight and go to the gym. You can fight this fact, hate it, disagree with it but it doesn't change the fact that 95% of men at first looking at the body of a woman.

As superficial as it might sound, that is unfortunately the hard truth.

Another factor is your behavior. If you are acting like a mean bitch or a psycho, it is a turn-off for men, too.

Getting a man is a combination of being a CARING PERSON and an ATTRACTIVE PERSON.

Men:
Some men struggle to get women. If you dress like a dork, act like a nerd or have low self-confidence, then you will have a hard time getting a girl. Some men are also acting like pigs and they physically don't take care of themselves.

You don't necessarily need to look like Brad Pitt because women care much more about the personality of a man.

Women like self-confident men who are successful and MAKE MONEY. Think about it this way: if you were a woman and you would give up your job, have a baby and be 100% dependent on another person, then you would also care about financial security. You can't be angry with a woman for focusing on money.

So if you are a man struggling to get a date then you should WORK ON YOUR CAREER, DRESS BETTER, GET INTO SHAPE and WORK ON YOUR MANNERS.

False belief 5: I can't be successful because I have this disadvantage...

There is no secret to success. In the end it all comes down to hard work, making a few extra calls, and doing what is necessary to win clients (= who pay money for a product or service = income for you).

Most people don't use have excuses or see themselves as a victim when it comes to their own lives. No matter how difficult your situation might be there are always people who had it more difficult and still they overcame all obstacles and succeed despite their problems.

Let's talk about W. Mitchell for example. W. Mitchell had a terrible motorcycle accident that burned 65% of his body and burnt off his fingers. Most people would have felt defeated but not W. Mitchell. He decided to live his life and stay positive. He even took up flying because it was one of his dreams. But then four years later, he had a plane crash that paralyzed him from the waist down. Now you can imagine that most people would have given up on life altogether but not W. Mitchell. He ended up marrying a beautiful woman and he made over $65 million with his business.

He is probably one of the most positive people in the world. He said: *"Before I was paralyzed there were 10,000 things I could do. Now there are 9,000. I can either dwell on the 1,000 I have lost or focus on the 9,000 I have left."*

If W. Mitchell was able to overcome these obstacles, then you can overcome your "little problems" for sure.

> You are never as broken as you think you are. Sure, you may have a couple of scars and a couple of bad memories, but then again...all great heroes do.

Don't be pussy or a coward

> A coward dies a thousand deaths – a hero only one. (W. Shakespeare)

True strength comes when you are able to stand up for what you believe in. When you are able to confront other people and say what is right.

I once had a friend who was kind of skinny but he was a tough cookie. He would confront anyone anywhere if they got in his way. His strength was very admirable.

He told me that he got beat up a couple of times because of his confrontational nature but he would never be able to live with himself if someone didn't show him respect. But most of the time people would back down if he confronted them because he didn't seem to have any fear. He was a little bit like the character from Scarface. No fear and no worries.

The interesting thing is that strong people respect other strong people. You don't have to be rude but stand up for what you believe is right.

When I was younger I was quite afraid of confrontation. I wanted to please everybody. I didn't like tension in the room. But secretly I admired the quality of people who were strong and not afraid to speak up.

Today, I have learned that life is too short and that you can't make everyone happy. You must speak up and you must be strong in this world. Don't ever be afraid of other people. Don't be a coward or a pussy. If someone is crossing the line, you must put him in his place.

Knowledge is power

> The rules have changed. True power is held by the person who possesses the largest bookshelf, not gun cabinet or wallet. (Anthony J. D'Angelo)

If you can't get ahead in life then the reason might be that you are lacking knowledge or education. But education doesn't necessarily mean going to school and getting a degree. A lot of things that students learn in University are "somewhat useless" in real life.

The right kind of knowledge is power. If you read one book per week for one year you will have read 50 books. If you choose to read books in your field, it will make you a real specialist in that field.

If you read 50 books a year and you do this for 10 years it is the equivalent of two full University degrees.

We are in the Information age and everything is available to us. You can learn absolutely everything about every possible topic. A lot of information is available for free but there are thousands of courses, seminars, books or schools that you can find online.

If you make learning a powerful and driving force in your life, you will differentiate yourself from the masses and excel.

> If you are not willing to learn, no one can help you. If you are determined to learn, no one can stop you.

If you make the decision not to watch 2 hours of TV each day but to read books instead for the next 10 years about business, sales, marketing, investing, success and personal development, you will become a millionaire.

Actually, the world is changing so much that now knowledge about the Internet and marketing is the new power. Studies have shown that 85% of all buying decisions start on the Internet. If you learn to become really good at Internet marketing, sales psychology and using technology you will be part of the newly rich of this millennium.

Live a happier life

There are 4 easy tips to live a happier life:

1. Practice gratitude
2. Spend time in the "flow"
3. Learn to say "NO"
4. Unplug and spend more time in nature

No matter where they are or what they are doing happy people recognize that they always have something to be grateful for.

People who practice gratitude are happier, less stressed and less depressed! Happy people can easily find gratitude in the world around them, whether they are looking at the sky or even in smallest of things, like a delicious meal, a good book, or a smile from a stranger on the street.

Each of us has a choice on how we focus our attention. Choosing to focus on gratitude for the beauty and uniqueness of life instead the problems will make you feel happier and more relaxed.

Find an activity in which you can totally immerse yourself. When we are in flow, such as when we are running a race, writing a song, or reading a great book, our self-awareness dissipates, time seems to stop, and we become focused, peaceful, and attentive to the task at hand. People who frequently experience flow tend to be happy, productive, creative and focused.

> Saying YES to happiness means learning to say NO to things and people that stress you out.

Happy people know that they must say NO to people, ideas, and behaviors that do not feel right. Saying yes to everyone and everything can lead you to feel overwhelmed, increase your stress, and leave you less time and resources to take care of yourself! This is especially true when you agree to do things that you are uncomfortable with or feeling like you are being pressured into situations that you don't like.

The stress that results from feeling overwhelmed can severely dampen your happiness. Learn to say "NO" if it is not right for you. Put your own happiness first.

Unplug and spend more time in nature. Although it may feel natural after a lifetime of conditioning, **human beings were not designed to spend our day hunched over a desk with electronics plugged into our ears and eyes**. No, we are meant to be spending time outside, away from the buzz of technology, the radiation from cell-phones and the blaring of screens. Happy people understand that it is their human birthright to give themselves quiet time to reflect and find serenity.

> Time outdoors in nature has been linked to happiness because light elevates people's moods, as does vitamin D, a byproduct of spending time outside.

Fight "Fido"

In German we have a saying: "Den inneren Schweinehund überwinden".

Basically, it means that you have lazy combination of a pig and a dog inside of you and you need to overcome your own lack of will power. You are fighting a fight with yourself. Your inner dog or "Fido" wants everything to be comfortable and easy. He doesn't want to work or suffer. Fido is like a little voice inside of you that tells you to quit or to eat that extra piece of cake when you know you shouldn't.

But in order to succeed in life you must fight your own "Fido" and do the things that are uncomfortable. You must fight against your own weakness and laziness.

I once was a seminar and we talked about our own Fido. It was actually quite funny and entertaining because we all have an inner Fido inside of us that is lazy and wins in situations when things are difficult or uncomfortable.

The trainer said to us that we should make a pact with Fido. And this is how it goes: *"Listen Fido, you can have all the lazy time, food and pleasures of life is you stay quiet for the next 5 years. I will give you everything that you have ever dreamed of. But the deal is that you must shut up and let me do my work for the next 5 years so that I can make all the money for the both of us!"*

> We all must suffer one of two things: the pain of discipline or the pain of regret and disappointment. (Jim Rohn)

Our inner Fido can really screw up things for us if we let him. Without self-discipline, it is nearly impossible to be successful.

Program yourself with positive affirmations

> Yesterday I was clever and I wanted to change the world. Today I am wise so I am changing myself. (Rumi)

Many of the great self-help teachers tell you to use daily affirmations. John Assaraf, for example, taught me these two very powerful affirmations:

1. *Money is flowing to me from both expected and unexpected sources.*
2. *I am making space for more success to come into my life.*

If you say these affirmations over and over again and you emotionalize it, then your sub-conscious mind will eventually accept them as truths.

Another great way is to ask yourself positive questions like these:

1. *Why am I so lucky to attract millions into my life?*
2. *Why am I so successful with everything that I start?*

Your subconscious mind will then try to find the answers to those questions and the reasons why will be reinforced into your life.

And the last tip is from Brian Tracy. He teaches people to say these things over and over:

1. *I am the best!*
2. *I can do it!*

People who are strong and successful do a lot of self-talk to motivate themselves so that they can perform better.

Professional fighters pump themselves up before going into a fight. They says things like "I am the best!" and "I am going to win!". They repeat it over and over again and it becomes their driving force.

You can do it, too. It is very powerful and will help you to achieve your goals.

Who says you have to be realistic?

Person: I want a magical unicorn for Christmas.
Santa: Be realistic.
Person: Ok, I want 5 minutes to myself each day to have my coffee hot and pee in peace.
Santa: What color unicorn would you like?

Honestly, you don't have to be realistic at all. Some people are so unrealistic but they believe in their dreams so much that they end up surprising everyone around them because they made it happen.

No one should be able to tell you what you can do and what you can't do.

Do you want to make a $100,000 per month? Is that realistic? For some people it is very realistic. For others it seems totally out of their reach.

But if you open up your mind and start to wonder how you could do it, you start to come up with ideas and possible solutions.

Let's try it right now:

- If you get 20 clients per month (=1 client per working day) that pay $5000 for your consulting services, then you make $100,000 per month.
- If you sell 1000 products online per month and charge $1000 for your product, then you make $100,000 per month.
- If you raise $1 million from investors and you get a 10% commission, then you will make $100,000 per month.

You see? It is possible. I could come up with 20 more ideas or ways. I didn't say it was easy but it is possible. The next step is to make a plan of action.

But most people don't even dare to dream that big. They don't set their goals that high. (They are maybe somehow afraid that they spend too much energy or something like that.)

Set your goals high – even if you only hit 30% of it, it is still $30,000 per month. If you set it at $10,000 you will not really break through. You will not give 100%.

Becoming great is really just a decision. If you want become a leader in your field then you must make that choice. I always wondered why somebody didn't do something about that, and then I realized that I am somebody.

You can be somebody. Dare to set high goals and then go for it!

Making the right decisions and letting go of old things

> You must be brave enough to release something GOOD to make space for something GREAT.

If you are not happy with your life, then change it now. No one is forcing you to live the life that you currently live. It's never too late to make things right.

You are not a tree – you can move and change your life at any moment in time.

You can do, be or have whatever you like. You were born into a free country as a free person. You are the only one who has complete power and control over your life.

Sometimes you realize that you have come off track so much that you must change again. But everything happens for a reason. Maybe you need to get off track to learn something so that you could evolve and become stronger.

Someday soon, you will look back at this time in your life, and it will make perfect sense why everything happened like it did.

Sometimes you must make the decision to let go of the past and start new. If you can let go of old things you can attract new and better things into your life.

This also means that you need to part from some people. I used to have friends who liked to party a lot. But the problem is that they will not move forward and they will drag you down if you don't cut them lose.

> They say: "*See you at the club!*"...I say: "*I never see you at the bank!*"

In order to evolve you need new and better fitting friends. This tip alone can change your life. Surround yourself with the right kind of people and things will change for the better.

Respect, manners and character

> Show respect even to people who don't deserve it, not as a reflection of their character but as a reflection of yours.

Rudeness is the weak person's imitation of strength. But that doesn't apply to you. You should always keep your composure like a gentleman.

True strength comes from within. You don't need to get loud to get respect. In fact, people will respect you much more once they see how you hold up in difficult situations.

No matter how bad a situation is or how badly someone has treated you, you should always behave in a manner that shows your character.

There is really no excuse for bad and rude behavior.

> The Dalai Lama has got nothing on me. (Quote from the movie: Delivery Man)

Always live in truth with all people and circumstances. Be a good person and do good things in this world.

You can only help other people if you become a strong force yourself. Develop into the person who has character and who people will look up to.

Forgive yourself for everything "bad" that you have ever done

> And God said "Love Your Enemy", and I obeyed him and loved myself. (Khalil Gibran)

Forgive yourself for not knowing what you didn't know before you learned it.

Let go of guilt. Have no regrets. Forgive yourself. Embrace your mistakes.

We all make mistakes and no one is perfect. Living in denial about your mistakes or getting wrapped up in your ego will only you make you miserable and block you from learning valuable lessons that will help you grow and improve.

By embracing your mistakes, you will be able to forgive yourself, and the bonus is that other people might actually like you more!

Making mistakes makes competent people seem more attractive, and more human to others. Happy people seem to intuitively know this, embracing mistakes as learning experiences and not judging themselves too harshly.

Another important factor is to forgive others. This one can be challenging for the many of us who have been wronged by other people in our lives. Forgiveness does not mean that what happened was ok, it just means you no longer want to carry the pain. Forgiveness is not for the other person – it is for you. You no longer need to feel bad. You can let it go. Drop the negative energy and free yourself from it.

> Never complain. Never explain. (Benjamin Disareli, British Prime Minister)

The more you complain about your problems, the more problems you will have to complain about. Complaining is a very negative activity that will have a very strong influence on you and your general mood. Complaining is what weak people do because they give away their power of a situation to other people.

If you are not happy with a situation, then change it but never, ever complain!

Developing a strong character

Determination, perseverance, dedication, focus and not giving up are qualities of a fighter. You need to discover the fighter in you. Everyone has a fighter inside. All you need is the right motivation to let him out.

> Don't give up. The beginning is always the hardest.

When you feel like giving up, remember why you held on for so long in the first place. When things go wrong as they sometimes will or you are struggling in an uphill battle, rest if you must, but don't ever quit.

Attitude is a reflection of character and character is a reflection of habit. Giving up often can be a habit. Make it a habit that you follow through on things. Make it a habit that you keep your promises.

Your character is a reflection of your habits. If you have gotten off track then go back to the starting point. It's never too late to turn it all around. If you are doing anything that you should be doing, then stop immediately. Life is way too short to continue in the wrong direction. But the longer you do, the less time you will have to travel in the right direction.

Developing a strong character takes time. Having a strong character means to be honest with yourself and with the people around you. You don't compromise your values to please anybody and you keep true to your goals and values.

When you do the right thing in the right way, you have nothing to lose because you have nothing to fear.

Having a strong character means that you have decided what your goals are, what you stand for, what you don't stand for, you have clarity and you have made a commitment and decision to pursue your goals.

What gets measured gets done

> Set clear goals and standards for each person and for each aspect of your business. What gets measured - gets done. Brian Tracy

Unless you have definite, precise, clear set goals, you are not going to realize the maximum potential that lies within you.

I always used to afraid to set goals that were "too low". I always wanted to keep my options open so that just in case it went better than expected I would achieve a higher goal.

But the truth is that will not achieve anything without clarity. The trick is to set a goal and define it to the last detail. Just make a decision and set a goal that can be measured. Try to plan your goals in numbers so that you can see if you make progress or not. Setting clear and measurable goals is a great help.

Always think in terms of "numbers". You will be surprised how much more efficient your life will become once you "control your own numbers". Facts and numbers will help you to realistically see where you are at any point in time. It will help you to determine what needs to be done in any given situation.

If you are not a numbers guy or gal, you should become one when it comes to goal setting and planning.

I would recommend you going away for a couple of days into the mountains where no one can disturb you and then make a plan for the entire year. Plan every single detail.

> Never doubt what you can do because you can do anything you set your mind to.

Protecting your own energy: criticism and negative people

> Criticism belies a need for recognition, appreciation, or validation. None of which, however, can be obtained through criticism.

Don't be distracted by criticism. Remember: the only taste of success some people have is when they take a bite out of you.

People who criticize a lot are poor souls. They feel like they need attention or recognition because of their own inferiority.

People who can, do. People, who can't, criticize. (Frank Sonnenberg)

Be an encourager. The world has plenty of critics already. Negative people don't want solutions. Solutions mean they have to work to find something else to be negative about.

Your value doesn't decrease based on someone's inability to see your worth.

Don't allow other people's egos to distract you from your mission. Surround yourself with those on the same mission as you. And leave the negative people behind. You have to do what is right for you. No one walks in your shoes.

You need to protect your own energy and happiness. If people are critical of you, then ignore them. Delete their emails; ignore their phone calls and don't read their stupid comments on the Internet.

Some of the greatest people in the world like Anthony Robbins for example have been attacked and criticized. The Internet is anonymous and people can hide.

But don't let that pull you down. Everyone and I mean everyone has been attacked or criticized if they were successful. That is just the nature of things. Not everyone is going to agree with what you do or what you say. There are always one or two assholes out of 100 people. That is normal.

But that shouldn't concern you. You don't provide your products for the critics. You develop your products for the people who appreciate you and what you have to offer.

You will only attract "your kind of people" anyway. The kinds of people who are on the same wave length like you. Go boldly and confidently in the direction of your dreams and do it for the right crowd.

If you live for people's acceptance you will die from their rejection. You are not free until you have no need to impress anybody.

Never try to convince a negative person of your point of view. They don't want to change or agree with you. Let them be.

Keep away from people who try to belittle your ambitions. Small people always do that, but the really great make you feel that you, too, can become great. Strong people don't pull others down – they lift them up.

And for your enemies or critics: **Defeat your enemies with success.**

> People will love you. People will hate you. And none of it will have anything to do with you. (Abraham Hicks)

Develop a new mentality for success and change the world

> People who are crazy enough to believe that they can change the world are usually the ones who end up doing it. (Steve Jobs, founder of Apple)

Plan your long-term goals and life. What is your vision for your life? What do you ultimately want to accomplish?

What does your heart secretly wish for? What would you dare to dream if you knew that your success was guaranteed?

> Once you have mastered time, you will understand how true it is that most people overestimate what they can accomplish in a year - and underestimate what they can achieve in a decade! (Tony Robbins)

I believe that we are who we choose to be. Nobody is going to come and save you. You have to save yourself. Nobody is going to give you anything.

You have to go out and fight for it. Nobody knows what you really want except you. Don't give up on your dreams.

Nothing can change who you really are – not a bad day, week, or year. You will always rise above every obstacle and lift off. It is your very nature.

Times have changed and you must learn the new rules to succeed in the new economy.

Times have changed and how you make money today is different than just 10 years ago. The rules have changed and some people still live in the past and can't let go or accept that the game is different today.

Things that used to work in the past, no longer work. Many people need to shift their focus because otherwise they will go down. You need to learn that the world has changed and there are new opportunities available to you. The world of technology has changed how people make money.

The power of your own power is more important than ever. You must learn to adept and how to play the game in the new millennium.

Be strong and courageous. Lead the way for others and live the life of your dreams!

CHAPTER 17

STRATEGY AND PLANNING

How to plan effectively to achieve your goals

> Failing to plan is planning to fail. (Brian Tracy)

Most people invest more time in planning a 2-week holiday than the planning of their entire lives.

Statistics show that people who plan are 4 times as successful as people who don't plan. Most people never take a look at their lives and ask if their life is going, as it should. They are too busy trying to make money.

A strategic plan is a long-term plan. It covers the next 3 to 10 years. If you don't plan your life you might end up in the same place in a couple of years from now. That's why you need medium and long-term goals.

When I started my sales organizations in Switzerland I needed to plan one or two years ahead. I needed to think like a chess player and assume that not everything would work out. I needed to have a plan B for every strategic move.

> Figuring out your "**worst case scenario**" can be an incredibly powerful practice that helps simplifying a decision.

The reason why I became a self-made millionaire in only 2 ½ years was only because I had great **clarity**. I always knew what the next step would be. I had prepared my master plan in a journal that I had previously written into every day for two years.

My advice is this: **go away for a long weekend somewhere quiet**. Ideally somewhere in the mountains where you have no distractions and think about all your goals and how you plan to accomplish them. Doing a strategic goal-setting plan for your life where you spend several hours alone writing down your thoughts. This one weekend can change your life forever.

> The right STRATEGY can save you a decade of hard work.

Why is strategic planning so important? Well, there are a lot of very talented people in this world who are not where they could be because they are using the wrong strategy for their goal achievement. Don't make the same mistake. Take the time and make a plan for yourself.

The right strategy can make all the difference. It can change the outcome 10 times and people who don't apply the right kind of leverage will start to doubt themselves and never really accomplish what their true potential could have been.

> You can VISUALIZE the outcome all you want.
> But if you don't have the right strategy, you
> will fail miserably. (Raul Villacis)

Step 1: Goal setting

> There are no unrealistic goals – only the
> wrong strategies. (Jürgen Hoeller)

The first step to achieve anything in life is goal setting. You can't hit a target that you can't see. You need to be clear about what you want to achieve.

If you don't know what you deserve, you will always settle for less. You will wander aimlessly and wonder how life has ended up here.

You must find your dream first, and then the path is easy.

If you don't know what you want, you will never find it.

Ideally, you want to have short-term goals (12 months), medium-term goals (3 to 5 years) and long-term goals (10 years or more).

You should set goals in the following areas of your life:

1. Financial goals
2. Career goals
3. Personal goals
4. Thing goals
5. Fitness and health goals
6. Relationship and family goals
7. Spiritual goals
8. Self-development goals

In my opinion the most important goals are the **12-month goals**. You should make a list of the **10 most important goals** that you want to achieve in the next 12 months.

12-month goals are motivating and require you to take action. Long-term goals like "I want to become a millionaire" are great but they often leave you without any concept of what actually needs to be done.

Step 2: Leverage

> Success is 20% skills and 80% strategy. (Jim Rohn)

When it comes to strategy, using **leverage** is key. Without leverage you are constantly struggling because you are only using your own time and energy.

Let me give you a few examples:

1. If you sell your own time for $20 per hour and you work 10 hours per day, then you can make $200 per day. But if you have 10 people working for you and you sell their time for $20 per hour and pay them $10 from it, then you can make $2000 per day. Your 10 employees are your leverage in this example.
2. You can set up 3 personal meetings with clients per day and give a sales presentation or you can record your sales presentation and 1000 people watch it online each day. The Internet gives you the necessary leverage.
3. Instead of trying to save money every month to open up a second location for your business, you could get a loan/financing for $1 million from a financial institution and open up 10 more locations immediately. The money or extra financing is your leverage in this case.

You see? You need to use **leverage** in order to get ahead faster and make more money.

You need to think differently and smarter. You don't need to work just harder and do what you have always done. You need to use the power of leverage to get ahead faster. Just because you did things a certain way in the past doesn't mean that it was the best and fastest strategy.

Step 3: Time management

> When you wake up in the morning you can't just wait to see what kind of day you will have. You have to decide what kind of day you will have. (Joel Osteen)

Ideally, you want to have your long-term goals tie into your short-term goals and eventually your daily goals.

What works best for me is to create **a list of the 5 most important tasks each day** before I start working in the morning.

In general, I found that short term goals that are 12 months or less, motivate the most and get you to take action.

Most people overestimate what they can achieve in one year and underestimate what they can achieve in a decade. So set your **12-months goals** and make them achievable and realistic. But also dream big and have your long-term vision.

> Only a broke man can give you all his time.

The difference between rich people and poor people is how they use their time. A successful person has his day planned and he can't usually spontaneously spend an hour with a person having a casual conversation.

A successful person has the day structured into time blocks that help him to achieve his goals. Only a broke or unsuccessful man has lots of time available.

Step 4: You cannot delude yourself into success

> We can talk facts or we can talk feelings. The first step is separating the two.
> (Sonya Teclai)

In order to get ahead in life you must focus on what you can actually do versus what you wish or hope for. Being realistic and using common sense is what will get you ahead.

In my twenties I used to work for AWD, a financial planning sales organization. The head was Carsten Maschmeyer who ended up becoming a **billionaire**. I used to have lots of direct interactions with this man because every two months we attended one of his seminars for a weekend. He is hands down the best sales person that I have ever met in my life. One time we talked about recruiting new employees. He told us that his secret of success was simple. If his competitor interviewed 5 candidates, he called up two more and set 7 appointments. Effectively, this was just setting 2 more meetings but the bottom line was the deciding factor. He ended up with the largest sales organization in Europe because he just did a little bit more than the others. I never forgot this lesson.

Success is not something magical or mystical. The difference between a normal success and a huge success is just **going the extra mile each day**.

People who dream about success and don't take action every single day will never move forward in life. You need to focus your time and energy on **income generating activities** (meetings with clients, sales, phone calls with potential customers, marketing activities, recruiting new sales people, etc.) That is the secret.

Step 5: Psychology and motivation

> Without the right PSYCHOLOGY, which is your driving force, you won't achieve anything.

Desire is always first. You need to know **why** you want something. You must have a compelling reason. Your motivation to do better than average must be rooted in a deep desire inside of you. Otherwise you might as well live with the minimum and survive on basic things. But that's not what life is all about.

Your words are an extension of your thoughts. Change your thoughts and you will change your life. You can have, do or be anything that you want in this world.

> If you knew how powerful your thoughts are, you would never think a negative thought.

Words matter. What you say or think matters. Your subconscious mind will take everything in and try to manifest it into the real world. That's why you should always try to keep your thoughts, words and goals positive.

Step 6: Develop a vision

Where do you see yourself in 10 or 20 years? Where do you want to ideally be? What does your life look like? How much is your company worth? What do you want to be known for?

This image of your ideal future should be imagined in great detail. This will be your **driving force.**

In order to make this picture clearer I recommend that you buy yourself an empty journal and write into it daily. You should also cut out pictures from magazines and glue them into your book. The more visual it is the better.

By the **law of attraction** you can't help but eventually get exactly what you ask for and put into your **dream journal**.

> A man without a vision for his future always returns to his past.

Everything in the physical world is made out of atoms. Atoms are made out of energy. And energy is made out of consciousness. Your thoughts and images are real and they are energy. They need to be manifested into the physical world. That's why you need a clear vision. Writing down your vision is the first step to manifesting it into the real world.

Step 7: Stress – follow your plan and don't get stressed out

> And then one day I decided that hurry and stress were no longer going to be part of my life. Stress is self-created and I decided to stop manufacturing it. (Brendon Burchard)

Stress is an alarm clock that lets you know you are attached to something that is not true for you.

Whenever you feel stressed you need to stop and realize that you are doing this to yourself. If you focus on your goals and execute accordingly, then there is no reason to feel constantly stressed. If you are clear about what you want and what needs to be done, then there should be no stress.

We are only stressed and run around like a chicken with its head cut off when we have no clarity. It is during times when we have too many factors that are uncertain.

Sometimes it helps to stop what you are doing and look at your life by taking a step back.

Anxiety and stress happen when you think you have to figure all at once. Take it day by day. Solve one problem at a time and be more rational about everything.

> "I can't take it anymore!"... *"Then give!"*

Stop worrying, panicking and stressing. Breathe. Remember, you made it this far through difficulties that seemed impossible. Remember how many times you were saved at the very last minute – this time is no different.

Sometimes things don't work out for a reason. Whatever happens, happens. Don't stress. There are things that you can control and there are things that you cannot control. Knowing which ones you can control and letting go of what you can't control is wisdom.

> God, grant me the serenity to accept the things I cannot change; the courage to change the things I can; and the wisdom to know the difference. (Serenity Prayer)

Again: **There are things you can control and things you can't control.** Once you understand this and live by it, your life becomes a lot calmer.

Step 8: Business Systems

> I love my boss! (PS: I work for myself.)

There are many great multi level marketing companies out there. In fact, when I was in my early twenties I was part of such an organization myself. It taught me valuable lessons about sales, recruiting and success.

But if you really want to succeed in life, then you must start **your own company or your own system**. You need to be **at the founder level** of an organization and not part of a bigger organization and falsely believing that you have your own business. Understanding the difference between making the rules for others and working in a system that provides you with rules is key to getting ahead in life.

Don't get me wrong. I like multi level marketing organizations. They teach you great things and you can make good money. But in order to excel you need your own system in your own company. Then you hire others and tell them "the lie" that they have their own business within your company.

In order to make more money you need to create a business system and that operate without your daily involvement and can be operated by others who bring in sales.

Step 9: Face your financial fears

> When you are afraid to lose, you normally lose. (Paulo Coelho)

You will only get ahead with a realistic assessment of your situation and brutal honesty with yourself. But once you have done that, you can actually work on improving your weaknesses and take action. It hurts to look at yourself honestly and see your shortcomings. But if you continue to live in a world of illusions, then nothing will ever get better. Have the courage to be honest. Once you can let go of all that isn't you, then you can realistically make progress.

When you are honest with yourself about fears of success or failure, they can no longer control you. Be free of hidden fears by exposing them to the light of awareness, and you will realize that you in fact have nothing to fear.

Deep down you worry whether you deserve to receive abundance. And because you are struggling with fear of both success and failure, **you are stuck in indecision and inaction.**

Fortunately, once you admit these fears to yourself, they lose their power to unconsciously control you. Every person struggles with self-doubts. Thankfully, you are blessed with the gift of self-awareness. You can take an honest inventory of your thought processes and admit that you have sometimes sabotaged your own success. Your new decisions are no longer guided by fear.

> Quit overthinking, replaying failed scenarios, feeding self-doubt and seeing the good in everyone but yourself. You deserve more.

What you allow, is what will continue. So stop now and change your financial life.

Step 10: Set up companies all over the world

> By owning your own business you have put yourself in a position where creating wealth is at least possible.

As a regular employee there is not even a chance to get ahead financially. But this is not the only reason why you should have several companies.

You should incorporate several strategic companies. Sometimes you will need to have a different company for accounting purposes. Very often you will need to charge an expense from one company and you can't have your personal name involved. You should always have several companies and accounts set up with different bank and in different states or even different countries. I have companies and accounts in three different countries.

You can make money by having a consulting agreement from a different company that you secretly own. Often I use a nominee director to hide who is really behind the company. This is crucial in some instances in life. Sometimes it is to save you out of a tight financial situation, a reputational risk and sometimes to pay fewer taxes.

I have had lots of companies set up in Nevada due to the tax laws there but also in other countries like Switzerland where I am originally from.

> Set up a few companies with different banks and protect yourself legally and financially.

Step 11: Expect problems

> You are surrounded right now by unlimited opportunities disguised as insurmountable problems. (Brian Tracy)

Problems are a normal part of business and of life. Expect problems to come into your life. No plan is ever going to be achieved 100% smoothly. There are always unexpected problems that get in the way. But once you know and expect that, you can plan accordingly. In business, things usually cost twice as much and take twice as long as originally anticipated.

But talking about our problems is one of our greatest addictions. Break the habit. A problem is only a problem if you see it as a problem. Welcome a problem with open arms. It is not the end of the world but an opportunity for you to grow. Sometimes the easiest way to solve a problem is to stop participating in the problem and working towards a solution. Always ask yourself: what can I actually in this situation right now? And what is out of your immediate control?

You need to increase your capacity to deal with any problem. No one is coming to the rescue. If you want to solve a problem and get ahead, you must do it yourself. And you must develop that "courage muscle" to deal with it head on. If God wants to give you a present, he will wrap it up as a problem.

> A situation is never desperate. Desperate is only a defeated attitude. (Actual quote from Norman Meier during an argument)

If there is no way, create one. There is always a way or a solution. You just have to find it. A situation is never final. You can always change your situation. You just need to be creative, positive and not accept defeat. There is always a way if you try hard enough. It is all a mental game.

Step 12: Being normal versus being unique

> To be normal is the aim of the unsuccessful.

Being "normal" is so overrated. Be your weird, strange, unique self. That is where your true light shines. Don't cover up your light by trying to be someone that you are not. Your true light will attract the people that you truly need, while your dulled light will attract those who your EGO feels it needs and not genuine and serving of your souls truth. So be yourself and your true light guide you.

> The most important kind of freedom is to be what you really are. (Jim Morrison)

In order to be successful in life you must find out who you really are. If you can be yourself and live a life that is true to who you are, then you will be successful. Besides goal setting you need to do **soul searching** and find out who you are.

> Everyone has the power for greatness, not for fame, but greatness, because greatness is determined by service. (Martin Luther King Jr.)

Nobody can beat you at being you. It is important to accept who you are and use it in your strategic plan.

Step 13: Resourcefulness versus resources

> It is not the resource but the resourcefulness of a person that makes all the difference.

What are resources? Resources are things like money, time, contacts, etc.

But the problem is that most people lack money when they try to start their own business. So the resource is missing. But this is not the main problem. Each one of us has the ability to use our talents.

What we consider possible or impossible is rarely a function of our true capacity. It is more likely a function of our beliefs about who we are.

A person who is successful is a resourceful person. This person can **achieve his goals despite lack of money or resources.** A person who is excited and has a solid plan can motivate others to give them the resources. A resourceful person has ideas, talents, energy, etc. Being resourceful is much more important than having money. If the idea is good, the money can be found.

We live in the age of the Internet and all the information and contacts are available online. We just have to find them.

Step 14: Generating leads and sales – your number 1 task!

> Sales are the BLOOD of a business. If you don't like sales, you will bleed to death.
> (Raul Villacis)

In this world, you are either selling or being sold to. Either way, you have to choose a side. If you understand sales, which is the highest paying profession; you will eventually become a millionaire. Those who know how to sell know that it dramatically enhances the life of everyone around them.

You can sell vacuum cleaners, vegetables or stocks. The process is the same. But you will make most money when you sell stocks – especially stocks of your own company or project. Once you decide to raise money from investors and sell them shares of your company, you will not only get a commission but your company also gets funded. If you own shares in your own company, then you have the chance to get rich. That's why I decided to only sell shares of my own deals that I am involved in and never someone else's deal.

Sometimes ONE CUSTOMER can change your business and life.

Business is a numbers game – work them! Your greatest asset is your earning ability and your greatest resource is time. Once you understand how important sales really is you will make it your number one priority.

There will always be a surprise if you contact enough people. Often your best customers come from the least expected sources.

If you make 100 calls per day and get 5 good leads, then you can sell your way into financial independence. You need to make sure you talk to enough people each day to have the odds in your favor.

No conversations = no sales = no money = no future

Step 15: Clarity with a business plan

Any goal can be achieved if you break it down into enough small parts. (Brian Tracy)

Many years ago I listened to a program from Brian Tracy. He said that you must take the time and write a business plan. He said that it is **a crucial factor for success** because it forces you to think about every little step. A written plan will provide you with clarity and it is absolutely necessary if you want to achieve your business goals.

Honestly, I never took this seriously until last month. I decided to write a 60-page business plan for my energy and resource company. I could not believe what happened afterwards. Once I decided to define what the main goals and milestones should be, the Universe provided me with the right people and contacts to make it happen. In the same week I was able to find two financial advisors who committed to raise $6 million and 5 new oil projects. I was stunned. Also, I now know what needs to be done in detail and whether or not it is realistic to achieve my goals in time.

I also asked myself what I wanted to achieve in life in general. My number one wish or answer was: $100 million net worth.

At first, this seems like wishful thinking and totally unrealistic. However, there are people in this world who do have such a fortune. How did they get it, I wondered?

Well my answer was as follows: I needed to start my own company, own 20 million shares of it and then eventually get the share price to be $5. 20 million times $5 is $100 million.

The only way you can do this is with a company that will go public in the stock market (IPO) and since my expertise is in the energy and natural resource market, this was the company that would help me to get there.

In my business plan I need to raise $6 million in the first 12 months so that I can buy oil projects that produce 300 barrels per day and have a profit of about $5 million per year. This should give me an approximate valuation of about $100 million in the stock market. The next phase is to expand and raise an additional $10 million. Based on that I can continue to execute my business plan and achieve a share price of $5 in the next 5 years. The plan has a lot more details and mini steps that are very realistic.

Simply the fact that I have defined the main goals has helped me to take the right action. I now sound much more convincing when talking to business partners or clients because I have clarity.

It took me about one week to write the plan but it is the foundation for a new company and new success.

Step 16: Self-confidence is the basis for success

> What we consider possible or impossible is rarely a function of our true capability. It is more likely a function of our beliefs about who we are. (Tony Robbins)

Greater self-esteem produces greater success, and greater success produces more high self-esteem, so it keeps on spiraling up.

All limitations are self-imposed and chosen out of fear.

What would you dare to dream if you knew you could not fail? What would you choose as your goal if you knew that success was guaranteed?

No one is really better or smarter than you. Others have simply found a better strategy, decided what they wanted with great clarity and worked hard every to achieve it. If someone else has done it, then you can do it, too.

The starting point is self-confidence. You need first to believe that you can do it.

> 6 months from now you can be in a completely different place mentally and financially. Keep working and believe in yourself.

Step 17: Hard work

> Hard work beats talent when talent doesn't work hard. (Time Notke)

Talent, knowledge and credentials don't mean anything without persistence and a strong work ethic.

What does hard work mean?

- It means working 10 to 12 hours every day.

- It means having the self-discipline to work on uncomfortable things.
- It means to put in the hours and effort when it would be more convenient to take it easy.
- It means never to be lazy.
- It means working six days per week.
- It means planning your week in advance and following through.

> Everybody wants to be famous but nobody wants to do the work. It could be in 30 days or in 30 years. Eventually, your hard work will pay off. (Kevin Hart – comedian)

The best tip I could give you is to be active. Don't be a talker, be a doer. Success doesn't come from what you do occasionally. It comes from what you do consistently.

Step 18: Be a leader in your field

> If you want to make everyone happy, don't be a leader – sell ice cream.

Focus on one area and decide to become the best in that field. Once you decide to become the best in your industry, you will realize that there are not too many people at the top.

For a long time I struggled with finding my niche or area of expertise. I was a great sales person and team leader but I also knew finance.

I realized that my specialty was Private Equity. This means selling shares of private, unlisted companies to private investors and then taking a company public.

Finding my niche or area of expertise didn't happen overnight. It was a process that took many years. My first success was with my gold company Hemis where I raised $40 million from 500 private investors, took it public in the stock market and achieved a market capitalization of $300 million.

But the company didn't last. It took me another 10 years of trial and error to finally find my area and myself.

I know not only raise money from investors and lead my sales organizations but I also focus on training and educating others on my website www.normanmeier.com

You will know your field if you cannot imagine doing anything else anymore. And once you know what it is, you need to decide to become the very best in your field.

Step 19: Gratitude and positive attitude

> Every time you praise something, every time you appreciate something, every time you feel good about something, you are telling the Universe: "More of this, please!"

If you get into a state of appreciation, you will start attracting more money. It is the law of attraction. If you have positive vibes, you will attract more positive vibes. The same is true of the opposite: if you are constantly negative, you will only attract negative things into your life.

Don't be naïve or a dreamer who is not prepared, though. Realistically cover all bases but then expect the best to happen.

My advice in regards to strategy is as follows: **Always expect the best and be positive!**

Your energy is one of the most important things when dealing with clients or business partners. If you are honest, positive and happy, it will have an effect on your business dealings. If you are 100% convinced of your company and believe in your products, your clients and employees can't help but to believe in you, too.

Step 20: Just do it!

80% of success is showing up. (Woody Allen)

No one is born an expert. It is the result of endless trials and errors. The biggest mistake you could ever make is being too afraid to make one.

In case of doubt, just try it. Once you did it, you will know what to change or improve. But don't be paralyzed and take no action. Just do it. That should be your motto.

You can set a goal and assume certain things. You can make an initial plan and set time lines. After a while you will see that it was maybe too optimistic. That's ok. Then just adjust your plan. No plan is ever fixed. Your goals shouldn't change but your plan does.

If you want to start an online business and you have never done it, then do the following things outlined below. Since those people have already gone before you and proven that success is possible, a smart approach for you could be like this:

1. Find out who the real big players are and learn from them
2. Read 10 books about online marketing
3. Buy their programs and courses and learn from them
4. Go to their seminars and learn
5. **Reverse engineer** their marketing process
6. Find your market / niche / product
7. Set goals
8. Hire external consultants from upwork.com to help you
9. Create a high quality product
10. Get started with your marketing process (Place an ad on Facebook or Google)

There are a number of people who made more than one million dollar per year with their online business. Just like you, they started with nothing and had to figure out what strategies work and which ones don't.

Step 21: Dealing with doubts

> When you doubt your power, you give power to your doubt.

Doubt is only removed by action. And you will only take action if you have clarity. If you know what needs to be done. That's why your starting point is to make an action plan.

You should know every single day what the goals and the activities are. It all starts with your plan.

Unfortunately, there is never a guarantee whether or not you will accomplish your goals. If you want security and certainty, you are on the wrong planet. Life is always full of unforeseen problems but also positive surprises. But it starts with clarity and knowing what you need to do.

> Discontent, blaming, complaining, self-pity cannot serve as a foundation for a good future, no matter how much effort you make. (Eckhart Tolle)

If doubts creep into your mind, then you must go back to WHY you want your goals in the first place. You must remind yourself each morning what your main goals in life are by writing them down. Write down the 10 most important goals each morning for 5 to10 minutes and dwell on them. Doubts can only be removed with positive thoughts.

If you are insecure, guess what? The rest of the world is, too. Do not overestimate the competition and underestimate yourself. You are better than you think.

Step 22: You deserve everything

> You don't get in life what you deserve but
> what you set as a goal for yourself!
> (Harald Psaridis)

You get exactly what you ask for. Then you realize you have get better at asking. The Universe cannot play a bigger game until you do. But once you make a decision, the Universe conspires on your behalf. It is almost strange or funny how that works. But in my experience it happened every single time when I made a firm decision. The Universe will bring you the people, money or circumstances that you need in order to achieve your goal.

You are not the product of your circumstances. You are a product of your decisions. So make some decision today! Make written goals and develop a strategic action plan.

> Timing, perseverance and 10 years of trying will eventually make you look like an overnight success. (Biz Stone)

CHAPTER 18

DAILY RITUALS AND HABITS FOR SUCCESS

Good habits are the key to success

Successful people are simply those with successful daily habits.

Your habits and daily rituals are what will make you successful. It is the little things that you do every single day that determine your long-term success.

Poor habits will give you poor results.

10 years of watching useless reality TV shows will make you dumb.
10 years of eating junk food every day will make you fat.
10 years of being around unsuccessful people will make you fail, too.

But…10 years of reading, learning, working on your business and improving yourself will make you a more successful person.

Change your daily habits – change your life.

I am sure you have heard this quote: "The definition of insanity is doing the same things and expecting a different result."

Even though it might be obvious, it is harder for people to change their thinking and their actions than you might first expect.

Letting go of old habits or old ways of thinking and taking on new things is difficult for a lot of people. But life is change and only those who can adapt to change will survive.

Right now we live in a new time and things are changing. The way we make money has changed and a lot of old business models are dying and with it, the people who can't let go. The Internet has killed some old jobs and also created new opportunities.

Change requires courage. If you are open to change yourself and the way you think and act, you have a chance to come out on the other end as the new winner.

Time management and daily activities

Consistency is more important than short-term highs.

Achieving a big goal is a series of achieving many little goals or tasks first.

People don't realize that you can't be successful in anything if you don't put in the hours. This means working hard and long hours. But not just for a few weeks but over a longer period of time. Anything that is worthwhile to achieve, takes time. Anything that has great value is not easy to obtain. But nothing is really difficult if you break it down into small little steps. And those little steps are daily activities that are tied into the big end goal. In the end it all comes down to your daily activities or habits.

You have to put in many, many, many tiny efforts that nobody sees or appreciates before you achieve anything worthwhile. (Brian Tracy)

The perfect day (for you)

Imagine your life is perfect in every respect: what would it look like?

Basically, you have to ask yourself what your long-term goals are and then ask yourself what it will take to get there. What daily activities do you need to incorporate in your daily plan to ensure that you can achieve your goals?

Typically, your goals are not just financial goals or things. You also need to have goals for your fitness, health, relationships and happiness along the way.

But for most people a typical day looks like this: 8 hours of sleep, 8 hours of work and 8 hours for the rest.

How can you rearrange the remaining 8 hours, your weekends and the time when you work? How could you improve the quality of your sleep so that you have more energy and can be more productive? What are the things that make you happy and that you want to have in your life regardless of money and success?

Each one of us has different goals. But in the end we are all just human and have similar needs and desires. We all want to feel happy and be successful in at least one area.

For many successful people a good day looks like this:

5 am to 8 am	Exercise, Yoga, mediation, inspirational reading, dreaming, Goal setting
8 am to 6 pm	Work
6 am to 10 pm	Dinner, family, reading

How could you change your day to incorporate new, beneficial habits?

Most successful people get up very early. Most get up between 4 and 6 am. They do the most important things long before the rest of the world wakes up. No really successful person sleeps past 6 am.

If you develop the habit to get up a 5 am for example and do important things until 8 am before you go to work, your life will change dramatically.

Are you a morning person or a night person? Many people have to "force" themselves out of bed until getting up early becomes a habit but afterwards they have no more problems getting up early. But for some people it is be better to work during the night and be more productive that way.

You need to do what is right for you. Some people are "night people" and that is when they perform better. My own mother is almost 70 but she can't help but getting to bed at 2 or 3 am.

How much sleep do you really need?

This varies from person to person but you should sleep at least 6 hours per day. Anything less will mess with your health and energy level.

On the other hand sleeping more than 8 hours is unnecessary.

But there is no point in sleeping only 5 or 6 hours and then being tired, sluggish and unproductive all day. If you only function at a level of 50% of your productivity, then there is no point in cutting back on sleep.

Sleep and rest is important for your mental, emotional and physical state. A good quality of sleep will balance your hormones and make you healthier and give you more energy.

In order to improve those parts of your life consider getting a new bed, new pillow or new mattress.

Replace some old habits with new ones

The average person watches 4 hours of TV each day.

What old habits can you replace with new and better ones?

Bad habits:

- TV at night
- Facebook, Twitter and other social media
- Unimportant Internet surfing
- Spending time with unimportant people
- Sleeping in unnecessarily
- Smoking, alcohol, drugs and other addictions – they steal your life energy
- Bad nutrition and fast food
- Comfort shopping
- Gambling
- Video games
- Obsessively checking smartphone
- Going to the club or bar
- Staying up late
- Unnecessary house cleaning and rearranging things
- Binge watching movies and recorded shows
- Worrying and pondering about things that you cannot change
- Bullying and attacking other people
- Wasting time with the wrong person in a relationship way longer than you should and you know it
- Getting too drunk, having a hangover and wasting the whole next day
- Trying to keep up with the Jones and showing off things for no good reason
- Rationalizing that you are "still young" and "still have time"

Which ones are you guilty of?

There are a lot more bad habits like for example "picking your nose" but the ones that you should really focus on are the bad habits that are **time consuming** and take away valuable time for things that could get you ahead in life.

The goal is to free up some extra time and replace old, time consuming activities with new ones that help you to achieve your goals.

If your goal is to make more money, then you should put aside a few extra hours per day to work on your business, go to school or learning about a new topic.

Self-discipline is a habit

They say that is takes 21 days to develop a new habit. In my opinion it takes less time. But it also depends on the habit and the person. If you make a decision and that decision is really firm, then you can change things immediately.

> What you lack in talent can be made up with desire,
> hustle and giving 110% all the time. Don Zimmer

How you do anything is how you do everything. Self-discipline is the most important habit. But what does self-discipline really mean and where does it come from?

Self-discipline means setting a goal, working hard on it every single day **whether you feel like doing it or not**. It means that you are even working on your goal even if you are not in the mood. You do certain activities that will help you to achieve a greater goal.

Self-discipline is **the price** that you have to **pay in advance** for success.

So the starting point for self-discipline is to define what you really want. You need to set a goal and be very clear about it. Then, you need to have the desire to make it happen. It basically comes down to the 3 D's:

1. Desire
2. Determination
3. Discipline

You will only have the power and energy to make it happen if you **emotionalize your goal on a daily basis.** Desire and determination have to do with how you feel about your goal. It is your driving force.

New habits that you should incorporate into your life

There are a number of habits that you should incorporate into your life if you want to be more successful. You need to replace old habits that were time consuming with new ones.

> Incorporating a new habit into your life should be like brushing your teeth on a daily basis. It should feel so normal that you don't even have to think about it.

The following is a list of habits of other successful people. If you do the same things that other successful people do, you will achieve the same results.

New habit 1: Exercise every single day

> When in doubt, go work out!

Without physical energy, you cannot perform well. But the effect on your mental and emotional state is why you should do it. Exercise will give you more energy and the power to execute. It will make you feel more self-confident and more balanced.

If you walk two miles per day, you will reduce your risk of heart attack by 50%.

Daily exercise doesn't only have a positive effect on your body alone. It also will increase your energy level, your relationships, your emotional balance and your mental state. It will have a positive effect on your business success and all other areas in your life.

It is too important not to have in your daily routine. Humans need to move their bodies to be physically and mentally healthy – even if it is only 30 minutes per day.

The best way to start with this habit is to have your workout clothes and shoes next to your bed. When you wake up in the morning you put on them on and leave the house within 5 minutes. Don't even give yourself a chance to question it. Just do it. Once you start to "wake up" you are already half way through your exercise routine.

New habit 2: Eat healthy

> The higher your energy level, the more efficient your body. The more efficient your body, the better you feel and the more you will use your talent to produce outstanding results. Tony Robbins

My friend and realtor Dennis is 46 years old and he is in great physical shape and has a lot of energy. When I asked him what he is doing, he told me his secret: every morning he uses his **juicing machine** and make a shake with **green vegetables** for himself and for his wife. He does it every single day and he looks amazing because of it. This onc daily habit changed not only his energy level but also helped him to increase his business tremendously.

Add lots of **vegetables and organic food** into your daily diet. Replace noodles or French fries with vegetables or salad. You can still eat your meat but just replace the carbs with veggies.

Eat **real food** and avoid processed food products. Your energy level will increase and you will lose excess body weight.

They say one apple a day will keep the doctor away. David Wolfe says: one avocado per day keeps the doctor away forever!

> Give up carbs? Over my bread body!

Give up carbs at night. If you eat carbs after 6 pm, they will most likely be turned into body fat. There is a rule called "salads at six". If you want to lose excess weight, then simply apply this rule and eat a salad with some lean protein every night. This habit alone will help you to easily lose 10 or 20 pounds.

Drink water and tea only. Replace soda drinks and alcohol with water or tea. This is a good habit and will keep you healthy.

Simply do a few dietary changes and your whole life will improve.

New habit 3: Money and spending

> Wanting to look rich is what keeps most people poor.

If your goal is to have money, then you need to develop the same habits that rich people have. You need to be smart about how you spend your money, save it, invest it and not spend it foolishly when you are emotional.

For many people spending money or shopping is almost like a drug to make themselves feel better. They have accepted poor spending habits into their lives and that is why they never have money.

New habit 4: Meditation

You are a spiritual being. Incorporate meditation into your life and you will get more clarity, reduce stress, lose fears, develop more appreciation and happiness, get piece of mind, develop intuition, become mentally sharper, expand your awareness and consciousness and gain more confidence. Some people meditate for 10 minutes per day while others do it up to one hour.

New habit 5: Write down your goals daily

> Goals that are not in writing are merely wishes or fantasies.

Write down your most important goals daily and dwell on them. The act of writing them down daily will get you your focus. Spend 5 to 10 minutes doing this and you will achieve anything that you desire. It is important to **emotionalize** your goals and imagine yourself already having them achieved.

New habit 6: Personal development and learning

> Invest 5% of your income in yourself (personal and business development) in order to guarantee your future.

There are things that you don't know yet or that you are not aware of. And that is the reason why you are not where you want to be in life. Maybe you lack a certain mental attitude or specific strategy.

Other successful people have spent their lifetime finding out how to be more successful. You can learn from others and you don't need to make all the mistakes yourself. You can save 10 years of your life by listening to motivational and educational programs.

You should feed your brain with positive and empowering information each day. Don't listen to the news or the radio. Use the time to get influenced in a positive way.

The average American sits over 600 hours in his or her car in one year. Use those 600 hours to learn something new and to stay motivated.

Remember: If you are not where you want to be, then there is something that you don't know **yet.** It is as simple as that.

New habit 7: Write into your personal journal

Buy a journal or book with empty pages and write into it every single day. Write down your goals, new ideas, and things that you have learned or heard, important quotes, plans and insights.

Cut out pictures of your ideal house, cars or other things that you want and glue them into this book.

This is your most important book. It is a collection of the things that you want to have, be or achieve.

Before I became a self-made millionaire I wrote daily into my journal for about two years and all of a sudden I had an epiphany. I realized what I need to do and only 2 ½ years later I made millions.

> One good idea is all you need to save yourself years of hard work.

New habit 8: Work on the 5 most important daily goals

> Make a daily list with the 5 most important tasks.

Time management is crucial for success. We all have 24 hours but how we spend them makes the difference between rich and poor, successful or unsuccessful.

One of the best habits that I have learned is to write down the 5 most important goals for the day and then prioritize them in order. Then start working on your list. If you only achieved one, two and three but not four and five, then you can still be satisfied because you worked on the most important things during your day.

If you are a manager, don't spend an hour with your employee discussing unimportant things. Some of the best managers that I have worked with spent 5 minutes on a problem and then basically almost threw me out of their office so that they could continue with working on their own goals.

Be effective and clear in your meetings and your communication. Prepare well, set goals and don't socialize too much.

Get an assistant for all the little things and always ask yourself if you absolutely have to do a certain task or if someone else could do it.

Always ask the question: Who else could do this? Get an assistant for all small and unimportant tasks. Giving away those little jobs and focusing only on the important things is a habit that will get you far. Once I got my first assistant things started to take off because I could free up time to sell more.

New habit 9: Dream every day

All successful people are big dreamers.

The best way to dream and is to **"think on paper"**. Take a legal pad of paper or your journal and write down what you want to achieve.

Draw diagrams of your strategy, flow charts or write down sales targets. **Don't ever feel you're wasting time strategizing. You are the military general of your life**. Winning, plotting and strategizing is your job.

Write down your strategy and hang it on a whiteboard in your office so that you can see it every day. Change your plan of action as necessary or needed.

Print out a picture of your dream house or dream car and hang it there, too.

If you want to buy a house, then go house shopping and look at homes in the area that you would like to live.

New habit 10: Don't check emails in the morning

> One small positive thought in the morning
> can change your whole day.

Always start your day on a positive note. When you get up in the morning, don't check your emails, your phone and messages.

A negative message can also ruin your day and dampen your positive mood.

Most people do exactly that and then "react" to what life throws at them. But successful people decide first what the five most important goals for the day are and then they work solely on those. That is how you get ahead.

If you are constantly reacting to the needs of others, you will spend time doing things that are not getting you ahead. You won't have enough time to work on your goals.

Check emails later in the day and reserve some time to answer them. But don't keep looking at them constantly and respond immediately. Nothing is that important that it cannot wait 24 hours.

New habit 11: Always keep a book with you

> Read one book per week. That's 50 books per year. This is
> equal to an additional University degree in 10 years.

Whenever you go anywhere there are times where you have to wait for something. Those times are usually "dead times". Examples: Waiting for food in a restaurant, waiting at the doctor's office, picking up your kids from school, etc.

Use that time well. Always have a book with you and read during those times. Make sure you read something about success, sales, marketing, personal development, business or about your industry. Don't read novels. Read something useful where you can learn new things.

Do you believe that you can increase your financial success by reading books about personal development, business success, marketing, sales and strategy? You bet!

New habit 12: Manage your telephone/smartphone

You don't have to be available for the world 24 hours per day. Turn off your phone when you are doing something important or manage in such a way that an assistant will get the call.

Some people expect you to return their calls or messages immediately and get mad if you wait a day. But you need to focus on your priorities and you can't let other people dictate your time management.

People have become addicted to their smartphones and spend more and more time looking at their phones than being present. Remember that you should focus 100% of your attention on work, on a certain task or having a meeting with another person. Constantly checking emails or messages is not just rude but also very ineffective.

My friend Mariano got rid of his smartphone and bought a cheap, regular phone that can only call people. No Internet, no emails and no Facebook. This helps him not to constantly think about work or clients and he can enjoy his free time and his relationships with the people that are most important to him.

Also make sure that you don't have distractions or any interference when you are working. Get an assistant to shield you from people who steal your time and energy. Set clear rules for your employees and only give your private phone number to the most important people in your inner circle. Everyone else will get the secretary's number. The same applies to your personal email.

You alone are in charge of how you spend your day. No one else should dictate what you should do. No one else should be able to put pressure or stress on you just because they want something from you.

New habit 13: Work on it until it is 100% finished

> Once you start an important job, stay with it
> until it is 100% complete. Brain Tracy

If you have an important project, then work on it until it is 100% finished. Don't break it up into smaller pieces because it will take longer and if you have to start all over again to get into your topic. It will take much longer to complete if you do it in several parts.

You will increase your productivity and results if you focus on the most important tasks and finish them.

If you have several things unfinished you will feel like you haven't accomplished anything and you will eventually lose your motivation and momentum.

New habit 14: Combine activities to increase productivity

Try to read while you eat. Work out while you listen to motivational or educational audio books. Read a book while you are waiting for an appointment. Little things like that can increase your productivity enormously.

Some people are more creative when they are listening to music in the background while they are working. Others always bring a legal pad of paper and a pen with them wherever they go.

And of course you should listen to personal development programs while you drive your car instead of listening to the radio.

New habit 15: Focus 80% of your time on income generating activities

> You need to be constantly selling a product every single day – either in person, online, over the telephone or in your store.

This is the most important habit of them all. You need to be constantly selling or marketing your product. In the end, failure in business has only one reason: lack of sales.

A lot of new entrepreneurs fail in business because they focus on things like cleaning up their office, alphabetically labeling binders or doing some other unimportant work to avoid selling. They are afraid of rejection or failure and that is why they do everything else first instead of talking to clients.

Ask yourself the following question: Who else could do this task besides me so that I can free up more time to sell more products to clients?

Generating new client leads and getting new sales is everything. If you have money in your life as a supporting role, it can solve 95% of all problems.

New habit 16: Listen to inspirational audio CDs in your car and when you exercise

> You change what you are and where you are by
> changing what goes into your mind.
> Zig Ziglar

Before I became a self-made millionaire I was listening to inspirational and motivational audio programs every single day. I would go for a walk with my dog and listen to a program with my CD player. When I went to work, I listened to a program in my car.

I mainly listened to programs of Brian Tracy, Anthony Robbins and programs from people about personal and business success.

I can honestly say that my success was possible because of this one habit. I got to a point where I felt like I knew just as much as all the gurus. And when I started to take action and things took off because I knew exactly what to do.

A few years later, I was struggling in my business and then I decided to listen to my programs again. And guess what? The positive messages every day were a great influence on my attitude and things started to improve again.

You need to feed yourself with positive messages and knowledge instead of useless information from the Internet, negative news reports or the radio.

What you put into your mind is so important. Make it only positive and empowering.

New habit 17: Eat that frog – don't procrastinate

> If you procrastinate when faced with a big difficult problem... break the problem into parts, and handle one part at a time. Robert Collier

People procrastinate because they are afraid. But the key is to overcome the fear and deal with the problem.

If you ignore a problem, difficult person or situation, it will not go away on its own. It will usually get worse if you ignore it.

Sometimes it is better just to deal with the problem at hand, get it resolved and move on with your life.

Make it a new habit to deal with difficult people or situations **immediately** before the problems become bigger. Develop the courage by facing the situation right away. Waiting or procrastinating will rob you of your emotional energy. Usually, if we worry about a problem for too long, we start to feel bad, lose our happy spirit and waste valuable time.

"To eat that frog", means dealing with difficult situations right away even if it is hard at first. But once you have dealt with it, you will feel much better and you can continue to work on your goals.

Make it a new habit to make that difficult phone call right away or facing a certain person.

But to "eat that frog" also means to start with a big project that you have been avoiding. Just do it. Develop the habit of tackling big or difficult problems right away. Don't overthink it and just take action.

New habit 18: Simplify your life

> Our life is frittered away by detail... simplify, simplify. Henry David Thoreau

Get rid of things that have been sitting on your desk for weeks or months can be very liberating. Cleaning up your desk, your house and your life feels good.

It creates space for new things to come into your life.

Sometimes you have to refocus and decide what is important and what is not that important. Get rid of all the things that don't help you anymore.

There is a simple test that I often do. I have a box with things that I will deal with "later" or "not right now". After a few months the box gets really full and then I start to go through it. I try to be radical and throw away almost everything because if I didn't deal with it until today, then I will most likely not deal with it later, either. I ask myself the question what the consequence would be if I didn't deal with it and if it would really be so bad. In most cases I can get rid of it and throw it in the garbage.

If you simplify your life you will focus on the few important things in your life. You will have more power to execute and unimportant details won't distract you.

New habit 19: Reduce stress by dealing with bills once a month only

Most people are constantly stressed over bills. Every day or every second day they get a bill in the mail and they start to get stressed out. The constantly think and worry about bills and things that they have to pay.

Years ago I read one tip that changed my life in that regard. I still do it the same way after almost 20 years and it keeps me sane.

I have one box assigned to bills. Each time I get a new bill in the mail I put it straight into the box. I don't look at it or even worry about. Then once a month I spend one hour going through bills and pay them. That is when I deal with them.

This strategy has helped me to worry less about money and paying bills. I can focus on work and life with less stress.

New habit 20: Act as if...

Confidence has no competition.

If you want to be king one day, you have to start acting like a king already today. If you want to be successful in your field, then you must already do the things that other successful people in your field do.

You need to act as if you have already achieved your goal. I am not talking about spending money that you don't have. I am talking about the habits that you need to incorporate into your daily life that will ensure your success.

Most people are holding themselves back due to fear and self-doubt. If you act with confidence even if you are not yet where you want to be, you will convince other people of your greatness.

If you want to go to the top of your field, you must already act with confidence and it will only be a matter of time until you get there.

New habit 21: Make 5 extra sales calls per day

Most people hate cold calling. But do you think that if you made 5 extra sales calls per day, which equals an additional 1250 extra calls per year, that it would increase your overall yearly financial result? Of course it will!

You don't need to suffer for hours or days and get rejected over and over again. Make a pact with yourself and make 5 additional sales calls each day. Make it a new habit and just add it to your daily routine. It is a small thing but it can dramatically improve your overall result.

Some people simply get upset because they didn't achieve what they intended to do. But you can't get upset with yourself if you didn't do what was necessary. You can't dream of results and don't do anything for it.

> Don't get upset with the results because of the things that you didn't do.

It's hard to get what you never ask for. You need to do things that will help you to get ahead. In a lot of cases this means selling a product to a client or convincing a person in some way to accept your proposal. Make it a new habit to ask. Don't ever be afraid to ask. Sometimes simply the act of asking will change everything.

New habit 22: Develop a life-long perspective for your goals

Where do you want to be in five years?

If you don't start today then you will still be in the same place in two years and nothing has changed.

Getting started is better than not getting started – even if it is not perfect in the beginning.

The key is creating something great is to get started and then you can improve what you have as time goes on.

> Your dream doesn't have an expiration date.
> Take a deep breath and try again.

Setting goals

> If what you are doing is not moving you towards your goals, then it is moving you away from your goals. (Brian Tracy)

The most effective goal setting exercise that I have ever encountered and used is this: Set 10 new goals for the next 12 months.

This is very effective because 12 months is not too long and it forces you to take action in the short-term.

Some people have done this and one week later, they have achieved their whole list. Some people set those 10 goals and to their surprise they achieved their goals in as little as three months.

When I did this exercise I set 10 huge goals and after two years I had accomplished 7 out of the 10 goals. But my goals were things like having 100 employees, becoming a millionaire, etc.

Setting 10 goals is a very powerful exercise and it can really change your life. Don't downplay it just because you heard about goal setting already a hundred times.

Whatever your goals are, they have to be broken down into monthly, weekly and daily goals. That is where you decide what your activities should be daily. Those daily activities become your new habits.

> The key to success is to focus on the things
> we desire and not the things we fear.

The power of clarity

> Think before you act but then act decisively. Fortune favors the brave.

In order to be very effective you need to be very clear what you want to achieve. The clearer you are in regards to the details of your goals, the more likely you will achieve them because you will do exactly the things that are required to get there.

You should plan your week in advance and reserve slots for client meetings. I call this the "submarine game". As kids we used to play this game where you had to place your submarines on a chessboard. The other player had to find out where the slots were and sink your boats. Just like you have to sink a submarine, you can place a client meeting in an open slot.

If you organize your week in advance even if you don't have any client meetings yet, you will try to fill the open spaces that are assigned for those times and make sure that the rest of your life is also incorporated into your schedule.

> The first step to getting anywhere is deciding you
> are not willing to stay where you are anymore.

Sometimes you need to first experience fully what you don't want in life to understand what it is that you really want.

Define your own happiness

What makes you happy?

Most people are constantly unhappy because they haven't reached their financial goals yet. They are constantly suffering and feeling down. But this is not necessary. You can be happy for no reason. You can be happy now and grateful for what you have today. But this doesn't mean that you can't have more. You deserve everything that you want in this life. You just have to make a decision to get it and then work on it daily.

But there are also things besides money or things that make you feel good. Maybe you like spending time with your animals, your family, going hiking or surfing at the beach.

Life is a combination of many things. Decide what makes you happy in your daily life and then incorporate those things. Maybe you would feel good if you incorporate one thing once a week. Maybe just doing that is enough to feel a certain need.

Example: I love animals but because my wife is allergic to animals, we can't have any. That is why I go once a week to the animal shelter and volunteer. This way I can get my "animal fix" and it makes me happy. Once a week is enough. Daily would be too much.

No one is in charge of your happiness except you.

Balance in life

Good habits improve other areas in your life. A good habit in one area will have a positive effect on other parts in your life. Everything is connected. You can't be feeling sluggish and be successful in business. You can't have problems in your marriage and have the power to conquer the world. You need to have a good balance in all areas to do well in other areas.

Just as your car runs more smoothly and requires less energy to go faster when the wheels are in perfect alignment, you perform better when your thoughts, feelings, goals and values are in perfect balance.

You need to be strong, determined, goal oriented and hard working if you want to achieve your goals but you can only do this if you have physical, mental and emotional energy. You can't be wildly successful if you have constant stress or worry.

That is why you should look a good look at your life and determine what other area than money or business success is important to you.

> Nobody on his or her deathbed has ever said: "I wish I had spent more time at the office."

Other areas of life are:

- Relationships
- Family and children
- Health
- Hobbies
- Spiritual beliefs
- Social activities
- Education
- Travel
- Etc.

It also makes your life more enjoyable if you reward yourself at the end of each day or week with something small. This will keep your momentum going because then you are not just suffering for a long-term goal that is still far away but you will have little mini-milestones or successes to be happy about.

In order to improve your relationship you should plan regular dates or lunches with your partner. This habit will help to keep things positive.

The 6 best doctors in the world

> Let food be thy medicine.

1. Food
2. Exercise
3. Sunshine
4. Fresh air
5. Nature
6. Love

A lot of people have poor habits when it comes to nutrition and their bodies. But in order to feel good about ourselves we need to have healthy habits to have a good life.

A lot of medical problems come from poor lifestyle habits. You can heal yourself by changing your habits. Your body can heal itself and recover from almost anything.

If you start eating healthy, organic foods and exercise daily you will dramatically increase your health and energy level.

If you incorporate things like Yoga or meditation into your life, you will develop a new level of mental and emotional stability.

> Nature is cheaper than therapy.

In the end all that matters are your three main **energy levels:**

1. Physical energy
2. Emotional energy
3. Mental energy

You cannot function well if you are constantly stressed, under pressure or have negative influences in your life.

> Take control over your environment and ensure that it is predominantly positive.

Your personal and professional life needs to be positive if you want to live a positive life. Nothing is more important than **piece of mind**.

Character and habits

Character is a series of habits over a long period of time.

Success and having a strong character go hand in hand. You cannot be successful if you have a weak character. And your character comes from your daily habits.

Your life will only get better if you get better. The better person you become, the better people you will attract and better opportunities will come your way.

Never stop doing your best just because someone doesn't give you credit. You need to do things for yourself and not because you want praise or recognition from other people.

Ultimately, you become what you do on a daily basis and what you think about all the time. Therefore, keep your thoughts and actions positive.

Your habits shape your life. If you want a good life, then you should have good and supporting habits.

Dealing with your problems and pain

A lot of people use food and overeating as "emotional protection". They still suffer from an emotional event that was painful and they have never really recovered from it. In order to make themselves feel better, they use food.

Other people use drugs, alcohol, cigarettes, gambling or shopping to cover up the pain. But those things are negative habits and eventually they will harm your life in the long run.

The key is to deal face on with your problems or pain so that it can go away. You need to get rid of those old, bad habits that you used as a coping mechanism and replace them with new and better habits. But this is only possible if you deal with the problems from the past. Otherwise you will always feel like you are in pain and the only cure will be those bad habits.

Many people fall into the **victim role or victim mentality**. They keep saying to themselves that they are powerless and that is why they can't change their lives. But **you are NEVER the victim.** You alone make yourself the victim. In reality you are lacking love or attention. You want to be rescued or saved but no one is coming for you.

Maybe you were exposed to criticism, emotional pain or even physical pain and you never got over your problems. But in order to improve your life again, you must let go of the past because you can't change it anymore anyway. You need to get your own power back.

The power of your own power

People don't need to be saved or rescued. People need knowledge of their own power and how to access it.

Everything happens for a reason. Sometimes the reason is that you acted stupid, made bad decisions or had poor habits.

The key to achieving any goal is self-confidence. You can develop more self-confidence by being self-disciplined. You set a goal and then do the daily things (habits) to achieve that goal. Once you have achieved a goal, it will increase your level of self-confidence. The more things that you have achieved in your life, the more self-confident you will feel. Eventually, you will feel like you can accomplish any challenge if you set your mind to it.

> Do something every day in the direction of your dreams.

The only things that are holding you back are fear and doubt in yourself. Stop being afraid of what could go wrong and start being positive about what could go right.

Incorporate new habits that will help you to have little successes every day, week or month. This will increase your self-confidence and belief in yourself.

Change one habit at a time until it becomes normal

Changing your life all at once is challenging. That is why I suggest something that works for me. Instead of changing 10 habits at a time, I start incorporating one habit a time. Then I add another one and another one until all new habits have become normal.

Example: I replace soda drinks with water for each meal. That is the first habit that I change. It is one small new habit but it can drastically improve your health. After a couple of weeks you get used to it and it becomes normal. Then I switch French fries or noodles with vegetables or salad until I get used to that. And so on.

The key to becoming successful is changing one little habit at a time. Over time you will have changed many habits and you got used to them. But overall, your entire daily routine has improved your results.

Don't give up – anything worthwhile takes time

> The moment you are ready to quit is usually the moment right before a miracle happens.

Everything happened exactly as it should have. Maybe you needed to "waste" time to come to the realization that you want to fully live your life now.

But today that you are aware of what you want or no longer want in your life, you have a new chance to chance your life again.

Set new goals and develop new habits that will help you to achieve those goals.

You only have to succeed the last time.

Anything that is worthwhile to achieve takes time. It might not be easy but that is why not everybody can have it. Give yourself time but develop new habits that will help you to get there.

If you never give up, you will achieve anything that you set your mind to. Success is a habit and so is failure. Giving up is a habit for some people. If you decide to follow through no matter what life throws at you, there is no limit to have you can achieve.

I wish you all the strength and energy to make your life wonderful!

CHAPTER 19

THE POWER OF CLARITY

Life is like a buffet

Life is like a buffet. Everything is available in abundance. You can have, do or be anything that you want in this life but you need to make a decision first. You need to be clear about what you really want.

You can have **anything but not everything.** There are too many things or options to choose from. There is not enough time in one lifetime to do everything. That's why you must choose.

The starting point: desire

What does your heart desire? What do you want to have, who do you want to be and what do you want to do in your life?

What would you dare to dream if you knew you could not fail?

We all want things. We all are motivated to make something out of our lives. The starting point of any achievement is always **desire**. What is it that you desire? What would you like to accomplish? What would you like to do, have or be?

A desire is an emotion. It is a feeling of something that you long for. As you feel the emotion, you also have **wishes or thoughts**. These thoughts, wishes or desires always come first. Before you set a goal, you have these emotions, thoughts, wishes and desires. The trick is to take these wishes and **try to define them in detail** so that you know what you have to do to get them.

All successful people are big dreamers. Usually, we try to compensate in life for the things that we didn't get in our childhood. We all come into this life with certain dreams, wishes, talents and abilities. It is up to us to find out what these are and then to pursue them.

Manifestation: brining a wish or thought into the physical world

Most people have dreams and wishes and often they are fleeting. Unless you do something specific, like the simple **act of writing them down**, your dreams and wishes will eventually disappear again.

You can have, do or be anything in this life. The world is full of options for you. Anything is available for the taking. **You can do anything but not everything**. That's why you must at some point in your life **make a decision** of what you actually want.

A wish that is not written down is not a goal.

The first step of setting a goal is the physical act of **writing it down on paper.** You take something from the spiritual world (like your dream or wish) and bring it into the physical world by writing it down on paper and defining it or describing it in great detail.

A dream written down with a date becomes a goal.
A goal broken down into steps becomes a plan.
A plan backed by action makes your dream come true.

Difference between a goal and a wish

Goals that are not in writing are merely wishes or fantasies. A goal must be measurable. It must also have a deadline.

It was be something realistic even if it is a big goal. It must be something that is doable and possible in the physical world. You need to take that picture in your head and try to **describe and define it as a logical and measurable thing**.

You can't hit a target that you can't see.

Anything else is still wishy-washy and unrealistic daydreaming and you will never achieve a goal that you cannot define clearly. **Clarity is key** when it comes to goal setting. You need to know exactly what it is that you want.

It is better to make a clear decision and get it than to always keep your options open. If you don't define it clearly, you will never get it. Once you have achieved a goal, you can always set a new goal and get more of the same if you like.

Alice in wonderland: *What road do I take?*
Cat: *Well, where are you going?*
Alice: *I don't know.*
Cat: *Then it doesn't matter. If you don't know where you are going, any road will get you there.*

Big goals

How do you eat an elephant? One bite at a time!

How do you reach a huge goal? One small step at a time! It is the same principle like eating an elephant. You can't expect to be able to eat the elephant in one bite or in one day. It is physically impossible. But it is possible to do it with a little bit of time and with mini-goals along the way.

> You can achieve any big goal if you break
> it down into enough small steps.

If you take a big goal and really break it down into small, measureable steps or milestones, you can achieve anything. If you can analyze what needs to be done and write it down as an action plan with daily goals, then nothing is unachievable.

You get in life what you have the courage to ask for. So you should ask for big goals. And if you have to think anyway, why not think big? **Nothing is really difficult if you break it down into small steps.**

> No dream is too big when you truly understand
> that abundance is your birthright.

Lack of self-confidence and doubt in your own abilities are the only reason why you don't set big goals.

Time frames

> There are NO unrealistic goals – only unrealistic time frames.

You can achieve any goal that you set for yourself. The only factor that is you must consider is **time**. Some goals take twice as long as we normally anticipate. Sometimes the only reason why you are not achieving your goals is because you have unrealistic time frames.

That's why you must plan with great clarity and break down each goal into monthly, yearly and daily goals.

> Unrealistic time frames trigger stress. You have time. Give yourself the time you need.

If you set a goal with the wrong time frame, meaning you give yourself too little time to achieve it, it can actually backfire. If you get the feeling that you are too far away from reaching your goal, you can get demotivated and even give up all together.

That's why you need to give yourself enough time and even plan some extra time for potential problems that could come along your way (which they will).

> Just because it takes longer for you to achieve the same goal, doesn't mean that you have failed. You just need a bit more time.

In general, most business undertakings take twice as long and cost twice as much as you originally anticipated. But once you know that, you can consider that in your planning.

You don't need to stress yourself out because you are not yet a millionaire at 30. You can still achieve any goal that you have set for yourself.

When things don't happen right away, remember this: It takes 6 months to build a Rolls-Royce and 13 hours to build a Toyota.

You can achieve anything. The impossible just takes a little bit longer.

Make a specific goal and plan of action

> Clarity is power. Make a plan for each undertaking that forces you to think through every single step before you even begin.

When I started an oil company, I knew that I wanted to make it successful and take it public in the stock market. I also wanted to eventually end up with $100 million in stocks.

So I asked myself the following question: How can I pull this off for real? What would I have to do to build an oil and resource company that is worth $500 million with me being the main shareholder.

So I decided to write a 60-page business plan and tried to cover each individual step to make it happen. I realized that I needed $6 million from investors (pre-IPO), $30 million (post IPO), 5 projects that would produce 300 barrels of oil per day in the beginning and I needed a sales team who could help to raise the money.

If I personally owned 20 million shares in the company and the share price would eventually be at $5, then I would have $100 million in personal net worth.

The more details I wrote down, the clearer became my plan.

> A business plan forces you to think through every single detail and factor to realistically make it work.

And then something interesting happened. Two days after I had written everything down, I was approached by 2 Germans who work with financial institutions to help to raise money for start-up companies. A month later, an M&A (mergers and acquisitions) company from Germany agreed to raise the $6 million in 6 months.

> I realized that the Universe will bring you the people, the money and the circumstances into your life once you decide exactly what you want.

The law of attraction works once you are absolutely clear in regards to your goals.

It is like being pregnant. When your wife is pregnant you start to see pregnant women all over the place. Before that you weren't really seeing them even though there was probably the same amount of pregnant women walking the streets.

When it comes to our goals it is the same. Once we have a specific focus, we start to see the things that will help us to achieve our goal.

Visualization / Emotionalize your goal

> Don't project your goals into the future – say it like you own it now / today!

Dreaming is an important part of becoming a millionaire. Everything starts with a thought, wish or a dream. The more you dream about it and imagine how it would be, the more likely will you achieve your dream. The Universe conspires on your behalf.

Dwell on your ideal future and write down your plans in a dream journal. The next and maybe one of the most important steps is to **expect it**. Cut out pictures from magazines and put them in your dream journal or hang them on your wall.

Every day visualize your ideal future for 5 minutes. Imagine a mental picture and try to see every possible detail. Dream and imagine. This exercise every morning will be like an order for your subconscious mind to make it a reality.

It is important to believe that you already have it today. Imagine yourself having it and describe how it feels.

> Set a goal but be flexible about the plan. The Universe often has a faster way than you.

Let the Universe do its magic. Your way or strategy is not necessarily the best or fastest.

You must be absolutely clear about your goal, but be flexible about the process of achieving it. Often, the Universe will show you a way that you couldn't think of before. The main thing is the goal and not the way you go about it. So be open to other options and flexible about the process.

Law of attraction

> You will attract what you focus on daily.

You must decide exactly what it is you want in life. No one can do this for you. If you don't have any goals, then you work for someone else who has goals. Basically, you work for his or her goals.

The book / movie "The Secret" was very popular a few years ago. It seemed to be a revelation to many people. Basically, it was describing the law of attraction. The law states that you will attract what you focus on. If you focus on making money, you will attract money.

One of the things I personally learned when I became a millionaire is this: **If you don't make making money your number one focus, you will never have it.** Making money means being results-oriented. It means focusing on generating sales and revenue. You need absolute clarity in regards to your actions and what you want to accomplish on a daily basis. You need to set clear daily goals and then have the self-discipline to follow through.

Determination and dedication

> *There is no talent here. This is hard work. This is an obsession. Talent doesn't exist. We are all human beings. You could be anything if you put in the time. You will reach the top and that's that. I am not talented. I am obsessed.* (Conor McGregor)

Some people have amazing talents and it is clear what they should be doing with their lives. Maybe you don't have any particular talents that stand out. But that's ok. Most people don't have them, either.

You have to ask yourself what you want out of your life. If you have a burning desire to do something, then deep down inside you also have the ability to make it happen even if you initially don't have the talent.

There are a lot of successful and skilled people who had no talent but worked hard to gain certain skills.

Ask yourself what you want to achieve and then work hard to develop the necessary skills. You wouldn't have the dream if deep down you didn't have the necessary talent to achieve it.

Self-discipline

> Once you set a goal, you must do things on a daily basis whether you feel like it or not.

The big secret of life is that there is no secret. You can reach any goal if you are willing to work for it. Without self-discipline you will never achieve anything. Life doesn't give you what you want. It gives you what you work for.

When I got out of shape I decided to go to the gym every single day whether I felt like it or not. I decided that if I went every day and worked out that I can't help but get fitter. At first, I went to the gym and gave up after 10 minutes. My workout was totally inefficient. But the next day I was there again. And then the next day and so forth. Eventually, my workouts got better and better and after 3 months I lost 30 pounds. The main thing for me was to go every single day – no matter what.

If you decide to run 5 miles every day and watch what you eat, then you will get fit and lean. It works whether you believe in it or not. It works because there are certain physical laws that apply to all of us.

If you are in sales, then you must work with numbers and make a certain amount of calls each day. If you stick with the numbers and have the self-discipline, you will by the law of averages be successful. There will always be a positive surprise and result if you talk to enough people each day.

> Less thinking and more doing.

Once you have decided to do something, don't overthink it. Just do it.

Laziness

> There are NO lazy people – only people WITHOUT MOTIVATING GOALS. Laziness doesn't exist.

Laziness doesn't exist. Laziness only means that you have no real goals. If you had a goal that was motivating enough, then you would not be sitting on your butt. You would be actively pursuing your goal.

Maybe the reason why you can't get motivated is because you have the wrong goal. Maybe you have someone else's goal or you feel like something is expected of you but deep down you don't really want to do it.

In the end it all comes down to desire. What is it that your heart desires?

> Set a goal that makes you jump out of bed in the morning.

Another important factor is that you don't make your goal a MUST. You can say it would be nice to own a Ferrari or you can say, "I absolutely MUST have a Ferrari". Once you make your goals a MUST, then you find the REASONS why you have to achieve it.

False security

No amount of security is worth the suffering of a **mediocre life** chained to a routine that has killed your dreams.

> If you end up with a boring, miserable life because you listened to your mom, your dad, your teacher, your priest or some guy on television telling you how to do your shit, then you deserve it. (Frank Zappa)

If you don't set goals and stay in a job that doesn't fulfill you, then you are wasting your life and talent. There is no real job security anymore. In two weeks you could lose your job and then you are on the street. The only security that you have is yourself. That's why you need to set goals and make decisions.

Control – check your numbers

Once a week you should make a quick analysis of your numbers.

We all tend to get emotional and act based on how we feel. But this is a sure way not to reach your goals. That's why you need to check your numbers and activities. You need to make a pact with yourself to make an exact number of calls or meetings with clients and follow through exactly.

Business is a numbers game and goal achievement is a numbers game, too. You reach goals by doing certain things on a consistent basis. Therefore you must know your numbers and control them every day, week and month.

Otherwise you are like a lost lamb or a running around like a chicken with its head cut off. Completely unrealistic goals are a form of self-delusion and you cannot delude yourself into success. **You need clarity and numbers give you clarity.**

10 things you can control

> There are things in life that you can control and there are things that you can't control. Knowing the difference is wisdom.

1. Your attitude
2. Your thoughts
3. The people you surround yourself with
4. Your physical well-being
5. Your daily habits and self-discipline

You can't worry about the things that you can't control. You only drive yourself crazy. But there are things that you have control over. Those things are either actions you can take or your attitude.

If you do your best in any given moment with the things and tools that you have at this moment, then you did all you could do and you shouldn't worry about what you couldn't control anymore. If you can't change a situation and there is nothing you can do about it, then you can at least change your attitude towards it.

Remember: **Do what you can with what you have now**. Better tools will eventually come your way.

Truth

The best and worst thing about the truth is that is gets instant results. Do not fear the truth. Let it liberate you. Allow it to give you the gift of clarity so that you may move forward more focused.

No one is coming to the rescue to save you. This life of yours is 100% your responsibility. No one will help you out of the graciousness of his or her heart. If you want to change your life for the better, you need to do it yourself. No one will do it for you.

Deep down you know exactly what you are capable of. There is even moments where you get a glimpse of all the potential you have. You can get there. You just have to be willing to sacrifice the habits, things and situations that are standing in the way of your success.

You need to get clarity, set goals, develop self-discipline, be courageous, work hard, sell more and develop a smart business system that can help you grow financially.

> When someone tells you it can't be done, then it's more so a reflection of their self-imposed limitations and not your potential.

Keep your goals to yourself

> Keep your goals to yourself. Don't tell your friends.

People will discourage you from following your dreams. Most people don't want you to grow and get better. It is not necessarily a conscious but rather an unconscious thing. Your friends don't want to feel like a failure next to you if you surpass them.

That is also the reason why a lot of successful people change the people they associate with. They surround themselves with better people who are equally or more successful.

If you keep yourself surrounded with people who will constantly discourage you or who cannot imagine what it would be like to have millions for example, then your chances of reaching your goals drastically decrease.

Just keep doing your thing and work on your goals in private until you have a certain amount of success to show for.

Self-discovery

> Find out who you are and what you are good at. Use only your God-given talents.

What is the purpose of your life? What are your God-given talents and abilities?

What is it that I am great at? What am I gifted at? Find out what that is. Everybody has one thing that they are great at.

Millions of people go to work every day and hate their jobs. But if you find out what you are really good at, develop your skills further and then make it your own business, then you will always succeed.

You cannot fail if you do what you were meant to do.

You just have to find a way to turn your talent into something that you can make money with. You have to develop products and services that other people are willing to pay money for. This could be your knowledge that you turn into a seminar, a book, a course, personal coaching or something else.

Every one of us has one thing that they are great at – one thing that they excel at. What is your one great talent?

> Life isn't about finding yourself – it is about creating yourself. (Mamdouh "Big Ramy" Elssbiay – professional bodybuilder)

Dreaming is powerful

> To accomplish great things, we must not only act, but also dream; not only plan, but also believe. (Anatole France)

The Universe is an interesting place. Everything starts with a thought or a dream. Everything that was once small and is now big started with a person having an idea, a thought or a dream.

Thoughts and dreams are very powerful and they are the essence of creation. They are the beginning point of creating anything in this world.

Your intention is also important. If you have the intention to make something happen, you will activate the cosmic energies.

I want to encourage you to dream every day for 5 to 10 minutes. Think about what you would like to have, do or be. Dwell on your goals and imagine every little detail. See yourself as if you have already achieved your goals.

In the summer of 2004 I was on a vacation in Malta with my wife and son. I remember how I was sitting at the pool and I made a list of 10 goals. When I got back home I put the list away and two years later I accidentally found the list in one of my drawers. To my surprise I could cross off seven out of the ten things from my list and the remaining three things were almost achieved, too.

This list was an easy list to accomplish. Those goals were big goals. One goal was for example to have 100 employees and I had about 60 at the time.

But I had an epiphany in this moment. I realized how powerful goal setting and dreaming really is. It will change your life and everything in it if you dream big.

I want to encourage you to make your own list of the 10 most important goals in your life. And then go to work.

The first step is to dream. The second step is to WRITE IT DOWN. The third step is to do ONE thing like making a phone call, sending a message or inquiring about something. That is the starting point of every great accomplishment.

The crucial thing is **writing it down** because otherwise your thoughts can easily be lost or forgotten. The act of taking a thought and **putting it on paper** is the first step to manifesting it into the real world. You take the thought from the spiritual world (or the world of thought) and you put it into the physical world (where you want it).

> If you truly want to do something you will always find a way. If you don't, then you will find an excuse.

Business is a numbers game

> Sales and marketing = usually number 1 focus (80% of your time) to reach your goals.

Most goals have to do with money. **And money comes from other people or customers**. You need to sell a **product or a service** in order to get money. Therefore, logically, **sales and marketing is key** to reach most of your goals.

Business is a numbers game. The more people or potential customers you come in contact with, the higher is the probability that you will make a sale.

There are three things you can do:

1. You can learn absolutely everything about **sales and marketing** in order to get better at it.
2. You need to make sure that you **control your numbers** and do certain things (like for example calling up 100 clients) every day.
3. **Build a system,** build a sales organization and get some leverage so that even more people come in contact with your products.

> Most goals have to do with money. And that's why you must **focus on generating leads, revenue and sales**.

My business partner Philipp said to me that in order to be successful in raising money you must have three things:

1. The right contacts
2. The sales talent
3. The frequency and number of clients that you contact every single day

In the morning he makes phone calls from 9 to 12 and generates 10 new leads, he has to make between 50 and 80 phone calls every morning to get his 10 leads.

In the afternoon, he focuses on sales. He contacts the leads from the previous week and tries to sell them the shares.

Because he generates 50 new leads each week, he has about 200 new leads every month. In his second follow up call he gets rid of 80% of the leads by determining whether or not they still show interest and he finally ends up with 10 to 20 really good potential clients that he tries to convince.

He has the sales talent but he has regular lists or leads. But because he uses the frequency, he ends up with a positive surprise once in a while. Sometimes he gets a really good client that invests more than the average person. But he said that he would have never found that person if he didn't make all those initial marketing calls to generate 10 leads every day first.

Developing a vision

> People don't become successful just by
> accident – you first need a vision.
> (Arnold Schwarzenegger)

During the time of the gold rush, people found gold and overnight they became rich. But this is an exception. All successful people need to first have a vision and a goal before they become successful. It doesn't happen overnight and it is not by accident. It is the result of setting a goal and working hard towards it. Success is not possible without work. It is not something that happens automatic or by chance. You can't become a millionaire in 6 months and be totally unrealistic about it. That's not how life works.

Arnold Schwarzenegger used to hang posters of his idols in his bedroom and those pictures were the last thing he saw before he went to bed and it was the first thing that he saw when he woke up. He wanted to be muscular like Ray Park and other bodybuilders of his time.

> You inevitably attract into your life the people, circumstances, ideas, opportunities and resources that are in harmony with your dominant thoughts.

Not reaching your goals

> If the plan doesn't work, change the plan but never the goal.

Problems, obstacles and setbacks are a normal part of life and goal achievement. Nothing worthwhile is easy. Otherwise everyone would be doing it. That's why you must not get discouraged or give up when things get hard. Just the opposite: expect problems. They are a normal part of any plan or goal achievement.

Reasons why we lose motivation:

1. **Lack of confidence**: If you don't believe that you can succeed, what is the point in even trying?
2. **Lack of focus**: If you don't know what you want, do you really want anything?
3. **Lack of direction**: If you don't know what to do, how can you be motivated to do it?

That's why it is so important to have clarity. You need to have crystal clear clarity in regards to your goals and why you want to achieve them.

> The moment you want to QUIT is the moment when you need to keep PUSHING. (Dennis James, professional bodybuilder)

Sometimes your mood plays tricks on you. You don't feel like working out at the gym for example because you are not in the right mood. The trick is to **start anyway** and do a few exercises despite your mood. Very often you realize that once you started, your mood starts to change and you end up doing more than you thought you would.

<u>Reasons for struggle</u>

1. Haven't set any goals (not really)
2. Haven't set the right kind of goals
3. Vague dreams but no clarity
4. You use the wrong approach or strategy.

...that's why you don't take action and stand still or feel paralyzed. **Get clarity** and get unstuck. Life is movement. You need to keep moving forward. Without movement (=action) and growth, you are dead.

Mental law: The law of control

You feel positive about yourself to the degree to which you feel you are in control of your own life. You feel negative about yourself to the degree to which you feel you are in control of your own life.

If you feel in control you feel happy. If you feel the victim of your circumstances, you are feeling highly stressed and unhappy.

If you feel you are in charge of your own life, you feel good about yourself. You feel strong and powerful.

When you control your thoughts, then you control your feelings and then you control your actions.

Feeling like a victim of your circumstances

In our society there are a number of people who are led to believe that they are victims. They believe that there is nothing that they can do about their situation and that everything happens by accident.

There are people out there who believe that there is a conspiracy out there of a few rich people who control the masses, etc. and that you have no influence over the course of your life. Of course, this is all nonsense.

If you believe that there is nothing you can do, then you are convincing yourself and believing something that simply isn't true. When you get to that point, you are passive and don't take action.

It is called in psychology "*learned helplessness*".

People say things like: *"There is nothing I can do. The debts are too high, the economy is too bad and life is really terrible."*

Interestingly, the great majority of people today are feeling helpless and they are constantly complaining.

But this is not you. You should have the awareness that you can change your life no matter what the circumstances are. **And it all starts with setting goals**. Once you have a clear goal and focus, you will start to make progress.

Set a goal, make a plan and change the circumstances in your life.

Failing to plan is planning to fail.

Nature doesn't care

In our Universe we have physical laws (like gravity, etc.) and we also have mental laws (like for example the law of cause and effect). The mental laws are just as strong and true as the physical laws. Just because you can't see them, doesn't mean that they don't work.

You can't see **gravity** but you know it is there.

There are **high-pitched sounds or radio waves** that you can't hear like for example the sound of a dog whistle but the sounds still exist.

There are things like **infrared** that we can't see with our eyes but other animals have the ability to see them.

It is the same with the Universe (including the spiritual world) as well as mental laws. Just because you can't see certain things, doesn't mean that they don't exist.

What's the conclusion?

You can be a good person or a bad person but **if you do the things that other successful people did to have success, you will get the same results.** Nature does not have a moral compass.

If you do the causes (actions and thinking), you will get the results – as simple as that! It doesn't matter if you **deserve it**, whether you were a **good or bad person** or whether you **need it.**

> Nature is neutral. Nature doesn't care. If you do the same things that other successful people did, you will also get the same results.

Mental law: The law of cause and effect

For every effect in your life, there is a specific cause. Success is not an accident. Failure is not an accident. They both have specific causes. **Everything happens for a reason.**

There are two types of laws in the Universe:

1. Physical laws
2. Mental laws

If you drop something on the floor, it will fall. It is the law of gravity. You can see it work.

You can see the result immediately. Gravity is a physical law.

But with mental laws, **you can only see the results over time.**

Physical laws are just as fixed as mental laws. **And mental laws also work 100% of the time** – just like physical laws.

In all of human history, man has never invented a law. We talk about physics, mechanics and mathematics, etc. Nobody has ever invented the laws. **We have only discovered the laws that already exist.**

Whatever your spiritual beliefs are…if all these laws exist, then there must have been a lawgiver. They cannot just develop on their own from the big bang. Precise mathematical formulas, etc. are simply discovered but they have always been there.

The laws are neutral. They will work for you or they will work against you. Nature is neutral. Nature is like justice.

Nature doesn't say "*You will be a big success*" or "*You will fail.*" Nature doesn't care.

This was a big breakthrough for me. Nature doesn't care. If you do the same things like other successful people do, you will get the same results. And if you don't, then you won't. It is as simple as that.

Nature says "**here are the laws**" or "**the rules of the game**". And if you apply these laws, you will have a great life and if you don't, then you won't.

But there is nothing out there that determines what happens to us, it is all a mental game. Success and failure are all in your head.

In life we violate a lot of laws – especially the mental laws and **we suffer the consequences.**

If you jump off a 10-story building you will get splattered all over the sidewalk. And it doesn't matter whether you **believe** in the law of gravity or whether you **approve** of the law of gravity or whether you **have a different opinion** of the law of gravity.

The law of gravity will work on you regardless and you will get splattered on the sidewalk. The law is neutral. The law doesn't care. It is not going to say something like "*you shall be spared*" or "*you will be killed*". It just works they way it is supposed to work.

The law is there and all successful people try to live in harmony with these laws.

Once you live your life in accordance with these laws, incredible positive changes will happen to you.

In the middle ages people used to believe in coincidences, lightening strikes, Gods, etc. They were not aware of the mental laws but believed in coincidences and greater powers that had control over their lives.

But the truth is that you have control over your life. You have control over the outcome and the quality of your life. If you do the same things like other successful people did, you will get the same results.

If a person says "*I am overweight because of my glands*", then it is that persons' mouth and not glands that is malfunctioning several times a day. Losing weight has to do with the laws of the physical body. Everybody can do it if they following the physical rules.

We know how to be healthy and fit and to live a long time. If you go into **ketosis** (eat only protein and fat and zero carbs) combined with **intermittent fasting**, then you will lose weight 100%. Your body works just like any other human body. There are rules and laws that you need to follow in order to get the same results.

If you want to become a millionaire, then you simply have to do what other people did who started with nothing to become a millionaire. We know how to make all the money that we want because there are millions of people who have it. **There are certain things and strategies that you must know and apply.**

In general, you must sell a product or service to as many customers as possible by becoming very good at what you do, earn more money and don't spend it all.

Thoughts are causes and conditions are effects. Your thoughts create the conditions of your life.

Mental law: The law of belief

It is the foundation of all religions. Whatever you believe with feeling becomes your reality.

You biggest obstacles are usually self-limiting beliefs.

We have **conscious beliefs** and we have **unconscious beliefs**. You have to discover what your false, unconscious beliefs are that are holding you back.

You also need to **believe that you deserve success** and you need to **stop self-sabotaging yourself**. You need to become aware of your beliefs about money and success and get rid of anything that is no longer serving you.

You are exactly where you want to be in life

I had a friend say to me "*You are exactly where you want to be in your life.*" Ha! I most certainly was not! "*But you are*", he said, "*Because you took every step to get exactly where you are.*"

Once I wrapped my head around the idea, it became one of the most important phrases of my life. We are all exactly where we want to be. Take some time to really think about it. There is so much more truth and wisdom in this statement than you first realize.

If your life sucks, it is your fault! It is no one else's fault. You have allowed and accepted every circumstance in your life.

> If you want something more you need to do whatever it takes to change it.

If you want money, go get some. It is as simple as that. You make that decision.

I could defend myself on that point all day long. But the more annoyed and defensive I became, the more I realized one thing: On some level I was accepting my current life as the life that I felt I deserved.

I may not have gotten what I wanted so far but now I can change that. Immediately! Once I realized that I was the only person who was holding myself back and it was not the fault of someone else or circumstances, I actually get to change and improve my situation. I may not have held the reigns up to this point... but I certainly can from this point forward.

No one will do it for you. No one is coming one day and giving you a check for $1 million just like that. No one is coming to save you. You have to save yourself. This life is 100% your responsibility.

It's not easy to change your mindset from "victim of circumstance" to "in complete control". And it's not something that happens overnight. But all it takes is one tiny seed to begin that transformation. The first step is awareness.

Not that anybody is looking, but in the end you need to impress the one person that matters the most: yourself. You deserve everything that you want! Go get it!

We are all exactly where we want to be.

After you stop defending yourself you are forcing yourself to really think about yourself and your life. How have you gotten to this point and why are you not further along like you intended?

Do you deserve it?

Do you feel like you deserve money? Are you self-sabotaging yourself sometimes because on some level you don't believe that you really deserve it and that is why you punish yourself unconsciously?

Are you getting ahead financially and then you do something stupid by spending too much money and self-sabotage yourself again? What might be the reason?

What is your mental mindset when it comes to making money? Do you feel like you are not deserving of love because you don't love and accept yourself?

Do you feel like you need the recognition and approval of others to have money? Do you feel that you don't deserve love in your life because you have been bad in the past and made mistakes? Do you feel that you have low self-esteem because of lack of love?

Many of our problems come from our childhood and from parents. Typically, a lack of love or attention is the main reason. We all want to be accepted and loved and we will do the craziest things to get it.

But you are an adult now and you need to break out of the cycle. You need to forgive your parents and all the people in your past.

You deserve everything! You deserve love, money, a nice house, things, etc. just like anyone else. You deserve the $10 million villa just like the person who has it today. You don't need to drive a crappy car just because you don't feel good enough or deserving enough to drive a nice car.

You need to stop punishing yourself and self-sabotaging yourself because you are worthy and you deserve everything.

> 99% of all problems have to do with lack of love and feeling of deservingness.

Love yourself. Stop blaming others and **stop playing the victim**. Take back control.

You give away your own power to others and to circumstances if you keep playing the victim role. You think that the victim role will give you love or at least some attention but in reality it is pity.

You are in life exactly where you want to be, you have exactly what you think you deserve and not one bit more.

Being honest with yourself and others is the starting point to feeling good about yourself. Do good for others and it will make you feel better about yourself.

If you get a windfall of money it will amplify what is already inside of you today. If you are an asshole you will become a bigger asshole. If you feel like you need to cover up pain by shopping, drinking, drugs, gambling, etc. then you will do that even more and on a bigger scale.

Find out what kind of problems or pain you are trying to avoid. We all want to avoid pain. It is one of our two main motivations in life (= avoiding pain, gaining pleasure). But how is avoiding the pain hindering you from financial greatness? Ask yourself honestly.

> You are far more powerful than you have been lead to believe. Stop letting fear get the best of you. Remember who you really are. Take your power back.

Copy other successful people

> Anything that someone else has done you can do as well.

Remember: if someone has done it before you and built a great company for example, then you can do it, too. Often, all you have to do is the same things like a successful person and eventually you will get the same results.

Maybe you are using the wrong or an outdated strategy to achieve your goals and that's why you are not getting ahead fast enough. We often overestimate what we can achieve in one year but we greatly underestimate what we can achieve in ten years.

If you do what other successful people do, you will get the same results. What does that really mean? It means that you need to have a daily routine that ensures that certain activities get done.

Sales and marketing clarity

> Most entrepreneurs are living paycheck to paycheck because they can't solve one simple problem: getting customers.

They spend 90% of their time wasting on activities that don't bring results. You need to focus on two things:

1. Marketing (= lead generation) to create opportunities and
2. Sales (= getting customers) to make money

If you can't generate leads, you can't generate sales. It's as simple as that. That's why you must focus your time energy first on lead generation. You need to be clear about that fact.

Business clarity – what exactly do you need?

Business and sales success have a logical order. This is what you need:

1. You need a goal
2. You need a product or service
3. You need a marketing plan
4. You need a sales process
5. You need a people / team plan

Setting business goals

> Those who do not have goals are doomed
> forever to work for those who do.

<u>Focus on daily activities</u>

$100 per day = $30,000 per year
$200 per day = $70,000 per year
$300 per day = $100,000 per year
$500 per day = $180,000 per year
$1,000 per day = $360,000 per year
$3,000 per day = $1,000,000 per year

How to make $1 million per year

> **SELL A $200 PRODUCT TO 5000 PEOPLE**
> **SELL A $500 PRODUCT TO 2000 PEOPLE**
> **SELL A $1,000 PRODUCT TO 1000 PEOPLE**
> **SELL A $2,000 PRODUCT TO 500 PEOPLE**
> **SELL A $5,000 PRODUCT TO 200 PEOPLE**
>
> **5000 PEOPLE PAY $17/MONTH, FOR 12 MONTHS**
> **2000 PEOPLE PAY $42/MONTH, FOR 12 MONTHS**

1000 PEOPLE PAY $83/MONTH, FOR 12 MONTHS
500 PEOPLE PAY $167/MONTH, FOR 12 MONTHS
250 PEOPLE PAY $333/MONTH, FOR 12 MONTHS

You need to set goals for yourself and for your business if you want to get ahead in this life. Take a good look at these numbers and decide which ones make sense to you.

How to make $100,000 per year

SELL A $200 PRODUCT TO 500 PEOPLE
SELL A $500 PRODUCT TO 200 PEOPLE
SELL A $1,000 PRODUCT TO 100 PEOPLE
SELL A $2,000 PRODUCT TO 50 PEOPLE
SELL A $5,000 PRODUCT TO 20 PEOPLE

500 PEOPLE PAY $17/MONTH, FOR 12 MONTHS
200 PEOPLE PAY $42/MONTH, FOR 12 MONTHS
100 PEOPLE PAY $83/MONTH, FOR 12 MONTHS
50 PEOPLE PAY $167/MONTH, FOR 12 MONTHS
25 PEOPLE PAY $333/MONTH, FOR 12 MONTHS

Most people would already be happy to simply make $100,000 per year with their business so that they can survive and pay their bills.

Once you break it down to that level, it seems very doable and takes away the mystery of creating a six-figure income.

It is actually very encouraging to look at these numbers. It seems that almost anyone can do it if you make sure that you do the right things first.

How much does your product cost? ____________
How many clients do you need in 12 months? ____________
How many clients do you need in one year? ____________

Break down yearly goals into daily goals

$100 per day = $30,000 per year
$200 per day = $70,000 per year
$300 per day = $100,000 per year
$500 per day = $180,000 per year
$1,000 per day = $360,000 per year
$3,000 per day = $1,000,000 per year

If you want to make $100,000 per year, then you should focus your activities on making $300 per day. $300 per day seems very realistic and doable. It could be the equivalent of one sale (depending on your product).

Breaking down a larger goal into a daily goal will show you what kind of activities you need to do in order to achieve your goal.

If you want to make one sale or $300 per day, maybe this translates into having 10 sales calls with clients in a day. By making sure that you do the right kind of activities on a regular basis, you can ensure the achievement of your overall, big goal.

What gets measured gets done

Set clear goals and standards for each aspect of your business. What gets measured - gets done.

Always think and plan in numbers. Numbers motivate. **Measurable progress motivates.**

Unless you have definite, precise, clear set goals, you are not going to realize the maximum potential that lies within you.

I always used to afraid to set goals that were “too low”. I always wanted to keep my options open so that just in case it went better than expected I would achieve a higher goal.

But the truth is that will not achieve anything without clarity. The trick is to set a goal and define it to the last detail. Just make a decision and set a goal that can be measured. Try to plan your goals in numbers so that you can see if you make progress or not. Setting clear and measurable goals is a great help.

Always think in terms of "numbers". You will be surprised how much more efficient your life will become once you "control your own numbers". Facts and numbers will help you to realistically see where you are at any point in time. It will help you to determine what needs to be done in any given situation.

If you are not a numbers guy or gal, you should become one when it comes to goal setting and planning.

I would recommend you going away for a couple of days into the mountains where no one can disturb you and then make a plan for the entire year. Plan every single detail.

Make a decision – no decision is a decision to do nothing

> It is impossible to live without failing at something, unless you live so cautiously that you might as well not have lived at all – in which case you fail by default. (J.K. Rowling)

Being undecided and keeping options open is the same like making no decision at all. No decision is often worse than making a bad decision.

If you make the wrong decision, you can correct it and make a better decision afterwards. But waiting and not deciding can be much worse because you are not moving forward.

Expect problems along the way – normal part of success

Don't stop dreaming just because you had a nightmare. Problems and obstacles are a normal part of life. Don't get discouraged when problems arise. Be aware that they are simply part of the process. Accept problems as a normal part of life and just deal with them when they arise.

Who says you have to be realistic?

> Being realistic is the most common path to mediocrity. (Will Smith)

Honestly, you don't have to be realistic at all. Some people are so unrealistic but they believe in their dreams so much that they end up surprising everyone around them because they made it happen.

No one should be able to tell you what you can do and what you can't do.

Do you want to make a $100,000 per month? Is that realistic? For some people it is very realistic. For others it seems totally out of their reach. I have done it. I know it is possible. It is not easy but possible.

Ask Donald Trump is making a million dollars is easy for him. "Only a million dollars" is a disappointment for him. He has a billionaire mindset. He doesn't believe in scarcity. Do you believe in scarcity and that's why you are holding yourself back from abundance?

But if you open up your mind and start to wonder how you could do it, you start to come up with ideas and possible solutions.

Let's try it right now:

- If you get 20 clients per month (=1 client per working day) that pay $5000 for your consulting services, then you make $100,000 per month.

- If you sell 1000 products online per month and charge $1000 for your product, then you make $100,000 per month.
- If you raise $1 million from investors and you get a 10% commission, then you will make $100,000 per month.

You see? It is possible. I could come up with 20 more ideas or ways. I didn't say it was easy but **it is possible**. The next step is to make a plan of action.

But most people don't even dare to dream that big. They don't set their goals that high. (They are maybe somehow afraid that they spend too much energy or something like that.)

Set your goals high – even if you only hit 30% of it, it is still $30,000 per month. If you set it at $10,000 you will not really break through. You will not give 100%. Eventually you will figure out how to get 100%.

Becoming great is really just a decision. If you want become a leader in your field then you must make that choice. I always wondered why somebody didn't do something about that, and then I realized that I am somebody.

Give yourself permission to live a big life. Stop playing small! You are meant for greater things. Never doubt what you can do because you can do anything you set your mind to.

How long are you going to wait before you demand the best for yourself?

You are the only one who can change your life. No one else can do it for you. And no one is coming for the rescue.

If you want to make a million dollars, you need to know how many customers you will need to achieve that goal. Depending on your product price, you will know what your goal in regards to the amount of customers is.

Once you have clarity it is much easier to plan the necessary activities to guarantee that number. When you break it down into numbers, you will get more clarity and it will become easier to achieve.

There are no super-humans. Just humans. And one man can do, another can do as well.

Think outside of the box

Common thinking will only you get you a common life.

You can't become financially independent with a regular 9 to 5 job. You can't become a millionaire if you are employed like a regular person. You will need a different strategy.

Think outside the normal options.

If we demand one dollar from life, then life will punish us with one dollar.

If a beggar on the street asks you for change, you probably just keep walking. But what if the beggar asked you for $20 or even $100 and had a good story, would you give it to him? Probably yes. We all get in life what we ask for. If we ask for change, then will get change but if we ask for a larger amount, we will get it, too.

Life is too short not to be important. I had achieved my success because I set huge goals. But my goals were unrealistic and way too big for me at the time. But I grew into my goals. Don't be afraid to think bigger.

Being an entrepreneur can be very difficult at times. But then again, so is being a regular employee. If you want to achieve success out of the ordinary, you can't do it with a regular 9 to 5 job. It is not possible.

You have to think anyway, so why not think big?

But if you set goals, then you might as well set big goals because you have to work anyway. If you decide to earn a normal income like everybody else, then the struggle of being an entrepreneur is not worth it. But if you decide to make millions, then your only option is to think differently than 95% of the people. You must look for other options and business opportunities to make it happen.

We all work about 45 years from the age of 20 to 65. What you do in those 45 years is up to you. But working in a slave like environment that doesn't fulfill you and that will leave you with a regular income is probably not what you were born to do. Don't be afraid to fully embrace your destiny and start a business with your talents and strengths.

Entrepreneurship is the key to wealth, security and impacting the world. Start your own business and change the world.

> If you don't design your own life plan, chances are you will fall into someone else's plan. And guess what they have planned for you? Not much. (Jim Rohn)

Finding yourself

Who are you? Answer without: name, job, things you did, friends

> Consider how hard it is to change yourself and you will understand what little chance you have in trying to change others.

There is a huge difference between wanting to change and being willing to change. Almost everyone wants to change for the better but very few are willing to take the steps necessary to create that change.

You need to realize that you need to change in order to achieve your goals. I remember when I wanted to earn $100,000 in a month what I need to change in my personality and my habits so I was able to achieve it. You need clarity, more self-discipline, mental focus, etc. etc.

It is extremely liberating to see that **you are the cause of all your problems**. With that realization you will learn that **you are also your own solution**. When you stop blaming external forces and be 100% accountable and responsible for anything that happens in your life, you will become the ultimate creator of your destiny.

> Once your know your purpose, then you need to find ways to commercialize it.

Ask yourself the question: "How do I make money doing what I love?" Then ask yourself how you could create products that people are willing to pay money for.

Ideas: Courses, seminars, book, consulting services, coaching, etc.

Be aware of your personal power – other things than money

> Don't underestimate the power of your vision to change the world. (Leroy Hood)

If you lack money and you think that you cannot start a new business until you have money, then you are holding yourself back because of a false belief.

You don't always need a lot of money to get started. And you don't always need your own money, either. You have assets other than money. Most people underestimate those assets.

> You have ideas, time, skill, energy, knowledge, contacts and talent.

If you have a clear idea of what you want to achieve you will find that the money will come your way sooner or later. If the idea is good, the money will follow.

You also don't need success gurus or teachers. You have everything inside of you and you need to unlock this power inside of yourself. Most success teachers will motivate you and encourage you to dream big. That is great but no one really tells you how to achieve your goals. Success teachers don't teach you to make baby steps first and focus on simply daily tasks. But that is what you need to do.

There is no secret to success. There is no secret formula or club. You need to simply set a goal, make a plan by breaking it down into little steps and then go to work.

If there were a secret it would be this: You and your belief in yourself is the secret to success. If you were aware of your own power and capabilities, you would not be lacking self-confidence. If you lose your fear, you can accomplish anything in this life.

All the power you need already lies within you, not in outside circumstances. Don't give away your power to circumstances like luck, magic tools or other people. Everything you need to know and have is already inside of you. The real source of power is you!

All the real power is already within you and not anywhere on the outside. You are the master of your own circumstances. You don't really need anything to ignite your own power. All you need is to do is trust that you have the power, and then you will succeed.

> People tend to give away their power and believe that they are the victims of their circumstances. Once you claim your power back, you will succeed.

Find yourself and your business idea

> Think big – think $100 million! How can you create a $100 million company? You have to think anyway so why not think big?

Life isn't about finding yourself – it is about creating yourself. Opportunities don't just happen by accident. You create them.

Your big opportunity may be right where you are now. Typically, the things that you are already doing and that you are interested will give you a pretty good idea where to look.

There will be a time in life when all your instincts will tell you to do something, something that defies logic, upsets your plans, and may seems crazy to others. When that happens, it is a sign and you must follow your intuition. Ignore the odds and just go for it.

> There is no passion to be found in settling for a life that is less than the one you are capable of living. (Nelson Mandela)

Once you start understanding yourself, once you start executing on who you actually are versus who you wish you were, things start to change very quickly. Often people are living in a dream world and because of it, they fail to take the necessary action today.

It is important that you **find yourself** first. **Know who you are and what you are really good at**. And then make a plan and build your business based on your **talents and strengths.**

If you can't do great things, then do small things in a great way. Eventually things will take off.

Listen to your own voice and soul. Too many people listen to the noise of the world instead of themselves. Deep down you know what you should be doing.

> You are not too old and it is not too late.
> (Rainer Maria Rilke – 1875 – 1926)

Remember your light has the ability to light others. Ignite the world. Life is about moments: Don't wait for them – create them!

> Become an expert in your chosen field and sell yourself honestly. Those are the keys to the Universe.

Speaking things into existence works

Stop calling it a dream. It's time to call it a plan. Words are very powerful.

Speaking the truth will make you authentic and then you will attract what you want into your life. Once you become consciously aware of just how powerful your thoughts are, you will realize everything in your life exactly how YOU allow it to be.

The only thing standing between you and your goal is the bullshit story that you keep telling yourself as to why you can't achieve it.

> At the center of your being you have all the answers. You know who you are and you know what you want. (Rumi)

Your heart knows the way. Run in that direction. Believe in yourself.

Just do it – just start

You don't need anybody's approval and you don't need to be afraid of anybody's disapproval. JUST DO IT. You can't win if you don't begin.

Water will feed weeds or flowers. it doesn't discriminate. The same is true with energy. You can focus on positive things and they will grow or you can focus on negative things and they will grow, too. The choice is yours.

> *Go, go, go…Figure it out, figure it out, but don't stop moving*
> *Go, go, go…Figure it out, figure it out, you can do this*
>
> (Song "Flames" by Sia and David Guetta)

Goal Setting

Types of goals / categories

Personal goals
Business and career goals
Financial goals
Thing goals
Fitness and health goals
Spiritual goals
Relationship goals
Family goals
Educational goals
Self-development goals
Social goals
Pleasure goals / crazy funny goals

Time frames

Short-term	1 – 12 months
Medium-term	2 to 3 years
Long-term	5 to 10 years
Lifetime goals	longer

Definition of your goals (SMART)

People with clear, written goals, accomplish far more in a shorter period of time than people without them could ever imagine.
(Brian Tracy)

1. **S**pecific
2. **M**easurable
3. **A**ttainable

4. **R**eward (why?)
5. **T**ime-bound

Examples

Not ideal:	I want a new car
Better:	BMW 550i, Price: $95,000 (fully loaded package) by January 1st, 2016 As reward for promotion to team leader

Not ideal:	I want to lose weight
Better:	Lose 20 pounds of fat and gain 10 pounds of lean muscle mass and have a body fat percentage of 15% by May 31st of this year Ready for beach season – to show off new hot body

Not ideal:	I want to be rich
Better:	$1,000,000 in cash in my account by December 31st, 2020 To retire early and to make my mother proud

Common mistakes when setting goals

1. Fuzzy goals
2. Setting unrealistic goals
3. Setting unrealistic time lines
4. Setting other people's goals (not your own)
5. Setting negative goals

Dreaming and dwelling

Create a dream collage – cut out pictures of your goals.

- Use 5 minutes every day to dream about your goals.
- Rewrite your goals every day on a pad of paper.

- Dwell on your goals. Get emotional about them.
- To things that are signs to the Universe to show that you intend to achieve your goals.
- Create collage with pictures from magazines and put them into a journal or hang them on your wall.
- Visualize and emotionalize when thinking about your goals.

Personal goals

☑ Check the things that you want:

☐ Learn a language
☐ Get into shape
☐ Travel to ______________
☐ Learn this skill: ___________
☐ Do daily: ___________
☐ Move to ___________
☐ Meet person ___________
☐ Become famous for ___________
☐ Make, create, invent, ___________
☐ Visit ___________

Why? (Reasons) ____

Business and career goals

☐ Get promoted by ___________
☐ Become ____________
☐ Work for _____________
☐ Learn _____________
☐ End goal ___________

Why? (Reasons) ____

Financial goals

Income goal in 12 months ____________
Income goal in 3 years ____________
Income goal in 10 years ____________

Net worth in 12 months ____________
Net worth in 3 years ____________
Net worth in 5 years ____________

Other ____________

Why? (Reasons) ____________________________________

Thing goals

Car Type ________ Price ________ When ________

Motorcycle Type ________ Price ________ When ________

House 1 Type ________ Location ________ When ________
When ________ Special feature ________

House 2 Type ________ Location ________ When ________
When ________ Special feature ________

House 3 Type ________ Location ________ When ________
When ________ Special feature ________

Airplane Type ________ Location ________ When ________
When ________ Special feature ________

Helicopter Type ________ Location ________ When ________
When ________ Special feature ________

Other things ______________________________

Why? (Reasons) ________________________________

Fitness and health goals

Ideal weight ___________

Body fat % ___________

Lose fat ___________ pounds

Gain muscle ___________ pounds

Activities ___________ ___________ ___________

Nutrition ____

Other things ______________________________________

Why? (Reasons) _________________________________

Spiritual goals

What? _________________________________

Why? (Reasons) _________________________________

Relationship goals

- ☐ Find a man/woman
- ☐ Get married
- ☐ Have ____ children
- ☐ Improve the relationship

- ☐ Plan date nights and trips
- ☐ ________________

Other things ____

Why? (Reasons) ____

Family goals

- ☐ Have _____ children
- ☐ Go on holidays to ___________
- ☐ Daily rituals _________________
- ☐ _____________________

Other things ____

Why? (Reasons) ____

Educational goals

- ☐ Get a degree in ___________
- ☐ Learn about _____________
- ☐ Get a diploma in _____________
- ☐ Do a course in _____________
- ☐ Go to a seminar

Other things ____

Why? (Reasons) ____

Self-development goals

Learn ____
Read ____
Study ____
Course / Seminar / School _______________________________________

Other things ______________________________

Why? (Reasons) ______________________________

Social goals

Other things ______________________________

Why? (Reasons) ______________________________

Pleasure goals / crazy funny goals

Other things ______________________________

Why? (Reasons) ______________________________

Skills

Skills (learn, improve) ____________________
Languages (learn, improve) ____________________

Travel

Top 3 destinations? ______________________________

Summary of goals

Once you have made a selection of the things that you would like to have or do, you must prioritize. Chose which goals are more important to you and chose no more than 3 goals per category. In the end you should chose your top goal for each category and finally your overall top 3 goals.

Personal goals

1. ____________________ 2. __________________ 3. ________________

Business and career goals

1. ____________________ 2. __________________ 3. ________________

Financial goals

1. ____________________ 2. __________________ 3. ________________

Thing goals

1. ____________________ 2. __________________ 3. ________________

Fitness and health goals

1. ____________________ 2. __________________ 3. ________________

Spiritual goals

1. ____________________ 2. __________________ 3. ________________

Relationship goals

1. ____________________ 2. __________________ 3. ________________

Family goals

1. ____________________ 2. __________________ 3. ________________

Educational goals

1. ____________________ 2. __________________ 3. ________________

Self-development goals

1. ____________________ 2. __________________ 3. ________________

Social goals

1. ______________________ 2. ____________________ 3. __________________

Pleasure goals / crazy funny goals

1. ______________________ 2. ____________________ 3. __________________

Major goals in life

1. ______________________ 2. ____________________ 3. __________________

CHAPTER 20

MENTAL LAWS OF MONEY: THE PSYCHOLOGY OF FINANCIAL SUCCESS

Think and grow rich. (Napoleon Hill)

How can I write about this topic? What qualifies me to talk and write about it?

When I was in my twenties I hungry for money and success like so many others. I was doing well in my career but I did not have financial success like a millionaire.

One day I came across a book from Bodo Schaefer: "The journey to financial independence. Your first million in seven years."

I loved that book and I even went to his seminar. But besides starting to read about financial independence from him, I started to make plans, write in my journal every day, listened to motivational audio programs and read several other books.

After dealing with the topic of money and making the decision to become a millionaire, it took me 2 ½ years to make it happen. But I didn't just make one million. I made over 100 million! I had $1.3 million in cash and the rest was in stocks of my companies. But I also made over $100,000 every month.

I thought I had it all figured out. I was on top of the world and I believed that money would always be there for me.

But then I started to self-sabotage my success and myself. Eventually, I lost everything again. Just a few years later I was broker than broke.

How was it possible that I could let that happen? How could I go from millions to zero in a matter of years? What went wrong?

> Success or failure is all in your head.

My fast rise to success and my fall from grace thereafter taught me valuable lessons about myself. Today, I am back on top and now I know the reasons why everything happened the way it did.

In the end, it is all in your head. It is a mental game. Success or failure is all in your head.

You are exactly where you want to be in life

I had a friend say to me "*You are exactly where you want to be in your life.*" Ha! I most certainly was not! "*But you are*", he said, "*because you took every step to get exactly where you are.*"

Once I wrapped my head around the idea, it became one of the most important phrases of my life. We are all exactly where we want to be. Take some time to really think about it. There is so much more truth and wisdom in this statement than you first realize.

If your life sucks, it is your fault! It is no one else's fault. You have allowed and accepted every circumstance in your life.

> If you want something more you need to
> do whatever it takes to change it.

If you want money, go get some. It is as simple as that. You make that decision.

I could defend myself on that point all day long. But the more annoyed and defensive I became, the more I realized one thing: On some level I was accepting my current life as the life that I felt I deserved.

I may not have gotten what I wanted so far but now I can change that. Immediately! Once I realized that I was the only person who was holding myself back and it was not the fault of someone else or circumstances, I actually get to change and improve my situation. I may not have held the reigns up to this point... but I certainly can from this point forward.

No one will do it for you. No one is coming one day and giving you a check for $1 million just like that. No one is coming to save you. You have to save yourself. This life is 100% your responsibility.

It's not easy to change your mindset from "victim of circumstance" to "in complete control". And it's not something that happens overnight. But all it takes is one tiny seed to begin that transformation. The first step is awareness.

Not that anybody is looking, but in the end you need to impress the one person that matters the most: yourself. You deserve everything that you want! Go get it!

We are all exactly where we want to be.

After you stop defending yourself you are forcing yourself to really think about yourself and your life. How have you gotten to this point and why are you not further along like you intended?

You don't have to change your life overnight. And besides, you cant. But you do have to get a clear vision of your dream, and then figure out what it would take to turn that dream into a reality. And from there, you must take action on it every single day - no matter how small.

Nobody wants to wait two years for something they want today. But if you don't start taking action on it today, you will still be in the exact same position two years from now.

I suggest that you put your goals down on paper today and that you map out the steps it will take to turn your dream into a reality. Can you do it in this year? Can you do it by 2020?

Figure that out, and then take action towards it every single day. That is how you change things in your life.

Just because you aren't where you think you should be in your life doesn't mean you're not exactly where you are meant to be.

Sometimes we get caught up in the idea that we need to achieve certain things by a certain time of our lives. When we don't it's easy to feel like a failure or beat yourself up for not being where you expected.

Perhaps you wanted to:

- Be a millionaire by the age of 30.
- Be a New York Times bestselling author, selling millions of books.
- Be discovered by Hollywood and won an Oscar
- Marry your soul mate and have 3 kids by 35
- Own your dream house

Stop beating yourself up for not being further along. Everything happened for a reason and you are exactly where you are supposed to be. Judging yourself for not being where you think you should be won't get you where you want to go. Judging yourself just keeps you stuck further where you are now. It doesn't help. Only moving forward helps.

But today if you don't like where you are, you have the power to change it! Just because you made your bed doesn't mean you have to lie in it. You can remake your life at any moment, if you choose to do so. Now that time has come...

False beliefs about money

Many people have false beliefs when it comes to money and because of that they will never attract money into their lives. Your beliefs about money determine how much you have.

Whatever your limiting beliefs about money are is what determines how much you will attract into your life.

We all have certain beliefs when it comes to money. Unfortunately, a lot of those beliefs are false beliefs and they are holding you back from having a lot of money. But money in itself is neutral. You give money a meaning. You make it good or bad.

Do you say things like…?

- Money doesn't grow on trees.
- I must work really hard to make a lot of money.
- I will never be able to afford that.
- You can only make money if you have a degree.
- I don't deserve to make money.
- I have bad karma because I am an unlucky person.
- Money is the root of all evil.
- People with money are all crooks.
- Money doesn't buy happiness.
- Money is not that important.
- I'm just not good with money.
- It's selfish to want a lot of money.

Money in itself is neutral. It is the beliefs about money that are the real problem. You will never become a millionaire if you have limiting beliefs about money. If you feel like you don't deserve to be rich or if you think that money is bad, then you cannot by the Universal law of attraction attract money into your life. You might make some and then lose it again or sabotage yourself but you will not be able to keep it.

So ask yourself which false beliefs about money do you still have today? You need to realize that those false and limiting beliefs are BS.

Examples for false believes about money:

- Money finances wars and kills innocent children
- People with money cheated their way to riches
- People only care about money but things like love are more important. That is why I refuse to have money.

But money can also create positive things:

- Build hospitals for sick children
- Feed the poor and homeless
- Find a cure for cancer and other illnesses
- Provide a happy and secure life for your family

Money can make you very happy and it is of course not the only thing that is important in life. But money can do a lot of good things in this world. It can help people, it can finance cures for illnesses, it can give people education, it can reduce stress, it can save lives, it can make you happy and it can give you freedom. It good or bad based on how you look at it.

You see, you need to let go of the negative views because they are holding you back. Remember what your parents used to say to you when you were growing up. Often, we simply accepted their statements as truths and we still carry them with us.

Do you deserve it?

Do you feel like you deserve money? Are you self-sabotaging yourself sometimes because on some level you don't believe that you really deserve it and that is why you punish yourself unconsciously?

Are you getting ahead financially and then you do something stupid by spending too much money and self-sabotage yourself again? What might be the reason?

What is your mental mindset when it comes to making money? Do you feel like you are not deserving of love because you don't love and accept yourself?

Do you feel like you need the recognition and approval of others to have money? Do you feel that you don't deserve love in your life because you have been bad in the past and made mistakes? Do you feel that you have low self-esteem because of lack of love?

Many of our problems come from our childhood and from parents. Typically, a lack of love or attention is the main reason. We all want to be accepted and loved and we will do the craziest things to get it.

But you are an adult now and you need to break out of the cycle. You need to forgive your parents and all the people in your past.

You deserve everything! You deserve love, money, a nice house, things, etc. just like anyone else. You deserve the $10 million villa just like the person who has it today. You don't need to drive a crappy car just because you don't feel good enough or deserving enough to drive a nice car.

You need to stop punishing yourself and self-sabotaging yourself because you are worthy and you deserve everything.

> 99% of all problems have to do with lack of love and feeling of deservingness.

Love yourself. Stop blaming others and **stop playing the victim**.

You give away your own power to others and to circumstances if you keep playing the victim role. You think that the victim role will give you love or at least some attention but in reality it is pity.

You are in life exactly where you want to be, you have exactly what you think you deserve and not one bit more.

Being honest with yourself and others is the starting point to feeling good about yourself. Do good for others and it will make you feel better about yourself.

If you get a windfall of money it will amplify what is already inside of you today. If you are an asshole you will become a bigger asshole. If you feel like you need to cover up pain by shopping, drinking, drugs, gambling, etc. then you will do that even more and on a bigger scale.

Find out what kind of problems or pain you are trying to avoid. We all want to avoid pain. It is one of our two main motivations in life (= avoiding pain, gaining pleasure). But how is avoiding the pain hindering you from financial greatness? Ask yourself honestly.

The millionaire mind mindset

Childhood influences shape our financial blueprint. These influences can lead to self-defeating thoughts and habits.

If you are not doing as well as you would like then this means that there is something that you don't know. All rich people think in very similar ways. It is not an exact science but most rich people think very similar and most poor people think completely differently when it comes to money.

> All you have to do is to start thinking the same way that rich people do and you will get the same results.

Psychology of money and success is the basis for financial success. It all starts first in your head before you can change your outer circumstances.

Ask yourself the following question: How were my own thoughts holding me back from wealth?

You need to recondition your mind. You need to play to win and not get constantly sidetracked. Don't even consider quitting until you are a millionaire.

Do not entertain certain thoughts if they don't empower you toward your vision of wealth

Combine the inner game of money (mindset) with the. outer game (tools and strategies). Then your results will go change dramatically for the better.

You don't have to learn but mainly to "unlearn" some of the old ways of thinking that have gotten you exactly where you are right now!

Outer laws of money are things like business knowledge, money management, and investment strategies. These are essential for financial success. But the inner mental attitude is much more important and comes first.

> It is not enough to be in the right place at the right time. You have to be the **right person** in the right place at the right time.

Do you truly feel that you deserve wealth?

Have you heard of people who have "blown up" financially? Have you noticed how some people have a lot of money and then lose it again? Or people have excellent opportunities, start well but then something happens and the deal goes sour on them? From the outside it looks like they have bad luck, a downturn in the economy or a partner that cheated them out of money. But the real reason is that they had the wrong financial mental attitude. Their internal money belief system was wrong. That is why if you come into big money when you are not ready for it on the inside, chances are your wealth will be short-lived and you will lose it all again.

You need to develop the internal capacity to deal with large amounts of money. You need to be able to deal with bigger challenges that come with more money and success. If you can't handle it, then this is the primary reason why you don't have a lot of money in your life.

Do you realize that Donald Trump could never "just be a millionaire"? If Donald Trump only had a net worth of $1 million, do you think he would feel good and successful about himself? He would probably feel like a financial failure! That is because his financial "chip settings in his brian" are set for billions and not millions. (Donald Trump made about $10 billion in his career to date.)

Most people are unconscious about their own financial mental mindset.

> The key to success is to raise your own energy; when you do, people will be naturally attracted to you. And when they show up, bill them! (T. Harv Eker)

A tree grows big because of its roots

When it comes to nature, we can learn again from the law of growth. A tree can only create large fruits (= equivalent to money) if the roots (= foundation) are big and strong.

If you want to change the fruits so that they will be bigger, you must first change the roots. If you want to change the visible, you must change the invisible.

What is deep in the ground is invisible but it will create what is visible on top. If you want to change your life, you must change your thinking.

Example: Printing out a letter

Let's say that you have just written a letter on your computer. You hit the print key and the letter comes out of your printer. You look at your hard copy and all of a sudden you find a typo. You decide to take your good eraser and erase the typo on the paper. Then you hit print again and out come the same letter as before with the same typo.

At this point you are wondering how this could be because you just erased the typo earlier. But this time you are committed. You take an even bigger eraser and you rub even harder on the paper to get rid of the typo. Just to be sure you even study a 300-page manual called "Effective erasing". Now you have all the "tools" and knowledge that you will need and you think you are ready. Now you hit print again and the same letter comes out as before. You start to scream and cry in disbelief and with amazement. How is this possible? Haven't you done everything that you could? You start to feel like you are in the twilight zone.

But the real problem cannot be solved in the physical world or in the printout. It can only be changed in the "program", the mental world. You can only change it in your computer (=mind).

We live in a world of cause and effect. Money is simply a result. Health is a result. Weight or illness is a result.

This is why a lack of money is never, ever a problem. A lack of money is only a symptom of what is going on inside your head.

Lack of money is the effect but the root of the problem is in your mental mindset.

> The only way you can change your "outer world"
> is to first change your "inner world".

If things aren't going well in your outer life, it is because things are not going well in your inner life. It is that simple.

Every child that comes into this world has no idea about money. It has no attitude or opinion. Every child is taught how to deal with money and how to think about it. The same is true for you and for me. These "false teachings" are the reason why you have no money. It is a false conditioning. But this false conditioning is set on autopilot and runs for the rest of your life. That is why you need to become aware of what your own self-limiting beliefs about money are and then you need to unlearn these false ideas and replace them with the kind of thinking that rich people have so that you can also become rich.

You first need to change your programming before you can get results in the outer world or in your bank account.

Sometimes people link up "having money" with being greedy or being a bad person. And because you don't want to be a bad person, you cannot attract and keep money. It goes against your very core.

But money in itself is neutral. It can do good things and it can do bad things. But it is up to you what kind of belief you have towards it.

The first step to change this cycle is awareness. You can't change something unless you know that it exists in the first place.

The second step is to understand how and why your false beliefs were holding you back in the past. What was the reason?

The third step is to disassociate yourself from your false beliefs and then to recondition yourself with better beliefs that will help you.

They say that the apple doesn't fall far from the tree. Most of your issues come from your parents and your childhood. As kids we tend to model the behavior of our parents.

You can have all the knowledge and skills in the world but if your financial mindset / blueprint is not set for financial success, you will always struggle financially. Or in other words: You will always be doomed.

If your motivation for having money comes from things like fear, anger or the need to prove yourself, money will never bring you happiness.

Seeking security comes from insecurity, which is based in fear.

Money is not the root of the problem: fear is. But what is worse is that fear is not just a problem. It is a habit. Therefore, some people will make more money and become more and more afraid.

They say: If I make too much money, I will be punished in high taxes. Then they will do something to self-sabotage themselves so that they don't have to pay so many taxes. Sounds silly but it is very true for many people.

Some people have a major inferiority complex and they think that making a lot of money will make them "good enough". Let me tell you this: no amount of money will ever make you a better person or good enough. If you have the need to constantly prove yourself, it will become a driving force in your life and you will be your own slave of your own expectations and never happy.

If you feel that money can erase some pain from the past to prove that you are good enough, then you are also fooling yourself. No amount of money will ever make you feel good enough if you don't feel that you are good enough without money.

Mental mindset of rich versus poor people

Change your thinking – change your life

Rich people	Poor people
I create my life	Life happens to me I am a victim of circumstances or people I blame this person or this circumstance…
I am responsible	justifying… Complaining…
Play money game to win	Try not to lose the money game
I am 100% committed to becoming rich	I want / would like to be rich
They know exactly what they want	They don't know what they want

Think in big dimensions / numbers	Think on a small scale
Deliver value to the marketplace	Expect something from others
Focus on opportunities	Focus on problems and obstacles
Admire other successful people	Have envy, resent more successful people
Associate with positive and other successful people	Associate with negative/unsuccessful people
Try to copy / model rich people	Criticize rich people and are jealous of them
"If they can do it, I can do it, too."	Don't believe things are possible
Willing to sell and promote themselves	Believe that selling is negative
Become a leader in their field	Are followers / sheep
Have passion and enthusiasm	Are negative and numb to new things
They are bigger than their problems	Big problems overwhelm poor people
Don't avoid problems or try to get rid them They try to grow so that they can face any problem or situation	Avoid problems and try to get rid of them
They are ready to face any problem	Give up when the problems are too big

They believe they are worth it to be rich and deserve wealth	They don't really believe that they deserve money and wealth
Want to give and provide value for others	Expect a paycheck for time at job
Focus on doing things excellent and with high quality	Only deliver the minimum or what is expected
Choose to get paid based on results	Want to get paid based on time.
Think they can do several projects	Poor people think in terms of "either/or"
Think about increasing their net worth	Think of getting more working income
Make money a focus and priority	Have no clear focus or plan. Live day by day.
Manage their money actively Have their money work hard for them	Don't manage their money at all or well Work hard for their money
See money as seed money to make more money in the future	Don't invest. Think only about spending.
They act in spite of fear, doubt, worry, Inconvenience, discomfort or mood.	They let fear stop them.
They are action and goal-oriented.	They don't take action.
Don't avoid things that are hard.	Are only willing to do what is easy.
Constantly learn and grow	They think they already know.

Change your thinking: the important questions to change your financial mindset

1. Which false beliefs have held me back from a life of wealth?

   ___

2. What were the things or phrases that my parents used to say in front of you?

   ___

3. Which false beliefs are you still struggling with today and why?

   ___

4. What could you do differently and how could you change some of those false beliefs?

   ___

5. Which new empowering beliefs will you use going forward in your life?

   ___

It is not either money or happiness

> You can have money and be happy at the same time! It is not an either/or question.

You can have both at the same time! You can also be happy and have no money or you can have money and be unhappy.

The two things are NOT related. Money can make you very happy. But it makes other unhappy.

Happiness is a decision. It is a mental state of mind that is not bound to people or circumstances. Once you realize what happiness is and how it works, then you can be happy just like that – for no particular reason.

And you should be. Being happy and being positive will help you and empower you much more in life than negativity will ever do.

I think that in general money can buy you a lot of things that can add to your already existing happiness. It can do great things to your life. I would rather have money than not have money. But my happiness is not dependent on it.

The truth about success and the law of nature

Have you read all the books about success, attended all the seminars or listened to all the success gurus? And despite all this info are you still not any further in life financially?

This is what had happened to me. I became a success junkie. In ten years I had read over 500 books, listened to over 100 audio programs and attended countless seminars. I read so much about success that I could easily get a degree from a university for it.

But something was missing. I was willing to learn, to plan, to set goals and I was always thinking positively. But my net worth had not improved. What was it that the success gurus were not telling me? I dreamt of millions but I had to worry how to pay my rent next month. I totally disillusioned myself.

Then I realized something. Reading another book or attending another seminar would not make any difference anymore. I basically knew everything already. So I decided to do something different.

> You can't go against the laws of nature.

Interestingly, I was not alone in this situation. Thousands of people like me were addicted to success knowledge, spent thousand of dollars on material but did not earn one cent more. I was living in a dream world and was hoping to find an idea that would make me a millionaire over night. But I forgot one very important thing: one specific law of nature - the law of growth.

We live in world governed by law: the laws of nature. They are also called the natural laws. The laws of natures also apply to business and financial success.

The law of cause and effect says that there must first be a cause or an action before you will have an effect or a result. So you can only earn money if you plant the seeds. You can only become successful if you first do something else first.

When it comes to money, the law of growth is a key factor. If you want to have a million dollars you first must have $1. And then $2, then $100, $1000 and so on…

> The law of growth is a natural law of the Universe and cannot be avoided.

Step by step:

- How can someone earn one million dollars without having made $100,000 before?
- How can someone earn $100,000 without having made $10,000 before?
- How can someone earn $10,000 without having made $1,000 before?

You need to work in accordance with the law of growth in order to grow your own net worth. Success is a series of little steps and a growing process.

It is quite simple:

- Do you want to lose 50 pounds? Then you need to start losing the first pound.
- Do you want to marry to woman of your dreams? Then you should go on a first date.
- Do you want to earn a degree? Finish the first lesson.

You need to prove first that you can handle a smaller amount of money before the Universe will give you millions to manage.

How money feels in your hands

$2000 cash in your wallet feels better than $2000 in your bank account.

Believe it or not but most millionaires always carry a lot of cash in their wallet: typically, a few thousand dollars. Now why is that? Why don't you carry lots of cash with you?

Having a lot of cash in your wallet also influences your subconscious mind in a positive way. If you have the feeling that you always have lots of money available right now you program your mind to attract more money.

Most millionaires often look at their money and play with it. It makes them feel good. I do have a lot of rich friends and most of them do carry lots of cash. It is no myth.

If you previously had false and limiting beliefs about money, this is one way to change it.

Now what could you say that goes against carrying all this cash in your wallet?

Some people will immediately say something like: *"Are you crazy? That is just not smart because…*

1. *You could loose it,*
2. *Someone could steal it,*
3. *You could spend too much."*

But this is exactly small-minded thinking. This is exactly why you don't have money in your life.

If your life is ruined because you are afraid to lose $2000, then you won't attract more money into your life. If you are afraid to someone could steal it, it is the same. And of course, don't spend it. The reason why you have $2000 in cash is to program your mind to become more comfortable with money.

And on another positive note: in a case of an emergency you always have enough money with you.

The feeling of always having enough money will give you power. It will give you a feeling that you are already rich.

If you want to become king, you have to act like a king already today.

You have to act as if and soon things will be accordingly. If you want to be rich, you should act like a millionaire today and start with copying their habits.

Go to the bank now and get that cash!

Playing the lottery and the effect on your subconscious mind

> I have great news for you: You are NOT going to win the lottery! Ever!

I remember the time when I used to play the lottery. I used to say to myself: "Well, someone has to win. Why not me?"

Playing the lottery is one of the most dangerous things that you can do when it comes to money and your mindset.

Statistically looked at chances are 54 million to 1 that you are going to win. If you play the lottery twice a week for 100 years, you will have played 11,200 times. If you play for one or two dollars each time, it won't be much money that you invested.

But the problem lies somewhere else and is much deeper:

The problem with playing the lottery is not the money that you spend but the effect that it has on your subconscious mind.

> If you play the lottery you basically tell your subconscious mind that you are not capable of making millions yourself with your own abilities. You surrender to chance and luck.

And by doing it on a constant basis, just like a habit, you program your own mind that you are a victim of luck and circumstances. You program yourself over and over again that you will never have the capacity to make it happen on your own and with your own abilities. 11'200 times!

I urge to stop playing the lottery right now if you are because you are never going to win. Use your head and create millions with your own talents and your own creativity. Believe in yourself from now on.

Give a sign to the Universe by quitting. It is almost the same like stop drinking or taking drugs for good. You life will improve. Quit playing the lottery and new opportunities will come your way!

Sending a sign to Universe by giving away money

> Give and donate money. You send a sign to the Universe that more money will always come your way in abundance. There is no need for a scarcity mindset.

Another important psychological thing is to give away or donate money. Whenever you go to a drive through at McDonald's for example or buy groceries at the store, there is often a box for change to donate for a good cause. I want to encourage you to always put your change in that box and to tip well at a restaurant.

What does that have to do with becoming a millionaire? If you believe in karma, it means that if you do good in the world, you will get something good back even if no one sees it or knows about it.

But the other and more important factor is that if you give away money and don't hold on to it tightly because you are cheap, you send a message to the Universe. This message is that you have more than enough money and money is available to you in abundance so that you can give away money and it doesn't matter to you.

It also sends a message to your subconscious mind that even if you give away some money you know that it will be easy for you to attract new money into your life again. You don't worry about making more money in the future because you believe in your abilities and you trust in the Universe that new or other moneymaking opportunities will come your way.

You see, if you are small-minded and cheap than your money belief system is also small and limited. If you worry that you will not have enough money, you will be right. If you worry that by giving away money you will have less, you attract less. So be aware of your thoughts and beliefs about money.

If you think that saving alone and not spending is the only way, then you limit yourself to a very small kind of thinking.

All millionaires donate money for good causes. And they didn't start with donating money once they had millions. They did it all along even when they still had little money.

So start today. You need to trust me on this one even if you are unsure. Start with what you can do. Typically, you should give away about 10% of your money to a good cause. You will be surprised what good things life has waiting for you if you donate money.

Become the mentally powerful person who can make $1 million

Your life only gets better if you get better. You can only be wildly successful if you improve yourself first.

Do you really need a million dollars in your bank account to live a good life? Do you really need to make $100,000 per month to have your expenses covered and be happy?

The answer is: no. Then why bother?

It is not the money itself that is key here but the **person** that you have to become that can attract that kind of money into his or her life.

What kind of person does it require? What would you have to do and be in order to make that kind of money?

Every master was once a disaster. (T. Harv Eker)

What kind of personality traits and habits do you have to develop?

How do you have to change your thinking?

Can you be successful with a regular job and a ceiling on your income?

Do you need to think outside of the box?

Do you need to use a new strategy with much more leverage to make that kind of money?

The goal is to become the person who is capable of making that kind of money. You need to become a **mentally stronger person**. You need to **change your thinking** and your strategies. It all starts in your head.

The power of clarity

Dreaming is powerful and important because it is the **starting point** of every financial success or manifestation.

But in order to get ahead **after** you developed your dream, you can only move forward if you have the 3 C's: Crystal Clear Clarity.

> Motivation is not enough – you need Crystal Clear Clarity!

Goal setting is "boring" for many people because they think they know everything about it already and have heard it a million times. But those people are still in the same position as they were years ago and nothing has changed.

People are lazy and don't really take the time to analyze what they really want. They say that they want something but deep down they don't really believe themselves. They still believe that somehow, one day, something will happen and then they will get it by chance.

But that is not how success works.

You need to get absolutely clear into the very last detail what you want to accomplish. Then you need to look at all the individual steps involved, the price you have to pay for it and then decide if you want to get it.

> You say you want it but you don't really believe it. Once you get clear about what you really want, the motivation will show up.

For a while I got really confused about this fact. When I first became a self-made millionaire I knew that **clarity was absolutely required and responsible** for my success.

Then I started to listen to Kevin Trudeau, the infomercial king and author of "Cures they don't want you to know about" and his motivational CDs about manifestation: Your wish is your command.

Kevin made millions but he ended up in prison. He has positive messages and wants to encourage people, which is a good thing. Through a personal connection from a friend I was actually to be in email contact with him while is in still in prison for fraud. The problem with his message is that it confuses people. It gets them happy and motivated but their lives never actually change.

His message is this: Dream, imagine but don't worry about the details. Let the Universe take care of the details. That is how you reach goals.

Dreaming and trying to leave all the detail up to the Universe is **one strategy** and I have tried it. But it honestly didn't get me anywhere! It was time for me to get back to what I know to work and to be true: Getting crystal clear clarity! And guess what? Things started to take off again when I applied clarity. So long Kevin...

I believe in the power and magic of the Universe. Don't get me wrong. I am all about the Universe if you know my books and me. But it is **the starting point for manifestation**. The second phase is goal setting and clarity.

Realistic view of the situation

> No matter the situation, never let your
> emotions overpower you intelligence.

My friend and mentor David Garcia is a master in this. He can access any situation and see the reality of it. He never uses wishful thinking and he never is disillusioned about the facts and the truth.

He is not negative at all. He is the most realistic person that I know. But this ability alone has made him a multi-millionaire many times over.

I often "fight" with him about things because I don't want to be a negative person. I am sometimes overly optimistic but the truth is that I can only progress and move forward if I take off my pink sunglasses and see things for how they really are.

> The truth and honesty hurts but you are not getting anywhere without the truth.

You need to be brutally honest and open with yourself and make an honest analysis of your financial situation. You can only improve your financial situation if you lay it all out on the table and be completely honest with yourself.

You can only improve ANY situation if you really know the truth and the facts. Otherwise you live in la-la-land and you are disillusioning yourself from reality. Once you can accept this, you will make progress. Otherwise it is not possible or a simple matter of luck or chance.

The same is true for anything else in life like relationships, health, etc.

> The truth can sometimes taste bitter, yet it is better to live with reality than to stumble through a world of illusions.

You don't want to go through life living in a world of illusions and then one day when you are older you wake up and realize that you are still a loser in your own sense.

Sometimes people don't want to hear the truth because they don't want their illusions destroyed. But that is not going to help you in the long run. You cannot hide from the truth and you will only be happy if you face the truth and do something to change and improve your situation.

The penguin principle

> You will only excel and be successful if you do something that is in your "element".

Dr. Eckart von Hirschhausen from Germany is a doctor that became a TV legend and motivational speaker.

When Dr. Hirschhausen was young, he got a job on a luxurious cruise ship. He was all excited about it but after a couple of days of being seasick he wished he had never gotten on board. The cruise ship stopped in Norway where he went to visit a zoo.

In that zoo he was watching penguins how they were waddling slowly on land and he thinking to himself that a penguin was a false construction by God. The penguin was unable to walk properly, had no knees and no wings to fly. He thought what an unlucky position to be in. He pitied the penguin.

But then the penguin jumped into the water and all of a sudden he could see that the penguin was moving and twirling ten times faster than a Porsche. And that this point he realized two things:

1. He was judging too quickly
2. Once the penguin was in the right element, the water, he would be better and faster than anyone else.

If you focus on your weaknesses, you will never be successful. The penguin is at his best when he is in the water or his **element.**

7 years of psychotherapy won't turn the penguin into a giraffe. No matter how hard he tries.

The right environment is also crucial – if you can use your strengths instead of weaknesses, you will be much better off. If you put the penguin in the middle of the desert he will be useless. But if he is in the water he is in his element.

If the penguin is in the desert, it will never perform at his best. But if you put him into water, he will excel. The same is true for you. Don't try to be someone that you are not.

You should only focus on your strengths. You will be much more successful if you do that. Step one is to find out who you are and what your strengths are. Then develop a business idea based on your strengths. Get help, like an assistant or contractors for the areas of your weakness. You don't have to be good at everything. No one is and you don't have to be. But be the best or in the top 10% in your area.

Dr. Hirschhausen is a medical doctor but he decided to quit his medical career because he is strength for improvisation and being a bit chaotic at times are not really well received in the medical field. He realized that he was not in his element as a doctor and he would perform so much better on stage or on TV with his real strengths. He is great at giving speeches and presentations and in his element he excelled in his career.

His advice to the world (and you): Don't hesitate and stay stuck like a penguin in the desert. Move forward until you find the water – your element. And then: Jump and swim! You will know when you are in your element when things flow easily and you are great at what you do.

An accountant with a more introverted personality is not going to be successful in a sales job and a sales person who is extroverted will be bored to death if he has to deal with numbers all day.

You can only do well if you are doing something that is in alignment with your personality structure. You can only do well if you have a strengths and talents and focus on those. Don't ever try to focus on your weaknesses and think you will do well in those areas. If you do that, life will always be hard.

Providing real quality value for others

How you do anything is how you do everything.

If you are sloppy and unorganized in other things, you will never be successful in business, either.

You need to develop good habits and quality in order to attract better things in your life.

The get paid the best, you must become the best.

People who are in the military develop habits of self-discipline, structure and organization. These traits or qualities help them to do well in whatever they do.

But because their environment is also reinforcing high standards, they do better in whatever they do. If your peer group is doing well then you will automatically try to match the behavior of your peer group, too.

Surround yourself with better people and strive for excellence and high quality in everything that you do. This will attract better things into your life and will make you rich.

Laziness and money

> Don't save your energy for the future. Ever! Give everything right now and don't hold back.

When my grandmother was on her deathbed she told me a few important things about life. One of the things that she said was that I should never be lazy. She said my father was the best during his time at the University because he was always active and never, ever lazy.

Being active and self-disciplined can come a long way. Whatever you do for work or in life, do it well and give everything. Don't save your energy for anything. You should develop the habit of always giving your best in any given situation.

Be helpful, do what you can and do it well. The activity that you are doing right now is all there is right now. There is nothing else.

Many people totally underestimate this kind of habit or quality. They feel like they have to give the minimum and that any extra effort is not necessary. But you never know what doors can open if you give more than is expected of you.

Some people got to the top of their companies because as a regular employee they thought ahead, were the first and the last in the office and gave more value than was expected of them. Eventually, they caught the attention of their superiors and got promoted faster than the others.

> I have found that luck is quite predictable. If you want more luck, take more chances, be more active and show up more often. (Brian Tracy)

The same is true for creating sales. Don't stay in your comfort zone and do the minimum. The best and most successful sales people are not necessarily better or more skilled than the other sales people. They simply don't hold back and give everything.

This one quality alone can make you a millionaire.

Make it a focus and priority

> If you don't make money your number one priority, you will never have it.

Your energy will go where your focus is. You need to make money a major focus in your life.

You can't take the topic lightly because the only thing in regards to money that is easy is to lose it. And without money your life is hard and more difficult.

There are very few things in modern life that are doable and possible without money. If you have money in our society and time, you will have a much better life. You can "fight it" or be "against it" but it won't help. Unless you move to the woods and eat worms and berries all day, you will never be happy.

The past is a different chapter of your life

> At age 57... Louise Hay was bouncing checks, Colonel Sanders was living out of his car and Stephen Covey had never even published a book...It's going to be OK.

The best days of your life have not happened yet!

When you hit rock bottom before and survived, there are very few things in life that can scare you. Be grateful for the experience because it made you so much stronger.

Everything happens for a reason and in order for you to master the future you needed to get stronger first. God's plan was to toughen you up before you can go into battle.

We all wish we could erase some dark times in our lives. But all of life's experiences, bad and good, made you who you are today.

> The Universe is not punishing you or blessing you. The Universe is responding to the vibrational attitude that you are emitting. (Abraham Hicks)

From now on you must change your frequency. You must change the vibrations, thoughts and signals that you send out. If you positively change your thoughts, positive things will happen.

> SHI(F)T HAPPENS

Sometimes things will first get "worse" before they will get better. But in order for new and good things to come into your life, the old and bad things need to go away first. They need to be replaced. You need to clean up the things that were holding you back.

Sometimes it means that you will lose your job, lose people and relationships or other things that "provide" you with something right now. But you will only move forward better and faster if you can clean up your life. You will need space for better things and people in your life.

There will be a shift and it won't always seem to be obviously good at first. If you change jobs or the way you make money today, you might find yourself with less money at first because you had to give up a certain activity. But you needed to be free and have time to work on making real money or millions. You needed to let go of something else first to have the time and energy to focus on your new path.

The limit is what you believe to be the limit

> The most common way people give up their power is by thinking they don't have any. (Alice Walker)

If you set your income expectation at $5,000 per month because you believe that is all that you "deserve" and that this is your potential, then guess what? You will not aim for more and most certainly not make more!

In my personal situation I "limit" myself at $100,000 per month. If I make this, I am happy and feel successful. If I make less than that, I feel like I am not working with my real potential.

But who says I shouldn't focus on $500,000 or a $1 million per month? The answer is: ME! I am the one limiting myself.

There are thousands of people who make a million dollars per month. Are they smarter or better than me? No! They simply have decided to raise their bar. And you can do the same. What is your absolute MUST that you must have? What is the standard that you allow yourself to have?

If you don't set that standard, no one else will. You decide if you drive a crappy car or a great car. You decide if you go to a 5 star hotel or the rotten 2 star hotels. It is all a decision whether you realize it or not. You give yourself the standard that you feel that you deserve – the standard that you feel comfortable with.

But honestly, you don't have to be realistic at all. Some people are so unrealistic but they believe in their dreams so much that they end up surprising everyone around them because they made it happen.

No one should be able to tell you what you can do and what you can't do.

> Miracles start to happen when you give as much energy to your dreams as you do to your fears. (Richard Wilkins)

Do you want to make a $100,000 per month? Is that realistic? For some people it is very realistic. For others it seems totally out of their reach.

But if you open up your mind and start to wonder how you could do it, you start to come up with ideas and possible solutions.

Let's try it right now:

- If you get 20 clients per month (=1 client per working day) that pay $5000 for your consulting services, then you make $100,000 per month.
- If you sell 200 products online per month and charge $500 for your product, then you make $100,000 per month.
- If you sell one house for $3 million each month and you get a 3.5% commission, then you will make $100,000 per month.

You see? It is possible. I could come up with many more ideas or ways. I didn't say it was easy but it is possible.

Why don't you make list of 20 ways or possible solutions even if they sound crazy at first. Start brainstorming. That is how things get started.

But most people don't even dare to dream that big. They don't set their goals that high. (They are maybe somehow afraid that they spend too much energy or something like that.)

Set your goals high and by high I mean at least $100,000 per month – even if you only hit 20% of it, it is still $20,000 per month. If you set it at $10,000 you will not really break through. You will not give 100%. Remember it is a mental challenge. You need to become the person capable of making $100,000.

Becoming great is really just a decision. If you want become a leader in your field then you must make that choice.

> If you want to achieve greatness stop asking for permission and just do it. Become great!

I always wondered why somebody didn't do something about that, and then I realized that I am somebody. You can be somebody. Dare to set high goals and then go for it!

In order to become one of the great ones you must **make the decision** to become one of the great ones. It is as simple as that. You set the standard for yourself. You decide if you want to play in the big league or not.

Becoming a leader in your field requires you to move from a life of mediocrity to a life of greatness by doing everything in your personal power to improve yourself, your thoughts, your standards and your thinking.

Get started today. Do something every day to move forward.

> Momentum: A body in motion tends to stay in motion.

Don't stop. Keep going. Believe you can make it happen.

PART 3

THE $100 MILLION BLUEPRINT

CHAPTER 21

IPO PLAN

Share structure at beginning

20 million preferred shares
80 million common shares
100 million shares total authorized

Shares for key people / management

10 million preferred shares should be issued at the start for the key people
Key person 1: 5 million preferred shares
Key person 2: 5 million preferred shares

Why preferred shares?

1. Special dividend rights
2. 10x voting rights compared to common shares (not to lose control)

10 million preferred shares are not yet issued – 2 x 5 million options for be included in the management agreement for the key people (to be issued at a later date)

Common shares for investors / Private Placements

1st round of financing: $0.25

2nd round of financing: $0.50
3rd round of financing: $0.75
First price at IPO: $1.00

1 million shares @ $0.25 = $250,000
1 million shares @ $0.50 = $500,000
1 million shares @ $0.75 = $750,000

Total money raised from investors: $1,500,000

Commission for sales organizations / brokers

- 10% commission = $150,000 90% = for company = $1,350,000
- 30% commission = $450,000 70% = for company = $1,050,000
- 50% commission = $750,000 50% = for company = $750,000

Remarks

- A 10% commission is standard for pre-IPO deals for a regular broker dealer
- 30% is a more realistic number since a sales organization will have extra expenses for office, administration and marketing
- 50% is a high commission but is also paid out in rare cases. Some companies have a hard time raising capital and the only way for them to get money in the bank is to pay 50% to a sales organization.
- Typically, a commission of more than 10% is frowned upon by the SEC but it is not illegal if it is properly disclosed.
- Make sure you have a good accountant who can declare excess commissions as company marketing expenses to acquire shareholders. If you do it the wrong way, you won't be able to pass your audit.

Expenses for IPO

Initial set-up:

- Incorporation - $1000
- Bank account
- Legal set-up to raise money - $5000
- Project acquisition / option / contract - $10,000
- Management - $10,000
- SSA, PPM, Form D (SEC) - $5,000

Legal fees:

- Retainer from securities lawyer: $5000
- S-1 Registration Statement: $25,000
- Additional work for comments: $10,000

Accountant:

- Financial statements and book keeping: $5000 (per quarter)

Auditor:

- Audited financial statements: $10,000 (per quarter)

Market Maker:

- no money
- Legal fees for comment for FINRA: $10,000

Transfer Agent:

- Set-up - $500
- Issuance of share certificates - $5000
- CUSIP number - $500

Employees:

- CEO / president: $5000 per month
- CFO / treasurer: $5000 per month
- Administration: $5000 per month

Total estimated expenses for 6 months: $197,000

Total estimated expenses for 12 months: $307,000

Time frame for filings and IPO

Financial statements: after 2-3 months
Audit: after 3 months
S-1 Registration Statement filed with SEC: 2 months
Comments from SEC: 2 months
Form 15c2-11 filed with FINRA: 2 months
Comments from FINRA: 2 months

Realistic time frame from start to finish: 9 – 12 months

The less transactions you have in your corporate account, the simpler and cheaper your financial statements and audit.

Some people who have all the technical knowledge, experience and contacts can create a listed shell for less than $50,000.

Some directors don't take a salary in the beginning to keep the expenses low and to show investors that they have the company's best interest at heart.

Some directors take a salary of $1 because they want to make money with the shares and options.

Since there are a lot of things to consider, you should always consult with your securities lawyer. But be aware that most lawyers overcharge and take advantage of your lack of knowledge and inexperience.

Reverse take-over / merger through a listed shell

Current market price for a fully reporting shell: $350,000 to $500,000

Form 10 - $100,000 (but no free trading shares available in the first 12 months)

You can find listed shells on www.mergernetwork.com

First public price and valuation

You can determine with your market maker what the first trade should look like and therefore set the initial price.

If you have 13 million shares issued and outstanding and a share price of $1.00 per share, then your market capitalization is $13 million.

Make sure that your business model can support your valuation (market capitalization) with either actual earnings or with future potential.

Forward split

If you have 13 million shares outstanding and a share price of $1.00, you can do a forward split of 2:1. After the split you will have 26 million shares and a price of $0.50 but still the same value of $13 million.

A forward split can help to increase your share price. If a share price is cut in half, it is more likely to go back to its old level and therefore doubling the valuation of the company.

Reverse split

If you have issued too many shares and if your share price is too low, you can do a reverse split to "clean up" your share structure and make it more solid.

Example:

A company has 500 million shares outstanding and a share price of $0.10 per share. Because the share price is so low, it is hard for the company to raise money or to get the share price to a stable level. If you did a reverse split of 20:1, you will have $25 million shares outstanding and a share price of $2.00 per share.

PIPE financing

Once your company is listed you can do an additional round of financing. This is called a "Private Placement into a Public Entity" (PIPE).

Example:

Your share price is at $2.00 and you want to raise additional capital for your company. You could do a PIPE financing at $1.50 (a premium to the current market price) but with a 6-month holding period (Rule 144).

Increasing your share price and valuation

If there are more buyers than sellers, a stock will go up. If there are more sellers than buyers, then a stock will go down. It is simple as that!

You can either create new volume by doing stock promotion and marketing so that new buyers are interested in your deal or you can have positive earnings from the business be your driving force.

You want to make sure that not everybody will sell in the beginning when you go public. You can do this by adding additional selling restrictions in the SSA (e.g. 12 months) or by communicating with your clients and managing them properly.

Phase 1: $100 million valuation

If you have 50 million shares outstanding and a share price of $2.00, then your valuation is $100 million.

You need to have a business model that can support that valuation or it will be short-lived.

Your products or projects must have the potential to create a valuation in the future so there is room for the stock to go up.

Phase 2: $500 million valuation

100 million shares outstanding x $5.00 per share = $500 million market cap. / valuation

If 20 million belong to you personally, then your personal net worth is $100 million.

The remaining 80 million belong to shareholders.

At this point, the only way to grow the valuation is with the acquisition of new projects or with outside financing to expand your business model.

At this point you will have at least 400 shareholders and can qualify for a bigger stock exchange. (e.g. NYSE AMEX)

At this point, it is easier to get institutional investors or loans in the amount of $10 million to $50 million.

IPO plan (tasks and timetable)

1. Incorporation and initial set-up
2. Acquisition of project or business model
3. Management team
4. Issuance of initial shares
5. Financial statements
6. Audit of financial statements
7. SEC Filing of S-1 Registration Statement with securities lawyer
8. Answer comments from SEC
9. SEC declares S-1 effective
10. Filing of Form 15c2-11 with Market Maker
11. Answer comments from FINRA
12. FINRA declares filing complete

13. Obtain trading symbol
14. First trade with market maker to set first price
15. After 30 days more market makers will follow automatically
16. Generate volume with promotional marketing activities and positive corporate news
17. Exit strategy for initial investors
18. Focus on positive business development of company

CHAPTER 22

SHARE STRUCTURE

Ideal US states to incorporate a C-Corporation

1. Nevada (best solution and flexibility, but more annual fees, 24 hour service)
2. Wyoming (cheap annual fees, incorporation takes up to 10 days)
3. Delaware (typically for larger companies due to tax advantages)

Authorized shares at incorporation

Total amount of shares: 100 million
Common shares: 80 million
Preferred shares: 20 million

Par value

Smallest amount possible: $0.00001 (Nevada)
Typical par value: $0.0001

Preferred shares

- Preferred shares have special rights and are meant for founding members and management members.

- Preferred shares can have special dividend rights compared to common shares.
- Preferred shares should have 10x the amount of voting rights compared to common shares so that the founders don't lose control.
- This can be defined in the bylaws of the company and with a corporate resolution.

Possible price strategy

1. Financing round: $0.0001 (Founding members)
2. Financing round: $0.001 (Strategic partners or companies)
3. Financing round: $0.10 (Friends and family round, certain investors)
4. Financing round: $0.25 (first round for investors)
5. Financing round: $0.50 (second round for investors)
6. Financing round: $0.75 (third round for investors)
7. First price at listing: $1.00

Share issuance for founders and main management members

Person A: 10 million shares at $0.0001 = $1,000 needs to be paid into company account
Person B: 5 million shares at $0.0001 = $500 needs to be paid into company account
Person C: 5 million shares at $0.0001 = $500 needs to be paid into company account

Directors and officers

Directors:

- President, Treasurer, and Secretary (official titles at incorporation)
- One person can have all three titles

- There can be more than 3 directors. An additional person is simply a "director" of the company and needs to be filed with the secretary of state where the company is filed and incorporated.

Officers:

- These are management titles like for example: CEO (Chief Executive Officer), CFO (Chief Financial Officer) and COO (Chief Operating Officer)
- Another possible title can be VP (Vice President)
- All those titles are management titles and NOT official titles like President, Treasurer, and Secretary
- Typically, the President and the CEO are the same person but they can also be two different people.

Share issuance for strategic partners or companies

- When you are planning a share structure, you always start with the end result in mind.
- Once your company goes public, you will need to pay third parties like marketing companies, consultants or strategic partners in shares (rather than cash).
- It is best to issue a certain number of shares (e.g. 5 million shares) to a strategic corporation that you control so that you will have shares to give away later for services.
- The main reason for this is accounting. If you do a financing round at $0.50 and you want to issue 1 million shares for marketing services, then it would be equivalent to $500,000 for those services in the financial statements. Depending on the services that this person will provide (newsletter writer, etc.), it would seem excessive to pay such a high price for these services.
- If you have issued too many shares and you won't need them in the future, then you can always cancel those shares. That is much easier than issuing them at a higher price.

Share issuance for friends and family

- Some people like to offer shares to their friends and family for a low price.
- These shares are also called "love shares" because the person who buys them usually loves the person who starts that business.
- Sometimes it is the crucial amount of money to get things started. A new entrepreneur can raise for example $50,000 from friends and family for $0.10 per share and has the initial capital to get set up legally and acquire the first project or prototype.
- Since family members invest at $0.10 per share, the risk is much lower in case the price of the stock drops later on.
- All investors (friends and family, too) need to fill out a SSA (share subscription agreement) and transfer the money to the corporate account or send a check in the name of the company (not the name of the entrepreneur).
- Example: John Smith gets 100,000 shares at $0.10 per share and transfers $10,000 to the company account.

First round of financing at $0.25

- Based on the company needs, you need to define how much money you will require for Phase 1.
- Example: You want to raise $250,000 to complete your first project, then you will need to sell 1 million shares at $0.25.
- You will need to make a private placement memorandum (= legal prospectus) in which you will describe everything about your company. This is not just a business plan but also a **disclosure document** with lot of legal language and financial statements.
- Typically a PPM (Private Placement Memorandum) contains about 30 to 50 pages.
- You will need to define a time frame for your private placement. Typically a time frame could be 6 to 8 weeks.
- You will define a starting date and a date for when your private placement is finished.
- If you are not able to raise enough money during that time, you can close the private placement and accept the amount of money

that has been raised. E.g. Only $200,000 instead of $250,000 has been raised at $0.25 per share.

- You also have the option to extend the time frame for your financing round and extend it a few more weeks.
- If you get over-subscribed, you can either turn down the people who were late or you have the option to increase the amount that you wanted to raise at the $0.25 level. Being over-subscribed is usually a good sign because it shows that there is a lot of interest from the market.

Second and third round of financing

- Example for second round: 1 million shares at $0.50 for $500,000
- Example for third round: 1 million shares at $0.75 for $750,000

First price at IPO

- The first price has to be filed with FINRA in the document Form 15c2-11 and it can be a range. For example: $1.00 to $1.20
- It typically is close to the last round of financing. It should not be $5.00 for example if your last round was at $0.75.
- The company can decide where the first price should be. The market maker who will input the initial quote for the very first trade will assist the company with it.
- The market maker is a member of FINRA and the company needs to be sponsored by the market maker in order to obtain a ticker symbol.
- For the first month, there is only one market maker. Afterwards, more market makers will automatically be added.

SEC Filing and set up

- In order to raise money from private investors in the US, you must first file a Form D with the SEC.

- A Form D explains how much money you intend to raise and at what price.
- It also defines how much you will pay out in commissions.
- The first step is to get a company profile set up with the SEC.
- Then the second step is to file the Form D.
- You must wait 15 days after you filed the Form D before you are allowed to raise money.
- The SEC uses an electronic system called EDGAR.

Issuing shares / Transfer Agent

- The company can legally print its own share certificates and send them to investors.
- However, if the company intends to go public in the future, it makes more sense and looks more professional if the company gets set up with a transfer agent.
- A transfer agent issues shares, keeps track of the amount of shares that have been issued, replaces certificates and sends the shares physically (share certificate) or electronically to investors or the company.
- Before the company goes public, the transfer agent will issue a CUSIP number for the company.

From incorporating to money raising

1. Incorporation
2. Select management team
3. Open up the bank account (EIN = corporate tax number, 2 different IDs, articles of incorporation, initial list of officers)
4. Organize share structure and pay initial amounts into the account (to acquire shares for the management team members)
5. Develop business plan
6. Acquire first project ($10,000 - $50,000)
7. Hire corporate securities lawyer ($5000 retainer)
8. Hire corporate accountant ($3000 retainer)
9. Create marketing material

10. Create PPM – Private Placement Memorandum
11. Create SSA – Share Subscription Agreement
12. File Form D with SEC (Securities and Exchange Commission)
13. Set up company with a transfer agent to issue shares
14. Set up administration (office address, telephone, email, hire assistant part-time, computers, etc.)
15. Start selling shares (raising money for first round of financing)

Summary of shares issued and money raised

Preferred shares

Person A = 10 million shares (at $0.0001) - $1000
Person B = 5 million shares (at $0.0001) - $500
Person C = 5 million shares (at $0.0001) - $500

Total: 20 million shares issued - $2000 goes into corporate account

Common shares

Strategic company = 5 million shares (at $0.001) - $5000
Friends and family = 500,000 shares (at $0.10) - $50,000
First round of financing = 1 million shares (at $0.25) - $250,000
Second round of financing = 1 million shares (at $0.25) - $500,000
Third round of financing = 1 million shares (at $0.25) - $750,000

Total: 8.5 million shares issued - $1,555,000 goes into corporate account

Total / Summary

Shares issued = 28.5 million
Money raised = $1,557,000

Total amount of shares authorized: 100 million
Left to be issued: 71.5 million common shares

Valuation / price strategy

- If you have issued 28.5 million shares and you go public at $1.00 per share, then your market capitalization or value of the company is $28.5 million.
- Depending on your business model, this might be a fair valuation, a low valuation or over-valued.
- That's why you must decide how many shares you will issue and at what price level to have a realistic valuation when you are public.
- Many new companies make the mistake to issue too many shares at first and then get diluted.
- For example: a company has 500 million shares issued and is trading at $0.05 per share. The value would be only $2.5 million.
- If too many shares get issued and the price is low (e.g. $0.05) it is very difficult to raise more money.
- In that case the company should consider a reverse split so that less shares are outstanding.
- If your plan is to have a valuation of $100 million and your business model can support that number, then your price target can be at around $4 per share.
- If it makes sense based on your business and potential, then you can use the proposed numbers in our main example.
- The fewer shares that are issued, the better. This means that the company is tight and solid. This makes the company more attractive.

CHAPTER 23

SEC FILING

> Get registered and set up with the SEC. This will give you credibility and trust with your clients.

First, you must get registered with the SEC and their EDGAR system. In order to get registered, you must file the Form ID, which you can download from the SEC website (www.sec.gov).

You can use a filing agent or a securities lawyer to submit this form with the SEC. I always use a company in Canada called Computershare (www.computershare.com). They are considered an "e3 Filing Professional". Even though they are located in Canada, they do US filings, too.

The next step is to file the SEC Form D. The Form D says basically that you intend to raise money from private investors according to SEC Rule 506. You must announce it 15 days in advance before you can accept money from the public by filing the Form D. In this form you will state the total amount of the private placement amount and how much commission you will pay out.

After you have done these two filings, you will file the **S-1 Registration Statement**. This is your filing to go public. The S-1 Registration Statement is basically the same content like your PPM plus your **audited financial statements**. In this filing you will also mention the company's goals, all the potential risks involved, the shareholders, the management team and basically every single important detail about the company.

The key here is transparency and **disclosure**. The most important factor here is disclosure. The goal is to create a document that mentions all facts and potential risks so that an investor can make a proper decision whether he wants to invest or not.

The SEC is not looking for a "good business model". It just wants to make sure that all facts are mentioned and that the investors are properly informed.

Set up

- In order to raise money from private investors in the US, you must first file a Form D with the SEC.
- A Form D explains how much money you intend to raise and at what price.
- It also defines how much you will pay out in commissions.
- The first step is to get a company profile set up with the SEC.
- Then the second step is to file the Form D.
- You must wait 15 days after you filed the Form D before you are allowed to raise money.
- The SEC uses an electronic system called EDGAR.

Form ID and Form D

http://sedarfiling.com
The system for any SEC filing is called EDGAR. You must first register your company and get a basic profile set-up (Form ID). The second step is the filing of the form D.

This company in Vancouver can do it all for you for about 2x $100 = $200.

It is very simple.

Before you can start raising money in the US you need to file a form D with the SEC. You can download it here: https://www.sec.gov/files/formd.pdf

But before you can file the form D you must first register with the SEC EDGAR online system and get the company set up initially.

This company in Vancouver can help:

Computershare
e3 Filing Professional > e3 Filing
T 604 661 0200 **TF** 1 800 973 3274
F 1 866 503 1230 **E** e3filing@computershare.com **W** www.e3filing.com
510 Burrard Street, 2nd Floor
Vancouver, BC V6C 3B9
www.computershare.com

The cost is about $100 CAD for the registration and another $100 for the Form D. Once it is filed you can look it up online.

This will give the company also additional credibility and trust since it had to do a filing with the SEC. But the main reason is that it is a requirement to raise money.

CHAPTER 24

INTERNATIONAL CONNECTIONS AND LIST OF CONTACTS

Securities lawyer / law firm

Bacchus Law Corporation
925 W Georgia St #1820
Vancouver, BC V6C 3L2
Canada
Telephone number: +1 604-632-1700
http://www.bacchuscorplaw.com
Main person / lawyer: Penny Green

- Even though the company is located in Canada, they are also licensed to practice law in the United States.
- Penny Green can help with all company matters, SEC filings, PPM, etc.

Brunson Chandler & Jones PLLC
175 Main St
Salt Lake City, UT 84111
USA
Telephone number: +1 801-303-5730 (Main number)
Telephone number: +1 801-303-5737 (Lance Brunson)

Law Offices of Thomas E. Puzzo, PLLC
Securities Counsel, OTCQX Sponsor

3823 44th Ave, NE
Seattle, WA 98105
206-522-2256
Email: tpuzzo@msn.com

Ellenoff Grossman & Schole LLP
Corporate and Securities Law
1345 Avenue of the Americas
New York, New York 10105
Tel: 212 370 1300
Fax: 212 370 7889
Email: reception@egsllp.com
www.egsllp.com

Market Maker

Spartan Securities Group, Ltd.
Member FINRA/SIPC
15500 Roosevelt Blvd
Suite 303
Clearwater, FL 33760
Office: (727)502-0508
Fax: (727)502-0858
Main person: Micah Eldred

- This company is a FINRA member and a market maker and they can sponsor your company.
- They will file the Form 15c2-11 with FINRA so you can obtain your ticker symbol.
- Typically, they will require that you use their in-house transfer agent Island Stock Transfer in exchange for them sponsoring your company.

Transfer Agent

Pacific Services Group
6725 Via Austi Pkwy
Suite 300
Las Vegas, NV 89119
USA
Phone: (702) 361-3033
www.pacificstocktransfer.com

Quicksilver Stock Transfer
1980 Festival Plaza Dr #530
Las Vegas, NV 89135
USA
Phone: +1 702-629-1883
Fax: (702) 562-9791
http://www.qstransfer.com

Island Stock Transfer
15500 Roosevelt Blvd,
Suite 301
Clearwater, FL 33760
T: 1.727.289.0010
F: 1.727.289.0069
info@islandstocktransfer.com
www.islandstocktransfer.com
(associated with Spartan Securities – Market Maker)

Accountant Canada and USA

Gerald Wong
3740 Albert St 701
Burnaby, BC V5C 5Y7
Canada
Tel: +1-(604) 294-2818
Email: geraldwong@telus.net

- Gerald Wong has prepared over audited financial statements for over 200 public companies.
- He is self-employed and works from home.
- He is a great accountant who is extremely diligent and can help even with challenging financial statements.
- He has contacts to auditors for public companies.
- He is reasonably priced but requests a retainer before he starts working.

Accountant USA, Carlsbad

Van Riper & Messina CPAs, Inc.
2888 Loker Ave E #213
Carlsbad, CA 92010, USA
Phone: +1 760-931-5900
http://www.vanripermessina.com
Main person: Paul Messina
Email: info@vrmcpas.com

Incorporation companies USA

Silver Shield Services, Inc.
4590 Deodar St
Silver Springs, Nevada
89429
Tel : 1-775-577-4822
Fax: 1-775-546-9955
www.shieldcorp.net

EastBiz.com, Inc.
5348 Vegas Dr.
Las Vegas, NV 89108
Phone: (702) 871-8678
Email: info@incparadise.com
www.incparadise.com

Incorp Services, Inc.
3773 Howard Hughes Pkwy - Suite 500s
Las Vegas, NV 89169-6014
Phone: (800) 246-2677
Fax: (702) 246-2677
www.incorp.com

US Address, mailbox and mail forwarding services

Postal Annex
2647 Gateway Rd #105
Carlsbad, CA 92009
USA
Phone: +1 760-579-0044
https://www.postalannex.com/location/carlsbad/8008

Mail Link
848 N. Rainbow Blvd.
Las Vegas, NV 89107
USA
Phone: 702-258-2968
Fax: 702-258-3357
www.maillinkplus.com

Financial consultant / stockbroker USA / Real Estate Agent

Thomas Jandt
Newport Coast Asset Management
9050 Pulsar Court Suite D
Corona, CA 92883
Tel: (866) 766-1112
tom@hiltonthomas.com

- Thomas E Jandt is a financial advisor with Newport Coast Asset Management, which primarily works with Individuals and High Net Worth Individuals. Thomas Jandt operates out of Corona, CA.

Project acquisitions gold projects

www.bcgold.com
Main Person: David Zamida
Phone: +1 250-999-1221
Phone: +1 416-946-1456
Email: info@bcgold.com

Designer

Mariano Duyos
Buenos Aires, Argentina
www.marianoduyos.com
Email: mariano@marianoduyos.com
Skype: mariano.duyos

- Great professional designer for brochures, logos, print design, websites and marketing material
- Great English and communication skills
- Very intelligent and can help to finalize an idea or concept

Website programming / outsourcing

Jaydeep Namera
India
Email: jaydeep.namera@gmail.com

- Jaydeep is a programmer from India. His prices are very reasonable and he is very good at his job. His English skills are not great but ok.

Upwork

www.upwork.com

- Online platform to hire a person for any kind of job. If you need to outsource a job but you want it cheap, then this service is great.

Bank referrals USA

Chase (JPMorgan Chase Bank, N.A.)
2219 Palomar Airport Rd
Carlsbad, CA 92011
USA
Phone: +1 760-438-7791
Person: Nick Anderson (Business accounts)

Wells Fargo Bank
6961 El Camino Real
Carlsbad, CA 92009
USA
Phone: +1 760-929-9947
Ana Atempa (Business accounts)

Incorporation of a UK company

Companies Made Simple
20-22 Wenlock Road
London
N1 7GU
United Kingdom
Phone: +44-207 608 5500
www.companiesmadesimple.com

Incorporation of a Swiss company or buying an existing shell

Institut für Jungunternehmen AG
startup space
Wiesenstrasse 5
8952 Schlieren-Zürich
Tel.: +41 (0)44 730 11 60
www.ifj.ch

Blum Treuhand
Löwenstrasse 20
8001 Zürich
Switzerland
T +41 (0)44 488 40 60
F +41 (0)44 488 40 62
info@blum-treuhand.ch
www.blum-treuhand.ch

Websites

www.otcmarkets.com
(Official site for OTCQX, OTCQB and OTC Pink Securities)

Buying a listed shell

Deal Stream (formerly MergerNetwork.com)
www.dealstream.com

Immigration to USA / Lawyer

Clemens W. Pauly
815 Ponce de Leon Boulevard
Suite 209
Coral Gables, Florida 33134

USA
Tel : 305.967.6900
Fax: 786.509.7490
Website : www.CPauly.com
Email: pauly@cpauly.com

CHAPTER 25

PRIVATE EQUITY WORKBOOK

Subtitle: **How to raise money for your company and get it listed in the stock market**

> Private equity helps produce strong companies, promotes innovation and spurs job growth. (N. Robert Hammer)

Your company / idea

- Name:
- Basic idea:
- State incorporated:

Industries

- Natural resources and precious metals
- Oil and gas
- Biotechnology
- New technologies
- Real Estate
- Other industry:

Basics of Private Equity

- What is your overall goal with your company?
- How much money are you looking to raise?
- How do you plan on spending that money exactly?
- How many private placement financing rounds do you want to have before your company goes public?
- At what price levels do you want to raise money for each round?
- What does your share structure look like once you have raised all the money (pre-IPO)?
- What are your main goals / milestones for your company before you go public?
- What is your intended first price when you are listed?
- How do you justify the value / market capitalization?
- What do you need to do in regards to "proof of concept"?
- What do you need to do in regards to "proof of management"?
- What makes your company special or unique?
- How would you sell your company to an investor with one or two sentences?
- What is the potential of your company in millions / billions of dollars?
- What do you need to do in order to achieve this goal?

Initial share structure

Founder level: $________ $0.00001 (example)

Management: $________ $0.01 (example)

Family and friends: $________ $0.05 (example)

1st round of financing: $________ $0.25 (example)

2nd round of financing: $________ $0.50 (example)

3rd round of financing: $________ $0.75 (example)

First price: $_________ $1.00 (example)

Overall issued shares (pre-IPO)

Number of shares authorized: __________________ million shares

Number of shares in control of management: __________________ million shares

Number of shares in control of investors: __________________ million shares

Public company

- How many shares do you personally own in your company?
- What is your goal in regards to valuation / share price?
- What is your exit strategy for yourself?
- What is your exit strategy for your initial investors?
- What is your overall plan for the next 5 years?
- How do you ensure financing?
- Which law firm or lawyer do you work with?
- Who is your accountant?
- Who is your auditor?
- Which transfer agent do you work with?
- Do you have a corporate consultant who can advise you independently and who has your best interest at heart?
- If you wanted to raise money with a PIPE financing once you are public, at what level would you raise money and how much?
- How can you ensure a stable share price?
- What can you do to make sure that your share price is somewhat protected?
- Which investors should you get rid of or pay out? Which one causes you emotional stress?

Business Development

- What is the core income-generating stream of your business?
- How can you build value in your company so that you will be able to justify a certain market valuation?
- What is your first milestone in regards to business development?
- What things does your company need to fulfill before it will get listed?
- How can you show "proof of concept" by setting up initial operations, completing a first project or showing a prototype?
- What steps are necessary after you go public to increase your company's value?
- Who are the key people in your operations?

Going public process

- ☐ 35 shareholders
- ☐ Audited financial statements
- ☐ S-1 Registration Statement (SEC Filing)
- ☐ Project
- ☐ SEC comments answered
- ☐ SEC S-1 Registration Statement declared effective
- ☐ FINRA (former NASD) member = market maker will file form 15c2-11 on behalf of the company
- ☐ FINRA comments answered
- ☐ FINRA declares filing as effective
- ☐ FIRNA assigns trading symbol to company
- ☐ Market maker and company make first trade – set first price

Stock Promotion and marketing

- What is going to be your first target price when you are public?
- What kind of exit strategy do you have planned for your initial investors?
- What is the time frame for your promotional stock campaign?
- What is your budget for your campaign?

- Where other than your company can you organize the funds for your campaign?
- Who is in charge of your campaign?
- How can you ensure that the main stock promoter has your interests and the interests of the company at heart (and not just his own)?
- How can you ensure that the float of your free trading stocks is under control?
- What kind of contacts do you still need to ensure a successful campaign?
- How many shares do you want to sell during your campaign and at what average price level?
- How can you ensure that you won't hurt the company and still be able to sell stocks into the market?

The business of finding investors

- Where can you find the right names or lists of potential investors?
- Do you have a sales office set up?
- How many people do you want to hire first to get started?
- What is your goal for your team per month?
- What kind of training program can you provide for your sales people?
- How can you be a role model for others and lead by example?
- What are your numbers (Lists to leads to potential customers to customers)?
- What other activities than telephone sales can you do to find investors?
- What is your main advantage over your competition and why should an investor work with you instead of a bank advisor?
- How can you improve your own sales skills?
- How can you improve your own leadership skills?
- Do you have a database for potential investors?

Techniques to raise capital

- What are you going to say in your initial phone conversation with a client?
- What initial materials are you going to send out?
- What are you going to say in your second call?
- What are you going to say in your third call?
- How can you position yourself as an expert?
- Have you created a sales script? If yes, what are the key points?
- How can you fight fear of rejection and fear of failure?
- What is your personal money-raising goal per month and per year?
- Have you made a list with rebuttals for objections from investors?

The $100 million blueprint

1. Find a project that has a multi-million dollar potential
2. Form corporation and make set-up of share structure
3. Take company public (6 to 12 months)
4. Raise initial capital to fund or acquire project ($1 million to $5 million)
5. Develop project to a point where your achieve "proof of concept"
6. Create annual earnings of $5 to $10 million
7. Create a project with $100 million value potential
8. Get additional financing to expand company ($10 to $20 million)
9. Valuation: PE-ratio x annual earnings = market capitalization (Example: PE-ratio of 10 x $10 million annual earnings = $100 million valuation)
10. Expand and grow company

Recommended books

- Create Wealth with Private Equity and Public Companies (Norman Meier)
- How your company can raise money to grow and go public (Robert Paul Turner)

Recommended movies

- The Wolf of Wall Street (Leonardo Di Caprio)
- Boiler Room (Vin Diesel)
- Wallstreet (Michael Douglas, Charlie Sheen)

ABOUT NORMAN MEIER

As a successful businessman and entrepreneur he has accomplished success that many people only dream about. He built companies and financed them with millions of dollars and as a former stockbroker he has built more than 3000 clients, raised over $400 million from the private sector and $600 million from institutional clients.

Prior to founding Norman Meier International, Norman was the Chief Executive Officer and main shareholder of a publicly listed company with a market capitalization of over $300 million.

Norman Meier was born and raised in Switzerland and moved to America to fulfill his personal dream. Norman has traveled and worked in many countries all over the world and speaks five languages.

He has had successful careers in the financial industry, sales and marketing.

Norman Meier has produced many audio and video learning programs on the topics of business, financial independence, sales and marketing and personal development. He has written and produced several audio and video learning programs and published 12 books.

Norman Meier has been an investment professional since 1995 and is an expert in Private Equity. He has held executive positions with top-tier global investment firms such as MAN Investments and AWD in Switzerland, and Canaccord Capital Corporation in Canada.

Norman Meier started to study psychology at the University of Zurich and received a BBA, MBA and Ph. D in Human Behavior from Newport University. He has 12 different finance diplomas / designations and was licensed as a financial advisor in three different countries. He has been licensed in Switzerland, Canada and the US to sell securities and his record is absolutely clean and perfect.

He had originally received the Swiss Matura Type D (languages) and went to the University of Zurich to study Psychology. After his service in the army, he received a Financial Planning Designation of AWD Switzerland where he worked for over six years. He continued his journey to Canada where he finished several courses and received designations in from the Canadian Securities Institute (equivalent to FINRA in the USA):

- Canadian Securities Course (CSC)
- Derivatives Fundamental Course (DFC)
- Conduct & Practices Handbook Course (CPH)
- Options Licensing Course (OLC), Ethics Case Study Course
- Technical Analysis Course (TAC)
- Investment Management Techniques (IMT)
- Options Strategies Course (OSTC)
- Portfolio Management Techniques (PMT)
- Agricultural Markets – Risk Management (ARM)
- FCSI – Fellowship of the Canadian Securities Institute Designation
- Canadian Investment Manager Designation
- Derivatives Market Specialist Designation

In 2011 he became licensed with FINRA in the US and got his Series 7 and Series 63 license, which made him officially licensed to sell securities in the US.

Norman Meier was the manager of a FINRA licensed broker dealer in USA and CEO and president of a two public mining exploration companies. He was the founder and major shareholder of several gold and uranium exploration companies in the US and major shareholder of three sales organizations in Europe.

He built up a global team of over 60 employees in Switzerland, USA, Canada and Mexico. He was the president and founder of a Swiss financial services company with a license from a self-regulatory organization and a license from the Swiss Banking Commission.

Norman Meier has over 10 years of experience in the gold exploration and production industry. He has become a real specialist who not only understands the financial and business side of a public company but as well as the actual technical knowledge and processes in the gold industry. He (or though the companies that he worked for) held over 25 different projects all over the world. Most of these projects were gold, silver, copper and molybdenum.

Today, Norman is a Private Equity Specialist and has built an international Private Equity firm with offices and sales people all over the world.

He also developed the company Norman Meier International that focuses on personal and business development.

Norman competed in two bodybuilding competitions, was two times Swiss Aerobics champion, is a third degree black belt in Karate and was the first runner up in the mister Switzerland competition.

Norman is happily married and has four children. Besides spending time with his family, he likes working out, tennis, ice hockey, chess and he has a love for animals in need.

Printed in the United States
By Bookmasters